BradyPedia

The Complete Reference Guide to Television's
The Brady Bunch

By Erika Woehlk

BearManor
Media

Albany, Georgia

Published in the USA by
BearManor Media
P.O. Box 71426
Albany, GA 31708
www.BearManorMedia.com

Softcover Edition
ISBN-10: 1-62933-130-9
ISBN-13: 978-1-62933-130-0

Printed in the United States of America

Dedication

I dedicate Bradypedia to all fans of *The Brady Bunch*.

Table of Contents

Acknowledgments

I would like to thank many people who have supported me during this writing and researching process. First is my family whose support was unfailing: Anita Woehlk, Heinz Woehlk, and Mary Lou Woehlk. Then, although a Kickstarter project did not succeed, I'd still like to thank those who contributed by name: Adam & Andrea Davis, Brian Rogers, Daniel & Jessica Reeder, Pepé, Eric Shields, Melissa & Zebulun Lamp, Mary Kay Coker, David Moore, Christopher Davis, Sandy Hempe, Mark Barylski, Frank Laraia, Diane McKinney, Maureen & Ralph Norcie, Emily Lecaque, and Nicole Collins.

A big, giant thank you goes to Fuller French of the American Radio and Television Script (ARTS) Library in Ft. Worth, Texas. Without your generosity, some of this book's greatest revelations would not have been possible. Thank you.

Finally, I'd like to thank Sherwood Schwartz for creating *The Brady Bunch* and his son Lloyd for patiently answering my questions.

IntroDuction

There is hardly an American today who has not seen *The Brady Bunch*. It has never been off the air in the U.S. since the pilot episode aired in 1969. It has an almost universal appeal in terms of audience and its themes are timeless. So what makes *The Brady Bunch* so successful?

Most of us know that a man named Brady with three boys of his own married a woman named Carol with three girls of her own. But how did the show start, and whose idea was it? It's all due to a man named Sherwood Schwartz.

Sherwood had a successful career as a comedy writer for Bob Hope, Red Skelton and others. He was also the man who gave us *Gilligan's Island*, which ran from 1964-1967. While *Gilligan's Island* was still in production, he had an idea for a television show about a blended family (aka a step-family). In a 2005 interview, Sherwood explained he got the idea for *The Brady Bunch* from an article in the Los Angeles Times. "There were three lines in the LA Times that said over 29% of all marriages as of that date had a child or children by a previous marriage,"[1] he said. The article sent his head spinning and when it stopped he had the format for the Brady family. But network

Sherwood Schwartz in 1964

executives were not too keen on the idea because it was something that had never really been tested before. No television show up to that point had a premise that revolved around a blended family.

But Sherwood was convinced that the idea would work and he kept pitching it year after year. In 1968, a feature film debuted that was called *Yours, Mine and Ours*. The movie was about a man with ten kids who married a woman with eight. Then they had a baby of their own. The movie, starring Henry Fonda and Lucille Ball, was a hit with audiences across the country. To boot, the movie was based on the true story of the Beardsley family as told in the book Who Gets the Drumstick? (a great read, by the way). Also in 1968, movie goers were treated to *With Six You Get Eggroll*, a Doris Day film about another blended family. Now Sherwood had some hard proof that a blended family premise could work.

ABC-TV was the network that was willing to take a chance on Sherwood's show.

A large cast can be difficult to work with, especially with children and the labor laws about the hours a minor can be put to work. So originally, Sherwood's script contained just two children: Bobby and Cindy. Fuller French, director of the American Radio and Television Script Library says, "In Sherwood Schwartz's original, typed pilot, Carol is to marry Steve Bradley. They have one child apiece—Cindy is Carol's, Bobby is Steve's. Their housekeeper is a plump Swedish woman named Kris."[2]

Yes, it's true. The original story idea for *The Brady Bunch* had just two children, and Mike Brady was named Steve Bradley! Moreover, the series began life as *Yours and Mine*. Sherwood penned this series proposal in 1967, a year before the aforementioned film *Yours, Mine and Ours* hit the theatres. Nevertheless, to avoid confusion with the movie, the title of the series was quickly changed to *The Bartons* on April 10, 1967.

The series proposal and pilot script would go through several more drafts over the next year and a half. Additional titles were *The Brady Brood* and *The Bradley Bunch*. Ultimately, everyone settled on *The Brady Bunch*, but not after some frank discussions about the meaning of "bunch." The network wanted to avoid associations with the lawlessness of gangs like The Wild Bunch. On the other hand, "brood" conjured up images of farm animals. But, they finally agreed that *The Brady Bunch* sounded better than *The Brady Brood* and development got underway.

TIKI TALK

Sherwood's drafts show significant changes over time. Most of them only feature two children, and theirs are the only character names that never change. Only with the last set of revisions did the script finally include six children. These original drafts of the series proposals and pilot episode scripts are housed at the American Radio and Television Script (ARTS) Library in Ft. Worth, Texas.[3]

Yours and Mine. Larry Martin, age 30, is a construction engineer with one son, Bobby, age 7. Their housekeeper is Willie (short for Wilhelmina). Larry marries Judy Parsons, age 28, who has a 7-year-old daughter, Cindy. (no date)

The Bartons. Everything is the same as above, except Larry Martin has become Larry Barton and Judy Parsons is now Judy Martin. (dated 04/10/1967)

The Bradleys. Still the same cast, but Larry Barton is now Larry Bradley. (dated 04/13/1967)

The Bradleys. Steven Robert Bradley, age 33, with his son, Bobby, age 6, and housekeeper, Kris, who is "Swedish, middle-aged, and a fondness for her own cooking has made her plump." Carol Martin, age late 20s, daughter, Cindy, age 6, lives with her parents, Mr. and Mrs. Henry Tyler. (no date)

The Bradleys. Same as above, except this time Steve Bradley is an engineer for an aircraft company. (no date)

The Bradleys. Now there are four kids instead of two. Steven Paul Bradley is 36, and his two sons are Greg, 13, and Bobby, 9. Carol Ann Martin's two daughters are Marcia, 11, and Cindy, 7. (dated 05/1968)

The Bradley Bunch. Michael Paul Bradley, 36-year-old engineer, has three boys. Greg is 13, Peter is 9, and Bobby is 6. Their housekeeper is Kris. The ladies are Carol Ann Martin, Marcia, 11, Jan, 9, and Cindy, 5. (dated 08/09/1968)

The Brady Bunch. Mike Brady, age 35, lives with his sons Greg, 13, Peter, 10, and Bobby, 8. Carol Martin, 32, has daughters Marcia, 11, Jan, 9, and Cindy, 7. And then there were six! (no date)

The Brady Brood. Mike Brady, 36, is "nice looking in a rugged sort of way," Greg is 13, Peter is 9, Bobby is 6, Kris is the housekeeper, and Marcia, Jan and Cindy are 11, 9, and 5. (dated 09/10/1968)

The Brady Brood. Same as above, but Peter is 10 and Bobby 7. (dated 09/19/1968)

The "last final revised draft" is called *The Brady Bunch.* Michael Paul Brady is an architect, and the housekeeper is Alice (it's only this last draft where the Swedish Kris gets nixed!). Greg is 13 and "interested in muscles and athletics," Peter is 10 and "bright eyed and outgoing," and Bobby is 7 and "intense and serious." Carol Ann Martin's girls are Marcia, 11, who is "a big help to her mother," Jan, 9, is "quite shy," and Cindy, 5, is "still very much a little girl." (dated 10/02/1968)

Sherwood and company had to cast nine major characters: two parents, six children, and a housekeeper. Until the roles of dad Mike and mom Carol were cast, Sherwood decided to create two pools of kids. The audience would have a tough time keeping up with nine main characters at first, so why not make it easier? Create the dad and his three boys with all the same hair color and the mom and her three daughters with a different hair color, making it easier to determine which kids belonged to whom just by looking at them. Thus, eleven (not twelve; one kid was in both pools) child actors were selected to be potential Brady kids: one set with blonde girls and dark-haired boys, and a second set with dark-haired girls and blond boys.

Sherwood liked a guy named Gene Hackman for the role of Mike Brady. But the execs didn't like him, so he was written off. (Fortunately for Hackman, he soon made a star of himself on the big screen, as we all know.) Then Robert Reed auditioned. Bob was a handsome, serious actor from television's legal drama *The Defenders*. He, the producers thought, would be a good straight man opposite a comedic wife and housekeeper. As for Carol Brady, there was one brunette woman in the running, but her name is now lost. (She wasn't in the running long, though, because Robert Reed had dark hair.) After the mysterious brunette came blonde Joyce Bulifant. Then for the part of Alice the housekeeper, the producers liked Monty Margetts, a famed comedienne. She didn't work out and so Ann B. Davis, also a comedienne and famous for her role in *The Bob Cummings Show*, was selected in her place. Finally, Bulifant was eliminated and Florence Henderson of Broadway fame was asked to do a screen test. Everyone liked the test she did with Robert Reed and the rest is history.

TIKI TALK

The screen test, dated October 10, 1968, is titled *Bradys, Bradys, Bradys* and is the scene in the honeymoon suite where Mike and Carol open their champagne bottle and speak in innuendo. This, too, is housed in the ARTS Library.

So now producers had a dark-haired dad and a blonde mother. That meant the set of kids with dark-haired boys and blonde girls got the job. So long, bizarro Brady kid set #2; somewhere out there are five Brady kids who could have been. (Reddish-headed Mike Lookinland was part of both sets of kids, thus five unknown actors rather than six.) The names of the five kids who were so close to pop culture fame are now sadly lost to history. So Barry Williams, Christopher Knight, Mike Lookinland, Maureen McCormick, Eve Plumb, and Susan Olsen became Greg, Peter, Bobby, Marcia, Jan, and Cindy Brady.

The casting was complete, the set was built, the crew hired, and that meant that filming the pilot episode came next. The plot of *The Brady Bunch* may seem simple today, but in the 1960s it was a novel idea for a television show. Having a blended family on television was a first of its kind. Although the percentage of blended families Sherwood quotes is a little high (according to the most recent data available from the US Census Bureau (2004), 17% of all children lived in blended families; they have no data for any year in the 1960s or 1970s), there was still a relatively large number of this type of family in America. Sherwood wanted something that they could relate to <u>and</u> that average families could relate to as well. Thus, the "blending" took place early on – in the pilot episode – and the rest of the series focused on the Brady family's everyday life. The squabbles between the kids and the squabbles between the parents were universal enough that both blended and average families could identify with them.

The premise of the show was that Mike Brady is a widower with three young boys. Carol Martin is a single mother of three young girls. We are never told whether or not she was divorced or widowed. That is because Sherwood wanted her to be a divorcee (although his early scripts do say she is a widow). ABC was uncomfortable with that situation and so her status remained undefined. Mike and Carol fall in love and two or three months later they are married. Throw in a housekeeper, a dog, and a cat and viewers had plenty of action to watch in the pilot episode.

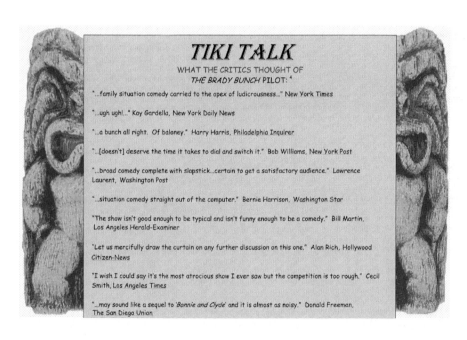

TIKI TALK

WHAT THE CRITICS THOUGHT OF
THE BRADY BUNCH PILOT: [4]

"...family situation comedy carried to the apex of ludicrousness..." New York Times

"...ugh ugh!..." Kay Gardella, New York Daily News

"...a bunch all right. Of baloney." Harry Harris, Philadelphia Inquirer

"...[doesn't] deserve the time it takes to dial and switch it." Bob Williams, New York Post

"...broad comedy complete with slapstick...certain to get a satisfactory audience." Lawrence Laurent, Washington Post

"...situation comedy straight out of the computer." Bernie Harrison, Washington Star

"The show isn't good enough to be typical and isn't funny enough to be a comedy." Bill Martin, Los Angeles Herald-Examiner

"Let us mercifully draw the curtain on any further discussion on this one." Alan Rich, Hollywood Citizen-News

"I wish I could say it's the most atrocious show I ever saw but the competition is too rough." Cecil Smith, Los Angeles Times

"...may sound like a sequel to '*Bonnie and Clyde*' and it is almost as noisy." Donald Freeman, The San Diego Union

Looking back on the show today, it seems strange that it was so ravaged by the critics when it first aired. *The Brady Bunch* is part of American culture; there's no denying that. But when the show first aired, the critics wrote scathing reviews because of its seemingly ludicrous opening episode – imagine newlyweds inviting their six children along on their honeymoon! – and somewhat absurd situations the family got itself into. But the viewers saw something that the critics did not. They saw a family with simple problems and a very happy home life: a family who was happy *despite* being blended, *despite* the boys' mother having died, *despite* Carol's first husband being AWOL, and *despite* all that was going on in the world at that time. Sherwood's series pitch includes this question, a basic theme of the series: "Can any of us really accept the new with the same care and concern and devotion which we have for the old?"[5]

Ann B. Davis, Susan Olsen, Mike Lookinland, Eve Plumb, Christopher Knight, Maureen McCormick, and Barry Williams in 1968, with scripts in hand ready to film the pilot episode

It's plausible that audiences across America liked to believe that such an ideal family could exist and therefore enjoyed escaping into the Bradys' world every week. Life in the US and the world was a bit tumultuous in this era. The year 1969 saw Richard Nixon take office; protests against the Vietnam War were picking up; there was a draft instituted for the War; the Edward Kennedy Chappaquiddick Affair occurred; the Charles Manson cult members murdered five people, and more. On the other hand, America landed the first men on the moon only two months before *The Brady Bunch* aired and hundreds of thousands of happy people attended Woodstock just the month before. There was so much going on that year that maybe *The Brady Bunch* was indeed a sort of escape for people: a place to go for thirty minutes and know that everything will turn out just right in the end.

Whatever it may have been, *The Brady Bunch* lived to see four more years of production. After five full seasons, the show was cancelled and many spin-offs ensued.

That brings us back to the original question. What made *The Brady Bunch* a success that morphed into a cult classic? Theories abound. First is the happy home life theory described earlier. Next is the theory that the actors were popular and gained a large fan following. Also a big contender: the inundation theory. After *The*

Brady Bunch was cancelled in 1974, the show was in syndication for the Fall 1974 season. It hasn't been off the air since. Schoolchildren would watch reruns after school every day. Subsequent generations of schoolchildren would do the same. It's kind of the same thing that happened with *Seinfeld* and *Friends,* and more recently *The Big Bang Theory.* They're on seemingly all the time and people just absorb them whether they consciously want to or not. As evidence, *The Brady Bunch* pilot episode in September 1969 enjoyed about 8 million viewers. By the time the spin-off movie *A Very Brady Christmas* aired in 1988, viewership had grown to over 22 million. Therefore, the answer to Sherwood's question in his series proposal is yes, we can accept the new and love them just as much as the old.

This book will take you through all *The Brady Bunch* and spin-off episodes one by one, will provide reference information on all the characters, include biographies of the actors and their families, and reveal lots of other neat-o information. So sit back and enjoy the show that makes us laugh and feel all warm and fuzzy inside!

---

[1]"The Brady Bunch Under One Roof," featurette from *The Brady Bunch: The Complete First Season,* Paramount Entertainment, 2005.

[2]Svokos, Heather. "Following the Scripts: Man Collects a Treasure Trove of TV History." PopMatters. Online. Retrieved 03/16/2016. www.popmatters.com/article/following-the-scripts-man-collects-a-treasure-trove-of-tv-history/.

[3]Quotes from these scripts are courtesy Fuller French and the ARTS Library. Scripts by Sherwood Schwartz.

[4]Broadcasting: The Businessweekly of Television and Radio. V. 38. (October 6, 1969): 46.

[5]Schwartz, Sherwood. The Bradleys. Series Proposal. (1967): 2.

CHAPTER 1: EPISODE GUIDE

THE BRADY BUNCH **(comedy)**
SEASON ONE 1969-1970
Fridays 8:00-8:30pm ET on ABC

Production Notes: The world is just getting introduced to that smiling family called the Bradys. In this season, the plots are simple and limited to one child at a time. The problems are straightforward and can be easily related to by almost any viewing audience member at some point during the season. Do you relate to Jan the middle child, Bobby the forlorn, or Marcia the over-achiever?

In the pilot episode, the Brady house is not the one that is seen for the rest of the series. The pilot episode was filmed with different sets and a different exterior shot of the Brady Residence (the house was reportedly the producer's neighbor's). Viewers also learn that Mike's first wife died but are not told what happened to Carol's first husband. Viewers never find out the fate of Mr. Martin...ever. They also never see Carol's parents after this episode nor do they ever again see Fluffy the cat. This episode was filmed almost a year before the rest of the season's episodes.

For more, read the Introduction Chapter.

#1 – The Honeymoon
Airdate: September 26, 1969
Nielsen Rating: 13.4
Directed by John Rich
Produced by Sherwood Schwartz
Written by Sherwood Schwartz
J. Pat O'Malley .... Mr. Tyler
Joan Tompkins .... Mrs. Tyler
Dabbs Greer ....Minister
James Millhollin.. Mr. Pringle

Mike Brady is a widower with three dark-haired boys and Carol Martin is a single mother of three blonde girls. Mike and Carol are engaged to be married. The blessed day arrives and the wedding is to be held in the back yard of Carol's parents, Mr. and Mrs. Tyler. Greg, Peter, Bobby, Marcia, Jan, and Cindy all accompany their parents for the wedding ceremony. Even Tiger the dog and Fluffy the cat are in attendance. Mike and Carol promise to love each other, honor, and obey and they kiss to seal the deal. Everyone is thrilled, including Fluffy the cat who lets out a congratulatory meow. Tiger, who is locked in Mike's car, hears the meow and jumps out an open window to chase the cat. It's animal mayhem as the dog and cat race through the Tylers' back yard, walking on guests and tables, causing ice to be spilled, and the cake to tumble down a collapsed table. Fortunately, Mike catches the cake on his haunches, but when Carol comes over to give him a hug, Mike falls over and becomes covered in wedding cake. He'll be sneezing rosebuds for weeks. After the ceremony, Mike and Carol dash off to a hotel to spend the night in the honeymoon suite. But back at Mike's house, Alice the housekeeper is in charge of three very depressed boys. Greg, Peter, and Bobby all believe that their dad yelled at them for Tiger and Fluffy's destruction and not the girls. They assume that that's the way it's going to be from now on: just because the girls are Carol's kids (and not Mike's) the boys will get blamed for everything no matter who is at fault. Similar sentiments are being voiced back at the Tylers' where Marcia, Jan, and Cindy are spending the night. The girls are sad that Carol yelled at them during the wedding, even though Cindy blames Tiger and the boys for the whole mess. Back at the hotel, Mike and Carol are beginning to feel guilty about the way they yelled at their children during the wedding. They feel the marriage got off on the wrong foot and that the children are suffering because of their disciplinary behavior. Guilty consciences get the best of the newlyweds and they go off in the night to pick up the kids and bring them back to the hotel so that amends can be made. When the whole gang arrives back at the hotel, it turns out that Jan brought Fluffy along in her cage. So not only will the couple be sharing the honeymoon suite with six children, they have a cat to contend with as well! Then Alice shows up with Tiger. With two pets, one housekeeper, six kids, and two parents, the bunch of Bradys is quite overwhelming. Alice will be there to watch the dog, cat, and kids while Carol and Mike can do what they please. The episode ends with the whole Brady Bunch marching up the stairs for their first night together as one big happy family.

TIKI TALK

In the first eight drafts of this pilot episode, there is no Tiger and no Fluffy. Instead, Bobby secretes a hamster named Skipper away in his suit jacket pocket. The hamster escapes at the end of the ceremony, Cindy screams, and Skipper runs amok through crowd where a lady kicks it, sending the hapless rodent flying into the punch bowl.

#2 – Dear Libby

Airdate: October 3, 1969
Directed by John Rich
Produced by Sherwood Schwartz
Written by Lois Hire
Jo deWinter ....Elizabeth Carter aka "Dear Libby"

Marcia discovers a letter to Dear Libby in the newspaper that is written by a parent of a blended family. The writer complains, *"Dear Libby, We have a terrible problem in my family. I have three children of my own and three additional children from a recent marriage. I had no idea three new children could cause so much trouble. Should I continue pretending to love these three new children and wait until they wreck my marriage, or should I get out now? --Harried and Hopeless."* Marcia shares the letter with the five other Brady children who all think the letter came from either Mike or Carol. The kids believe that they need to save their parents' marriage by being as well behaved as they can. Eventually, Alice, Mike, and Carol all find out about the letter to Dear Libby. Everyone is a suspect, but no one communicates with each other to find out if the Bradys really are the subject of the letter. In the end, the six kids and Alice send pleading letters to Dear Libby all begging to reveal the identity of the writer. Dear Libby is so moved by their letters that she makes a personal visit to the Brady household to clear everything up. She reveals that Harried and Hopeless lives in Kingsford, Illinois, far away from the Brady home. The kids, Alice, Mike, and Carol are all relieved and things return to normal.

#3 – Eenie, Meenie, Mommy, Daddy

Airdate: October 10, 1969
Directed by John Rich
Produced by Sherwood Schwartz
Written by Joanna Lee
Marjorie Stapp .... Mrs. Engstrom
Tracy Reed .... Miss Marlowe
Brian Forster .... Elf

Cindy is the lead in her school play, "The Fairy Princess." When she learns that she will only be able to invite one parent to attend the performance, Cindy does not know whether to ask her mother or her new father. It is a difficult decision for such a youngster, who is in an unfamiliar situation with her newly-blended family at home. Fortunately for her, Cindy's parents find out about her dilemma and convince the school to allow the children to give a special performance of "The Fairy Princess" just for the whole Brady family.

#4 – Alice Doesn't Live Here Anymore

Airdate: October 17, 1969
Directed by John Rich
Produced by Sherwood Schwartz
Written by Paul West

Fred Pinkard.. Mr. Stokey

When Bobby scrapes his knee falling from his bike, he comes running to Alice for first aid. Carol is a little hurt when Bobby says he prefers Alice as a nurse. Unbeknownst to Carol, Alice convinces Bobby that he should go to his mother anyway. Carol fixes him up and sends him on his way, relieved that Bobby changed his mind. Next, Alice sends a bickering Greg and Peter to Carol to settle their dispute about a missing baseball glove. When Carol solves their problem, the boys are impressed. From now on, the boys are comfortable going to their new mother for help. Alice feels like a third wheel and decides that the Brady family will be better off without her. She makes up a story about a sick aunt in Seattle and tells Mike and Carol that she is quitting her job as housekeeper to move to Seattle to care for the aunt. Mike and Carol have no choice but to let her go. The next day, Jan and Marcia accidentally overhear Alice talking on the phone. "Who needs an old Victrola when stereo comes to town?" Alice says. The girls have found out the truth about Alice's decision to leave and Marcia immediately informs Carol. Carol calls Mike and they hatch a plan to convince Alice that the family still needs her. "Operation Alice" is put into play and through a series of events, Alice realizes that the Bradys still need and want her around and she agrees to stay.

#5 – Katchoo
Airdate: October 24, 1969
Directed by John Rich
Produced by Sherwood Schwartz
Written by William Cowley

Jan is allergic to something, but the Bradys don't know what. At first, Alice and Carol fear that she is allergic to Mike, but thankfully that is not so. Unfortunately, they *do* believe that Jan is allergic to the family dog Tiger. The boys and girls are heartbroken when they learn that Tiger will have to be given away to their grandparents so that Jan can be healthy again. True to the Brady spirit, though, the family secretly gives Tiger four different baths the night before he is to be given away in a last desperate hope that once he's clean Jan will stop sneezing. The baths fail to stop Jan's allergy. But at the last second, Carol realizes that it is actually Tiger's flea powder that Jan is allergic to and not Tiger himself. They get rid of the powder instead of the dog and the day is saved.

#6 – A Clubhouse is Not a Home
Airdate: October 31, 1969
Directed by John Rich
Produced by Sherwood Schwartz
Written by Skip Webster

Four hundred forty-three cartons arrive from storage that belong to Carol and the girls. The cartons must be unloaded and added to the Brady household. The Brady boys do not appreciate acting as the girls' Sherpas and having to share the bathroom with perfume and hair ribbons. The boys and girls divide according to sex and treat the opposites with disdain. A Mike Brady lecture about sharing and equality works only long enough for the girls to decorate the boys' clubhouse with curtains. When the boys protest, Mike puts his foot down and insists that the boys need a place of their own. In retaliation, Carol and Alice hatch a plan for the girls to build a clubhouse of their own. They deliberately botch the job so that the men can take over and build a proper clubhouse. When it's all finished, the clubhouse is beautiful. And the boys' clubhouse? Well, Bobby took some nails out of its boards and the whole thing falls to the ground...back to square one with only one clubhouse in the yard. Mike and Carol learn that fighting will always be a part of having six kids in one household. Both clubhouses disappear from the Brady yard after this episode.

#7 – Kitty Karry-all is Missing

Airdate: November 7, 1969
Directed by John Rich
Produced by Sherwood Schwartz
Written by Al Schwartz and Bill Freedman
Pitt Herbert...Mr. Driscoll

Cindy's favorite doll, Kitty Karry-all, goes missing and Cindy accuses Bobby of stealing her. Bobby insists that he is innocent. He treats Cindy in kind when his own prized kazoo goes missing. Now the Bradys are left with two upset children, a missing doll, and a missing kazoo. Bobby has a change of heart for Cindy and spends almost his whole life savings ($4.00) to buy her a new Kitty Karry-all doll. Cindy, however, is unable to bring herself to love this new Kitty as much as she loved the original. Brought to despair, the Bradys take up a search for Cindy's original doll. When Mike and Carol catch Tiger stealing the second Kitty, they follow him to his doghouse where they discover both Kittys and Bobby's kazoo. Problem solved.

#8 – A-Camping We Will Go

Airdate: November 14, 1969
Directed by Oscar Rudolph
Produced by Sherwood Schwartz
Written by Herbert Finn and Alan Dinehart

Mike and Carol decide to take the kids and Alice for a three-day camping trip at a nearby lake. It will be the first time Carol and the girls have gone camping and the girls are a bit skeptical of the whole thing. The boys don't much like the idea of the girls going along either; they think girls don't belong in the great out-of-doors and will mess up their good time. But Mike and Carol insist the whole family go for some bonding time, and they all pile into the station wagon (yes, all nine of them!) and head to the lake. Once they get there, they set up camp and the boys, girls, and Mike decide to go fishing for lunch. Jan drops Greg's fish back in the lake because it felt "fishy," Marcia breaks Peter's fishing line, and Cindy falls in the water. No fish for lunch. But Mrs. Brady staves off everyone's hunger by unpacking some fried chicken and cold cuts that she brought along for emergencies. At first the boys are angry at the idea of not eating off the land, but their hunger gets the better of them and everyone goes to bed satisfied. When the girls are falling asleep, they are frightened by an owl hooting, a frog croaking, and the rattle snake-like sound of Alice's leaking air mattress. In return, Jan and Marcia decide to scare the boys by making them think that a bear is right outside their tent. They create the silhouette of a bear on the boys' tent, which makes the boys immediately run outside to look for it. There, they discover Marcia and Jan up to no good and everyone except Cindy gets involved in a chase. They end up in the girls' tent, which promptly collapses. Mike and Carol finally get the togetherness they have been looking for.

TIKI TALK

They filmed an alternate ending – or "tag" – for this episode that had the boys getting back at the girls for the bear prank. It had something to do with a rubber spider in the girls' room. This photo below is from the lost ending where the whole family tucks Cindy into bed, presumably after being scared by the spider. You can see the top of the girls' bedroom set in this image, too.

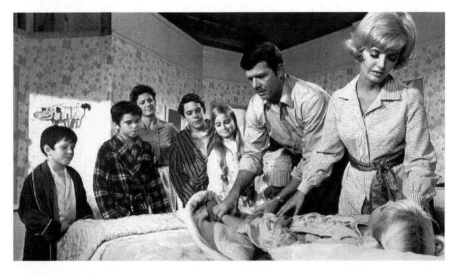

#9 – Sorry, Right Number
Airdate: November 21, 1969
Directed by George Cahan
Produced by Sherwood Schwartz
Written by Ruth Brooks Flippen
Allan Melvin...Sam
Howard Culver.. Mr. Crawford

The kids are racking up enormous phone bills and Mike has had it. He installs a second phone line for himself and Carol in his den with the hope that the phone can be used at all times for his own needs. The plan does not work because the kids are now using both phone lines to take care of their own business. Next, Carol starts timing the kids' phone calls with an hour glass, but that fails quickly. When Alice visits her boyfriend and butcher Sam, she sees a payphone in his butcher shop. That gives her an idea, which she quickly conveys to Mike. When Mike gets home from work, he unveils a pay phone in the family room that is for the kids' use only. He allots them twenty extra cents a week for their allowance that they can use for phone calls. Every call from the pay phone costs at least ten cents, and anything over the twenty-cent allotment must come out of the kids' allowances. Naturally, the kids are upset. Mike thinks he has solved the problem. When Carol is using her and Mike's extension in the den, Mike says that he needs to make a phone call to a potential client named Mr. Crawford. Carol cannot get her friend Martha off the phone, so Mike decides to make his important business call from the pay phone. Wrong decision. When he gets through to Mr. Crawford, the operator asks Mike to deposit another ten cents, and Mike is out of dimes. The call is disconnected and so is the deal with Mr. Crawford. Or so he thinks. Alice convinces Mike to call Mr. Crawford back using Sam's plethora of dimes and explain the situation to him. He does so and Mr. Crawford is so intrigued by the idea of a pay phone in a domestic household that he grants Mike the meeting he needs and also installs a pay phone in his own home for his three teenagers. Mike's multimillion-dollar factory deal goes through. The pay phone in the family room is disconnected because everyone has learned his lesson.

EPISODE GUIDE

#10 – Every Boy Does it Once

Airdate: December 5, 1969
Directed by Oscar Rudolph
Produced by Sherwood Schwartz
Written by Lois and Arnold Payser
Michael Lerner..Johnny

Cindy and Bobby watch Cinderella on television and Bobby takes the portrayal of step-mothers as mean seriously. His angst is compounded when Carol asks him to sweep out the fireplace. Next, he is too young to accompany Jan and Marcia to a movie, and when everybody leaves the house and nobody says goodbye Bobby thinks he is unloved and unwanted. His young psyche is damaged and he decides to run away from home. As he is packing, Mike and Carol come home from shopping and Alice tells them that Bobby is planning to leave. Mike goes upstairs to Bobby's room and tells him that he doesn't want any son of his staying when he doesn't want to. Bobby is confused by Mike's reaction, but sticks to his guns and decides to continue with his plan to run away. On the way down the stairs, he encounters Carol who has packed a suitcase of her own. She says that she will not let anyone leave home without her. Bobby is surprised and happy. He confesses his worries to Carol about being neglected because he is a step-son and a step-brother. Carol counters with, "The only steps in this house are those…the ones that lead up to your room." Mike and Carol's plan to let Bobby know that he is loved works and he decides not to run away after all.

#11 – Vote for Brady

Airdate: December 12, 1969
Directed by David Alexander
Produced by Sherwood Schwartz

Written by Elroy Schwartz

Stephen Liss .... Rusty

Casey Morgan .... Scott

Martin Ashe .... Mr. Dickens

Both Marcia and Greg have been nominated for president of the student body at Fillmore Junior High. Each is allotted ten dollars by the school to spend on advertising their campaigns. Marcia uses her money on posters and Greg uses his on cassette tapes to play his campaign promises from the school loudspeakers in the mornings. When Greg's tape turns up blank and Marcia's speech is missing, the kids accuse each other of sabotaging the other's campaign. The other kids take sides with Jan and Cindy supporting Marcia and Peter and Bobby supporting Greg. Tensions are high in the Brady household. Greg holds a campaign meeting with his buddies Rusty and Scott in the Brady back yard. Marcia overhears Rusty proposing that they start a rumor about her in order to make her lose the race. When Greg lashes out at Rusty for a rotten idea, Marcia is pleased to see that he is protecting her. Given this and the fact that Greg is a year older, Marcia graciously steps down from the race during her campaign speech in front of the school and Greg is elected president by default.

#12 – The Voice of Christmas
Airdate: December 19, 1969
Directed by Oscar Rudolph
Produced by Sherwood Schwartz
Written by John Fenton Murray

Hal Smith .... Santa Claus

Carl Albert .... Little Boy

It's the Bradys' first Christmas together and Carol is scheduled to sing at church services on Christmas morning. The house is decorated but nobody feels like celebrating after Carol comes down with laryngitis. Some of the kids even contemplate canceling Christmas so that their mother will not be disappointed in being unable to celebrate with them. But young Cindy asks Santa Claus for a special present for Christmas: give her mommy's voice back for Christmas Day. When the day arrives, Carol wakes up humming, her voice back to normal. It's a Christmas miracle and Mrs. Brady is able to sing her solo of "O Come, All Ye Faithful" at Christmas services.

#13 – Is There a Doctor in the House?
Airdate: December 26, 1969
Directed by Oscar Rudolph
Produced by Sherwood Schwartz
Written by Ruth Brooks Flippen

Herbert Anderson .... Dr. Cameron

Marion Ross .... Dr. Catherine Porter

All six Brady children come down with the measles. Carol calls Dr. Porter and Mike calls Dr. Cameron, both of whom make house calls. Dr. Porter, a woman, has been the girls' doctor for years and Dr. Cameron, a man, has been looking after the boys since they were born. Since the Bradys do not need two doctors, Mike and Carol must decide which doctor to keep in their employ. The boys are adamant that they should not have to be seen by a woman doctor and the girls feel just as strongly about not having a male doctor. What to do? Never fear, the problem is solved when the two doctors decide to combine their practices into one and the Bradys may call upon either one of them for future ailments. The boys can keep Dr. Cameron and the girls can keep Dr. Porter. (In this episode, viewers learn that Jan has had the chicken pox, Greg, Marcia, Peter, and Cindy have all had the mumps, Greg and Peter have had scarlet fever, and Tiger has had his shots for rabies and distemper.)

#14 – Father of the Year
Airdate: January 2, 1970
Directed by George Cahan
Produced by Sherwood Schwartz
Written by Skip Webster
Oliver McGowan ....Hamilton Samuels
Bill Mullikin.. Lance Pierce
Lee Corrigan ....Cameraman
Bob Golden ....Mr. Fields

Marcia discovers an advertisement in the local newspaper and decides to write an essay nominating Mike for Father of the Year. In order to write the essay in secret, Marcia goes to Mike's den in the evening when she is supposed to be in bed. Mike comes home from work and discovers Marcia up past her bedtime. After he sends her to bed, he accidentally spills white-out all over some blueprints and the notes for a speech he is supposed to give to the Creative Institute of Architects because Marcia left the cap off. Marcia is punished with an afternoon of chores. The next day the chores are not finished because Marcia is still working on her essay. She can't tell her father why she hasn't completed her punishment because she wants to keep her essay a secret. Thus, she is grounded for one week, which means she will be unable to accompany the family on a skiing trip. But being a great father, Mike has a soft heart and feels that it is okay to suspend Marcia's sentence to let her go on the ski trip. When he and Carol go upstairs to the girls' room to tell her, they discover that Marcia is not in her bed. She arrives a few seconds later by way of the trellis outside her second-story bedroom window. This time it's too much for Mike and he tells her that she is definitely not going skiing this weekend. Marcia is very upset, especially because the reason she was outside in the first place was to mail the essay to <u>The Daily Chronicle</u>.

TIKI TALK

Excerpts from Marcia's essay: "He is always fair and tries to be a real father to both his three sons and his three new daughters. My dad should be Father of the Year for hundreds of reasons...And Dad doesn't even play golf every weekend so he can spend more time with his family. Even when he punishes me it's because I deserve it...And even though he's only been my dad for a short time, no father could be a realer father than Michael Brady. Yours sincerely, Marcia Brady."

A few days later, a television crew and the publisher of The Daily Chronicle, Hamilton Samuels, show up at the Brady residence to surprise Mike with the Father of the Year Award. Naturally, Mike is surprised and flattered, but he is even more affected when he finds out that Marcia was the one who submitted the essay. Father and daughter hug and their picture goes in the paper.

#15 – 54-40 and Fight
Airdate: January 9, 1970
Directed by Oscar Rudolph
Produced by Sherwood Schwartz
Written by Burt Styler
Herb Vigran..Harry

The Brady kids have 94 books of Checkered Trading Stamps: 54 from the boys and 40 from the girls. They want a prize from the stamp store, and time is running out. There are only thirty days left to make a purchase and the kids can't agree on what to get. The boys want a rowboat and the girls want a sewing machine. Carol comes up with the idea of the kids choosing one thing that everyone could enjoy, but the kids can't make a decision about a product. Then Greg and Marcia decide to play for it, winner take all 94 books. The family conducts a contest to build a house of playing cards. Whoever knocks down the house loses and the winner gets to go to the store to redeem the books. During construction of the tenth story, the boys lose because of interference from Tiger and the girls go to get their sewing machine. Once in the store, though, the girls have a change of heart and choose a prize that the whole family can enjoy: a color television set for the living room.

#16 – Mike's Horror-Scope
Airdate: January 16, 1970
Directed by David Alexander
Produced by Sherwood Schwartz
Written by Ruth Brooks Flippen
Abbe Lane.. Beebe Gallini
Joe Ross ....Duane

Mike and Carol are reading the horoscopes in the newspaper. Mike's says, "A strange woman will soon come into your life." Sure enough, the next day Mike is introduced to Beebe Gallini, a rich and exotic woman who wants Mike to design her next cosmetics factory. Beebe is demanding some strange things: that her factory be pink and that it be shaped like a powder puff, for example. Mike is working overtime for her and is unable to take the boys on a Saturday fishing trip. So, Carol takes the boys fishing and Alice takes the girls horseback riding. Carol gets sunburned and falls in a pile of fish and Alice is thrown off a pesky pony. Things aren't so great at home without Mr. Brady there to fix toy airplanes and help with homework. Then Beebe decides to drop by the Brady residence and tell Mike that she now prefers her factory to be designed in the shape of a compact, complete with a flip-top lid. This outrageous request is the last straw for Mike. Fortunately, he doesn't get a chance to tell Beebe that he won't do it because Peter's airplane flies into Beebe's head and Bobby and Cindy squirt her with water pistols. She is so put off by Mike's little "creatures" that she fires him from the job and decides to get a different architect. This is okay with Mike because he feels he and his firm have been saved a lot of craziness. Mrs. Brady is glad to have her husband back at home where he belongs.

#17 – The Undergraduate
Airdate: January 23, 1970
Directed by Oscar Rudolph
Produced by Sherwood Schwartz
Written by David P. Harmon
Gigi Perreau ....Miss Linda O'Hara
Wes Parker ....Himself
Teresa Warder..Linda

Greg is flunking math because he has a big crush on his teacher, Miss Linda O'Hara, and cannot concentrate in class. Mike and Carol do not know what to do to help Greg overcome his crush, and all they know is that it is on a girl named "Linda." They naturally assume that she must be a schoolmate of Greg's. When Marcia brings home a new girl from school named Linda, Carol figures that she is the Linda whom Greg has a crush on. But when Greg comes home and is introduced to Linda, he shows no signs of knowing or liking her. Perplexed, Mrs. Brady is at a loss of what to do next. Then Mr. Brady comes home from work he opens the mail to find a letter from Miss O'Hara – Miss *Linda* O'Hara – asking him to come to her classroom tomorrow at 4:00 to discuss Greg's performance. The mysterious Linda is finally identified and Mike goes to meet her the next day. There he learns that Miss O'Hara is dating Wes Parker, a baseball player with the Los Angeles Dodgers. Mike brings Wes in to meet Greg and Wes convinces Greg to get an A in math. Problem solved!

#18 – Tiger! Tiger!
Airdate: January 30, 1970
Directed by Herb Wallerstein
Produced by Sherwood Schwartz
Written by Elroy Schwartz
Maggie Malooly..Mrs. Simpson
Gary Grimes.. Teenage Boy

Tiger runs away and Bobby is especially affected by his disappearance. Mr. Brady puts an ad in the paper offering a $42.76 reward for Tiger's safe return. If you think the dollar amount is strange, that's because each of the kids, Mike, and Alice all contributed different amounts:

Mike = $25.00	Alice = $5.00
Greg = $4.00	Marcia = $3.00
Peter = $2.14	Jan = $2.00
Bobby = $1.12	Cindy = $0.50

Alice comes up with a theory as to where Tiger went. Greg and Peter overhear her telling Mike and Carol that there has been a rash of burglaries in the neighborhood and that the thieves could have lured Tiger away so that they could have a crack at the Brady residence that night. The boys think Alice's theory is worth considering, so they booby trap the doorways downstairs. While they're setting the traps, Alice hears their noises and ends up walking right into one in the family room. She is covered with empty cans and string. Mike comes downstairs and he and the boys are about to hit her with a baseball bat because they think she is the burglar. Fortunately, Carol turns on a light and Alice is revealed to be herself. The next day, Tiger is still AWOL and the Brady kids and Mike mount a search throughout town to find him. Eventually Peter does and Mike and Bobby meet him at Mrs. Simpson's house where it is revealed that Tiger has fathered three puppies with Mrs. Simpson's dog. Bobby is pleased to see that Tiger is a father and they bring him home proudly; they leave Mrs. Simpson to deal with the pups.

#19 – The Big Sprain

Airdate: February 6, 1970
Directed by Russ Mayberry
Produced by Sherwood Schwartz
Written by Tam Spiva
Allan Melvin .... Sam

Alice trips over the kids' Chinese checkers game and sprains her ankle. With Carol gone to take care of her aunt for a week, there is no one left to do the household chores. How will the Bradys get along? Mike enlists the kids to take care of things and keep the house in shape while Alice recovers in bed. The kids are far from perfect housekeepers, though. Breakfast is burned, the doghouse is flooded, and the washing machine overflows and sends the wash floating into the dining room. When Carol calls to check on things, Mike tells her that everything is just fine. This causes Marcia and Greg to feel guilty about how they've behaved so far. The kids all band together and the household is now running like clockwork. Meanwhile, Alice has had to call off her date with Sam for Saturday night because she can't go to the Meat Cutters Ball with a sprained ankle. She thinks that Sam will take someone else to the Ball, but is happily surprised when Sam shows up at the Brady house with some nosegay and a plan to kiss her goodnight under the stars.

#20 – Brace Yourself

Airdate: February 13, 1970
Directed by Oscar Rudolph
Produced by Sherwood Schwartz
Written by Brad Radnitz
Molly Dodd .... Saleslady
Mike Robertson .... Alan Anthony
John Daniels .... Eddie
Brian Nash .... Joey Michelson
Jerry Levreau .... Harold Reynolds

It's Marcia's first date and two weeks before the school dance she gets braces. Marcia thinks she looks horrible with braces on and doesn't think that her date Alan will like her anymore. Alan comes by the house and tells her that he has to break off his date because he has to go out of town with his parents the weekend of the dance. Marcia construes his explanation to mean that Alan doesn't want to go out with anyone with braces so she breaks up with him. Carol, Alice, and Greg all get the idea that a date with a new boy will lift Marcia's spirits so they enlist Harold, Eddie, and Joey to ask her out. Marcia meets the three boys but quickly finds out they've all been bribed to take her to the dance. Now Marcia is feeling even lower than before. Then Alan's parents change their plans so he is free to go to the dance with Marcia again. This time, Marcia accepts his invitation. When Alan shows up to escort her to the dance, it turns out that he has gotten braces as well. The happy couple goes to the dance arm in arm.

#21 – The Hero
Airdate: February 20, 1970
Directed by Oscar Rudolph
Produced by Sherwood Schwartz
Written by Elroy Schwartz
Pitt Herbert..Mr. Driscoll
Dani Nolan...Mrs. Spencer
Dave Morick ....Earl Hopkins
Joe Conley.. Deliveryman
Randy Lane .... Steve
Iler Rasmussen.. Jason
Susan Joyce..Jenny
Melanie Baker... Tina Spencer

There's a new headline on the front page of The Daily Chronicle: *"Boy Hero – Peter Brady, 11, Risks Life to Save Young Girl."* Yes, Peter swooped in and saved Tina Spencer just as a wall of shelves was about to collapse on her in Driscoll's Toy Store. As thanks for his daring deed he gets his picture in the paper and Mrs. Spencer offers to buy him everything he wants from the Toy Store. Peter's head is swelling fit to burst. When The Daily Chronicle comes back and awards Peter the Outstanding Citizenship Award and $50, Peter elects to throw himself a party with his prize money. His siblings are fed up with his bragging and they let their parents know that they will not be attending. Peter overhears their conversation and insists that he can have a swell party without them. He invites all his friends, but the next day after school no one shows up. Peter has learned his lesson: "a guy can sure get messed up patting himself on the back." In the end, his siblings decide to attend and so do Mrs. Spencer and Tina.

#22 – The Possible Dream
Airdate: February 27, 1970
Directed by Oscar Rudolph
Produced by Sherwood Schwartz
Written by Al Schwartz and Bill Freedman

Desi Arnaz, Jr. .... Himself
Gordon Jump ....Collins
Jonathan Hole.. Thackery
Pat Patterson.. Collection Man

Marcia has a wild crush on Desi Arnaz, Jr. and she writes all about it in her diary. When Cindy accidentally gives her diary away to the Friend in Need Society, Marcia is devastated. Her secret thoughts are out there for the whole world to read, she fears. Mike and Carol decide to track down the diary and Mike learns that there are about a dozen used book stores in town where it might be. The two get together with Marcia and Cindy and go diary hunting. Meanwhile, Marcia has confessed her crush to Alice who just happens to know Desi's mother's housekeeper. Alice arranges for Desi to stop by the Brady residence and pay Marcia a visit. Marcia is very enamored with the famous teen idol and can barely believe her eyes when he walks in. Desi tells her that he is very glad to meet his number one fan and gives Marcia a peck on the cheek which she swears she will never wash again. Cindy and Carol return in time to meet Desi and give Marcia her diary back. It's a swell ending to a tragic day for young Marcia Brady.

#23 – To Move or not to Move
Airdate: March 6, 1970
Directed by Oscar Rudolph
Produced by Sherwood Schwartz
Written by Paul West
Fran Ryan.. Mrs. Hunsaker
Lindsay Workman ....Bertram Grossman

The Brady kids are fighting over the bathroom and for more privacy; all six children must share two bedrooms and just one bathroom. Carol and Mike decide that it is time to sell their home and move into a larger one with more bathrooms and bedrooms. Even though it was the kids' idea to move, they have a change of heart when they realize how many fond memories they have of this home. After all, this is the house where Peter got stitches in his nose, Bobby got a lump on his head, and Greg fell off the garage roof. The kids hatch a plan to "haunt" the Brady home. They've heard that haunted houses don't sell so well and they hope to scare off any prospective buyers so that Mike and Carol have to keep this house. The kids play recorded sounds of inhuman moaning and creaking boards. They slam doors when no one is looking and make loud crashes outside. Carol and Alice are thoroughly convinced that the house is haunted. Mike has been away working late during the week, so he has not heard any of the strange noises. He tries to convince Carol that the house is just settling. When Bert Grossman brings over a prospective buyer, the kids are up to their tricks. They play moaning noises. Bobby and Cindy dress up in sheets as ghosts and walk by Alice's room, which makes her scream bloody murder. The buyer is just about ready to walk away when Mike catches Bobby and Cindy in the act. The buyer thinks it's endearing that he kids are willing to go to such lengths to save their home. Mike and Carol decide not to sell and the Brady bunch can stay in the house that Mike built.

#24 – The Grass is Always Greener
Airdate: March 13, 1970
Directed by George Cahan
Produced by Sherwood Schwartz
Written by David P. Harmon

Mike and Carol come in from a long day of playing ball with the boys and taking the girls into the woods. Mike says that taking care of the boys is more difficult than taking care of girls and Carol contends the opposite. They can't settle the argument so Alice proposes that they change places for the coming weekend. Carol will teach baseball to the boys and Mike will help Marcia get her cooking badge in the kitchen. It sounds like a good idea, but things immediately go wrong. Carol is sliding into bases and batting hard enough that she can barely move after an hour. Mike spills a dozen eggs on the floor, creates a colossal mess in the kitchen, and falls again and again trying to clean it up. The couple makes amends and agrees that taking care of the opposite sex is indeed just as hard as taking care of their own. They go downstairs to enjoy Marcia's dinner of chilled tomato juice with lemon, egg salad, French fried potatoes, breaded veal cutlets, string beans, and cake with chocolate frosting.

#25 – Lost Locket, Found Locket
Airdate: March 20, 1970
Directed by Norman Abbott
Produced by Sherwood Schwartz
Written by Charles Hoffman
Jack Griffin...Security Guard

Jan receives a locket in the mail. There is no return address and no card inside; it's a real mystery who sent it. Greg discovers that the typewriter that typed Jan's address (4222 Clinton Way, City) drops its ys. Mike and Carol each secretly suspect each other of sending the locket to Jan and they check their spouse's typewriters to see if their ys are dropped. Mike's typewriter at work is perfect and Carol's portable at home is perfect as well. Thus, the mystery deepens. Then, Jan wakes up one night screaming that her precious locket is gone. A thorough search reveals nothing. Greg wants to reenact the events leading up to the disappearance, so all eight Bradys and Alice do exactly what they did the night before. When 10:00 rolls around – the time Jan screamed the night before – Jan suddenly remembers that she had been at her bedroom window looking out at the stars before she went to sleep last night. She hollers again and everyone comes running. When she and Mike peer down into the ivy in the trellis below her window, they find the missing locket. Jan's happiness is restored. But, the mystery of the unidentified sender still lingers until Alice pulls Jan aside one morning. Alice tells Jan that when she was growing up she, too, was a middle child. Her two sisters Emily and Myrtle were a lot like Marcia and Cindy. Alice understands firsthand what it is like to grow up as a middle child. Jan is pleased to hear that Alice understands her strife. It's then that Alice confesses that she sent the locket to Jan. Alice's aunt gave her the locket when she was a child and Alice decided to pass it onto Jan. Jan and Alice hug and the answer to the mystery is safe with them.

THE BRADY BUNCH (comedy)
SEASON TWO 1970-1971
Fridays 7:30-8:00pm ET on ABC

Production Notes: The Brady Bunch is back for a second season despite the predictions of most critics. Says Robert Reed of the occasion: "I was really surprised. But it's always nice to be accepted. You tell yourself you'd rather do something else, but it's always a matter of rejection."[1] Charles Witbeck of The Toledo Blade explains, "The premise of a widower with three boys marrying a widow with three girls in ABC's 'The Brady Bunch,' sounded like a show marked by a death wish last fall, but the intrepid Brady family is with us again for another season of mirth and canned laughter. Reasons for series survival remain a mystery. Being prejudiced, I like to believe that Alice the housekeeper, played by Ann B. Davis, is responsible for audience approval."[2] Indeed, the show defied the odds and whether it was because of Ann B., the wholesome storylines, or something else altogether, the nine blue-boxed smiling faces were back to entertain viewers again.

It's time to start the Brady kid age shuffle! It's hard to pin down just how old the kids are in any given year, and sometimes the gap between the kids changes. In general, most of the time Greg is the oldest, Marcia is one year younger than he is, then comes Peter two years after her, then Jan the next year, Bobby two more years later, and Cindy is last just one year behind Bobby. In other words, the boys are three years apart from each other as are the girls and the girls are one year behind the boys. But this isn't always true. For example, in this season, Cindy is 8 (remember last Christmas she was 6), Bobby is 9, Jan turns 12 in November, Peter is 12, Marcia is 14, and Greg turns 15 in November. Stay tuned for next season when Marcia and Greg's ages change the most.

#26 – The Dropout
Airdate: September 25, 1970
Directed by Peter Baldwin

Executive Producer Sherwood Schwartz
Produced by Howard Leeds
Written by Ben Gershman & Bill Freedman
Don Drysdale .... Himself

Mike is designing a home for baseball great Don Drysdale. Mike introduces Don to the Brady boys and Greg is especially impressed. Don gives him a tip on how to throw a better slider and tells Greg that maybe someday he can play for the major leagues. From that point on, Greg's head is swollen to popping. He imagines signing bonuses and all-star treatment are headed his way. He spends every waking moment reading about baseball and practicing and his school grades are taking a nosedive. The big game for his team the Tigers (last year Greg played for the Rockets) is on Saturday and Greg is their starting pitcher. The cocky young lad steps up to the mound thinking the opposing team will be lucky to get a foul tip off him today. Unfortunately for Greg, his pitching skills are not all that he thinks they are; the opposing team scores twelve runs in the first inning and Greg's coach takes him off the mound. Greg comes home from the game early, thinking that it is the end of the world. Mike is there to pick up the pieces and helps Greg understand that although he may not be another Don Drysdale, he doesn't have to go to the other extreme and forget about baseball all together. Greg is thankful for his dad's advice and the two go outside to play catch in the yard together.

#27 – The Babysitters
Airdate: October 2, 1970
Directed by Oscar Rudolph
Executive Producer Sherwood Schwartz
Produced by Howard Leeds
Written by Bruce Howard
Gil Stuart..Restaurant Captain
Jerry Jones...Police Officer

Mike and Carol have tickets to see a show and Alice has a date with Sam to hang curtains in his apartment. Who will watch the kids? Greg and Marcia overhear their parents talking about employing a babysitter for the evening. The two eldest Brady kids, 14 and 13, are utterly opposed to the idea because they feel quite capable of sitting for themselves and their siblings. They make their feelings known to Mike and Carol who reluctantly agree to give it a go. Greg and Marcia are put in charge for the night and Mike makes sure that Greg knows what to do in emergency situations. After Mike, Carol, and Alice are gone, they start to question their decision and want to check in on the kids. None of them wants to let the kids know they're being checked on, though, so they decide to sneak around the side of the house just to see that everything is okay. Mike makes a ruckus outside, which Greg hears from inside. He thinks a prowler is in the yard and calls the police to come check out the situation. The cops find a very embarrassed Mike, Carol, and Alice. They bumble their way through an explanation and are let go. They all apologize to the kids for not trusting them and decide to go back out to finish their evening plans. Parents…

#28 – The Slumber Caper

Airdate: October 9, 1970
Directed by Oscar Rudolph
Executive Producer Sherwood Schwartz
Produced by Howard Leeds
Written by Tam Spiva

E.G. Marshall ....Mr. J.P. Randolph
Chris Charney .... Paula Tardy
Hope Sherwood...Jenny Wilton
Barbara Henderson..Ruthie
Carolyn Reed .... Karen

Marcia is granted permission to hold a sleepover on the upcoming Saturday night. Her plans are derailed when she ends up with a week's detention. Mr. Randolph, her principal, accused Marcia of writing "Mrs. Denton? Or a hippopotamus?" on a drawing she did. Marcia claims the drawing is of George Washington and that she did not write the offensive remark. Mr. Randolph has no evidence to the contrary and therefore cannot believe her explanation. Mike and Carol find out about the drawing and her punishment, so they call off the slumber party. Marcia is distraught and thinks that her parents would rather believe her principal than her, which is true…at least until Mike decides to investigate for himself and meets with Mr. Randolph. Mike sees the picture and brings it home to Carol. They both decide that they should believe their daughter. Although there is nothing they can do about her punishment at school, they do lift her punishment at home and the party is back on. Meanwhile, the Brady boys are plotting some pranks to play on the girls at the party. They fill the sleeping bags with itching powder, plant a fake rubber spider in one of them, and plan to scare the girls with Halloween masks. Marcia is looking for the person who wrote the remark about Mrs. Denton on her paper. She blames her best friend Jenny for the deed and promptly repeals her invitation to the party. Jenny is mystified. The night of the party arrives and, counting the three Brady girls, there are 14 teenage girls camping out in the living room. Mike and Carol go out to dinner and Alice is left to police the gaggle. The boys' tricks are played and all the girls end up itching. Alice takes them upstairs to wash off, and on the way up Marcia's friend Paula confesses to the "joke" on Mrs. Denton. Paula had intended for the drawing to be seen by Marcia's eyes only. The girls decide to explain everything to Mr. Randolph on Monday morning. Marcia feels guilty about jumping the gun by blaming Jenny and calls her up to apologize and ask her to the party. Jenny shows up – but not before a bucket of flour is dropped on Mike's head – and all is well.

#29 – The Un-Underground Movie

Airdate: October 16, 1970
Directed by Jack Arnold
Executive Producer Sherwood Schwartz
Produced by Howard Leeds
Written by Albert E. Lewin

Greg's groovy history teacher assigns the students a project to portray the story of the Pilgrims. Greg decides to use Mike's 8mm home movie camera and write a script for the movie. He gets the whole family involved. The family have a lot of ideas of their own and soon Greg's project is commandeered. Mike, Alice, and Carol edit the script, Carol changes the costumes and the kids demand to play all the best parts. Greg becomes fed up and tells his parents that the movie is off. Realizing the error of their ways, Mike and Carol promise to give Greg total creative freedom from this point on. Thus, Greg's project is back on track. Greg writes, directs, and produces his movie, which he calls "Our Pilgrim Fathers or through Hardship to Freedom." Greg even puts in some fancy special effects like narration, music, and slow motion. Clearly, his school has great editing equipment, especially for its time. His teacher gives him an A for the film and Greg is already thinking of his next one: Paul Revere's ride.

EPISODE GUIDE

#30 – Going, Going…Steady

Airdate: October 23, 1970
Directed by Oscar Rudolph
Executive Producer Sherwood Schwartz
Produced by Howard Leeds
Written by David P. Harmon
Billy Corcoran..Harvey Klinger
Rory Stevens..Lester

Marcia has an unrequited crush on a boy named Harvey Klinger. Harvey hardly takes notice of her because he is preoccupied with his hobby, entomology. Marcia is down and out until her parents suggest that she try to take up Harvey's hobby, too. So, she engrosses herself in books about insects. She gets Harvey's attention at school the next day by planting an insect at his feet and exclaiming, "Look, a *lateral femorata!*" (There is actually no such thing as a lateral femorata. There are about 200 different kinds of femorata ranging from bees to beetles to walking sticks, but none of them is named "lateral.") Harvey is instantly entranced with both the bug and Marcia. The two decide to go steady, much to Carol's chagrin. Harvey and Marcia compare bugs in the Brady kitchen while Greg and Jan make fun of them out of earshot. The couple decides that they are like a woman of 20 and a man of 22 in Carol and Mike's generation and Mike decides to treat them as adults. He gives Harvey '20 Questions' about his plans for employment, education, and even retirement. After Mike's adult-like questioning, both Marcia and Harvey decide they should act their ages: 14 and 13. After she goes out with him for a while, Marcia decides that Harvey is boring and dumps him. She goes through a very quick string of boyfriends (Danny, Alan, and Lester) as Mike and Carol watch on, shaking their heads and chalking it all up to youth.

#31 – Call Me Irresponsible

Airdate: October 30, 1970
Directed by Hal Cooper
Executive Producer Sherwood Schwartz
Produced by Howard Leeds
Written by Bruce Howard

19

Jack Collins.. Mr. Phillips
Annette Ferra ....Randy Peterson
Barbara Morrison.......................................Drama Coach
William Benedict ....News Vendor
Gordon Jump.. Mechanic
Bob Peoples ....Mr. Peterson

Greg makes an important announcement to his parents: in thirteen months he will be sixteen years old and he would like to get a part-time job after school to start saving up money for his first car. Mike and Carol agree that Greg should be allowed to work as long as his grades are kept up. Mike arranges for Greg to come to work with him at his architectural firm as a janitor/delivery boy. Greg's ecstatic to have his very first job. He has been dating a girl named Randy Peterson and now he can brag to her that he is a working man and is saving up money for his very own car. He also tells her (before he knows what his actual duties will be) that he is going to build some really groovy buildings just like the Egyptian pyramids. Randy is impressed. On his first day of work, Mike asks Greg to deliver some designs for low-cost housing to the printers for copying. Greg takes the yellow canister with the plans inside and rides his bike to 12th and Sunset where the printing shop is. On his way there, though, he stops by the newsstand to buy the latest issue of <u>Car Sport</u> magazine for fifty cents. Unbeknownst to Greg, the top of the canister slips off and the plans roll out and into the street where they are promptly stepped on by pedestrians. When Greg arrives at the print shop, the plans are gone. Greg looks all over for them but cannot find them and arrives back home dejected. Mike is very disappointed and he has to call his boss Mr. Phillips to tell him what happened. Mike spends all night redrawing the designs. Mr. Phillips wants to fire Greg for his mistake, but the next day Mike asks his boss to give Greg one more chance. Mr. Phillips agrees, but lets Mike know that if Greg screws up again he (Greg) will be fired. Mike calls Greg at home and tells him the good news that he is being given a second chance. Greg hurries over and takes the second set of plans from his father and promises to hold on tight. Disaster strikes Greg again when the chain on his bike breaks. Fortunately, it happened right in front of his girlfriend and her father. Mr. Peterson offers Greg a ride to the print shop. When they get there, Greg goes around the back of the car to pick up his prints, but Mr. Peterson drives off with them. It looks like Greg has done it again! This time he is persistent, though, and tracks Mr. Peterson's car down to a mechanic's garage. Greg retrieves the plans and delivers them to the print shop before it closes. He comes home half an hour late to a worried Mike and tells his father that everything went just fine and the prints were delivered without a problem. Mike can trust his son and Greg keeps his job.

#32 – The Treasure of Sierra Avenue
Airdate: November 6, 1970
Directed by Oscar Rudolph
Executive Producer Sherwood Schwartz
Produced by Howard Leeds
Written by Gwen Bagni and Paul Dubov
Victor Killian .... Mr. Stoner

Greg, Peter, and Bobby find a lost wallet in an empty lot that contains $1100 and no identification. Mike turns the wallet into the police so that the rightful owner will have a chance to recover it. In the meantime, the boys are dreaming about what they can do with $366.66 each. The girls want in on the loot, too, but the boys are unwilling to share. The boys feel that since it was they who found the wallet only they should be entitled to the money. Mike realizes that the Bradys are rapidly becoming a house divided so he makes sure that his mantra of share and share alike is followed. If the money does go unclaimed, all six kids will split it and get $183.33 each. Peter learns from a friend's father that if the money goes unclaimed for six months that they can get it. Plus, if the Bradys want to assume liability they can keep the wallet in the bank and collect the interest it accrues. Pete and Bobby leave it to Mike to determine how to handle it. In the end, Mike doesn't have to make a decision because the wallet's rightful owner has claimed it. Mr. Stoner, the owner, stops by the Brady house to thank the boys for their honesty and gives them a $20 reward. The kids split the twenty bucks and give Mike the two cents left over.

EPISODE GUIDE

#33 – A Fistful of Reasons

Airdate: November 13, 1970
Directed by Oscar Rudolph
Executive Producer Sherwood Schwartz
Produced by Howard Leeds
Written by Tam Spiva
Russell Schulman...................................... Buddy Hinton
Paul Sorensen..Ralph Hinton
Ceil Cabot ....Mrs. Hinton

Cindy is being teased by schoolyard bully Buddy Hinton because she lisps. Peter rises to her defense, but ends up with a black eye and a new nickname "chicken." Mike and Carol try to straighten the situation out by talking to Buddy's parents, but both his mother and father couldn't care less if Buddy picks on little girls and starts fights with boys. From that point on, Mike gives Peter permission to defend himself. If reasoning doesn't work with Buddy next time, Mike says it's okay for Peter to fight him back. Peter goes into training and Greg and Mike teach him how to fight. The next time Peter and Cindy run into Buddy, Pete is ready. He tries reasoning with Buddy, but it doesn't work. Buddy tells him shut up or fight. So Buddy throws the first punch, misses, and Pete throws the next one and hits Buddy in the mouth. Buddy gets a loose tooth and now he himself speaks with a lisp. Cindy teases him, but Peter admonishes her for it by telling her that no one likes to be teased, even bullies. Buddy reconciles with the Bradys by coming over and asking to borrow Cindy's tongue twister book. It appears he's learned his lesson about picking fights and teasing...at least until episode #49.

#34 – The Not-So-Ugly Duckling

Airdate: November 20, 1970
Directed by Irving J. Moore
Executive Producer Sherwood Schwartz
Produced by Howard Leeds
Written by Paul West

21

Mark Gruner..Clark Tyson
Joseph Mell .... Druggist

The best looking boy in Jan's class, Clark Tyson, has eyes only for Marcia. Jan is thoroughly upset and jealous of her older sister. Why don't boys pay attention to me, she wonders. She thinks it's because she has freckles, but when she hears Peter talking about how much he likes another girl's freckles, she knows there must be some other reason. She thinks Clark doesn't like her just because she's her. Jan does not want to admit to her parents what she is thinking, so she invents a fake boyfriend named George Glass. She even goes so far as to make the operator call the house twice. When she picks up the receiver, she pretends it's George at the other end. The Bradys want to throw Jan a surprise 12th birthday party and everyone tries to find George so that they can invite him. When no one can, Carol and Mike realize the truth. Mike, Carol, and Alice all try to come up with a way to help Jan and Carol thinks of the idea of asking a boy from Jan's class what all the guys think of her. So, she asks Clark to come over for some dessert and poses the question to him. Clark says that Jan is a real neat "guy," but none of the boys really see her as feminine. Carol immediately pops Jan into a dress and parades her outside where Clark is playing. Clark's eyes bug out and he finally notices her for who she is: an attractive young lady. The family throws the surprise party for Jan and Clark comes as Jan's date.

#35 – The Tattle-Tale
Airdate: December 4, 1970
Directed by Russ Mayberry
Executive Producer Sherwood Schwartz
Produced by Howard Leeds
Written by Sam Locke & Milton Pascal
John Wheeler... Postman

Cindy is becoming notorious for tattling on her brothers and sisters. Mike and Carol try to impress upon her the importance of staying out of other people's business. At the same time, Alice is entering a jingle contest for the Ever Pressed Fabric Company. She comes up with two separate options: "For the fabrics that are best, put your faith in Ever Pressed. You will always look well dressed, in the east and in the vest," and, "Ever Pressed is just right for you if you are no matter who. Try our fabrics real soon in flannel, silk, or gaberdoon." She sends in the first one and soon she hears from the Fabric Company that she won the contest. Alice is so excited that she gives the postman a hug. Cindy is on the phone talking to Alice's boyfriend Sam at the time and tells him that she can't come to the phone because she is currently hugging the postman. Alice gets all gussied up for her date with Sam that night and when he doesn't show, she is perplexed. She gives Sam a call and he suggests that she go with the postman instead and hangs up on her. Now Alice is utterly confused. Cindy comes downstairs and pipes up that she spoke to Sam earlier and the truth comes out. Mike gives her a classic Mike Brady lecture and makes her promise that she will never tattle on anyone again. Cindy takes the lecture to heart. The next day the postman comes again and delivers another registered letter for Alice. She isn't home so Cindy signs for it and puts it in the front entryway. Tiger snatches the letter and takes off for his doghouse. When the Fabric Company calls Alice to congratulate her they tell her that she must redeem the certificate they sent her for a new hi-fi stereo set by midnight that night otherwise the offer expires. Carol and Alice begin the search for the letter. Carol asks Cindy if she knows anything. Cindy says she does, but she can't tell them where the letter is otherwise Daddy will send Tiger to Siberia. The truth slipped out of her mouth, but this time Cindy will not be punished. Alice finds her certificate in the doghouse and redeems it. She is nice enough to put the stereo in the family room so that the whole family can enjoy it. Cindy's tattling days are over.

#36 – What Goes Up...

Airdate: December 11, 1970
Directed by Leslie H. Martinson
Executive Producer Sherwood Schwartz
Produced by Howard Leeds
Written by William Raynor & Myles Wilder
Jimmy Bracken .... Jimmy
Sean Kelly .... Tim
Brian Tochi .... Tommy

Bobby is tagging along with his older brother Peter. Pete convinces his friends Tim, Tommy, and Jimmy that Bobby should be allowed to join their tree house club as their mascot. The boys agree only after Pete says that Bobby will pay dues. Bobby is excited and starts climbing the boards nailed to the tree trunk to get initiated. He falls from the top rung and sprains his right ankle. Bobby is nursed back to health quickly by his siblings, Alice, and parents. Mike even buys him a pet parakeet to keep him company. But after his ankle heals, Bobby becomes afraid of heights. He is worried that he might hurt himself again, but does not confide his fears to his family. It's only after he declines offers to coast down Maple Street, to climb the tree a second time, and to have a swinging competition with Jan that the family figures it out. To combat his fears, Bobby's family decides to get him back on the horse again. Greg builds some stilts, but Bobby doesn't want to walk with them. They all borrow a trampoline and the other kids and Alice give it a try and attempt to coax Bobby down from his room. The only thing that finally works in getting Bobby over his fear is when he puts his own safety aside in order to rescue his parakeet. Tiger scared the parakeet out the window. Bobby spots the bird in a tree above the swing set. He maneuvers his way to the top of the swing set where he stands up and gets the bird to climb onto his finger. The family is there to witness his triumph and Bobby has successfully overcome his fear.

#37 – Confessions, Confessions

Airdate: December 18, 1970
Directed by Russ Mayberry
Executive Producer Sherwood Schwartz
Produced by Howard Leeds
Written by Brad Radnitz
Snag Werris .... Hardware Man

Peter throws a very poorly aimed basketball in the house and accidentally breaks Carol's favorite vase. He's looking forward to an overnight camping week for the coming weekend, and now he thinks he's doomed to miss it. Big brother Greg hatches a plan to glue the vase back together and hold off Peter's confession until after the camping trip is over. All the kids are in on it because they all witnessed the broken vase. When Mike comes home with flowers for Carol, she thinks the flowers will look lovely in the very vase that Peter broke. Greg and Peter put the flowers in the damaged vase and pray that the glue is dry enough. Unfortunately for them, it's not and the vase turns into a fountain in the middle of the dinner table. Mike and Carol tell the kids they expect a confession after dinner. All the kids confess separately except for Peter. Carol deduces that Peter is the guilty one because he has something to look forward to for the weekend. Instead of punishing Peter, the parents decide to let his conscience do the work. They make Peter come up with punishments for his brothers and sisters. Additionally, they buy him a new lantern for the camping trip. When Saturday comes, the five Brady kids are diligently doing the chores Peter meted out for them. When Pete gets to the door to go away for his trip, his conscience finally gets the better of him. He confesses the whole ordeal to his parents. He has to tell his buddies that he can't go camping with them now. He also takes over all the chores he assigned to his siblings. Carol has one more left for him: re-glue the vase back together. When she tries to hand him the vase, she drops it. Pete is quick to say that they better tell Mike the truth before things get worse. Lesson learned.

#38 – The Impractical Joker
Airdate: January 1, 1971
Directed by Oscar Rudolph
Executive Producer Sherwood Schwartz
Produced by Howard Leeds
Written by Burt Styler
Lennie Breman ....Exterminator

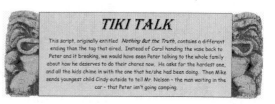

TIKI TALK

This script, originally entitled *Nothing But the Truth*, contains a different ending than the tag that aired. Instead of Carol handing the vase back to Peter and it breaking, we would have seen Peter talking to the whole family about how he deserves to do their chores now. He asks for the hardest one, and all the kids chime in with the one that he/she had been doing. Then Mike sends youngest child Cindy outside to tell Mr. Nelson – the man waiting in the car – that Peter isn't going camping.

Jan is playing practical jokes on her family members. First, she puts an ink spot on Alice's new coat. Then she scares her sisters with a fake spider in the cookies. Carol warns her to stop playing jokes because someday soon she's going to end up hurting somebody. Jan gives a sly little grin and sure enough the next day she is up to her tricks again. Greg brings home a science project for the weekend. He is supposed to teach a mouse named Myron to run a maze by Monday. Jan is enamored with Myron and her sisters and mother decidedly are not. Mike makes Greg keep Myron out in the garage so the girls don't have to worry about being squeamish. During the middle of the night Greg wakes up and realizes that the neighbor's cat Guinevere could get to Myron any second. He rounds up his brothers and they go outside and retrieve Myron's cage. Jan witnesses them bringing Myron into their bedroom. A bit later, she sneaks into the room, takes Myron out of his cage, and puts him in the girls' hamper. She hopes that Myron will scare Marcia and Cindy in the morning. When the boys wake up, they immediately notice that Myron is gone and begin a search for him. The little white mouse chewed his way through Jan's hamper and ends up in the kitchen where Alice spots him. Alice is unaware that he is Greg's science project, so she calls the exterminator. The Zap-it company arrives and sprays under the house. Greg thinks Myron has been exterminated. Jan comes up to him and confesses what she did last night and says that Myron must be in the hamper where she left him. The boys are very relieved and they and Jan run upstairs to find the mouse. But when they get there, all they see is a hole chewed in the hamper. Now Jan realizes that her joke backfired and that Myron is probably dead. Carol and Mike come home from shopping and work and see that the household is in mourning for Myron. Even Tiger seems to be upset. He's howling and the family goes out to investigate what the matter could be. When Mike peeks into Tiger's doghouse, he sees a tiny white mouse. It's Myron alive and well! Greg is overjoyed that he escaped the exterminator. Jan learns her lesson about playing practical jokes and Greg is able to continue working on his science project.

#39 – Where There's Smoke
Airdate: January 8, 1971
Directed by Oscar Rudolph
Executive Producer Sherwood Schwartz
Produced by Howard Leeds
Written by David P. Harmon

Craig Hundley	Tommy Johnson
Marie Denn	Mrs. Johnson
Gary Marsh	Phil
Bobby Kramer	Johnny

Jan and Cindy catch Greg smoking after school with some buddies of his. They tell Marcia who in turn tells Mike and Carol. The parents confront Greg about his smoking and he promises never to do it again. They let him get off with a warning. In the meantime, he is practicing with his friends and their band The Banana Convention. Greg plays guitar and sings and Tommy plays drums. The two other band members are Phil and Johnny and all three of them smoke. The band has a gig at Stephen Decatur High for Saturday. When Greg comes home from practice, a pack of cigarettes falls out of his jacket in front of Carol and Mrs. Johnson, Tommy's mother. Mrs. Johnson thinks they're Greg's, but Greg convinces Carol that they are not his. Carol says that maybe she'd better not join Mrs. Johnson's anti-smoking group after all. Greg becomes determined to prove to his parents that they were right in trusting him, so he sets out to find where the cigarettes came from. Alice discovers that the jacket he had thought was his really isn't because the lining has never been mended. At that moment of discovery, Tommy rings the doorbell and is there to exchange jackets with Greg. Greg grabs Tommy, tells him that he (Greg) was accused of owning the cigarettes, and makes Tommy tell the truth to Mike and Carol. Mrs. Johnson comes in in the middle of Tommy's confession and she, too, learns the truth: that Tommy is a smoker and not Greg. Carol is very nice about it and invites Mrs. Johnson and the anti-smoking group over for Friday night and Mrs. Johnson agrees. Tommy gets in trouble, Greg is off the hook, and The Banana Convention really bends the gig out of shape at Stephen Decatur High.

#40 – Will the Real Jan Brady Please Stand Up?
Airdate: January 15, 1971
Directed by Peter Baldwin
Executive Producer Sherwood Schwartz
Produced by Howard Leeds
Written by Al Schwartz and Bill Freedman

Pamelyn Ferdin	Lucy Winters
Marcia Wallace	Wig Saleswoman

25

Karen Foulkes .... Margie Wimple

Jan buys a brunette wig in order to distinguish herself from her two blonde sisters. Her siblings think she looks awful in it, but Jan is determined to prove them wrong by wearing the wig to Lucy Winters' birthday party. When she shows up at the party, Lucy and the other kids laugh at her. Jan runs off crying. Then Peter tells them it wasn't intended as a joke, and Lucy, Peter, and Margie Wimple track Jan down at home and ask her to come back to the party. They tell her her hair is the envy of them all and that she is fine just the way she is.

#41 – The Drummer Boy
Airdate: January 22, 1971
Directed by Oscar Rudolph
Executive Producer Sherwood Schwartz
Produced by Howard Leeds
Written by Tom and Helen August
David "Deacon" Jones .... Himself
Bart LaRue .... Coach
Jimmy Bracken .... Larry
Dennis McDougall .... Freddy
Pierre Williams .... Jimmy

The plots are starting to get a little more complicated because now there are two kids with problems in the same episode. Jan, Peter, and Cindy make it into the Glee Club, but Bobby does not. Apparently, Bobby has a voice that sounds like a croaking frog. He is very sad about the whole thing, but his parents are able to cheer him up by telling him that maybe instead of singing he should play an instrument. The next day he comes home with a drum set. Meanwhile, Peter is also on the football team and his teammates are giving him a hard time about being in the Glee Club. They call him a songbird and a canary and think that he's a sissy because he sings. Peter is thinking about quitting the Glee Club. He uses Bobby's drumming as an excuse at first. The drums are driving the family up the wall so Mike sends Bobby out into the garage to practice in his own "studio." Finally, Peter tells his parents the truth about the reason he wants to quit the Glee Club. They advise him to take a little bit longer to think about it. The next day at football practice, Deacon Jones is there to give the guys some pointers. The pro-footballer is friends with Peter's coach. When Pete is set to go against his teammate Larry, Larry says he doesn't want to tackle him because he might damage Peter, him being a frail singer and all. Deacon hears the taunt and tells the whole team that he sings, that Joe Namath, Rosy Greer, and others do, too. None of them is a sissy. Pete's teammates apologize and some of them even try out for the Glee Club now. The same day, Bobby decides that he has had enough drumming. He switches to the bugle. But when he gets up at 5:30 in the morning to play Revile, Mike wants to tie a knot in the bugle. In the end, Mike gets Bobby a baton, something quiet and easy for the poor kid. As soon as it's in Bobby's hands, it's out flying across the living room and breaking something. At least Bobby is determined not to give up.

#42 – Coming-Out Party
Airdate: January 29, 1970
Directed by Oscar Rudolph
Executive Producer Sherwood Schwartz
Produced by Howard Leeds
Written by David P. Harmon
John Howard .... Dr. Howard
Jack Collins .... Mr. Phillips

No, it's not what you think. This kind of coming-out party involves two tonsillectomies. Cindy and Carol both have inflamed tonsils and they must come out. They get ace medical treatment: an at-home visit to determine if the tonsillectomies are necessary, an overnight stay in the hospital, another at-home visit when they come home from the hospital, and a third the next day to make sure they're still doing well. Ah, 1971 doctors.... The surgeries throw a wrench in Mike's plans to bring the whole family and Alice along fishing with his boss Mr. Phillips. Mr. Phillips invited everyone for a day of deep sea fishing on his sailboat. They reschedule for the next weekend. The day Carol and Cindy come home from the hospital, Mike has to work. He gives Alice a call to check up on them, but Alice is out shopping and Carol answers the phone. Mike tells her she isn't supposed to be talking and especially isn't supposed to answer the phone. He hangs up. As a test, he decides to call back and pretend to be Carol's friend Ellie. When Carol answers the phone again, Mike puts on Ellie's voice and then switches to his own when he's sure that he has caught Carol in the act of talking again. He makes her promise not to pick up the phone any more. At home, the phone rings a third time, but this time it isn't Mike. It's Mr. Phillips calling to talk to Mike, who just left the office. Carol thinks it's Mike playing a trick on her again and says that she would never set foot on his (Mr. Phillips') broken down barnacle barge of a boat and hangs up. Mike walks in the door just after she hangs up. Whoops. Carol tries to explain to Mike what happened and then Mike calls Mr. Phillips to explain, but Mr. Phillips hangs up on him. Not too much longer, though, Mr. Phillips pays the Bradys a visit and brings Carol a dozen roses. He says he knows there must have been some explanation as to what happened and re-invites the Brady family to go fishing. They all agree and when Cindy and Carol are well, they go out on his sailboat. Alice gets sea sick right away, but the others all have a good time.

#43 – Our Son, the Man
Airdate: February 5, 1971
Directed by Jack Arnold
Executive Producer Sherwood Schwartz
Produced by Howard Leeds
Written by Albert E. Lewin
Julie Cobb .... Girl
Chris Beaumont .... Boy

Greg is fed up sharing his room with his brothers and wants to be treated as a man. Mike and Carol are sympathetic to his situation and Mike "volunteers" his den to be Greg's new room and moves his own drafting table to the family room. Greg decks his new bedroom out in funky psychedelic colors and lava lamps. He puts his mattress on the floor and calls a couple boxes his furniture. He's as happy as a clam in his new pad and feeling very confident: confident enough to approach a senior girl at his high school. When he gets nowhere the first time, he witnesses another boy have success with the girl (at least in asking her to the cafeteria to "rap" together), and he decides that he needs some new clothes. He asks Mike for a loan, who gives it to him, and the next morning Greg comes down ready for school looking like a ... well, like a hippy Greg Brady. He's got a leather vest with fringe, a blue spotted shirt, striped pants, and a pair of green-tinted shades. He tops the ensemble off with a beaded headband and a necklace. In his new duds, he approaches the same girl again at school and asks her out for the weekend. But poor Greg is shut down. The girl sees him as a young freshman and not quite a man. Greg goes home for the weekend with no plans. His family has been planning a camping and fishing trip to Mount Claymore for the weekend. Greg had been saying all week that he didn't want to go, but after thinking it over and in the face of having no other plans for the weekend, he decides to go along anyway. Mike and Carol and the other kids are happy with his decision and in the end Greg moves back into his old bedroom and Mike gets his den back. Greg was just growing up too quickly.

#44 – The Liberation of Marcia Brady

Airdate: February 12, 1971
Directed by Russ Mayberry
Executive Producer Sherwood Schwartz
Produced by Howard Leeds
Written by Charles Hoffman

John Lawrence	Man
Ken Sansom	Stan Jacobsen
Ken Jones	Himself
Claire Wilcox	Judy Winters

Marcia is interviewed by a local television station about women's rights. The interviewer asks her leading questions, which gets her to say such things like she doesn't get treated fairly at home by her brothers just because she is a girl. The broadcast is seen by Greg, Peter, Bobby, Mike, and Carol. The boys think Marcia is crazy for saying that she can do anything a boy can do, but her parents, especially Carol, are supportive of her opinion. In order to prove to her brothers that she can do anything they can do, Marcia decides to join Greg's Frontier Scouts group. The Scouts are made up of just boys, but when the two Scout Masters – Mike is one – check the guidebook, they find nothing that says that a Frontier Scout has to be a boy. Marcia has her in and begins preparing for her field initiation tests. Greg naturally wants revenge on his sister for doing such a "dumb" thing and decides that he will join Marcia's Sunflower Girls group. He checks out the Girls guidebook and doesn't find exclusive language for boys. But he does find something that says that Sunflower Girls have to be between 10 and 14 years old. Greg is 15 and he's too old to join. Bobby is 9 and too young, but Peter is 12 and is just right. It takes a lot of cajoling, but finally Pete agrees to fight back for all mankind. The boys tell Marcia their plan, expecting her to get angry, but she reacts just the opposite. Marcia is pleased that Peter understands her point, which is that anyone should be able to join whatever group he/she wants to. Greg is more or less at a loss of what to do next, but the boys all decide that Peter should go out selling cookies in a Sunflower

Girl uniform to try to get Marcia to see just how silly the whole idea is. Very reluctantly, Pete rings the doorbell for one house. He gives the Sunflower Girl spiel and the man is so much in admiration of Peter's guts that he buys a box of cookies. This is the final straw for Pete and he quits the Girls. The only thing left for Greg to do now is to make sure that Marcia follows every single rule for the Frontier Scout initiation tests…and he means every single one. When the time comes, Marcia puts up a tent, starts a fire with flint, bandages Greg, and follows a marked trail. Greg made sure the markers for the trail were really tiny so that Marcia would have such a hard time that she wouldn't be able to find her way back to camp before the timed exercise is finished. But luckily for Marcia, she is a very fine tracker and makes it back to camp with a minute to spare. Mike lectures Greg about how unfair he was through Marcia's tryout and makes him tell Marcia that she has made it into the Scouts. When Greg gets to Marcia's tent, she's asleep: totally worn out from the day's activities. It's time for the initiation ceremony the next day, but Marcia decides not to join the Frontier Scouts after all. She says that for her all she needed to do was prove that she *could* get in. Her equality proven, Marcia goes upstairs to read a fashion magazine and leaves a baffled Greg and Mike behind in the living room. This episode is the closest the writers get to addressing current events in the show.

#45 – Lights Out
Airdate: February 19, 1971
Directed by Oscar Rudolph
Executive Producer Sherwood Schwartz
Produced by Howard Leeds
Written by Bruce Howard
Snag Werris .... Store Owner
Lindsay Workman .... Schoolteacher
Joseph Tatner .... Warren

Cindy is scared of the dark. Why? Because she saw a magic trick at a birthday party where a lady disappeared in a box but never came back. Peter wants to try out for his school's Vaudeville Show as a magician, and Mike and Carol realize that this is the perfect way to help Cindy overcome her fears. If she becomes Peter's assistant, she will learn the tricks of the trade and not be afraid of the unknown anymore. So, Peter sets off on his way to becoming Peter the Great and learns quite a few new tricks. Mike builds him a disappearing cabinet of his own, which will be the highlight of Peter's act. Cindy is afraid to try it out herself, so Peter recruits Bobby for the test run. When Peter asks for Bobby to reappear, he doesn't. Cindy runs inside crying for Carol. Pete and Jan look all over for Bobby, who finally returns a little while later when Mike comes home. Bobby thought he was playing a trick on everyone and didn't realize how badly Cindy would take it. Mike makes Bobby go inside and apologize to his sister. She is very happy to see him again, but decides that she no longer wants to be Peter's magic assistant. Jan takes over her duties. When the day of the tryout comes, Jan calls the auditorium to tell Peter that she can't come over because she sprained her ankle in gym class. What is Peter to do? He can't do any of his tricks without an assistant. Fortunately for him, Cindy comes to his rescue. She, too, got a phone call from Jan and realized that if she didn't do anything, Peter wouldn't do very well in his tryout. So she shows up to save the day and braves the disappearing cabinet trick. She now likes the trick so much that she asks the judges if it's okay for her and Peter to do it again.

#46 – The Winner
Airdate: February 26, 1971

Directed by Robert Reed
Executive Producer Sherwood Schwartz
Produced by Howard Leeds
Written by Elroy Schwartz
Hal Smith .... Kartoon King
Kerry MacLane .... Boy

Bobby feels left out when Cindy comes home with a trophy from the playground. Every Brady kid has a trophy now except him. He feels like a loser and Mike and Carol try to lift his spirits by telling him he should pick one thing and stick with it. He decides to sell magazine subscriptions because third prize for the most subscriptions sold is a trophy – never mind that first prize is a college education. Bobby is doing really well; he even sells subscriptions to a lot of Mike and Carol's friends. But when Cindy lets it slip that their parents prompted their friends to buy from Bobby, he is rightfully angry and quits the contest. He says he will win at something by himself or not win at all. The next day Bobby is watching the Kartoon King Show on television when the Show announces that they will hold an ice cream eating contest. The first 6 callers can participate in the contest and the winner will get a year's worth of ice cream and a trophy! This is right up Bobby's alley and he calls and makes it onto the Show. The contest runs, but Bobby does not win. (Maybe it's because they served chocolate ice cream, which Bobby doesn't like.) Now Bobby really feels like the lowest of the low. He comes home from the contest with his parents and thinks that nobody is home. But then they get to the living room and his siblings and Alice turn on the lights and yell, "Surprise." They're throwing a party for him anyway because they want him to know that they are very proud of him no matter what he does. The kids even present him with a trophy of his very own. They doctored up Greg's with a piece of paper and wrote, "To our brother Bobby for trying harder than anyone we know. We're proud of him. Greg, Marcia, Peter, Jan, and Cindy." Bobby finally has his trophy.

BRADY TROPHIES

Greg = Student Body President plaque and some sort of academic or oratorical trophy
Peter = Outstanding Citizen Award plaque and a baseball trophy
Marcia = Volleyball trophy
Jan = Dance trophy
Cindy = Jacks trophy
Alice = Westdale High School, 19xx, 1st Place School Modern Dance Contest

In other episodes (even previous ones) there is a second baseball trophy and a football trophy on the boys' desk. Marcia also has more awards on her dresser in later episodes, including her own Outstanding Citizen Award (see episode #59).

#47 – Double Parked
Airdate: March 5, 1971
Directed by Jack Arnold
Executive Producer Sherwood Schwartz
Produced by Howard Leeds
Written by Skip Webster
Jackie Coogan ....Man
Jack Collins..Mr. Phillips

City Hall plans to build its new courthouse right on top of Woodland Park, the Brady kids' favorite park. They will have nowhere else to play ball, so the family decides to fight City Hall. The only trouble is Mike's firm has been given the contract to build the new courthouse. Mike's boss Mr. Phillips tells him that if he doesn't stop his family and the Women's Club from fighting City Hall, he will be fired. With such an ultimatum looming over his head, Mike is understandably worried. But he is as stalwart as ever and will not let a thing like losing his job compromise what he thinks is right. He tells his family that they should continue to fight City Hall no matter what. The Bradys collect signatures for petitions, hold a press conference on the steps of City Hall, and even picket City Hall. Then Mike has an epiphany – the new courthouse should be built on the city dump property instead of the Woodland Park area. He shows his plans to Mr. Phillips the next morning. Mr. Phillips thinks Mike's plan might work and takes it to City Hall straight away. City Hall agrees, assigns Mike to be the architect, and all is well!

#48 – Alice's September Song
Airdate: March 12, 1971
Directed by Oscar Rudolph
Executive Producer Sherwood Schwartz
Produced by Howard Leeds
Written by Elroy Schwartz
Allan Melvin ....Sam
Steve Dunne ....Mark Millard

Alice gets a call from an old flame, Mark Millard. He asks her out to dinner and Alice blows off Sam in favor of Mark. Yes, Alice is two-timing Sam right in front of his face! …Anyway, Mark is a very smooth talker and gives Alice all kinds of compliments. He takes her out to dinner and dancing every night for almost a full week. She is very enraptured with him and she and Carol talk about the chances of him popping the question to her. Mark is so slick with words, in fact, that he convinces Alice to get in on the ground floor of a very good investment opportunity. What kind of opportunity? What kind of company? What do they do? Alice doesn't know, but she thinks it's great anyway. She tells Carol about the opportunity and Carol is immediately suspicious that something just isn't right. Carol calls up Mike at work, who calls a friend of his in the District Attorney's Office. The DA tells Mike that Mark Millard is a gambler, preys on women to get their money, and has been married six times. Mike and Carol drop the bomb on Alice. Naturally, Alice is heartbroken and feels used. When Mark shows up a minute or two later to collect her money, Mike and Carol tell him that they're on to him and that the DA is coming by any minute to ask him some questions. Mark makes a break for it, but runs smack into Sam's frozen leg of lamb on the patio. He is knocked unconscious and Alice takes the opportunity to revive him by "watering" his face with a watering can. We assume the DA takes him in and there is no more need to worry about Mark. Sam and Alice are back together and hopefully Alice has realized that Sam isn't so bad.

#49 – Tell it Like it is
Airdate: March 26, 1971
Directed by Terry Becker
Executive Producer Sherwood Schwartz
Produced by Howard Leeds
Written by Charles Hoffman
Richard Simmons..Mr. Delafield
Jonathan Hole.................................... Wally Witherspoon
Elaine Swann ....Nora Maynard

Carol is secretly writing a story for <u>Tomorrow's Woman Magazine</u> about the Brady family. For one reason or another, she doesn't want her family to find out what she is up to, so she surreptitiously writes in the middle of the night. By coincidence, Mike runs into Carol in a restaurant the next day at lunchtime. Carol is forced to introduce him to Mr. Delafield, the editor of <u>Tomorrow's Woman</u>. Mike quickly learns the truth about what Carol has been up to and couldn't be happier for her. When he comes home from work, he sets her up in his den with her own table, typewriter, and all the accoutrements of writer. Carol writes away and soon her story is finished. She sends it off to Mr. Delafield. A week later, she gets a response: rejected. It seems Mr. Delafield wanted a more sugar-coated version of life at the Bradys' instead of the reality, which Carol depicts as occasionally bumpy. Mike takes it upon himself to ask Mr. Delafield to give Carol another chance and he agrees. So, Carol does a rewrite and this time Mr. Delafield is eager to publish it. The Bradys are very happy and proud of Carol. Mr. Delafield tells Carol that he and his staff and some reviewers will be by the house at 3:00 on Friday to take pictures and talk about her family. Carol mistakenly hears 4:00 instead of 3:00 so when they get there at three, she is in her dressing gown with her hair up in curlers. Sufficiently embarrassed, she bumbles her way through introductions. The kids arrive home from school. Marcia and Jan are arguing with each other, Cindy has the hiccups, Bobby tore his good pants, Peter has a black eye, and Greg has poison oak. All this happens right in front of the critics. Chief critic Nora Maynard tells Carol that she doesn't know what family she was writing about in her article, but it certainly wasn't this "delightfully normal" one. Mr. Witherspoon concurs. "Tell it like it is, Mrs. Brady," he says. After listening to his critics, Mr. Delafield apologizes to Carol. He's not going to publish her story the way it is. But, he will be glad to publish the *original* version, which would be to the critic's liking. Carol is grateful, but she promises never to write another story after this. Who would want to go through so much hassle ever again, eh?

THE BRADY BUNCH (comedy)
SEASON THREE 1971-1972
Fridays 8:00-8:30pm ET on ABC

Production Notes:
The week before episode #50 aired, the Brady kids were in a television special. *"The Brady Bunch" Visits ABC* aired as a preview to the upcoming cartoon season that featured, among others, a new Brady cartoon called *The Brady Kids*. The actors got to go behind the scenes of several kids' shows for ABC to promote the new 1971-2 season lineup. They got to meet the Jackson 5 (who also had a cartoon premiering) and the creatures of Sid and Marty Kroffts' Curiosity Shop. Airdate: September 10, 1971, 7:30pm on ABC.

Also in 1971, the magazine 16 SPEC's November issue made a startling announcement about the upcoming third season of *The Brady Bunch*: "Friday nights get off to a rousing start with that great series **The Brady Bunch** – which starts its third season this fall. Robert Reed and Florence Henderson will be back as the **Brady** parents who have their hands – and their house – full with their brood of active and adorable children! Barry Williams, Chris Knight, Maureen McCormick, Mike Lookinland, Eve Plumb and Susie Olsen will manage to get into the exact same kind of adventures – and misadventures – as **you** do, and it's this real-life quality that makes the show such a hit! And this year, there's going to be an addition to the **Brady** clan – a new baby! – which should mean even more fun and more predicaments for them all! It's also very likely that the **Bradys** will get into the recording studio again and release another LP – and maybe a single too! This is a terrific and talented 'family' who make Friday night TV a fun night!"[3] It's true: there were plans in the works for Carol to have a baby! Paramount leaked the rumor in order to get viewers eager for season three. Lloyd Schwartz says, "I believe there was an episode written of *The Brady Bunch* that had Carol having a baby, but I'm not sure."

Sherwood Schwartz's original series proposal for *The Brady Bunch* – back when it was called *The Bradleys* – included this line: "By the way, in the second year 'his' son and 'her' daughter are joined by 'their' own child."[4] So it was a plan in the works from the very beginning to create a yours, mine, and ours situation.

However, for better or worse, the plans were scrapped at the last minute and no little bundle of joy came to fruition.

The third season starts off with a three-part cliffhanger. The beginning and ending credits did not change from the second season – the same squares are used again this season.

The age shuffle continues: Greg is 16 by Episode 53, which aired on October 8. Last season he turned 15 in November. Cindy is 9. Jan is three years younger than Marcia. Marcia is still in junior high, even though she should be in high school now because she's one year younger than Greg who started high school last year.

#50 – Ghost Town, U.S.A.

Airdate: September 17, 1971
Directed by Oscar Rudolph
Executive Producer Sherwood Schwartz
Produced by Howard Leeds
Written by Howard Leeds
Jim Backus .... Zaccariah T. Brown
Hoke Howell .... Gas Station Attendant

Mike and Carol have a surprise for the whole family and Alice: a trip to the Grand Canyon! All nine of them cram into the station wagon, which is hauling a camper and all their gear. They set off on the road, happily singing songs all the way. The family stops at a gas station to fill up (Mike pays just $6.50 for a tank of gas and six sodas!) and the attendant tells them about a ghost town that is only 20 miles away. The kids convince their parents to camp out at the ghost town instead of the trailer park, so they head off down a dirt road to Cactus Creek. Cactus Creek is dry and deserted, but full of adventure for the kids. They climb on an old stagecoach and Greg makes a super 8 movie called the Great Train Robbery starring Peter as the crook. When the family sits down to a dinner of fried chicken, a man called Zaccariah T. Brown and his faithful mule Bessie surprise them. Mr. Brown tells them that his granddaddy built Cactus Creek during the gold rush. Mr. Brown offers to take the Bradys on a tour of the town. When they get to the jail, he says that Jesse James carved his initials on the jail wall. The Bradys all get inside the cell to find the initials and as soon as they're in, Mr. Brown shuts the door on them and locks them in. He tells them that he figures they're there to steal his gold claim. Of course they aren't, but Mr. Brown doesn't believe them, especially after Bobby says that they do want some gold. Zaccariah T. steals the Bradys' station wagon and camper, leaves Bessie behind, and leaves the Bradys shut in the jail cell. How will they ever break free? Well, Mike comes up with a plan after Bobby spots a spare key on a post. He throws everybody's shoes at the key in order to knock it off the post. Once it's off, he puts together a rope made out of everyone's socks with Carol's purse tied to one end. He throws the purse toward the key, which is now on the floor, and reels it in with the sock rope. The family is able to release themselves from the jail, but they are still stranded in Cactus Creek without food, water, or transportation. Mike decides that the only thing to do is walk back toward the gas station for help. Peter volunteers to go with him and the rest of the Bradys stay behind. The episode ends with "to be continued."

#51 – Grand Canyon or Bust

Airdate: September 24, 1971
Directed by Oscar Rudolph
Executive Producer Sherwood Schwartz
Produced by Howard Leeds
Written by Tam Spiva

Jim Backus .... Zaccariah T. Brown
Michele Campo .... Jimmy Pakaya

Part two of the three-part Brady cliffhanger starts with a recap of what happened last week. The Bradys are stranded in a ghost town, twenty miles from the nearest help. Mike and Peter are gone and the rest of the family starts to come up with other ways for them to be found. Greg finds an old telephone and rigs up some batteries to it. When he finally gets it working, it rings at the other end…the other end is also in Cactus Creek and Cindy answers the phone. So much for that idea. Jan, Marcia, and Alice try to carve out the word "HELP" in the dirt with the aid of Bessie the mule and a plough. Cindy, Bobby, and Carol gather wood for a signal fire. Just when they're putting the finishing touches on the fire, Mike reappears with the station wagon. It seems Zaccariah T. Brown had a change of heart and was on his way back to Cactus Creek to rescue them. He met Mike and Peter on the way. Now reunited, the Bradys are once again ready to continue their trip to the Grand Canyon. Mr. Brown gives them their car back and the Bradys hit the road. They arrive at the Canyon later that day. It's absolutely beautiful and everyone is happy. They spend one night in a campground and the next morning everyone rides down to the bottom of the Canyon on mules. The family plans to spend three nights at the bottom: one mile down from the rim of the Canyon. They set up camp. When it comes time for dinner, though, Bobby and Cindy are nowhere to be found. The youngest Brady kids wandered off in search of dinosaur fossils. When they encountered an Indian boy, they decided to follow him. But they never really caught up with the boy and Bobby and Cindy don't know how to get back to camp. The episode ends suspensefully with everyone searching for Bobby and Cindy. It's getting dark, and nighttime could be dangerous for two lost children in the wilderness.

#52 – The Brady Braves

Airdate: October 1, 1971
Directed by Oscar Rudolph
Executive Producer Sherwood Schwartz
Produced by Howard Leeds
Written by Tam Spiva
Michele Campo .... Jimmy Pakaya
Jay Silverheels .... Chief Eagle Cloud

The final episode of the Brady three-parter begins with the family searching for Bobby and Cindy, who wandered away from camp in the bottom of the Grand Canyon. Cindy is worried that they might not make it back to camp, but Bobby tries to keep her spirits up. Luckily, they spot the Indian boy again and this time they talk to him. Jimmy Pakaya has run away from home. He tells Bobby and Cindy that he will show them where their camp is. In return, Bobby and Cindy promise to bring some food to Jimmy later that night. The two youngest Brady kids are reunited with their family thanks to Jimmy's help. Bobby and Cindy don't tell Mike and Carol about Jimmy because Jimmy does not want to be discovered. The Bradys sing camp songs around a fire and eat hotdogs and beans. Bobby and Cindy sneak four hotdogs and some beans for Jimmy. When everyone else is asleep, the two kids steal away in the night and bring the food to Jimmy. The boy is grateful for their help. But the three of them are soon discovered by Greg and Peter, who noticed that Bobby wasn't in his sleeping bag anymore. Now Jimmy has been discovered. Greg thinks it's a good idea to tell Mike about Jimmy because they want to be able to help him. When they get back to camp, Bobby and Cindy explain everything to Mike. Mike goes back and gets Jimmy. Jimmy explains that he ran away from home because he wants to be an astronaut. His grandfather, he thinks, would not understand his wishes because in Jimmy's eyes he is more concerned about the past and about his heritage than modern professions like being an astronaut. Mike encourages Jimmy to tell the truth to his grandfather. Jimmy says he'll think about. In the meantime, Jimmy spends the night at the Brady camp. The next morning, Jimmy is gone. The Bradys fear that he continued on his run-away journey and Mike says that they did all they could for him. But Alice encounters a man, Chief Eagle Cloud, who turns out to be Jimmy's grandfather. The Chief and Jimmy are there at the camp to thank the Bradys for helping Jimmy. In return, the Chief asks the Brady family to come to their village where they will be inducted as members of his tribe. Of course the family agrees. They celebrate through song and dance and each of the Brady Bunch is given an Indian name. All is well and it looks like the Bradys have had an excellent and exciting vacation.

THE BRADYS' INDIAN NAMES

Mike = Big Eagle of Large Nest
Carol = Yellow Flower with Many Petals
Greg = Stalking Wolf
Peter = he rejects Middle Buffalo and Sleeping Lizard and ends up not getting a name at all!
Bobby = Little Bear Who Loses Way
Cindy = Wandering Blossom
Jan = Dove of Morning Light
Marcia = Willow Dancing in Wind
Alice = Squaw in Waiting

TIKI TALK

ALICE AND CHIEF EAGLE CLOUD SITTING IN A TREE...

Curious about what Chief Eagle Cloud says to Alice when he speaks to her in Navajo? Actually, he isn't speaking Navajo at all; he's speaking Mohawk! That's because the actor Jay Silverheels is Mohawk, but unfortunately he does not know many words in the language. Most likely the director told him to say something "Indian" as long as it sounded good. So, the only word he says in Navajo is "Yá'át'ééh," which is indeed "hello." But then he switches to Mohawk and says, "Where are you going, woman? I am an Indian. Where are you going? I love you." Little did Alice know he was professing his love for her!! (A big thanks to Brian Maracle for the translation.)

#53 – The Wheeler-Dealer
Airdate: October 8, 1971
Directed by Jack Arnold
Executive Producer Sherwood Schwartz
Produced by Howard Leeds
Written by Bill Freedman & Ben Gershman
Charlie Martin Smith ....Ronnie
Chris Beaumont ....Eddie

Greg is 16 and passes his driver's test. Now a licensed driver, he wants his own set of wheels. He has $109 in the bank. A friend of his is selling a car for $100 – right up Greg's alley. The car looks beaten down and the engine sounds horrible, but Eddie (Greg's friend) convinces him that it's a steal. All it will need is a little elbow grease to fix it up. Greg comes home with the car only to suffer the laughter of his siblings and an "I told you so" look from his father. Nevertheless, Greg is determined to fix it up. He repaints the car, rewires everything, and fixes the upholstery. He unveils the car's new look to his family and they're all dutifully impressed. But when Greg starts up the engine, things go haywire. The horn starts the wipers, the convertible top goes up and down for no reason, and the engine starts to smoke. So much for a little elbow grease. But, Mike says that things are okay because Greg learned a valuable lesson cheaply. *"Caveat emptor,"* he says. "Let the buyer beware." Greg has learned to be a responsible buyer from the whole experience. Or has he? Pretty soon he has a chump of his own over to the house taking a look at the car. He gilds the lily quite a bit and has his friend Ronnie convinced that the car is a good buy. Just as he is about to take a check from Ronnie, though, Greg has a change of heart and is unable to go through with the deal. He just couldn't do what was done to him. The car breaks down on his way home just in front of a junk yard. He sells the car to the junk man for fifty bucks. Greg is out fifty dollars from the whole deal, but is a lot wiser.

#54 – My Sister, Benedict Arnold
Airdate: October 15, 1971
Directed by Hal Cooper
Executive Producer Sherwood Schwartz
Produced by Howard Leeds
Written by Elroy Schwartz
Gary Rist .... Warren Mulaney
Sheri Cowart ....Kathy Lawrence

Greg is sore because Warren Mulaney beat him out for the first-string basketball team. Warren had already beaten Greg for Student Council President and Greg is bitter about it all because Warren goofs off when the coach isn't looking. Warren invites Marcia to go out with him and Marcia is excited because he's a high school boy and she is still in junior high. After she goes out to the pizza parlor with Warren, she decides that he isn't so great. Because of that and because Greg doesn't like him, she is ready to call off their relationship. But before she gets a chance to, Greg orders her not to go out with Warren again. This only incenses Marcia, who decides to continue seeing Warren just to spite Greg. Greg wants revenge so he asks out Marcia's enemy, Kathy

Lawrence. Kathy beat Marcia out for head cheerleader and when Greg brings her home, Marcia is upset. She and Greg end up arguing in the kitchen while Warren and Kathy are left alone. When Mike and Carol come home from some shopping, they walk into Marcia and Greg's fight. They get the scoop on what has been going on. They are very disappointed and tell Marcia and Greg that they've just been using Warren and Kathy. The two go out to apologize to their dates only to find that Warren and Kathy left together to go out for pizza. Kathy even asked Warren to go to the school carnival with her. Marcia and Greg learned their lesson. Everybody goes out to the Fillmore Junior High School Carnival where the Bradys have built a dunking booth and they all come home with prizes and happy as clams.

#55 – The Personality Kid
Airdate: October 22, 1971
Directed by Oscar Rudolph
Executive Producer Sherwood Schwartz
Produced by Howard Leeds
Written by Ben Starr
Sheri Cowart ....Kathy Lawrence
Monica Ramirez.. Kyle
Margie DeMeyer...Judy
Jay Kocen...Boy #1
Pierre A. Williams...Boy #2
Karen Peters.. Suzie

Peter is told that he has no personality and really takes it to heart. Poor Pete thinks he's just too dull for parties anymore. He feels sorry for himself until Mike and Carol convince him that if he doesn't like his personality he should change it. He tries Humphrey Bogart out for size and delivers his famous "pork chops and applesauce" line to Carol and Alice. Unfortunately for Peter, acting like someone else just isn't going to cut it. He needs to be himself, his parents say. So, Peter decides to learn a bunch of jokes and try them out on his friends. He holds a party for eleven of his friends and starts telling the jokes. The only trouble is that every time he tells one, someone else tells the punch line. Peter now is thoroughly convinced that he is dull. He mopes alone on the steps until a girl comes up to him and asks him what's wrong. Pete tells her that he is dull and she tries to convince him otherwise. Soon he has a harem of five girls surrounding him, all being very nice and telling him that he is great. Pete is finally happy with being dull because he can now get the sympathy of girls!

#56 – Juliet is the Sun
Airdate: October 29, 1971
Directed by Jack Arnold
Executive Producer Sherwood Schwartz
Produced by Howard Leeds
Written by Brad Radnitz
Randy Case .... Harold Axelrod
Lois Newman...Miss Goodwin

38

Marcia is cast as Juliet in the school production of "Romeo and Juliet." Peter and Jan will play palace guards and Carol is in charge of writing the program and selling ads. It's a family affair, but at first Marcia thinks she will have nothing to do with it. She cannot see herself in the part of Juliet. She tried out for the nurse and that is what she wanted; she just can't picture herself as the beautiful and noble Juliet. Mike gives her a pep talk and tells her that you are what you think you are. If you think you're beautiful and noble, you will be. When all her siblings give her compliments to boot, Marcia can finally see herself in the role. So, she begins rehearsing with Harold Axelrod, who will play Romeo. After a few rehearsals, Marcia begins to change. Suddenly she is the queen of the theatre and starts criticizing Harold, the staging, and even Miss Goodwin, the play's director. She is difficult to live with and wants to take closet space away from her sisters. The final straw comes when Carol witnesses her at rehearsal one day and realizes what a selfish diva she has become. Marcia's comments are slowing down the production and she is being so stubborn that the rehearsals cannot proceed as planned. Together, Carol and Miss Goodwin decide to fire Marcia from the play and let her understudy take the part of Juliet. Naturally, Marcia is devastated. She learns the hard way the same lesson that Peter learned when he was a hero – a guy can sure get messed up patting himself on the back. In the end the girl who is supposed to play Lady Capulet comes down with the mumps. Marcia graciously and humbly offers to take the part and all is well. The Bradys are very proud of their three young actors, even though Jan did end up saying "who goes there" before Peter said "hark."

#57 – And Now, a Word from Our Sponsor
Airdate: November 5, 1971
Directed by Peter Baldwin
Executive Producer Sherwood Schwartz
Produced by Howard Leeds
Written by Albert E. Lewin

Paul Winchell	Skip Farnum
Bonnie Boland	Myrna Carter
Art Lewis	Felder
Lennie Breman	Truck Driver

The Brady family is "discovered" by television commercial maker Skip Farnum. He invites the whole family and Alice to be part of a commercial for Safe Laundry Soap. Everyone is very excited and the kids start dreaming of spending their money before they even have it. Mike and Carol are discussing the commercial and get to the topic of Safe soap itself. Carol tells Mike that they switched from Clear and Bright to Help to Champ the Dirt Fighter to Safe and then to Best. Mike is surprised when he hears that Best cleans better than Safe. What kind of people would they be if they went on television touting a product that they believe to be inferior? Because of this, Mike decides to call Mr. Farnum and tell him the commercial is off. Sighs and disappointment are all around, but not for long. Mr. Farnum informs Mike that the commercial is for a new product: New and Improved Safe. The Bradys have never used it! So, the family joyously goes forth with plans for the commercial. In order to represent themselves truthfully, they have a wash-a-thon of New and Improved Safe versus Best. The Safe product wins because it gets the kids' dirty clothes cleaner. Now everything has fallen into place except for one more thing: the Bradys don't know how to act. So, Carol calls her friend Myrna

Carter who is an actress for advice on how to act in the commercial. Myrna tells Mike and Carol that they are too dull and that they need to spice up their act by "motivating." Mike is supposed to be very pleased with his clean shirts at work, so he is very happy when he comes home with a box of Safe for his wife. Carol, too, is supposed to be very happy and think, "Wow, he brought me a box of that stuff!" With these thoughts in mind, the Bradys feel they're ready for Skip Farnum to film on Saturday. Farnum arrives and begins filming with no rehearsals. He shoots Mike and Carol first, but is appalled at their fake, over-zealous acting. He switches to the kids who are supposed to enter the room looking dirty. The kids went way overboard and look like they've been trekking through a swamp. Mr. Farnum is none too pleased. He tries getting a shot of Alice, but she prances into the room with a dress on and curls in her hair. Cut! Mr. Farnum fires the Brady family. He wonders what happened to his natural, real family and walks out on the job. Naturally, the Bradys are disappointed; Myrna's advice backfired. However, the contract they signed with Farnum Enterprises states that they will still get paid. As to manner of payment, Carol is at a loss until a truck drives up with a delivery of 48 large containers of Safe Soap. Each container contains 42 boxes of Safe, meaning that the Bradys now have over 2,000 boxes of soap. The Brady family will never run out of laundry soap again!

#58 – The Private Ear
Airdate: November 12, 1971
Directed by Hal Cooper
Executive Producer Sherwood Schwartz
Produced by Howard Leeds
Written by Michael Morris

Peter is up to something…he is secretly tape recording his siblings' conversations and then letting the secret-teller know that he knows about their secret. Shame on him! As soon as he lets the secret-teller know, the person who was confided in is accused of blabbing. Everyone is mad at everyone else. Marcia thinks Jan told on her, Greg thinks Marcia told on him, and Bobby thinks Cindy told on him. They all erupt into arguments at the dinner table. Mike and Carol notice that Pete is not involved in the arguments, so they correctly draw the conclusion that he instigated all of this. They call him into Mike's den and make him confess. Pete says he didn't think his tape recording antics would turn out like this, and Mike and Carol make him go apologize to his siblings. Greg and Marcia think Peter got off too easy, so they hatch a plan for revenge. They plant a story on a cassette tape about Mike and Carol planning a surprise party for Peter this weekend because he got an A in geometry. Peter hears the recorded message and starts dropping hints to his family members about what he would like for presents. The day of the supposed party arrives and Peter is all revved up. Greg and Marcia are getting a kick out of Peter's excitement, but what they don't know is that Mike and Carol discovered the taped message they intended for Peter. Their parents have decided to actually throw Pete a party so that Greg and Marcia learn *their* lesson. Right before their parents arrive back home, Greg and Marcia decide that perhaps the medicine they spooned Peter was too bitter, and they apologize to him. Then the front door bursts open and Mike and Carol walk in with an armful of presents for Pete. Everyone is surprised, especially Greg and Marcia. Peter gets a tape recorder of his very own and leaves a new message on it for Greg and Marcia to listen to. He apologizes for what he did to them and forgives them for what they did to him. Everyone's even, and all is again well.

#59 – Her Sister's Shadow

Airdate: November 19, 1971
Directed by Russ Mayberry
Executive Producer Sherwood Schwartz
Produced by Howard Leeds
Teleplay by Al Schwartz and Phil Leslie
Story by Al Schwartz and Ray Singer
Lindsay Workman..Principal
Gwen Van Dam...Mrs. Watson
Peggy Doyle..Teacher
Julie Reese .... Katy
Nancy Gillette..Pom-Pom Girl

All day long, Jan hears how great Marcia is at this and how wonderfully Marcia did that. Marcia, Marcia, Marcia! Poor Jan feels like she's in her sister's shadow all the time and cannot make a mark of her own. She hides her sister's awards in the closet out of spite. (*Marcia has an Outstanding Citizenship Award plaque, a yellow First Place Swim Meet ribbon, was Class President of Fillmore Junior High, a blue First Place Art Show ribbon, a Debating Team plaque, and a Volleyball Trophy!*) Her parents tell Jan that she needs to find out what she's best at and do her best with it. So, Jan decides to try out for the Pom-Pom Girls, something Marcia has never been accepted to (even though Marcia did try out once). Jan practices and practices. When the day of the tryouts comes, poor Jan is beaten by Gloria Harper, Katy Rand, Judy Smith, and Laura Richmond. She doesn't make the squad, but she does find out that she has the best essay on Americanism in the school and is going to be presented with an Honor Society Award. This Award masks the disappointment she had with the Pom-Pom Girls and Jan is finally happy with herself. At home, she goes over her score as discovers that she should have gotten a 93 instead of the 98 that the judges gave her. Now Jan has a moral dilemma. Should she tell her teacher the truth and let Nora Coombs take the Award (Nora scored a 95), or should she accept the Award because no one will ever be the wiser? Jan has an internal dialogue, and the next day at the Award ceremony, she does the right thing. She tells her teacher that a mistake was made in scoring and that she is not the rightful recipient of the Honor Society Award. Her honesty causes a stir and now Cindy is coming home from school complaining about Jan, Jan, Jan!

JAN'S ESSAY ON AMERICANISM
93 points, not 98!

Spelling	15
Grammar	14
Neatness	14
Originality of Idea	15
Composition	15
Presentation	10
Literary Style	10

#60 – Click
Airdate: November 26, 1971
Directed by Oscar Rudolph
Executive Producer Sherwood Schwartz
Produced by Howard Leeds
Written by Tom and Helen August
Elvera Roussel ....Linette Carter
Bart LaRue...Coach

Greg is anxious about telling Carol that he is trying out for the high school football team. Carol is apparently notoriously against the sport because she doesn't want her sons to get hurt (never mind that Peter played football last year!). Greg and Mike ask her permission and together they convince her that Greg will be learning a lot about sportsmanship, winning gracefully, and losing with dignity. Carol reluctantly agrees and after tryouts, Greg makes it to the first string football team. His girlfriend Linette is proud of him. At the first practice game of the season, though, Greg is injured; Carol's worries have not been for naught. Greg comes home from the doctor with news that an X-ray shows he has a hairline fracture in one of his ribs. Carol and Mike decide that Greg should stay off the team until his rib heals, even though the doctor said that Greg could conceivably play if he wore a rib protector. Greg feels like Mike betrayed him by siding with Carol. He tells his father that if he can't play football he doesn't want anything to do with it. Teenagers can be fickle, though, because when Linette asks Greg to go to the football game on Friday, he goes. He takes pictures of Linette doing her cheerleading at the game. Unfortunately for Westdale, they lose 6-7. But when Greg gets home to develop his pictures of Linette, he finds out that he has a shot of the Westdale pass receiver making a fair catch that the referees called out-of-bounds during the game. Westdale should have scored a touchdown on that play, but the referees made the out-of-bounds call instead. Mike drives Greg over to his coach so that the coach can see the evidence in black and white. When Mike and Greg get home, they tell Carol that Greg is back on the team…as official photographer.

ALICE'S CAKE RECIPE

During this episode, Alice is trying to remember the secret ingredients to a special family cake recipe. Thanks to Bobby, she is able to write the ingredients down permanently so the culinary legend will not die with her generation. Bake at your own risk!!

1 tsp cinnamon	2 cups flour
$\frac{1}{2}$ tsp ginger	1 tsp baking powder
vanilla extract	$\frac{1}{2}$ tsp baking soda
$\frac{1}{4}$ lb butter	$\frac{1}{2}$ cup raisins
1 cup brown sugar	$\frac{1}{2}$ cup chopped nuts
3 egg yolks	$\frac{1}{2}$ cup chopped dates

#61 – Getting Davy Jones
Airdate: December 10, 1971
Directed by Oscar Rudolph
Executive Producer Sherwood Schwartz
Produced by Howard Leeds
Written by Phil Leslie and Al Schwartz
David Jones.. Himself
Britt Leach ....Manager
Marcia Wallace... Mrs. Robbins
Kimberly Beck...Laura
Tina Andrews .... Doreen
Whitney Rydbeck.. Page

Marcia is the head of the Fillmore Junior High Senior Prom Entertainment Committee. She and two other girls on the Committee are tasked with engaging the musical entertainer for the Prom. After Jan runs upstairs to tell Marcia that Davy Jones is in town, she gets an idea. Wouldn't it be neat if Davy Jones sang at her Prom? Her friends are skeptical that she can engage him for the evening, but Marcia pulls out a personal letter handwritten by Davy Jones to her. In the letter, Davy promises that when he is in town he will be glad to show his appreciation to her in any way. Marcia says she'll get him. The trouble is, her friends believe her and start spreading the word before she even gets a chance to ask him. By the time Marcia shows up to school the next day, the Art Club has already hung a banner welcoming Davy Jones. What is Marcia to do? The only thing she thinks of is that she just *has* to find Davy Jones. She finds out what hotel he is staying in (the Royal Towers) and tries to call and send a telegram, but all lines of communication are jammed. Out of ideas, Alice and Sam come up with one that just might help Marcia out. Sam is friends with the cook at the Royal Towers. He can get Greg and Marcia into the hotel disguised as busboys. The plan works and Greg and Marcia get into Davy Jones's room on the pretense of picking up his breakfast dishes. Too bad he isn't there. But his manager tells them that he is currently recording at Atlas Records. Marcia rushes over there. This time she strikes pay dirt and gets to watch Davy record his song "Girl." As soon as she's discovered by the manager, though, he tries to throw her out. No fans allowed when the master is recording. Marcia pleads her case, but it's no dice with the manager. All he promises her is a copy of Davy Jones's latest album. Davy, however, heard what Marcia said. He shows up at the Brady house after his recording is finished and personally delivers the album his manager promised her. Marcia is star-struck, but not enough to stop her from asking him if he will perform at her Prom. Davy says "Okay." Marcia has all the luck, right Jan? Well, Marcia is indeed very lucky this time because not only does she get Davy Jones to perform at her Prom, she also musters the courage to kiss him twice – once on each cheek. So Davy goes down in Marcia's book as star close encounter number two after Desi Arnaz, Jr. He asks her to be his date and of course Marcia agrees.

DAVY JONES' LETTER TO MARCIA

Miss Marcia Brady
President, Davy Jones Fan Club
Dear Marcia,
I want to thank you for your interest in my career. Without the help
of people like you, my career would not be possible.
If I'm ever in your city, I'll be happy to show my appreciation any way I
can.
With best wishes, I am your friend, always.
Davy Jones

#62 – The Not-So-Rose-Colored Glasses
Airdate: December 24, 1971
Directed by Leslie H. Martinson
Executive Producer Sherwood Schwartz
Produced by Howard Leeds
Written by Bruce Howard
Robert Nadder.......................................Gregory Gaylord

It's Mike and Carol's third anniversary. (Yes, even though they got married presumably in September 1969, they are celebrating their anniversary in December. That's okay, though, because next year they celebrate in January.) Mike has a surprise for Carol. He has had the kids' portrait taken and plans to give it to her on their anniversary. In the meantime, Jan is having trouble. She comes home from the park with the wrong bicycle. Her grades are slipping at school. She squints. Carol and Mike determine that she needs to get her eyes checked. Sure enough, Jan needs glasses. Jan is upset at the prospect because she doesn't want to look like a drip. She wants to impress a boy named Bernie and doesn't think that wearing glasses is the way to do it. So after her appointment with the optometrist, Jan only wears her new glasses when she feels like it, which isn't very often. She is riding her bike home from the library after seeing Bernie and not wearing her glasses. Apparently she has problems with depth perception, too, because she crashes into the end of the garage: right were Mike was hiding the photograph for Carol. The picture frame is ruined and the picture is bent all out of shape. Jan feels very guilty about the whole incident, but not guilty enough to confide in her father. So she rallies her siblings to sneak back to the photographer's and get a new picture taken and framed. They do exactly that and Jan even wears her new glasses in the photo so that her parents will be proud of her. The trouble is, though, that Jan didn't have glasses on in the original picture. When Mike presents the photo to Carol on their anniversary, he immediately notices the difference. He pulls Jan aside and makes her tell the truth. Jan confesses everything. It turns out that in order to pay for the second photo she sold her bicycle. Mike figures that losing her bike and feeling super guilty are punishment enough for her. She has definitely decided to keep wearing her glasses at all times now. Mike even tells her that he might be able to get her bike back. Carol is very pleased with Mike's present. Six beaming Brady faces now grace their bedroom wall.

#63 – The Teeter-Totter Caper
Airdate: December 31, 1971
Directed by Russ Mayberry
Executive Producer Sherwood Schwartz
Produced by Howard Leeds
Written by Joel Kane and Jack Lloyd
Dick Winslow...Mark Winters

Bobby and Cindy are feeling left out. No one will let them help with projects around the house and everyone except them is invited to Carol's cousin Gertrude's wedding. The two youngest Bradys are down in the dumps until they come to a decision. They will do something important, something that will get them noticed and that will make a lasting mark on the world. They'll show everyone that little kids can do important things, too. Unfortunately, they can't think of anything important enough. But when they are waiting for their cartoons to come on TV, they see a broadcast about two college boys who tried to break the world teeter-totter record of 124 straight hours. Eureka! Bobby and Cindy decide that they will try to break the record themselves and at 8:03 the next morning they begin their crusade. Greg and Peter give them a hard time about it, but they say "just you wait." Soon a reporter with The Daily Chronicle shows up in the Brady back yard. He's there to do a story on Bobby and Cindy. Now the other Bradys are impressed and they finally realize what the kids have been trying to do. Carol and Mike are very supportive and even let Bobby and Cindy stay on the teeter-totter through dinner. Sometime after dark the two kids become very sleepy. Eventually they fall asleep and their record-breaking attempt is over. Mike and Carol take them back inside. The next morning Bobby and Cindy come downstairs upset with their parents for letting them fall asleep. But their consternation disappears as soon as they see the morning paper. Their pictures are there in black and white and there is a story to go along with it. Satisfied that they have made a mark on the world, Bobby and Cindy have gotten their point through. Mike even tells them that they probably have made a world record for kids their age on the teeter-totter.

FROM THE DAILY CHRONICLE

Caption: "Bobby Brady (10) and Cindy Brady (9 ½) are flying high trying to break the existing teeter-totter record."

Story: "Bobby and Cindy Brady set out yesterday to break the world's teeter-totter record. They began their assault on the record at 8:03 in the morning and as of the taking of these exclusive photographs, the two have been teetering and/or tottering for several hours. The current record set by Ralph Nelson, 19, and Alan Rudolph, 20, is slightly over 124 hours. The young Bradys feel that with a serious effort the record is within their grasp."

N.B.: The current teeter-totter record is actually 75 hours 10 minutes, set in 2004. There is no actual record for 124 hours.

#64 – Big Little Man
Airdate: January 7, 1972
Directed by Robert Reed
Executive Producer Sherwood Schwartz
Produced by Howard Leeds
Written by Skip Webster
Allan Melvin.. Sam

Greg won't let Bobby help him fix the shutter on the girls' window. Bobby is perhaps still feeling left out of things he thinks he should be able to do (remember the last episode) and so when Greg goes inside to answer a phone call, Bobby climbs up the ladder. He's on the very last rung and can barely reach the shutter. He stands on his tiptoes and then the ladder shakes and falls out from under him. He is left hanging for dear life onto the window sill. He screams for help and Greg comes to the rescue and pulls him through to the inside of the house from the girls' room's window. Bobby thanks Greg for saving his life and promises him that he will pay him back some day. Later on, Bobby is again feeling low – quite literally. He doesn't like being short. When Sam comes by to drop off some meat for Alice, Sam calls him a "shrimpo." Sam's remark hits Bobby hard and he goes upstairs to his room. Sam goes up there to apologize and console Bobby by telling him that when he was a kid he was really small, too. But then in one year he grew six inches…maybe Bobby can grow that much, too. His spirits lifted, Bobby decides to start stretching himself by hanging onto the top bar of the swing set in the back yard. He hangs for a long time and measures himself. Amazingly he grew 1 ½ inches! He tells his parents the good news. Unfortunately, his excitement is very short lived. Marcia, Jan, and Cindy each confess to moving the mark Bobby was using to measure himself down ½ inch each. It's a dirty trick, Bobby thinks. He storms upstairs convinced he's never going to grow in his whole life. The next day Bobby comes home from school with a black eye. He started a fight with Tommy Huxley because Tommy was acting like a big shot. Carol treats him and talks to him. She says that a lot of people can prove their strength in this world through brain power instead of through brawn. So, Bobby goes to the library and tries to learn everything he can. He's doing really well at it, too. But eventually he tires of it. During all this time, Greg has been looking for a part-time job so that he can buy a used surfboard. "This stoked-up hotdogger needs some extra bread so he can latch onto a heavy board and hit the lineup," he says. Coincidentally, Sam is looking for a new delivery boy for his Butcher Shop. Alice gets Greg the gig and soon enough Greg is able to buy his surfboard. Bobby is home one day when everyone except Alice is gone. Alice realizes that she needs two pounds of sausage for dinner and decides to let Bobby go to Sam's by himself and bring home the meat. Bobby goes to the Shop to find Greg there working alone. It's almost closing time and all the meat is in the locker, so Greg goes in there to fetch it. Bobby follows him into the meat locker and closes the door behind himself. Immediately, Greg is mad because he knows that the door doesn't work two ways. You can get in, but you can't get out. Greg and Bobby are trapped in the freezer! Greg tries to break the handle open with the axe, which doesn't work. Finally, he breaks the small window seated in the freezer door. He is too big to fit through the window, but Bobby is just right. Bobby never thought that he would be happy to be small, but in this case his size is an advantage. He squirms out through the window and calls Sam to come and help them open up the door. Sam, Alice, Mike, and Carol all come to the rescue and are able to get Greg out of the freezer. True to his word, Bobby has saved his brother's life as payback for Greg saving his. Bobby is now content with being who he is.

46

#65 – Dough Re Mi

Airdate: January 14, 1972
Directed by Allen Baron
Executive Producer Sherwood Schwartz
Produced by Howard Leeds
Written by Ben Starr
John Wheeler... Mr. Dimsdale

Greg has written a surefire hit song, "We Can Make the World a Whole Lot Brighter," but he needs $150 to reserve the studio to record his song. Greg only has $43.12 saved up. He wants to record the song at Dimsdale Recorders, the best recording studio in town. When Peter hears Greg talk about the Studio, he wonders if Mr. Dimsdale is his friend Johnny's dad. Indeed he is and Peter goes down to the Studio himself to ask Mr. Dimsdale if he could do Greg a favor and cut the price. Mr. Dimsdale says no, that he's already given him the best price in town. But while he's there, Peter gets to watch a new group record a song: the Five Monroes. Pete gets an idea. If the Five Monroes can make money because they're a family group, the Bradys ought to be able to make more because there are six of them. He rushes home to tell Greg his plan. It just might work, Greg thinks. He gets all the other kids to chip in their money to put toward the recording session. The others can only contribute ten dollars total. Greg is short $96.88. After he pleads his case, Greg strikes a deal with Mike. Mike will take fifty cents out of each kid's allowance until the $96.88 is paid off. In return, Mike will give Greg a check for the money so that the kids can record his song this Friday. Greg makes the deal and the Brady Six is on its way to stardom. (It will take the kids 33 weeks to pay off the money they owe Mike!) The group practices the song in front of Carol, who acts as director. The song sounds groovy. The next day during a rehearsal, though, Peter's voice begins to crack. He's 13 years old now, and it's time for a change. The Brady kids can't very well record Greg's song with Peter's voice changing all the way through it, can they? Yes they can! Greg comes up with a great solution – instead of dumping Peter or letting him sing badly to "We Can Make the World a Whole Lot Brighter," he writes a new song called "Time to Change." Peter is the featured vocalist in this song because it's all about changing – especially voices. So the kids go to the Studio on Friday just like they planned, but they record the new song instead. Pete's voice cracks like a champion, just as it is supposed to. The recording is a success. This is the first time viewers get to see the Bradys singing together, but definitely not the last.

#66 – Jan's Aunt Jenny

Airdate: January 21, 1972
Directed by Hal Cooper
Executive Producer Sherwood Schwartz
Produced by Howard Leeds
Written by Michael Morris
Imogene Coca .... Aunt Jenny

The Bradys are cleaning out their attic. In the process, Jan runs across a picture of Carol's Aunt Jenny taken when she was Jan's age. Aunt Jenny bears an uncanny resemblance to Jan, so Jan decides to write her a letter enclosing a picture of herself. In return, Jan asks Aunt Jenny to send her a recent photo. When Aunt Jenny's letter and photograph finally arrive, Jan is dismayed when she sees the picture. To Jan's eyes, Aunt Jenny is ugly. Now Jan thinks she's doomed to look just like her when she grows up. A short while later, the Bradys receive a second letter from Aunt Jenny. She is coming to City and will arrive tomorrow! Everyone is excited except Jan. Aunt Jenny arrives in a limousine with a police escort. She comes bearing gifts. Bobby gets a basketball autographed by Wilt Chamberlain, Peter gets magic handcuffs that belonged to Houdini, Marcia is given a shofar – a horn used to celebrate Rosh Hashanah – that Golda Maier originally gave to Aunt Jenny, and Jan is presented with a portrait of Aunt Jenny done by an artist called Pietro. (Viewers don't get to see Greg or Cindy's gifts.) Aunt Jenny is a world traveler and knows practically everyone; she's quite the celebrity. But Aunt Jenny immediately senses that Jan is not comfortable being around her, so she drags the truth out of Mike and Carol. But, Jan gradually warms up to her. She is very impressed with Aunt Jenny, who gets phone calls about being given a llama, about dining on a boat, and even a marriage proposal from a US Senator. When Aunt Jenny gets a fourth phone call, she has to leave in a rush because she is supposed to fly to Paris. Jan is disappointed that Aunt Jenny won't be staying any longer. Aunt Jenny is glad to see that Jan has come to like her. She promises to visit again and with that she's off. A month or so later, the Bradys receive a package from her with a plaster leg cast. Aunt Jenny sent them the cast after she got it off her leg (she broke it skiing in Switzerland) because it is autographed by a lot of famous people including Paul Newman, Peggy Fleming, and Sir Edmund Hilary. Jan is duly impressed and now she doesn't care if she ends up looking like Aunt Jenny or not; she plans to take life one day at a time.

#67 – The Big Bet
Airdate: January 28, 1972
Directed by Earl Bellamy
Executive Producer Sherwood Schwartz
Produced by Howard Leeds
Written by Elroy Schwartz
Hope Sherwood...Rachel

Bobby arrives home from school elated that he can do five chin-ups – the most in his class. Greg thinks that's great for a kid Bobby's size but says that he can do twice as many with no problem. Bobby seizes on that statement and makes a bet with Greg. If Greg can't do twice as many chin-ups than he can by the end of the week, Greg has to do everything he says for a whole week. And if Greg *can* do twice as many as Bobby then Bobby has to do everything Greg tells him to for a whole week. It's a deal. Bobby starts lifting weights and practicing immediately, but Greg doesn't do anything. Greg is very confident that he can beat Bobby: no problem. When the end of the week arrives, the contest is on. Bobby does eleven chin-ups. It's Greg's turn next and he has to do 22 in order to beat Bobby. Unfortunately for Greg, he only manages to do 19 chin-ups. Bobby is the winner! Bobby has Greg shine his shoes, take out the garbage, drive Marcia and Jan to the library, polish his bike, sandpaper his skateboard, hose off the patio, and more. In the meantime, Mike gets a letter from Freemont High School, his *alma mater*. It's his 20th anniversary and he wants to go with Carol. Mike tells her that his high school nickname was "Hot Lips" and that he went with a girl named "Bobo" in his senior year. Carol makes a bet with Mike that she can figure out who Bobo is in three guesses or less. Mike agrees and the stakes are the same as they were for Bobby and Greg: the loser has to do whatever the winner says for a week. The week goes on and Bobby overhears Greg making a date with a girl named Rachel for a double-feature at the drive-in. When Greg hangs up, Bobby tells him that he wants to go, too. Greg becomes really upset because he feels that dates are not part of the bet he made; he does not want the "All-American kid" tagging along. Mike and Carol have to settle the argument and they rule in Bobby's favor. So, Greg takes him along on his date. Bobby sits in the back seat and Greg and Rachel sit in the front. Every time that Greg and his girl get close together, though, Bobby cries out, "You're blocking my view!" Bobby asks Greg to get him popcorn and pizza. He also asks Greg to put the top of the convertible down because he is getting hot. As soon as Greg does so, Bobby whips out an umbrella because he thinks it's going to rain. Greg replies that if it's going to rain, he'd rather have the top up. So, he puts the top of the convertible back up, but Bobby still has his umbrella open. The tip of the umbrella rips through the soft top and creates a hole. Now he's done it. When Greg and Bobby get home, they have to tell Mike about the hole. It will cost around $150 for a new top. Bobby is very apologetic and says that he has learned his lesson. He will never bet on anything again; even if you win, you lose. If he can ever boss anybody around again, he will never be mean. And most important of all, never keep an umbrella in a convertible. Bobby's lessons learned, it's time for Mike and Carol to settle their bet. They have returned home from the reunion and Mike tells Carol it's time for her to make her guesses about who Bobo is. She gets it right the first time: Irene Hesselroff. It just goes to show you that no bet is sure.

#68 – The Power of the Press

Airdate: February 4, 1972
Directed by Jack Arnold
Executive Producer Sherwood Schwartz
Produced by Howard Leeds
Written by Ben Gershman and Bill Freedman
Milton Parsons .... Mr. Price
Angela Satterwhite .... Diane
Bobby Riha .... Harvey
Jennifer Reilly .... Iris

Peter becomes a reporter for the Fillmore Junior High School paper. He has his own column, which he calls "The Whole Truth." He also gives himself a nickname, "Scoop Brady." Pete is really excited about his new job at school – so much so that he spends all his time on his column instead of on his schoolwork. He learns quickly that flattery will get him appreciation from his schoolmates. He gets invited to a lot of parties, he is given candy bars, pizza, sodas, and more. Pete thinks it's great. But finals week is approaching and Peter has one of the most difficult teachers in the school for science: Mr. Price. Both Marcia and Greg have already gotten through Mr. Price's finals, so they give Peter advice on studying. They tell him that making mnemonics is a good technique. Unfortunately for Peter, he ends up getting a D on the final; he didn't really study much at all. But then Peter has an idea. Why not write a flattering article about Mr. Price? Perhaps after he sees how much Pete admires him, he will give him a better grade. So, Peter gets to work on the article and rushes it over to his editor when it's finished. Soon after, though, Mike and Carol find out what he's up to. They discovered his test paper in his jacket pocket and learned from the other kids about the article on Mr. Price. "There is a thing called 'power of the press' and with that power comes responsibility," Mike tells him. Peter realizes that he has abused his power. The next day he visits Mr. Price and apologizes to him. Peter asks what his final grade will be and Mr. Price tells him he'll get exactly what he deserves. Peter ends up with a C. Altogether, the Bradys got 12 As, 29 Bs, and 7 Cs. Assuming no weighted classes, that's a 3.10 grade point average for the Brady kids.

#69 – Sergeant Emma
Airdate: February 11, 1972
Directed by Jack Arnold
Executive Producer Sherwood Schwartz
Produced by Howard Leeds
Written by Harry Winkler

Alice is going away for a week's vacation and in her stead the Bradys hire Alice's cousin Emma. Emma is a Master Sergeant in the Army and has twenty years' experience keeping order. She immediately starts trying to whip the family into shape by requiring the kids to do calisthenics at six o'clock in the morning. The kids must also make their beds according to Army regulations and they are all assigned chores to do around the house. Emma's Army ways are even present in the kitchen at dinner time. She makes Potatoes MacArthur, Beef Eisenhower, and Succotash Pentagon. Mike and Carol think that the chores and exercises are good for the kids…until they get drafted themselves. The next morning Emma has all 8 Brady family members out in the yard doing pushups. The day after that, they all go for a jog together. Mike and Carol are beginning to feel that Emma has gone too far. They try to think of a way to give her a three-day pass and make her take a break from her hard work, but it's no go. In the process, they don't want to hurt Alice, either, by dismissing her cousin. So, they decide to stick it out to the bitter end. Sergeant Emma's last day arrives and Carol wants to throw a party for Alice when she returns. But Emma catches sight of the cake and assumes it's for her; no one has ever thrown her a party and she is very touched. Now the Bradys have to pretend the party really is for her, and they do just that. In the end, they realize that Emma isn't so bad, but that they appreciate Alice all the more.

#70 – Cindy Brady, Lady
Airdate: February 18, 1972
Directed by Hal Cooper
Executive Producer Sherwood Schwartz
Produced by Howard Leeds
Written by Al Schwartz and Larry Rhine
Eric Shea ....Tommy Jamison

Like Bobby a few episodes earlier, Cindy is feeling too small and too young. She wants to be like her older sisters and go out on dates to the pizza place. She puts on her mother's dress and high heels and fixes her hair in a more adult fashion, but her parents tell her she is trying to grow up too fast. The next day, though, Cindy receives a note and a candy bar from a secret admirer. Maybe she can get a boyfriend at age nine after all. Every day for the next week or so Cindy receives more surprises from her secret admirer: a hair ribbon, some flowers, and a huge plastic engagement ring. She even receives a phone call from the admirer who tells her that she is very pretty. The audience get to learn that Bobby is really her secret admirer. He understands her woes because he has experienced similar feeling about being too young. So, he decided to pretend to be Cindy's secret admirer so that she could feel grown up. Bobby never planned on having to reveal himself. When Cindy asks the admirer to come over the next day Bobby can't think of an excuse and Cindy hangs up the phone expecting someone to come over tomorrow after school. Now Bobby is in a pickle. He's not sure what to do because he clearly can't let Cindy know that it was he who gave her all the presents. So he decides to write a note to her telling her that his family is moving to Europe and he can't visit her. But when he goes outside to leave the note and the candy bar in the middle of the night, the door slams shut behind him and he is locked out. Mike hears the noise the door made and comes downstairs to investigate. He finds not only Bobby but also the note and the candy bar. He figures out immediately that Bobby is the one pretending to be Cindy's secret admirer and orders him upstairs. Although Bobby's intentions were good, Mike and Carol tell him to let Cindy know the truth the next morning. When the morning arrives, Bobby finds himself unable to tell Cindy what he has done; he would just feel too bad bursting her bubble. So he hatches a plan. Bobby bribes a boy at school that day, Tommy Jamison, to come over to the Brady house and pretend to be Cindy's secret admirer. Bobby will give Tommy his Kennedy half dollar in return. Tommy follows through with the deal and shows up with some flowers for Cindy. Cindy is very pleased to meet him and she is all dressed up and acting womanly. She takes him outside to talk but all Tommy wants to do is play on the swing set, climb a tree, or play on the teeter-totter. Cindy replies that she is too mature to play like a child anymore. Tommy decides that she is too old for him and makes to leave. Cindy gets scared and stops him saying that she really is a kid, too. She likes playing on jungle gyms and she even collects lizards. Tommy is impressed that she collects lizards because he does, too. The two kids play on the teeter-totter together just like good friends would. Bobby witnesses everything from inside the house and when Mike and Carol come home they ask him for an explanation of who Tommy is. Bobby explains his plan to them. Tommy comes knocking on the sliding door and tells Bobby that he can keep is half dollar; Bobby doesn't have to pay him to play with Cindy because she's real neat. It looks like Bobby lucked out with his plan and Mike and Carol are okay with Bobby keeping his secret to himself. In the end, Tommy even gives Cindy a lizard, which promptly escapes into the kitchen and scares Alice.

#71 – My Fair Opponent
Airdate: March 3, 1972
Directed by Peter Baldwin
Executive Producer Sherwood Schwartz
Produced by Howard Leeds
Written by Bernie Kahn
William Wellman, Jr. ....Colonel Dick Whitfield
Debi Storm... Molly Webber
Lindsay Workman ....Mr. Watkins
Suzanne Roth ....Suzanne

Something horrible has happened at Fillmore Junior High. Marcia is very angry with her classmates for nominating Molly Webber for Hostess of the Senior Banquet. It seems they did it as a joke – Molly is awkward, shy, and not very attractive. Molly is slated to run against the most popular girl in school and doesn't stand a chance at winning. Marcia complains about the situation to Mike and Carol who tell her that if she's so upset about it, she should do something to fix it. So Marcia comes up with a plan. She will do a complete makeover for Molly just like Professor Higgins did to the plain Cockney girl in *My Fair Lady*. She brings Molly home from school and starts work right away. She teaches Molly about poise, balance, being friendly and keeping eye contact with everyone. She replaces Molly's glasses with contacts and gets her a groovy new wardrobe. Soon Molly is ready to reveal herself to her classmates, but does a trial run at Marcia's house first. All the Bradys and Alice are duly impressed with Molly's turn around. She looks like a knock-out. At her debut in school the next day Molly is a big success. She's pretty, talkative, and no longer clumsy. But then disaster strikes – the other girl has to drop out of the elections and the runner-up has to take her place to run against Molly. And who is the runner-up? It's Marcia, of course! Now Marcia must decide to run or not to run. If she drops out, she will be doing Molly a favor by letting her be hostess. After the time and effort she put into helping Molly, Marcia feels that it would be unfair to run against her. On the other hand, Marcia herself would love to be Hostess. But she decides to put her own feelings aside and drop out of the race. When she tells Molly, Molly replies that that is too bad. She said it would have been a close race and accuses Marcia of dropping out because she is scared of losing to her. Well, that remark does nothing except incense Marcia. She decides to stay in the race and run against the "monster" she has created. Unfortunately for Marcia, the faculty end up choosing Molly as the Hostess. Molly won because of a speech she gave that Marcia herself wrote! Poor Marcia...she really would have liked to have been Hostess and dance with Colonel Dick Whitfield, an astronaut and Host for the evening. Most of all, though, she is hurt because Molly turned against her. At home that night the doorbell rings and Marcia answers. It's Molly and she has something to say. She apologizes for her behavior and hopes that Marcia understands. She even told the principal what happened. Marcia is beginning to come around and forgive Molly when Molly drops a bomb. She says that the principal agreed to have *co*-Hostesses for the evening. Colonel Whitfield pops into the doorway (he came with Molly) and asks Marcia if she would be willing to serve as co-Hostess with Molly. Of course Marcia can't refuse. She and Molly accompany the Colonel to the dance and all is well.

#72 – The Fender Benders
Airdate: March 10, 1972
Directed by Allen Barron
Executive Producer Sherwood Schwartz
Produced by Howard Leeds
Written by David P. Harmon
Jackie Coogan .... Harry Duggan
Robert Emhardt .... Judge

Carol comes home from the supermarket with a dented fender. It seems a man backed into her car as she was backing out of a parking space. They agreed at the time to fix their own cars and to exchange addresses. When Mike comes home from work, he finds out what happened. He's a little upset, but very understanding. He plans to take Carol out to dinner, but just as they are getting ready to leave, a Mr. Duggan stops by the house. Mr. Duggan is the person that backed into Carol's station wagon and he has an itemized list of damage done to his car that he wants the Bradys to pay for. The list totals $295.11, which comes from repairs to the taillight, fixing the crushed fender, repainting the left side, and realigning the frame. It seems he's not going to let things go so easily. Mr. Duggan tells Mike his side of the story: that Carol was the one who didn't look back and he is the one who did. Mike must decide who to believe and naturally he sides with Carol. Mr. Duggan says that's fine and I'll see you in court! Bobby and Cindy overhear the exchange. They ask their parents if they will have to testify in court. Mike says it's a possibility because they were in the car with Carol at the time and they could serve as witnesses. The kids say that's what they're afraid of. They never saw their mother look back; they think that maybe the accident was her fault. That night Mike and Carol talk about it and decide to pay Mr. Duggan off. They just couldn't let their own kids testify against them. When Marcia hears the news she goes to her parents' bedroom to set them straight. She was in the car, too, and she *did* see Carol look back. With two conflicting versions of the events, Mike decides to recreate the crime before they commit to paying Mr. Duggan. In the same manner the family solved the mystery of Jan's missing locket two years ago, they hope to solve the mystery of the car accident. In true Brady fashion, everyone gathers in the driveway the next morning for the recreation. Carol, Marcia, Bobby, and Cindy are all in place in the station wagon and Greg is driving the convertible acting as Mr. Duggan. Marcia remembers that Bobby and Cindy were arguing about spilling some ice cream and the two youngest Bradys start the argument up again to honor the recreation. Greg begins backing up the car just like Mr. Duggan did. Mike realizes something – if Bobby and Cindy were arguing the whole time, how could they be sure Carol *didn't* look back? Eureka! The mystery of the two conflicting accounts has been solved. Carol feels confident enough to go to court now, so that's what they do. Carol, Marcia, Bobby, and Cindy are there to testify and Mike goes along for moral support. Mr. Duggan shows up in a neck brace claiming that he now has whiplash. It's obviously a false claim because the Bradys saw him after the accident and he was fine. Mr. Duggan presents his side of the story first to the judge and it's what the Bradys expected: that the accident was Carol's fault because she's a woman driver. Carol is up next and she gives her own account. The judge briefly asks the kids what they saw. Mike wants to make sure that the judge really, truly understands what a liar Mr. Duggan is, so he drops his briefcase loudly on the floor. With the bang, Mr. Duggan quickly snaps his head around to see what caused it. His "whiplash" didn't affect him a bit and the judge is fed up with Mr. Duggan's lies. He sides in favor of Carol Brady. Mr. Duggan is outsmarted by a woman, her pesky kids, and her sneaky husband. Season three ends with success for the Brady Bunch.

THE BRADY BUNCH (comedy)
SEASON FOUR 1972-1973
Fridays 8:00-8:30pm ET on ABC

Production Notes: Paramount Studios had just hired a new Executive Vice President, Emmett G. Lavery, Jr. and Bruce Lansbury was promoted to Vice President of Creative Affairs from his role as producer on *Mission: Impossible*. So the premiere of season four was ramped up and featured a three-part cliffhanging trip to Hawaii. The Hawaiian episodes were filmed on site, and all the actors seem to have enjoyed the experience. This season also featured more singing by the Brady kids. Their off-screen musical careers were taking off, and viewers this year were treated to the Silver Platters singing "Keep On" and "It's a Sunshine Day." The tunes would appear on their album "The Kids from the Brady Bunch," which was released by Paramount and ABC records. (See the music chapter for more.)

#73 – Hawaii Bound
Airdate: September 22, 1972
Directed by Jack Arnold
Executive Producer Sherwood Schwartz
Produced by Howard Leeds
Written by Tam Spiva

Don Ho.. Himself
Sam Kapu..Himself [uncredited]
David "Lippy" Espinada............................... Mr. Hanalei
Dennis M. Chun.................................... Young Workman
Elithe Aguiar...Hula Instructor
Patrick Adiarte .... David

Mike has a surprise for the whole family – his boss Mr. Phillips is sending everyone, including Alice, on a trip to Hawaii! Mike will be working with Kipula Construction Company to supervise construction of a building he designed, but the rest of the family is free to relax any way they choose. All eight Bradys and Alice fly on United Air Lines 748 to Honolulu. The Bradys are met by beautiful sights, including a few Hawaiian women who dress them with leis as soon as they exit the aircraft. David, a worker for Kipula, escorts the Brady family to the Sheraton Hotel in Waikiki. From here the adventure begins. The family goes sightseeing and visits King Kamehameha's Palace, Pearl Harbor, and the beach. Next, Mike takes Peter and Bobby to the build site where Bobby discovers an old island tiki. Unbeknownst to Bobby, the tiki idol is taboo and brings bad luck to anyone who touches it. Bobby happily strings the idol around his neck and soon enough unlucky things start to happen. First, Bobby squashes his ukulele after listing to Don Ho and Sam Kapu sing "Sweet Someone." Then a heavy wall hanging almost falls on Bobby's head, Alice's back goes out while she is wearing the idol during a hula lesson, and worst of all Greg wipes out during a surfing contest while wearing the idol. Greg had entered the contest because David (their guide from Kipula) was acting as judge. Greg rented a surfboard and hit the waves. He was doing quite well when suddenly a rogue wave knocked him off his board and straight into a head of coral. Oh, no! Will Greg drown? Stay tuned for next week's episode to find out.

#74 – Pass the Tabu
Airdate: September 29, 1972
Directed by Jack Arnold
Executive Producer Sherwood Schwartz
Produced by Howard Leeds
Written by Tam Spiva
David "Lippy" Espinada......................... Mr. Hanalei
Cris Callow.. Mandy
Patrick Adiarte... David
Vincent Price... Professor Hubert Whitehead [uncredited]

This episode picks up where the last one left off. Greg has just fallen into the Pacific and the viewers don't know what will happen. The narrator recapping last week's events ends his dialogue with, "[Greg's] surfboard has floated ashore but Greg is nowhere in sight." Mike says, "There he is," not two seconds later, though. So much for dragging out the suspense! Greg is okay except for a skinned neck and a brief moment of confusion. Momentarily, the tiki idol has been lost at sea, but Jan miraculously recovers it on the shore. She returns it to Bobby the next day, but only after she takes up a secret hitchhiker in her beach bag: a giant, hairy spider. That evening back at the hotel, the spider escapes Jan's bag and makes its way into the boys' room. Bobby has since learned from David that the tiki idol is *bad* luck instead of good and wants to wash his hands of it. Peter eagerly volunteers to take charge of the idol and believes it will make a great souvenir. He puts it over his neck and the boys shut off the light to fall asleep. Peter is soon visited by the eight-legged creepy-crawly beast and opens his eyes to find it staring him down on his chest. Pete freaks out and the boys raise a ruckus getting rid of the spider. Mike tells them to be quiet and humanely disposes of the spider himself. That's the last straw for the Brady boys and they decide that the legend is true concerning the idol. They want to know how to properly rid themselves of their ill luck and so enlist the help of Mr. Hanalei, an aged Hawaiian gentleman familiar with the story of the tiki. He also happens to work for Kipula Construction Company, and the boys have no problem finding him and asking him for his advice. Mr. Hanalei says that the tiki must be returned to its rightful resting place on the tomb of the king for which it was made. The tiki is the king's guardian and the boys' bad luck will disappear once the idol is returned to the king's grave. Mr. Hanalei gives them some general directions to where he believes the burial ground is. Early the next day, Greg, Peter, and Bobby sneak away on a quest to find the burial ground. Nobody knows precisely where they're going – they didn't tell their parents. Even though Marcia, Jan, and Cindy know their plan, they don't know exactly where to look for them should something happen. Sure enough, by the time dusk arrives the boys are not back at the hotel. They discovered a mysterious cave in the middle of a Hawaiian forest. Once inside, they are stalked by a scary-faced man who could only be up to no good. To be continued!

#75 – The Tiki Caves
Airdate: October 6, 1972
Directed by Jack Arnold
Executive Producer Sherwood Schwartz
Produced by Howard Leeds
Written by Tam Spiva
Vincent Price ....Professor Hubert Whitehead
David "Lippy" Espinada...Mr. Hanalei
Leon Lontoc...Mayor's Representative

The Brady boys are inside a cave deep in the Hawaiian forest attempting to return a taboo idol back to its resting place guarding the grave of the first king. Peter and Bobby are spooked by the atmosphere and weird noises they hear, but Greg tries to be rational and calm them down. Greg, though, has a good reason to be scared, too, because they are being stalked by a crazy archaeologist. Professor Hubert Whitehead has staked a claim to the cave and its contents and does not want any intruders taking the credit for his discovery. The Professor tries to scare the boys away at first, but when that doesn't work he resorts to capture. He trusses them to three man-sized tikis while threatening them at spear point. He wants to know what the boys are doing in the cave. Bobby explains that they're there to return the idol. "You found the find that I didn't find!" the Professor exclaims. He thinks the boys found the idol in the cave and stole it. It takes a lot of clever convincing, but eventually the boys make it understood that they found the idol in Honolulu. They are innocent of thievery and just want to return the idol and go home. Meanwhile back at the hotel, Mike and Carol are very worried about the boys...they should have been back hours ago. The girls spill their guts about the boys' true intentions for the day and Mike and Carol rush over to Mr. Hanalei's house to get directions to the burial ground. They believe that something must have gone wrong. Mr. Hanalei denies culpability but gives the Brady parents directions on how to find the boys. Mike and Carol set off at once and in the forest they find a trail of popcorn that Bobby left. The trail leads right to the cave. Immediately upon entering, they find Bobby, Peter, and Greg tied up and rescue them. Mike demands an explanation from Professor Whitehead. He explains everything and offers an excuse of, "All I ever really wanted was a place of my own in the academic world." Mike swallows it hook, line, and sinker and everything is A-okay. The Bradys even go the extra mile and report the Professor's find to the State and serve as witnesses to his discovery. Even though the guy's off his rocker – aside from kidnapping three minors, he talks to a statue he named "Oliver" – the local museum immediately grants him his own eponymous wing where his discoveries can be displayed. The mayor holds a luau honoring Professor Whitehead and the Brady family. It's reminiscent of the celebration the Brady family took part in at the Grand Canyon, complete with native dance. Everyone is joyful and they all go home happy and tan.

#76 – Today, I am a Freshman
Airdate: October 13, 1972
Directed by Hal Cooper
Executive Producer Sherwood Schwartz
Produced by Howard Leeds
Written by William Raynor and Myles Wilder
John Howard .... Doctor Howard
Vickie Cos .... Kim
Kelly Flynn .... Tom Peterson
John Reilly .... Dick Corset

It's Marcia's first day of high school and she is very nervous. Mistaking her nerves for a stomach virus, Carol calls the doctor who then correctly diagnoses her as worried and flustered. It seems that Marcia thinks she will be a nobody in high school. Even given all the awards she received in junior high and all the friends she made, she is extremely worried that no one will like her. It's a common worry plaguing youth and Carol convinces her that she has to face her problem and go to school the next day. To help her ease into high school life, Mike recruits Greg to introduce his sister to some of his friends at Westdale. Greg agrees and the next day Marcia makes a complete fool of herself (and by extension, Greg) in front of his friends. Now doomed to obscurity in school, Marcia comes home upset and angry. Mike and Carol try to put her straight by saying that she should join a school activity. Surely she can meet some new people and make a good impression that way. Marcia takes their advice seriously…perhaps too seriously because she signs up for every club on the bulletin board! On her résumé go: poetry, nursing, ceramics, scuba, archery, karate, music, composition, art work, and four that aren't even on the board – yoga, stamp collecting, drama and the Westdale Boosters. Actually, the Boosters have to approve Marcia's application before she can be allowed to join. They only take three freshmen each year, but considering Marcia's junior high record of success, she is a likely candidate. Sure enough the next day the Boosters hold their meeting at the Brady residence and tell Marcia she's in. The offer, however, is quickly rescinded after Peter sprays the whole Booster Club with mud from his homemade volcano. The Boosters are so upset at becoming messy that they kick Marcia out of the club. Marcia makes a quip like, "If you want to see something stupid you should see your face," and off they go. Marcia takes the banishment very well and decides to drop all of her clubs except ceramics. She now realizes that she does not have to conform to other people's expectations to be popular.

#77 – Cyrano de Brady
Airdate: October 20, 1972
Directed by Hal Cooper
Executive Producer Sherwood Schwartz
Produced by Howard Leeds
Written by Skip Webster
Kym Karath..Kerry Hathaway

Jan makes a new friend at school, Kerry Hathaway, and brings her home to introduce her to the family. When Peter meets her he's instantly in love. He vies to go out with her and phones her that evening. But when Kerry answers the phone she doesn't remember who Peter is and he hangs up heartbroken. Pete's next tactic is to approach her at school and impress her with his groovy duds and aftershave lotion. Unfortunately for Peter his clumsiness gets in the way when he drops her books in a mud puddle and then accidentally splashes Kerry with water. She storms away. Peter is batting 0-2 and confesses his problems to his parents. Mike comes up with the idea that Peter should write a letter to Kerry. That way he can take his time to formulate exactly what he wants to say. Pete does just that and Alice helps him write down Elizabeth Barrett Browning's Sonnet #43.

SONNET #43

How do I love thee? Let me count the ways.
I love thee to the depth and breadth and height
My soul can reach, when feeling out of sight
For the ends of Being and ideal Grace.
I love thee to the level of everyday's
Most quiet need, by sun and candle-light.
I love thee freely, as men strive for Right.
I love thee purely, as they turn from Praise.
I love thee with the passion put to use
In my old griefs, and with my childhood's faith.
I love thee with a love I seemed to lose
With my lost saints, - I love thee with the breath,
Smiles, tears, of all my life! - and, if God choose,
I shall but love thee better after death.

Unfortunately for Peter, this is strike number three and he's out. Kerry loved the poem, but Pete forgot to sign it! Nevertheless, Peter is determined and he gets an idea. Marcia tells him about *Cyrano de Bergerac* and Peter recruits Greg, aka "Old Silver Tongue," to be Cyrano to his Christian. Greg reluctantly agrees. The two Brady teens go over to Kerry's house with Peter dressed up in a suit and Greg hiding behind a bush feeding him lines.

Kerry is impressed and confused and walks outside to talk to Peter face-to-face. When she gets there she sees Greg behind the bush and jumps to the wrong conclusion: Greg is the one who has fallen for her, not Peter. Peter and Greg are both surprised that their plan backfired and Pete is super angry at Greg for stealing his girl. Of course Greg didn't really "steal" her, but Peter doesn't see it that way. Greg tries to tell Kerry the truth about what happened, but she won't listen. In the end, Greg must take drastic measures to convince Kerry to break up with him and to take Peter into her arms instead. Greg and Marcia concoct a wild plan wherein Greg will act like a jerk – he tells Kerry that if they go out she can't see other people but *he* can – and come onto Kerry really strong. Then Marcia will enter the picture as "Debbie," Greg's ex-girlfriend still vying for his love. The plan is put into action and it seems all is going well until Peter walks onto the scene. Greg and Marcia are busted and the truth comes out. They only set Kerry up because Greg didn't want to go out with her. Peter is ashamed of their behavior and says that if Kerry were his girl he'd treat her like a queen. Kerry finally understands that Pete is a stand-up guy and he gets his girl after all.

#78 – Fright Night
Airdate: October 27, 1972
Directed by Jerry London
Executive Producer Sherwood Schwartz
Produced by Howard Leeds
Written by Brad Radnitz

The Brady boys play a trick on the Brady girls and scare them into thinking that there is a ghost in the attic. The girls are onto them, though, and discover proof in the boys' room: a slide projector and a rope. The girls decide that they will not be had without a fight and they challenge the boys to spend the night in the attic by themselves for the whole night. If they come downstairs for any reason, the boys lose the bet. They all agree to wager their allowances and the deal is sealed with Mike and Carol's permission. (Even Bobby is in on the bet despite his promise last year to never bet again after his bet with Greg went bad.) The boys don't know it, but the girls have rigged up a tape player to play a spooky voice from inside an old trunk and a "ghost" to pop out of the trunk and scare them. The joke works and Bobby and Peter are run right out of the attic. The boys end up "poorer but wiser" when they fork over their week's allowances to the girls. But the joke isn't over yet. Alice tells Marcia and Greg that she isn't scared of *anything* (despite ample evidence to the contrary in the past – ghosts, mice, lizards, and the ocean have scared her before). The eldest Brady kids recruit their siblings to put Alice to the test. When she returns home from a date with Sam, the kids plan to scare her silly with a glowing skull, a tape recorded scream, and a fake ghost. Everyone is in place. The front door opens and the kids put on their show. Unfortunately, it's their parents who came home first and not Alice. Mike and Carol were attending an art show where Carol entered a fired clay bust of Mike in a contest. She won third prize for the bust. Now at home, Mike places the bust on the ledge in the entryway and makes his way to the fuse box to turn the lights back on. Before he can get to the fuse box Alice comes home, too. She sees the bust on the ledge, thinks it's an intruder, and whacks it hard with her purse. The bust shatters into a million pieces just as Mike gets the lights turned back on. The kids' joke backfired and Mike's head paid the price. Jan especially should have known better. Presumably she already learned that you can carry a joke too far when she lost Myron the mouse. Nevertheless, she learns the same lesson again and all the other Bradys learn it too.

#79 – The Show Must Go On??
Airdate: November 3, 1972
Directed by Jack Donohue
Executive Producer Sherwood Schwartz
Produced by Howard Leeds
Written by Harry Winkler
Allan Melvin .... Sam
Barbara Morrison .... Mrs. Tuttle
Brandy Carson .... Woman
Karen Foulkes .... Muriel
Frank DeVol .... Father
Bonnie Ludeka .... Daughter

Westdale High School is putting on a show called "Family Night Frolics." The intent of the show is to raise money for equipment for the school. Participants are high school kids and their parents. Marcia convinces a reluctant Carol to do a duet with her: a rendition of "Together" from *Gypsy*. Then Greg comes home the next day and says the Night needs more acts. Would Mike be willing to do a dramatic reading accompanied by Greg on the guitar? Sure he would! says Carol. The reading is Longfellow's poem "The Day is Done," which Greg, Peter, Bobby, and Mike all think is dullsville. But Mike comes up with an idea to spice up the act. When it comes time for their performance, Marcia and Carol are first. They do beautifully and the guys are up next. Bobby and Peter are on the catwalk above the stage throwing down props when they're called for. When Mike says "a feather is wafted slowly downward," the boys throw some feathers onto the stage. When Mike reads another line about rain, Bobby and Peter throw buckets of water over the performers. Both sets of Bradys are instant hits and the Family Night Frolics succeeds.

#80 – Jan, the Only Child
Airdate: November 10, 1972
Directed by Roger Duchowny
Executive Producer Sherwood Schwartz
Produced by Howard Leeds
Written by Al Schwartz and Ralph Goodman

Jan is fed up with having five brothers and sisters to hog the bathroom, phone, and generally just get in her way. She wishes she were an only child like her friend Donna. She makes her wishes known to her parents and siblings. At first, the other five Brady kids are indulgent and go out of their way to make Jan feel privileged. But then she discovers their motivations (to play along with her until she gets over her "phase") and tells them she wishes they never existed! From that point on, the others are invisible to her. She can do whatever she wants whenever she wants at home because her siblings will ignore her. She even decides to forgo the family trip to a ho-down in favor of spending the weekend with Donna. Time goes on and with that passage Jan becomes somber and realizes what she is missing by not having five siblings to talk to and do things with. She has a heart-to-heart with Mike who tells her that maybe her brothers and sisters will be more willing to take

60

her back among their ranks than she thinks. So Jan apologizes to her siblings for the way she treated them and all is well. Everyone goes to the ho-down and Jan even invites her sibling-less friend Donna along for the fun.

#81 – Career Fever
Airdate: November 17, 1972
Directed by Jerry London
Executive Producer Sherwood Schwartz
Produced by Howard Leeds
Written by Burt and Adele Styler

Mike discovers that Greg received an A on an English composition about choosing a career. In the paper, Greg said he wanted to be an architect like his father. Before Greg gets the chance to tell his father the truth (that he has no idea what he wants to be), Mike runs with the idea. He is so excited that Greg wants to follow in his footsteps that he volunteers the use of his den to Greg anytime he wants it. Now Greg feels stuck. He doesn't want to disappoint his dad by telling him the truth. What can he do? He and Marcia hatch a plan to get Greg out of being an architect. Once Mike sees what a horrible architect Greg will become, he's got to admit that his son doesn't belong in the business, right? So, Greg draws up some crazy house plans that include a moat around the domicile and shows them to Mike. Mike takes a look at the plans and says that they show promise. Mike's too worried about hurting *Greg* to tell *him* the truth so he comes up with a plan of his own: give Greg his old drafting kit, a book on perspective, and unlimited use of his den. Surely that will bring Greg's skills around. Not so. This time Greg determinedly comes up with an even more horrendous drawing. In the meantime, the other kids are coming up with career ideas of their own. Peter and Jan want to be a doctor and a nurse and start reviewing medical books to find all kinds of neat diseases to cure. Peter even gets the idea that he is sick with one of the fatal diseases until his parents reveal to him that he was reading the medical book incorrectly and all he really has is poison ivy. Bobby and Cindy have the career fever, too, and they ask Alice to give them special diets so they can practice becoming an astronaut and a model. Back to Greg and he has just shown his father his latest creation. It's abysmal and Mike and Carol don't know how to break the news that Greg would starve as an architect. They needn't worry, however, because Greg confesses to them first. Mike and Carol are pleased with the news; they want him to be whatever he sets his mind to.

THE KIDS' CAREERS		
Greg	Anything but an architect	An obstetrician
Marcia	(unknown)	A fashion designer
Peter	A doctor	A businessman
Jan	A nurse	An architect
Bobby	An astronaut or football player	A racecar driver
Cindy	A model or lady wrestler	A deejay

#82 – Goodbye, Alice, Hello

Airdate: November 24, 1972
Directed by George Tyne
Executive Producer Sherwood Schwartz
Produced by Howard Leeds
Written by Milt Rosen
Mary Treen..Kay
Snag Werris..Mr. Foster
Harry Crigger..Customer

Alice makes the worst mistake a housekeeper can make: getting too emotionally attached to the family. That is, at least, according to her friend Kay. It all started when Peter broke a lamp in Mike's den. Alice was witness to the accident. When Carol got home from shopping and discovered the broken lamp, she forced Alice to tell her everything she knows. Carol punished Peter (and Greg, who was a participant in the event) by taking away his allowance for one week. The next day, Carol asked Alice who was using the record player in the family room. Alice replied that she saw Marcia using it last night. Now Marcia can't use the record player for a whole week because she irresponsibly left it on all night. Alice tops off her week by forbidding Bobby and Cindy to go swimming at someone's house in the nude. The kids really wanted to go but Alice wouldn't let them without their parents' permission. So Alice has now set herself up as a spy out to get the kids in trouble. That's the kids' take on it, anyway. They all band together and decide to ignore Alice. That way they'll teach her a lesson about tattling on them. Poor Alice is in tears and goes to Kay's house to talk the situation over with her. Kay tells her that she got too attached and that she should find another job where she won't have to worry about the family she works for. Thus, Alice sadly decides to leave the Brady household for good. She tells Carol the next day and gives Carol about 8 hours' notice of her departure. Carol is saddened to see Alice go, but does nothing to stop her; all Carol does is shrug. True to her word, Alice is gone by the time the Brady kids get home from school that afternoon. Kay is working in her place until the Bradys can find a full-time replacement. At first the kids are confused at Alice's departure, but they are determined to get over it. It doesn't take long for them to realize what a good friend they had in Alice, though. Kay is nothing like her predecessor; she doesn't play games or watch TV or do anything fun. Eventually Greg and Marcia confess to Carol that they were the ones who drove Alice off. Kay overhears their confession and decides it's time to let the kids know where Alice is. She tells them that Alice is working as a waitress at the Golden Spoon Café. All six kids converge on the Café after school the next day. They discover Alice and she is pleased to see them. The kids apologize to Alice for making life difficult in the Brady home and ask her to come back. Alice is moved to tears by their request and quits her waitressing job on the spot. She comes back home where she belongs to the relief of Carol and the kids. Mike is mysteriously absent through the whole series of events.

#83 – Greg's Triangle

Airdate: December 8, 1972
Directed by Richard Michaels
Executive Producer Sherwood Schwartz
Produced by Howard Leeds

Written by Bill Freedman & Ben Gershman
Tannis G. Montgomery .... Jennifer Nichols
Rita Wilson .... Pat Conway

EPISODE GUIDE

Greg is approached at school by a lovely girl named Jennifer Nichols. Jennifer has heard a lot about Greg and the two of them make a date for Saturday at the beach. Greg will teach Jennifer how to surf (and they'll both show off their California-sculpted bodies to each other). Greg has fallen for Jennifer hard and even asks her to come home to meet his parents. Jennifer gives Mike and Carol a supreme snow job and they suspect she's up to something. Indeed she is. Jennifer knows that Greg is the chairman of the head cheerleader selection committee, and she wants his vote. To complicate the situation Marcia is trying out for head cheerleader, too! Greg must now decide to vote for his girlfriend or his sister: a tough choice. But, since there are three other members of the committee, Greg realizes that he doesn't have to vote unless there is a tie. He thinks he's off the hook. When the day of the tryouts arrives, Marcia, Jennifer, Pat, and another girl all do their best. The three judges cast their votes and Greg tallies them up: one for Marcia, one for Jennifer, and one for Pat. A three-way tie! Now Greg has to cast a vote in order to break the tie. In the end he votes his conscience and for who did the best at the tryouts. He elects Pat Conway as head cheerleader. Marcia is very understanding, but Jennifer acts the opposite. She hangs up on Greg when he calls to talk about it and never wants to see her "Greggie" again.

#84 – Everyone Can't be George Washington

Airdate: December 22, 1972
Directed by Richard Michaels
Executive Producer Sherwood Schwartz
Produced by Howard Leeds
Written by Sam Locke & Milton Pascal
Sara Seegar .... Miss Bailey
Barbara Bernstein .... Peggy Arnold
Jimmy Bracken .... Freddie
Sean Kelly .... Stuart
Michael Barbera .... Harvey
Cheryl Beth Jacobs .... Edith
Angela B. Satterwhite .... Donna

Peter tries out for the part of George Washington in the school play but ends up being cast as Benedict Arnold. Peter finds himself in the same situation his sister Marcia was in a year ago: cast for a role he didn't want. As they did with Marcia, Peter's parents encourage him to fulfill the role despite his reservations. Thus, Peter plugs courageously onward and begins rehearsing for the challenging part of Benedict Arnold. The tide turns when Pete's classmates find out what role he's playing. They start calling Peter a traitor and give him a really hard time. Naturally Peter does not put up with such razzing and makes up his mind to quit the play. But he can't quit because he promised his parents he wouldn't. Therefore, he feels that the only recourse is to get himself thrown out of the play. He tries badgering Miss Bailey to change the script. This only succeeds in getting him a bloody nose from a fellow actor – Peter insinuated that his fellow's character should be the traitor and not he.

Next, Peter tries pretending that he forgot his lines and that he twisted his ankle. Miss Bailey promptly solves those problems as well. His final attempt is to pretend that he has laryngitis. Miss Bailey lets him go this time. Meanwhile, Jan has been hard at work readying the sets and props for the performance. She makes a phone call to Miss Bailey to let her know that the sets are ready. But when she gets off the phone she informs Mike and Carol that the play has been cancelled because Peter has laryngitis. Miss Bailey could not find a replacement in time. Mike and Carol know just what to do about this development. They march up to Peter's room and get the truth from him. Now that everything's out in the open, Peter is told that the cancellation of the play is his fault. He quit because he didn't want to play a traitor. Now he's become one himself. That revelation is enough to get Peter back on stage where he belongs. The play goes on as planned and Pete is a big success.

#85 – Love and the Older Man

Airdate: January 5, 1973
Directed by George Tyne
Executive Producer Sherwood Schwartz
Produced by Howard Leeds
Written by Martin A. Ragaway
Don Brit Reid......................................Dr. Stanley Vogel
Allen Joseph.......................................Minister

Marcia is in love with her dentist, Dr. Stanley Vogel. She fantasizes a marriage ceremony and having kids with him. When Mike comes home from the dentist and asks Marcia if she is free at 7:00 on Friday for Dr. Vogel she is totally amazed and happy. An older man! But what Marcia doesn't know is that the message was convoluted – Dr. Vogel wants Marcia to babysit for his kid. He is a married man and doesn't want to date Marcia. But the poor teen's mind jumped to the conclusion she had been hoping for. She readies herself for her "date" by canceling one for the same night with a boy in Greg's class. She thinks the boy is too immature for her. After all, Teen Time Romance said that a woman should marry someone ten to twelve years older than she. But when Thursday arrives Marcia receives devastating news from Jan. Jan found out that Dr. Vogel is married. Marcia couldn't possibly play the role of the "other woman" and so at her appointment for a filling that day with the dentist she breaks her date. Dr. Vogel understands that Marcia got things confused (even if *she* never realized it) and lets her go gently. After the whole escapade is over Marcia reschedules the date with Greg's friend. Perhaps she was trying to grow up too quickly.

#86 – Law and Disorder

Airdate: January 12, 1973
Directed by Hal Cooper
Executive Producer Sherwood Schwartz
Produced by Howard Leeds
Written by Elroy Schwartz
Shawn Schepps .... Jill
Harlen Carraher...................................... Steve

Cindy Henderson ....Girl
Jon Hayes ....Jon

Bobby's whole class hates him. The poor elementary school student was appointed Safety Monitor by his teacher. In other words, he's now the class fink. Bobby comes home distraught. His parents are right there to pick up the pieces and they tell him that maybe there was a reason his teacher picked him. Maybe she thinks that he is responsible and can do a good job. If Bobby just put is mind to it and chooses to be effective and efficient, he could really learn to like the position. His parents' encouragement cheers him up and Bobby spends the night reading all about the school regulations. The next day, his "SM" armband brazenly tied on, Bobby sets to work stopping students from chewing gum, roughhousing, and running in the halls. He even writes up his own sister Cindy for running in the hallway! It doesn't take long for Bobby's newfound power to go to his head. He begins putting together a report on Alice and his siblings for violations they have committed at home. On the way home from school one day, a girl named Jill runs up to Bobby and implores him to rescue her cat Guinevere. The only thing is, the cat is inside a condemned house with a "no trespassing" sign. Bobby is a stickler for the rules now that he's a Safety Monitor and at first refuses to enter the premises. But Jill's pleas get to him and he does decide to rescue Guinevere. In the process he gets soot all over his good clothes. Guinevere is reunited with Jill but now Bobby has to find a way to get his clothes clean without his parents knowing. So, he comes home to an empty house – lucky him! – and throws all his clothes into the washer with almost an entire box of Safe laundry soap. The soap is enough to fill the entire service porch with suds and Bobby practically drowns in them trying to shut off the washing machine at the end of the cycle. Now Bobby's luck changes and Alice and Carol come home from shopping and discover the avalanche of suds. They rescue Bobby, who has learned a few very important lessons from the whole experience. He now knows that rules are in place to protect people but that sometimes rules can be broken if there is a good reason. For instance, he broke the no trespassing rule for a good reason. Greg and Jan had good reasons for breaking the rules they broke as well. No longer will Bobby write reports about his siblings and no longer will he try to act like a cop at home. He'll also tell the truth, read labels on clothes that say "dry clean only," and never use a whole box of laundry soap again.

#87 – Greg Gets Grounded
Airdate: January 19, 1973
Directed by Jack Arnold
Executive Producer Sherwood Schwartz
Produced by Howard Leeds
Written by Elroy Schwartz
Gracia Lee ....Jenny
Hope Sherwood ....Rachel

Bobby tells his parents that Greg is a great driver: so great that he avoided a near collision caused by his inattention to the road. Mike grounds Greg for one week because of his irresponsible driving. Greg is not to drive the Bradys' cars during that time. But Greg needs to get tickets to a rock concert for himself and his girlfriend Rachel. The tickets are only available at the stadium and the only way to get there is to drive. What to do? Easy – borrow a friend's car. His parents never said don't drive *any* car for a week, they just said don't drive *their* cars. After Mike and Carol find out what Greg did they ground him for another ten days, which means Greg will miss the concert. That evening Greg approaches his parents. According to him, there has been a misunderstanding. His parents might have *meant* no driving period, but they never *said* it. Greg wants to hold his parents to their exact words. Mike and Carol reluctantly agree to let Greg off the hook for his extra ten days' sentence even though they know he knew exactly what they meant. They make Greg promise to live by *his* own exact words, too. Hopefully for Mike and Carol Greg will learn a lesson from all this. The day of the concert arrives. Greg is getting ready to pick up Rachel when Bobby and Peter approach him and ask him if he's ready to drive them to a frog jumping contest. Greg had promised them the week before that he would take them to the contest. But now that Greg has a date he shouldn't have to take his little brothers out should he? Yes, he should, say Carol and Mike. Greg's exact words were that he would take Bobby to the contest. He put no stipulations on the promise and therefore he is obligated to follow through. There's no more concert in Greg's evening, but there is a chance that he can take Rachel to a late drive-in movie. After he dutifully brings Peter and Bobby back from the frog jumping contest (their frogs placed 35th and 49th), he and Rachel go to the drive-in. Unbeknownst to Greg, the frogs are still in the back seat of the convertible. During the movie, the frogs escape and jump all over poor Rachel and their food. Greg comes home that evening with a new attitude. He's sorry for holding his parents to their exact words and sorry that he acted like he did.

#88 – Amateur Nite
Airdate: January 26, 1973
Directed by Jack Arnold
Executive Producer Sherwood Schwartz
Produced by Howard Leeds
Written by Sam Locke & Milton Pascal
Harold Peary ....Mr. Goodbody
Steve Dunn..Pete Sterne
Robert Nadder.. Alfred Bailey

It's Carol and Mike's fourth anniversary. As a present for their parents, the six Brady kids pooled their money and bought a silver platter. Jan went the extra mile and had the platter engraved: "Mom and Dad Happy Anniversary All Our Love Greg Marcia Peter Jan Bobby Cindy." What Jan didn't realize, though, was that the engraving was 85 cents per *letter* instead of for the whole thing. She now owes the department store $56.23 ($53.55 for the engraving plus $2.68 in tax) and she and the other kids are broke. Bobby and Cindy try to get a loan from a bank, Greg tries to get money from a friend who owes him, and Marcia tries to sell her watch all to no avail. Jan is successful in signing the kids up for an audition for the Pete Sterne Amateur Hour, a local televised talent competition. Everyone is excited at the prospect of appearing on television and the chance of winning the $100 prize. The kids work up a singing and dancing routine and audition. Mr. Sterne likes the group and signs them up for the coming Saturday's show. The kids bill themselves as "The Silver Platters" and sneak away to the studio on Saturday morning. The studio provides them with costumes and they sing and dance their hearts out. Unfortunately, they end up in third place and are awarded a plaque for their efforts. So much for being able to pay for the engraving. Or is it? When the kids get home they are surprised to find that

Alice, Mike, and Carol all saw their performance on television. What's more, they got a call from the silver salesman and went to the department store to pick up the platter themselves. The kids are very pleased with the outcome and their parents couldn't be more proud.

#89 – Bobby's Hero
Airdate: February 2, 1973
Directed by Leslie H. Martinson
Executive Producer Sherwood Schwartz
Produced by Howard Leeds
Written by Michael Morris
Burt Mustin .... Jethroe Collins
Richard Carlyle .... Mr. Hillary
Gordon DeVol .... Jesse James
Ruth Anson.. Miss Perry

Mike and Carol are called in to see Bobby's elementary school principal. It seems Bobby wrote in an English composition that Jesse James is his hero. Furthermore, he brought a cap gun to school. Bobby's parents haul him into the den for a stern talking-to. They tell him that Jesse James is no kind of person to pick for a hero and that he had better stop playing around with cap guns. The message doesn't sink in. The next day Bobby is up to his antics masquerading as Jesse James around the house and "holding up" his brothers and sisters. To drive the point of Jesse's criminal ways, Mike and Carol allow him to stay up late and watch *Jesse James on the Vengeance Trail* on television. But Bobby is absolutely engrossed in the film because all the unsuitable scenes have been cut. Not one murder appeared in the edited version and Bobby came away appreciating Jesse James even more than before. So Mike takes it upon himself to learn more about the real folk figure. He checks out some books at the local library and stumbles across one written by a man whose father was murdered by Jesse James. It just so happens that the author of the book, Jethroe Collins, leaves near City. Mike calls him up, explains the situation, and asks Mr. Collins to come over to the house to straighten Bobby out. Mr. Collins obliges and tells Bobby the truth about Jesse James: that he was a mean, rotten, dirty killer who shot people in

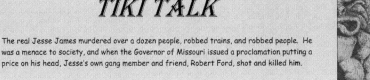

TIKI TALK

The real Jesse James murdered over a dozen people, robbed trains, and robbed people. He was a menace to society, and when the Governor of Missouri issued a proclamation putting a price on his head, Jesse's own gang member and friend, Robert Ford, shot and killed him.

the back for no reason. Mr. Collins goes further and tells young Bobby that when he was a kid he would have nightmares about what happened the day his father was shot in a train robbery. Bobby is reluctant to believe the older gentleman's story at first. But that night he has a terrible nightmare. He dreams that Jesse James robs *his*

family on a train ride. Then Jesse shoots and kills everyone. It's a horrible dream and Bobby wakes up yelling. Finally the truth about his hero has sunk in. Bobby goes into his parents' room to tell them that he has come around. He never wants to see a gun again. He turns in his holsters and caps to Mike who says that he's proud of Bobby for making the right decision. The next time Bobby picks a hero he'll make sure he is a real good guy.

#90 – The Subject Was Noses
Airdate: February 9, 1973
Directed by Jack Arnold
Executive Producer Sherwood Schwartz
Produced by Howard Leeds
Written by Al Schwartz and Larry Rhine
Nicholas Hammond .... Doug Simpson
Stuart Getz ....Charley
Lisa Eilbacher ....Vicki

Marcia has a date for Saturday night with Charley. Then Doug Simpson, the football-playing big man on campus, asks Marcia out for the same night. She's so flattered that she yes and doesn't realize until Doug has left that she already had a date for that night. Now she has to try to gently break the date with ordinary-guy Charley so she can go out with super-hunk Doug. Greg gives her some advice. "Tell him that something suddenly came up," he says. "That always works." So Marcia feeds Charley the line. Charley is disappointed but understanding. He wants to try for a different night but Marcia says she'll see. The next day everything seems to be right on track for Marcia. Then Carol asks her to go outside and tell Peter and Bobby to come in and clean their room. Marcia opens the sliding door and *wham!* gets hit right in the nose with a badly-thrown football. Marcia's nose swells up like a balloon. The doctor says it's not broken. Nevertheless, it will take a few days for the swelling to go down. At school the following day Marcia tries to hide her injury from Doug. She thinks that if he sees her nose the way it is that he will break his date with her. She has good reason to worry because as soon as he sees her he makes up an excuse. "Something suddenly came up," he says and walks away. Marcia is upset and sulks outside in the Brady yard after school. Charley comes by to deliver some wallpaper samples to Mike and Carol and discovers Marcia moping on the swing set. He gets his first look at her swollen nose but reacts in the opposite way than Doug. He says it's a shame that she's hurt but he wants to take her out anyway. He likes Marcia for her and not for her looks. Marcia is too depressed to realize what she has in Charley and fends off his advances for the time being. Friday comes around and Marcia runs into Doug at school again. But this time her nose is completely healed. Doug sees that he made a mistake in canceling the date earlier and asks her out again. Marcia, now a little wiser, declines. Not only is she wiser, but she also feels guilty for what she did to Charley. She confesses her sins to Charley. He is forgiving, though, and asks her if she would still like to go out with him on Saturday. Marcia accepts the offer gladly. Then Saturday night at the pizza parlor she and Charley run into Doug Simpson. He starts teasing Marcia for going with Charley and Charley steps up to defend her. The two boys end up in a fist fight and this time Doug is the one who ends up with a swollen nose. Marcia learns her lesson about being shallow, Mike and Carol repaint their bedroom, and all is well.

#91 – How to Succeed in Business
Airdate: February 23, 1973
Directed by Robert Reed
Executive Producer Sherwood Schwartz
Produced by Howard Leeds
Written by Gene Thompson
Jay Novello ....Mr. Martinelli

EPISODE GUIDE

Peter is VERY happy. At fourteen he's landed his very first part-time job. He'll be working at Martinelli's Bicycle Shop every afternoon and on Saturdays repairing bikes. Unfortunately for Pete, he's not very mechanically inclined. After only three days on the job Mr. Martinelli fires him. Peter doesn't have the heart to tell his parents that their son is a failure. Instead he lets them believe that he has been promoted to a bike salesman. Poor Pete spends his afternoons in Glenville Park feeding the pigeons. When Mike and Carol decide to take Peter up on a suggestion he made (while still employed) that they buy bicycles for themselves, they find out the truth from Mr. Martinelli. Peter's parents ride up to him on their new bicycles in the Park and let him know that they know what happened. Peter is embarrassed but he feels a lot better now that everything is out in the open. The whole family and Alice all go for a bike ride together and everything is swell.

#92 – The Great Earring Caper
Airdate: March 2, 1973
Directed by Leslie H. Martinson
Executive Producer Sherwood Schwartz
Produced by Howard Leeds
Written by Larry Rhine & Al Schwartz

Cindy watches Marcia try on a pair of Carol's clip-on earrings. She wants to try them on herself but Marcia says no. When Marcia leaves the room to go answer a phone call, Cindy disobeys her and tries on the earrings anyway. The earrings are special because Carol's mother Mrs. Tyler gave them to her. But when Cindy is called out of the bathroom the earrings disappear. They're nowhere to be seen and that's when she enlists Peter to help her find them. Peter has been reading about detective work and Sherlock Holmes. He tries opening the drain in the bathroom sink but the earrings aren't there. He questions everyone in the family on their whereabouts at the time of the disappearance but gets nowhere. He even takes everyone's fingerprints. Nothing works. He and Cindy are unable to solve the case. Mike and Carol are preparing for a costume party. The couple is going as Marc Antony and Cleopatra. Carol wants to wear the earrings she loaned Marcia. When Carol asks Marcia to retrieve them for her, Cindy has to tell the truth about their disappearance to her sister. Marcia drags Cindy downstairs and makes her tell Carol what happened. Mike takes over "The Great Earring Caper," as Peter calls it. He gets everyone's story and the Bradys piece together what happened. The earrings made their way downstairs and into the washing machine. Everyone runs to the service porch to retrieve them. Unfortunately, one of the earrings didn't survive the rinse cycle and is mangled beyond repair. Carol has to go to the costume party without her jewelry. She promises to have a long talk with Cindy the following day.

#93 – You're Never Too Old
Airdate: March 9, 1973
Directed by Bruce Bilson
Executive Producer Sherwood Schwartz
Produced by Howard Leeds
Written by Ben Gershman and Bill Freedman
Florence Henderson.............Great-Grandma Connie Hutchins
Robert Reed.....................Great-Grandpa Henry "Hank" Brady

Great-grandma Connie Hutchins is visiting the Brady family from Kentucky. Mrs. Hutchins is Carol's grandmother and she is full of live and verve. She jokes around and exercises like she's half her age. She is a refreshing visitor indeed. When Marcia and Jan overhear their parents wonder why Mrs. Hutchins never remarried they get an idea of their own. Why don't they set their great-grandmother up? And who better to set her up with than their own great-grandfather Judge Hank Brady? The girls call Mike's grandfather over to the house on the pretense of helping Marcia with some civics homework. When he gets there Marcia and Jan proceed to introduce him to Mrs. Hutchins. Mrs. Hutchins is outside playing basketball with the boys. She impresses the Judge with her energy and they sit down to lemonade together. Then all the Brady kids conspire to leave the "couple" alone at the house for a candlelight dinner. Alice goes along with their plan and makes a fantastic meal. Romantic music is playing in the background and Mrs. Hutchins asks the Judge to dance. He, however, has a different idea. He accuses Connie of setting the whole evening up in an effort to court him. Naturally, Connie is affronted by his accusations because there is no truth to them. The two of them resort to name-calling and Judge Brady leaves the house alone. Marcia thinks that everything is spoiled and Greg tells her not to mess with other people's lives anymore. She doesn't listen to Greg. She and Jan think up a new way to get their great-grandparents together. They "accidentally" have them meet at the park. Once the two elderly folk are together they settle their differences in a grown-up manner. They even start to like each other. Then that night the Bradys are all woken up by some banging noises downstairs. It seems that Great-Grandma Hutchins is making a getaway. Mike and Carol catch her in the act. She confesses to them that she and the Judge are eloping to Las Vegas! All is well that ends well. Who knows what the marriage of two great-grandparents does to the rest of the Brady family tree....

#94 – You Can't Win 'em All
Airdate: March 16, 1973
Directed by Jack Donohue
Executive Producer Sherwood Schwartz
Produced by Howard Leeds
Written by Lois Hire
Edward Knight.. Monty Marshall
Vicki Schrek...Woodside Girl
Harlen Carraher..Clinton Boy
Claudio Martinez ....Woodside Boy

Miyoshi Williams..Clinton Girl
Tracey M. Lee..Woodside Girl

Bobby and Cindy's school is having a contest to see who gets to appear on a television show called "Question the Kids." Kids from each grade are nominated to take a knowledge test and the top four performers in the school get to go on TV. Bobby is very self-assured and approaches the test without studying. Cindy, on the other hand, studies her heart out and goes into the exam attempting to do the best she can. Well, when the results are in Cindy is chosen and Bobby is not. Bobby learns a lesson about being cocky. But his sister Cindy is soon on her way to cockiness herself. She acts like a movie star around the house and spends hours fixing her hair and trying on dresses for the show. Meanwhile, Mike and Carol are planning a dinner for their friends the Bernsteins, Swansons, Clarks, Metzgers, Allens, Kauffmans, and Burkes. At first they want to barbeque but that's too many steaks to buy. Then they think of a Mexican dinner but there are still too many people to cook for. They finally settle on a smorgasbord for 26 guests on the night of the 10th. Then Cindy's school calls to let them know the day of her television appearance: the 10th. It's back to the drawing board. Cindy gets all dressed up for the quiz show. Her siblings want nothing to do with her, but as soon as she leaves the house they rush to turn on the TV so they can watch their youngest sister bomb out. Cindy and her classmates are in the television studio getting prepped for the show by the host, Monty Marshall. Monty tells them that as soon as the red light goes on on the top of the camera they'll be on the air. Despite a previous appearance on a local television show, Cindy gets an enormous attack of nerves when that little red light turns on. It's all she can do to stare at the camera speechless. Through the whole show Cindy doesn't raise her hand once to answer a question. Thusly humbled, Cindy comes home expecting her siblings to make fun of her non-performance. But in true Brady style they forgive her for the way she acted before the show and tell her that they are proud of her for just getting on "Question the Kids." Cindy has grown and Mike and Carol's smorgasbord is rescheduled for the 24th...at least until Carol learns that that's the weekend Mike will be out of town.

#95 – Room at the Top
Airdate: March 23, 1973
Directed by Lloyd Schwartz
Executive Producer Sherwood Schwartz
Produced by Howard Leeds
Written by William Raynor & Myles Wilder
Chris Beaumont...Hank Carter

Greg's friend Hank Carter is on spring break from college. Hank drops by the Brady house to visit with Greg and tell him all about college life. Hank even asks Greg if he will move in and become roommates with him... right now. Greg still has one year of high school left but that doesn't stop him from wanting to take Hank up on his offer. Greg is fed up with sharing a room with Peter and Bobby and always having to jostle for a chance at some measure of privacy. When he asks Mike permission to move in with Hank Mike turns him down. Greg has to wait until he graduates from high school next year before he'll be allowed to leave the house. On the flip side, the whole family is busily cleaning out the Brady attic. Everything must go and soon enough the entire attic is cleared out. Greg now has a great idea for a compromise. He wants to move into the attic and convert it into a bedroom. He runs the idea by Mike who says yes. The trouble is Marcia has the same idea for herself. Carol gives *Marcia* permission to move on up. When Marcia and Greg find out that they've both been promised the attic at the same time, Mike and Carol have to calm them down and solve the conflict. It's only fair, they say, to let Greg have the attic since he is one year older than Marcia. Naturally Marcia feels the decision is utterly unfair. She cries about it when Greg comes into her room downstairs to return a record album to her. All those tears really get to Greg and he folds and says that Marcia can have the attic after all. Delighted, Marcia hugs her brother and promptly moves all her stuff upstairs. Bobby and Peter are none too happy about this latest development. They were excited about getting Greg out of their room because that meant that they would each have more room to spread out as well. Thus, they conspire to get Marcia out of the attic. Peter has his friend Charlie call the house a few times pretending to be girlfriends of Marcia's. Marcia has to go all the way up and down the stairs from the attic to the living room three times before she figures out that she's being set up. Immediately she suspects Greg of orchestrating the prank. Greg denies it and fingers Bobby and Peter who confess their guilt. Marcia realizes that she may have been too hasty and selfish in taking the attic from Greg and offers it back to him. Greg accepts and once again the rooms go switch-a-roo. Greg is in the attic where he belongs, Bobby and Peter are in the boys' room, and Marcia, Jan, and Cindy are still in the girls' room. Everyone falls asleep content.

THE BRADY BUNCH (comedy)
SEASON FIVE 1973-1974
Fridays 8:00-8:30pm ET on ABC

Production Notes: In this final season of the show, the kids are growing up even more quickly than ever. Bobby has his first kiss (which, by the way, is the only on-screen kiss for any Brady kid, excepting that planted on Marcia by Desi Arnaz, Jr.). Greg's a senior in high school and Cindy is twelve years old. The beginning of the season starts out with a musical episode: one that would become notorious to fans as the Johnny Bravo episode. Then ten episodes later the Bradys take another family trip. Last season it was Hawaii, the year before the Grand Canyon and now Cincinnati, Ohio. Why Cincinnati? Well, originally the producers wanted to send the bunch to a more exotic locale like Italy, the Far East, or India. Robert Reed said at the time, "'They talked about taking the show abroad, so right away I thought of Rome…So I went to a language studio near my house…I studied so that I would have Italian by the time we got to Rome. So, what happened? They took the show to the Far East.'"[5] That's right! There were plans to bring the Brady clan all the way to the other side of the world in this vague region called the "Far East." However, budget constraints and the Hollywood writers' strike got in the way and something domestic was chosen instead. The year before the network had sent *The Partridge Family* to the King's Island Amusement Park in Cincinnati and it worked out well. Thus, feeling that luck would strike twice, the network sent the Bradys to the Park.

Toward the end of the season, ABC felt like it had to do something to liven up the show and attract new viewers. They tossed around season three's idea of Carol having a baby, but instead settled on an older child who would be the Brady kids' cousin. And so eight-year-old cousin Oliver invaded the Brady home. Today cousin Oliver is the poster child for when television shows "jump the shark." But honestly, there were different reasons that *The Brady Bunch* was not renewed and Oliver had nothing to do with them. Nevertheless, Robbie Rist is oft blamed for the downfall of TV's favorite family. But he's cool with that.

The real reasons that *The Brady Bunch* was not renewed are complicated. In Barry Williams' book <u>Growing Up Brady</u>, he says that it was a combination of factors. First, the kids were pushed by their manager Harvey Shotz to demand more grown-up storylines and more money. They also asked for 7 of 13 episodes to be singing ones. Robert Reed had walked off the set of the final episode, "The Hair-Brained Scheme," and executive producer Sherwood Schwartz was actually weighing the pros and cons of even asking him to come back for a sixth season as the Brady father. Finally, the actors' five-year contracts were up. Anytime that happens, it prompts a

Good-bye Taj Mahal, hello Ohio.

re-negotiation of show standards. Schwartz and the network were unwilling to meet the actors' demands. And so *The Brady Bunch* ended.

In retrospect, it is probably a good thing that it ended when it did. Who would want to see Mike punch Greg in the face (Barry's idea for Greg's character) and "little" Bobby with a steady girlfriend (Mike's idea)?

This year's age shuffle: the only ages that are revealed are that Bobby is 12 and Peter is 15. This tracks pretty well. Greg finished high school after four years. But because he started high school at fifteen (instead of fourteen), he graduates at age nineteen instead of the generally-accepted eighteen.

#96 – Adios, Johnny Bravo
Airdate: September 14, 1973
Directed by Jerry London
Executive Producer Sherwood Schwartz
Produced by Howard Leeds and Lloyd Schwartz
Written by Joanna Lee
Claudia Jennings .... Tammy Cutler
Paul Cavonis .... Buddy Burkman
Jeff Davis .... Hal Barton

The Brady kids are trying out for another local talent show, this one called "Hal Barton's Talent Review." Their tryout is a success and they are scheduled to perform on television the following Saturday. Their audition is more successful than they think, though. In the audience is a woman named Tammy Cutler, an Artist Manager for Big Hit Management Company. She gives her card to Greg and asks him to phone her at ten the next morning. The Bradys are super excited about the possibility of getting signed with an agent. The next morning they make their call and Tammy asks just Greg to come down to the office. Greg thinks that maybe Tammy believes he is the leader and can make the deal for all six kids. But the truth is that Tammy and her partner Buddy just want Greg. They want him to be the new Johnny Bravo: a hip, happening, groovy artist with big hits. When Greg finds out the truth, he is flattered but also feels a little guilty signing just himself and not his siblings. He comes home from the meeting and breaks the news to the other five who promptly call him a sellout. Greg, er Johnny, must now decide whether or not he wants a singing career or to go to college. Mike and Carol want him to go to school and *then* decide if he wants to be a singer. Greg has a lot to think about. Pretty soon his siblings come around and see his side of events. They apologize to Greg for the way they acted and tell him that they'll support him. It's nice to hear. Before his next meeting with Tammy and Buddy Greg has a meeting with his parents. He tells them that he has decided to be a musician and put off college. Mike and Carol aren't very happy with their eldest son. They make a decision of their own: to check out Big Hit Management Company when Greg gets back. Meanwhile Greg is signing contracts and doing a recording session with Tammy and Buddy. All is going well – he even has his own gaggle of crazed fans prepared at the drop of a hat to maul him in adoration. But then Greg gets to listen to the recording of himself and he's stunned. "That's not my voice," he says. Buddy replies that it's just a little electronic sleight of hand. But Greg has standards. He doesn't want to sound electronic or phony. If he's going to make it as a singing star he will do it on his own merits. He finds out that Tammy and Buddy were just using him because he fit the Johnny Bravo suit. So Greg rips up his contract and takes a walk. It's the end of Johnny Bravo but not the end of Greg Brady. He and his brothers and sisters go on as planned on the Hal Barton show and all is well.

#97 – Mail Order Hero

Airdate: September 21, 1973
Directed by Bruce Bilson
Executive Producer Sherwood Schwartz
Produced by Howard Leeds and Lloyd Schwartz
Written by Martin Ragaway

Joe Namath.. Himself
Tim Herbert... Herb Keller
Kerry MacLane .... Eric Parker
Eric Woods.. Tom Hamner
Larry Michaels...Burt Stevens

Bobby's new hero is Joe Namath, the quarterback for the New York Jets. He has a great dream about Joe where he (Bobby) is playing receiver and makes an amazing catch for the game-winning touchdown. The next day Bobby and three friends are playing football in the Brady backyard. His friends Eric, Tom, and Burt all claim that their fathers have had encounters with famous athletes. Has Bobby? Sure he has! Every time that Joe

Namath is in town he stops by the Brady house for dinner, Bobby lies. He didn't want to lose face in front of his friends and now he's in trouble. Joe Namath and the Jets are playing an exhibition game in town next week and Eric, Tom, and Burt all want to meet him. Surely Bobby can arrange that? Well, Bobby's in quite a pickle because he has never met Joe Namath and no one in his family has either. He has a choice now between telling the truth and somehow producing Joe Namath. He can't really tell the truth without the whole school realizing that he's a liar – his false claim has already traveled far. So, Cindy has an idea about how to help her brother out. She heard that a star went out of his way to go visit a girl who was sick in the hospital. So why wouldn't that work for Joe? Cindy writes a letter from Bobby (without his knowledge) that says he is very, very sick and would like nothing more than to meet Joe Namath. She mails it to the stadium where Joe's manager picks it up the next day. "Bobby's" heart-wrenching story is enough to get Joe to feel sorry for him and he calls the Brady household to schedule a visit after football practice. Cindy answers the phone and tells Joe to come right over. Then she has to tell Bobby about what she did and that he'd better get sick real fast. Bobby puts on some pajamas and practices moaning. Mr. Namath and his manager Herb Keller come at 5:00 and go up to Bobby's room to pay him a visit. They brought along a photograph of Joe so that he could sign it. Bobby is ecstatic at getting to meet his hero and asks Joe to write a lengthy note on the photo proving that he has been here and that he always comes to dinner whenever he's in town. That way Bobby can show the picture to his friends and his lie will not have to be found out. (It's a scheme not unlike the one pulled on 'Hannah Montana' in 2007. Maybe this episode is where the prankster got the idea??) Joe feels sorry for Bobby and leaves him in bed upstairs. When he gets downstairs he gets to meet Carol, Mike, Marcia, and Jan. He soon discovers that Bobby is not really sick and that he and Cindy pulled the wool over his eyes. At that moment the two youngest Bradys come downstairs and confess the truth to Joe. Joe is happy that Bobby is not sick and nice enough not to feel upset about the whole charade. He even goes into the back yard and throws some passes to a well Bobby and all his friends. It's a magical ending to a stressful week for young Bobby Brady.

#98 – Snow White and the Seven Bradys
Airdate: September 28, 1973
Directed by Bruce Bilson
Executive Producer Sherwood Schwartz
Produced by Howard Leeds and Lloyd Schwartz
Written by Ben Starr
Allan Melvin .... Sam
Elvenn Havard .... Policeman
Frances Whitfield .... Mrs. Whitfield

Cindy's teacher Mrs. Whitfield is preparing to retire. Cindy's class is going to present her with a set of first edition books worth $200. In order to raise the money Cindy volunteered herself and her family to put on a play of "Snow White and the Seven Dwarfs." Not only that, she recruited Mike to help with the sets. It's a full family production with everyone in a major role.

SNOW WHITE AND THE SEVEN DWARFS
CAST

Carol	Snow White
Mike	Prince Charming
Alice	Wicked Queen
Sam	Dopey
Greg	Doc
Marcia	Sleepy
Peter	Sneezy
Jan	Happy
Bobby	Bashful
Cindy	Grumpy

Production is underway. Cindy gets a call from the theatre she reserved double-checking the date. Unfortunately, Cindy gave the theatre the wrong date and now the theatre is booked. Cindy and the Bradys are out of luck and have nowhere to perform their play. But it's Mike to the rescue when he comes up with a plan to put the play on the Brady back yard. He'll use the arbor as the stage, rig a PA system, and put folding chairs on the lawn for the audience. Cindy is eternally grateful and now things are going double-time as preparations are made for Saturday's performance. When the day of the play arrives, there is another glitch. Alice ate the last apple in the house and now there's no prop to serve as the poisoned apple! Mike and Sam rush out to the market, buy an apple, are given a talking-to by the police because Sam parked in a red zone and they don't have a permit for the play, and arrive back home late. But the audience is patient and understanding. With everything now finally in place, the play begins. The performance is a success and Mrs. Whitfield is asked on stage so that Cindy can present her with the books. It's a happy ending for Snow White and the Brady bunch.

#99 – Never Too Young

Airdate: October 5, 1973
Directed by Richard Michaels
Executive Producer Sherwood Schwartz
Produced by Howard Leeds and Lloyd Schwartz
Written by Al Schwartz and Larry Rhine
Melissa Anderson..Millicent

Bobby has his first kiss. A girl named Millicent gives him a kiss because he stopped a boy at school from teasing her. Bobby is unwittingly entering the age of adolescence and doesn't quite know what to do about girls. He talks to his dad about Mike's first kiss. Bobby saw sky rockets when Millicent kissed him. Did Mike have the same reaction? Well, not exactly, but he was happy about it. Bobby wants to know how a person knows he's in love and Mike tells him to give it time and to be sure about what he's feeling. Bobby takes this to mean that he should kiss Millicent again and find out if he sees sky rockets a second time. So Bobby goes to Millicent's house and smooches her. Yes, it's sky rockets! But it also might be the mumps…Millicent is sick and thinks she has the mumps. She has to wait until the following morning to see the doctor to find out for sure, but in the meantime Bobby has been exposed. He doesn't want to expose anybody else, so he tries to spend the night sleeping in Tiger's dog house. Mike and Carol discover Bobby outside and then get the truth out of him. It used to be just Cindy who knew about Bobby's first kiss, but now everyone in the house knows. Poor Bobby's little heart is on his sleeve. Everyone is waiting anxiously for Millicent's phone call. Finally, she calls and Bobby learns that she doesn't have the mumps. Neither does he, then, and so he goes over to Millicent's house to spend time with her. That night everyone goes out to a Roaring 20's Party and Alice and Sam win first prize in the Charleston contest.

#100 – Peter and the Wolf

Airdate: October 12, 1973
Directed by Leslie H. Martinson
Executive Producer Sherwood Schwartz
Produced by Howard Leeds and Lloyd Schwartz
Written by Tam Spiva
Cindi Crosby .... Sandra Martin
Paul Fierro .... Juan Calderon
Alma Beltran .... Maria Calderon
Bill Miller .... Len
Kathie Gibboney .... Linda

Greg has a date with Sandra Martin. She is going to have to call it off, though, because her cousin showed up in town and she doesn't want to go out without her. Greg tells Sandra that he'll find a date for Cousin Linda so that they can double-date. However, no one seems to want to go out on a blind date. Greg can't find anybody. That is until he sees Peter. Pete's growing up fast and maybe, just maybe, he could pass as an eighteen-year-old from another high school. So Greg tells Peter his plan and Pete hops right on board. They invent a name for him – Phil Packer – and an identity as a suave ladies' man. Peter even glues on a fake mustache. Greg and "Phil" arrive at Linda's house Friday night for their double date. Linda turns out to be a babe and Peter is really excited, but very nervous, too. Greg tells him to just follow his lead. At the drive-in, "Phil" imitates everything Greg does. He's a bit clumsy and spills Linda's popcorn all over her. Then he accidentally starts munching on his own mustache. Linda suspects that she's been tricked into going out with a younger guy and confides her suspicions to Sandra when they get home. The two ladies decide to play a trick of their own on Greg and Peter. They call them up to ask them out for Saturday. The date is set but this time Linda and Sandra are going to pretend to fall all over Phil/Peter. They're at Marioni's Restaurant, which just so happens to be the place where Mike and Carol brought their dinner guests for the evening, a Mexican couple named the Calderons. The Calderons are kind of conservative and when they spy some teenagers a few booths over necking in public, Sr. Calderon is upset. The teenagers, of course, are Linda, Sandra, and Peter. Their unabashed behavior almost costs Mike the deal he's making with the Calderons. (For some reason Mike and Carol told them that those teenagers were their sons!) So, Peter has learned his lesson about acting older than he really is. Greg has learned his lesson about lying to his girlfriend. And best of all Mike's deal with Juan Calderon goes through.

#101 – Getting Greg's Goat

Airdate: October 19, 1973
Directed by Robert Reed
Executive Producer Sherwood Schwartz
Produced by Howard Leeds and Lloyd Schwartz
Written by Milton Pascal & Sam Locke

George D. Wallace ....Mr. Binkley
Sandra Gould ....Mrs. Gould
Margarita Cordova ....1st P.T.A. Lady
Selma Archerd..2nd P.T. A. Lady

The kids at Coolidge High School stole Westdale's bear cub mascot. The only thing for the Westdale guys to do is steal Coolidge's goat. So that's what Greg does. He sneaks Raquel the goat upstairs to his attic room where he hopes to hide her until the football game the next day. It's not long until he's found out by Marcia, then Mike, then Bobby and Peter. Mike thought at first that Greg had a *girl* named Raquel up in his room all night, but Greg cleared up the misunderstanding. That's what Peter and Bobby thought, too, but they discover Raquel the goat for themselves when they sneak up to Greg's room. The heat is on; the ladies from the P.T.A. and the boys' Vice Principal Mr. Binkley are all determined to find the culprits and make an example of them. Carol is on the P.T.A. but she doesn't know she's calling for her own son's blood. So Greg and Mike decide to effect a mascot exchange with Coolidge. They hope that if the exchange is made before the game that the heat will be off. After all, Mike stole his rival high school's mascot when he was a kid, so he can understand Greg's motivations. Mike was punished with a week's suspension from school and he hopes that Greg won't get caught. But when Mike and Greg get home from talking with the Coolidge guys, they find that the P.T.A. meeting has been moved to the Brady house! Raquel is at large because Bobby and Peter left the attic door open when they went upstairs. And now Greg has to find the goat and keep her hidden while the P.T.A. ladies and Mr. Binkley take a tour of the house. It's really hard to hide a goat. Raquel escapes Greg's clutches and runs right into the master bedroom where the tour group is. Now the jig is up and Mr. Binkley has to decide how to punish Greg. But Mr. Binkley is a bit of a softie, it turns out. When he was in school, he was suspended for a whole month for the same crime, so he goes easy on Greg and assigns him a 5,000-word essay on the evils of mascot stealing. He also tells Greg and Mike to hurry up and exchange mascots back with Coolidge otherwise he'll have to make Greg's punishment public. Greg and the Bradys are very grateful for Mr. Binkley's leniency and Raquel is returned to her rightful owners.

#102 – Marcia Gets Creamed

Airdate: October 26, 1973
Directed by Peter Baldwin
Executive Producer Sherwood Schwartz
Produced by Howard Leeds and Lloyd Schwartz
Written by Ben Gershman & Bill Freedman

Henry Cordon... Mr. Haskell

Michael Gray .... Jeff
Kimberly Beck ....Girl

Marcia gets a part-time job after school and on Saturdays working at Haskell's Ice Cream Hut. She's a great employee and spends a lot of time at the Hut: too much time according to her boyfriend Jeff. Jeff wants to take Marcia out but she can never go because she's either working, doing homework, or washing her hair. At the same time, Peter is looking for a job but is having no luck. At work one day Marcia convinces Mr. Haskell to take afternoons off. He's been working all day every day for twenty years and Marcia says he could use a break. Mr. Haskell takes her up on her suggestion and now there's an open afternoon position at the Hut. Marcia asks Mr. Haskell if Peter can get the job and Mr. Haskell agrees. All parties are happy. Peter's last job was with Mr. Martinelli's Bike Shop and he only lasted three days. The second time around Peter fares no better. He's lazy and does anything but work. He talks on the phone to his friends, eats ice cream, and listens to the football game on the radio. So, Marcia has no choice but to fire her own brother. She asks Mr. Haskell if he would be willing to take another chance on a Brady. He agrees and this time Jan goes to work at the Ice Cream Hut. She's super – a marked change from Peter. Then one day when Marcia and Jan are working Jeff comes into the Hut with another girl. He's trying to make Marcia jealous and it works. She squirts whipped cream all over Jeff and his date. They storm out of the Hut and Marcia has to foot their bill. Then Mr. Haskell comes in. He tells the girls he has some news. Semi-retirement is not working out for him. The only thing that makes him happy is working. So, he's going back to full-time, which means that he doesn't need one Brady girl. Marcia automatically assumes that she is the one who is going to stay. Mr. Haskell has other plans. He says that Jan is a better worker than Marcia and he will keep Jan on the payroll and let Marcia go. Marcia comes home furious with Jan for "stealing" her job. Jan says it's not her fault and then angrily offers to quit so that Marcia can have her job back. But the phone rings in the middle of their argument and it's Jeff calling for Marcia. Jeff wants to make up with Marcia and she's very amenable to the plan. She hangs up and lets Jan keep the job so that she can have free time to date Jeff. All is well. Peter even comes home with a new job at The Leaning Tower of Pizza Parlor.

#103 – My Brother's Keeper
Airdate: November 2, 1973
Directed by Ross Bowman
Executive Producer Sherwood Schwartz
Produced by Howard Leeds and Lloyd Schwartz
Written by Michael Morris

The Brady boys are outside doing handiwork on the house and garden. Peter pulls a hose toward himself to water the flowers, but the hose is wrapped around the foot of a ladder and the ladder comes crashing down. Bobby pushes Peter out of the way and a bucket of green paint gets dumped on Bobby. Peter says that Bobby saved his life; his head could have been crushed by the ladder. He's extremely grateful for his brother's bravery and makes a promise at dinner that night to be Bobby's slave for life. Peter voluntarily polishes Bobby's shoes, makes his bed, cleans out the closet, fixes the radio, works on the go-cart engine, oils his bike, takes out the trash, and more. But as soon as Bobby *asks* Peter to do something for him, Peter cops an attitude and accuses

Bobby of using him. Pete suffers through clipping the "stupid hedges" for Bobby instead of going on a date with Barbara just so Bobby can watch his friend Steve play baseball. When Bobby gets back from the game, Peter is still angry. The boys have an argument and end up putting tape across their bedroom, separating it diagonally into halves. Pete gets the side with the door to the hallway and Bobby gets the side with the door to the bathroom. That evening everybody is out of the house except for Alice, Peter, and Bobby. Bobby decides to apologize to Peter for using him, but Peter doesn't take kindly to his apology. Then Bobby throws a pillow in Peter's direction and destroys Pete's model airplane. Pete tries to corner Bobby and beat him up but Bobby shuts himself in the closet before Pete can lay a hand on him. The doorknob on the closet breaks off when Bobby slams the door and now he's trapped inside. Peter is downstairs talking on the phone for a long time before he goes back upstairs into the bedroom. He hears Bobby's cries for help, sticks the doorknob back on, and releases Bobby. Bobby says that Peter has now saved *his* life: he could have suffocated! Now they're even and they apologize for the way they treated each other.

#104 – Quarterback Sneak
Airdate: November 9, 1973
Directed by Peter Baldwin
Executive Producer Sherwood Schwartz
Produced by Howard Leeds and Lloyd Schwartz
Written by Ben Gershman & Bill Freedman
Denny Miller..."Tank" Gates
Chris Beaumont ....Jerry Rogers
Don Carter..Rich

Marcia is downtown putting up posters for Westdale High School: "All the way with Westdale. Massacre Fairview." Fairview and Westdale are preparing for the League Championship game. Greg plays halfback for Westdale (apparently Carol let him re-join the team after his season three rib injury). A guy named Jerry Rogers comes up to Marcia and offers to help her put up the rest of the posters, which is an odd request given that he's the quarterback for Fairview. Marcia's enamored with him and he gives her a ride home. She invites him in for a cold drink and Bobby spies Jerry trying to steal Greg's playbook. After Jerry leaves Bobby immediately tells Greg and Marcia what he saw. Greg believes him but Marcia doesn't. So they decide to set up a test; give Jerry another chance to steal the playbook. If he takes it he's worthy of the name "Fairview fink." If he doesn't, Bobby will apologize to Marcia. But if Jerry does take the playbook Fairview will have an unfair advantage over Westdale. So Greg, Peter, and Bobby quickly work up a phony playbook with which to tempt Jerry. They put their plan into action the following day. The playbook is in plain sight and unfortunately for Marcia, Jerry does steal the book. She's out one boyfriend. Mike catches wind of the plan and tells Greg that now Westdale has an unfair advantage and that Greg has sunk to Jerry's level. Greg, feeling ashamed, calls Jerry up and tells him that the playbook is a fake. Jerry doesn't believe him. Meanwhile, Carol has received a visit from her old high school boyfriend Tank Gates. Tank was an all-around sporty guy, playing practically every sport in high school. He played football in college and even ended up in the pros for a short time. Tank hasn't changed much since he and Carol went to Westdale. He's a big galoot and still crazy about his own accomplishments. He's in town for the big game of Fairview vs. Westdale. He hears the rumor that Fairview has Westdale's playbook and so he bets against his own *alma mater*. That turns out to be a mistake. Fairview's coach benches Jerry Rogers when he finds out what happened. Westdale won fair and square 20-7.

#105 – Try, Try Again

Airdate: November 16, 1973
Directed by George Tyne
Executive Producer Sherwood Schwartz
Produced by Howard Leeds and Lloyd Schwartz
Written by Al Schwartz & Larry Rhine
Judy Landon...Miss Clairette
Ruth Anson...Mrs. Ferguson
Darryl Seman ....Billy Naylor

Jan is feeling confident...confident that she's a no talent loser. She didn't get picked for the ballet recital, her tap dancing is atrocious, and her own brothers and sisters are letting her win at everything until she feels better. She finds out what they're doing and comes to the conclusion that she can't do anything well. Her parents tell her that she has to keep trying new things in order to discover her talents. Jan decides that she will give it one more try. She auditions for the lead in the school's production of "An American Girl in Paris," but totally bombs out. She forgets the lines (she only had one night to work on them) and spills paint all over Billy Naylor. But something good does come from the whole experience. She worked on a painting in order to make the audition scene seem more authentic. The teacher who is in charge of the play also happens to be the art teacher. She loved Jan's painting and asked her to enroll in her art class. Finally, Jan has found something in which she can be successful.

#106 – The Cincinnati Kids

Airdate: November 23, 1973
Directed by Leslie H. Martinson
Executive Producer Sherwood Schwartz
Produced by Howard Leeds and Al Schwartz
Written by Al Schwartz & Larry Rhine
Hilary Thompson ....Marge
Bob Hoffman..Attendant
L. Jeffrey Schwartz ....The Bear/Man

Mike has to submit some plans for an expansion to King's Island Amusement Park. He decides to take the whole family along so they can have a vacation at the Park. They arrive outside of Cincinnati on a warm and sunny day and immediately begin exploring the park. Everyone is excited about the rides and they all split up to go on their favorites. Even Alice rides some, including the roller coaster. Mike's meeting is at 1:00pm with Mr. Remington and Mr. Dempsey. He brought along his plans in a yellow cylinder. At lunchtime, Jan asks Mike if she can have one of the cylinders to protect her poster in. Mike agrees, transfers his plans to one cylinder, and places Jan's poster in the other. When lunch is over he mistakenly gives Jan the wrong cylinder. He discovers his error at the 1:00 meeting when he pulls out a poster of Yogi Bear instead of his architectural plans. Now he has to find Jan and the plans within the next half an hour because Remington and Dempsey have to catch a plane. Mike has thirty minutes to search the entire park for Jan, a task anyone who's ever been to an amusement park would find nearly impossible. Luckily for him, he finds her within twenty minutes. Unfortunately, Jan has lost the cylinder! Now the Bradys have ten minutes to search the *entire* park for the yellow cylinder and get it back to the manager's office. Impossible? Not for the Bradys! Jan finds it on a rowboat and she and Marcia are off running through the park toward the manager's office. They pass the cylinder on to Alice, who passes it to Bobby and Cindy, who pass it to Greg and Peter, who pass it to Carol, who takes it to the office just as Mr. Remington is leaving. Remington and Dempsey look over the plans on the plane and call Mr. Phillips to let him know they approve the plans. Mr. Phillips calls Mike to congratulate him and tells Mike to keep his family in Ohio at the park for three more days at company expense!

#107 – The Elopement

Airdate: December 7, 1973
Directed by Jerry London
Executive Producer Sherwood Schwartz
Produced by Howard Leeds and Lloyd Schwartz
Written by Harry Winkler
Allan Melvin .... Sam
Byron Webster .... Reverend Melbourne
Bella Bruck .... Gladys Harris

Jan and Marcia overhear Alice talking on the phone to Sam about an elopement. They jump to the conclusion that Alice and Sam are planning to elope. The truth is that the couple is attending Sam's cousin Clara's elopement – not their own. The Bradys don't know this, though. They piece together a circumstantial case that looks pretty convincing. First, there's Alice's phone call. Then Sam calls Mike to talk about finding a house for "a friend." Then Greg and Marcia encounter Reverend Melbourne in Sam's butcher shop, Cindy sees Alice buying a fancy dress, and Alice asks off for the coming Saturday night ostensibly to go bowling. Mike and Carol tell Alice that not only can she have Saturday off, but she can take a whole week off if she wants to. But then disaster strikes. Sam and Alice have a fight and Alice tells the Bradys that her bowling date is off. They take this to mean that the elopement is cancelled. Right away Greg and Peter talk to Sam and tell him that he should make up with Alice; Marcia and Jan to the same with Alice. Sam is the one who ends up coming around and arrives at the Brady house with a special package of meat for Alice and an apology. They make up and the bowling date is back on. The couple leaves Saturday evening for the semi-finals. The Bradys think that this is it; they're going to elope. So they put together some decorations, a cake, champagne, Bobby plays "The Wedding March" on the organ, and Greg is ready with his camera. When Sam and Alice arrive back home, they open the door to their own surprise party. Congratulations on your marriage! the Bradys say. Well, now the truth must be told. Alice and Sam did indeed go bowling tonight and it's cousin *Clara*'s elopement they're going to tomorrow, not their own. It was all a big misunderstanding and the Bradys sheepishly apologize. The next day Alice comes home from the elopement and tells Mike and Carol that she and Sam are engaged! The only thing Sam hasn't committed to is the year of the wedding.... (They finally do get married in late 1976.)

#108 – Miss Popularity
Airdate: December 21, 1973
Directed by Jack Donohue
Executive Producer Sherwood Schwartz
Produced by Howard Leeds and Al Schwartz
Written by Martin Ragaway
Darryl Seman .... Herman
Jerelyn Fields ....Shirley

Jan's classmates nominate her for the most popular girl in her class. She's very flattered and recruits Peter to be her campaign manager against her opponent. Jan starts making phone calls to her friends, passing out fortune cookies at school, and making promises to a lot of people. Her campaign promises range from babysitting for a friend's little brother to promising that Greg will help a boy named Herman with his algebra. Enough people in her class at Fillmore Junior High are convinced that Jan is a stand-up girl and she wins the election. Jan's thrilled with the win. Soon enough, though, things start to go sour for her. All those promises she made are catching up to her and she simply doesn't have enough time to fulfill them. Her friends are left stranded. She's quickly becoming the most *un*popular girl in school. Jan ignores their derision because she believes that as the most popular girl in school there can't be that many people who are upset with her. She goes home and writes a speech for the acceptance dance that sings nothing but praise for herself. Mike and Carol are not pleased with the way she is acting, but they consider her old enough to make her own decisions and don't make her change the speech. It finally takes something drastic – something that hits her where it hurts – to make the scales fall from her eyes. Jan finds out that the most popular boy is *not* going to ask her to the dance. He does not want to be seen or associated with her. Jan realizes how self-aggrandizing she's been. She takes the time to rewrite her speech, humble herself, and apologize to her family and her classmates for the way she has been acting. Jan vows to fulfill every promise she made during her campaign. Carol and Mike attend the ceremony (instead of having a second honeymoon) and supposedly Jan is well received.

#109 – Kelly's Kids
Airdate: January 4, 1974
Directed by Richard Michaels
Executive Producer Sherwood Schwartz
Produced by Howard Leeds and Lloyd Schwartz
Written by Sherwood Schwartz
Ken Berry..Ken Kelly
Brooke Bundy ....Kathy Kelly
Todd Lookinland..Matt Kelly
William Attmore, II...................................Dwayne Kelly
Carey Wong... Steve Kelly
Jackie Joseph...................................... Miss Jane Phillips
Molly Dodd..Mrs. Payne

TIKI TALK

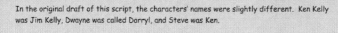

In the original draft of this script, the characters' names were slightly different. Ken Kelly was Jim Kelly, Dwayne was called Darryl, and Steve was Ken.

The Bradys have friends named Ken and Kathy Kelly. The couple has decided to adopt an eight-year-old boy named Matthew and they are sharing their good fortune with the Bradys by asking them for advice on raising kids. Mike and Carol are pleased and happy for the Kellys. And so Ken and Kathy come home the next day with a brand new son. Matt is very excited to have been adopted and loves his new room. That night, though, in a new bed all alone Matt is lonely. At the orphanage he had two really great friends, Dwayne and Steve. Now that he's been adopted and they haven't, Matt is sad. He confides his angst to his new parents and they hatch a plan. If Matt is lonely, why not give him a brother? How about Dwayne or Steve? Of course! So Kathy and Ken go the next day to the Terrace Adoption Home to meet Matt's best friends. It turns out that Dwayne is African-American and Steve is Asian. The Kellys decide that a boy is a boy is a boy and that they will adopt one of the boys no matter what. But which one? They're both equally deserving. So they decide to adopt *both* Dwayne and Steve. The process miraculously only takes one week. Ken brings home his surprise "guests" for dinner and Matthew is beside himself with joy when he finds out that the "Three Musketeers" are back together again. The Kellys now have three eight-year-old boys instead of one. They put bunk beds into Matt's room and let all the boys share the toys. But the Kellys have a creepy neighbor named Mrs. Payne who talks to Ken and tells him that she doesn't appreciate him having children. Boys mess things up, trample gardens, and break windows. "Especially the minorities," she adds contemptuously. Well, this does nothing but incense Ken and Kathy. They talk about Mrs. Payne that evening and Dwayne and Steve overhear them. Unfortunately, they only overhear part of the conversation and think that they are causing their new parents too much trouble. The two kids decide to run away in order to save Ken and Kathy from being kicked out of their organizations. As they leave they wake up Matt. Matthew tells his brothers that it's all for one and one for all and that if they're running away then he is, too. He decides to take Dwayne and Steve to the Brady house figuring that they have so many kids that they might not notice three new ones. They camp out on the lounge chairs on the patio and Greg discovers them after he comes home that night. The boys are brought inside where they are reunited with their parents. Ken and Kathy were extremely worried and are quite relieved to see the boys safe and in one piece. They tell them that there's nothing that Mrs. Payne or anyone else can say that would break up their family. The kids go home smiling and Ken and Kathy are grateful to the Bradys for what they did to help.

[See the end of this chapter for more on the Kellys.]

#110 – The Driver's Seat
Airdate: January 11, 1974
Directed by Jack Arnold
Executive Producer Sherwood Schwartz
Produced by Howard Leeds and Lloyd Schwartz
Written by George Tibbles
Herb Vigran..Examiner

It's time for Marcia to take her driving test. She makes a bet with Greg that she will score better on her test than he did. Greg had been deriding her because she's a woman. He's beginning to sound a little bit like Mr. Duggan – the man who sued Carol for backing into his car – "women drivers…ha!" He thinks it's an easy bet and they wager one month's chores against one another. Marcia scores a 98 on the written examination, but when it comes time to take the actual driving test, she freezes. She is unable to even start the exam and comes home dejected. Greg calls off the bet after he sees how upset Marcia is. Then Marcia gets a pep talk from Jan. With renewed fervor, Marcia makes a bet with Greg again. This time they wager one *year's* worth of chores against each other. Marcia passes the driving test with a score of 92. Up against Greg's 94 written and 96 driving, it turns out that they tied. Women can do just as well as men after all. But Greg and Marcia aren't satisfied with a tie. So Mike encourages them to have a driving contest. The whole family goes to an empty parking lot and sets up cones for a driving course. Whoever knocks over the least amount of cones and gets the closest to the final cone (without breaking the egg that sits atop it) wins. Marcia goes first. She doesn't knock over any cones and is able to stop an inch and a half from the final cone. It's Greg's turn. He completes the course without tipping any cones. But when it comes time to park next to the final cone, he freaks out, stamps on the gas and knocks the egg off. Greg loses and Marcia wins. Marcia is gracious and offers to let Greg off the hook. But Greg is stubborn and (or else masochistic) and does Marcia's ironing that afternoon.

#111 – Out of this World
Airdate: January 18, 1974
Directed by Peter Baldwin
Executive Producer Sherwood Schwartz
Produced by Howard Leeds and Lloyd Schwartz
Written by Al Schwartz & Larry Rhine
Brigadier General James A. McDivitt.................. Himself
Mario Machado.. Himself
Frank & Sadie Delfino ....The Kaplutians
James Flavin......................................Captain McCartney

Brigadier General James A. McDivitt, former Gemini astronaut, is making a guest appearance on a local television talk show. Peter and Bobby meet McDivitt after the show and ask for his autograph. They're amazed with his story about encountering a UFO while on the Gemini 4 mission. Bobby and Peter go to bed that night with visions of UFOs dancing in their heads. At midnight Bobby wakes up to a strange sound. He looks out the window and sees a glowing red object: a UFO! He quickly wakes up Peter who corroborates his sighting. They tell the family the next morning at breakfast. They all make fun of them but Bobby and Peter hold their ground. Later that night Marcia is upstairs in Greg's attic room and finds out the truth behind the UFO sighting. Greg set it all up as a way to get back at his brothers for them telling on him earlier that week. He put a plastic sheet in the yard, shined a red flashlight on the sheet, and blew a whistle to make the eerie sound effects. It's a good hoax and Marcia congratulates him for his ingenuity. Greg sets everything up again that night because Bobby and Peter want to sleep outside in hopes of seeing the UFO again and capturing a picture. They borrow Carol's camera and huddle up in sleeping bags. When the time is right, Greg shines the flashlight on the plastic curtain and voila, a UFO. Marcia and he have a good laugh over it. Peter and Bobby want their pictures developed right away and Carol agrees to do it before school the next morning. She develops them and is surprised to see that there is indeed something on the film. She shows the pictures to Mike. He makes the decision after work that day to call up Carter Air Force Base and report the sighting. The Air Force sends over a police captain to investigate the Brady UFO. The captain is two years from retirement, curmudgeonly, and very skeptical. He asks to see the Bradys' pictures. He takes a look at them and tells them that that blob on the photo could be anything. Then Greg comes home, sees the captain, and panics. His joke has gone too far and he summons Mike upstairs to show him what he's done. Greg demonstrates the rig to Mike. As he does so, the Captain downstairs sees the "UFO" for himself. He gets very excited and immediately calls up the police force to report the sighting for himself. He even asks Peter to take pictures of him as he's making what he thinks is an historic phone call. When he's off the phone, though, Mike comes downstairs and has no choice but to tell the Captain the truth. Naturally Captain McCartney is irate. However, he can't let his comrades know that he was had by a teenager. He agrees to keep quiet about the whole thing if the Bradys will, too. It's a deal.

#112 – Welcome Aboard
Airdate: January 25, 1974
Directed by Richard Michaels
Executive Producer Sherwood Schwartz
Produced by Howard Leeds and Lloyd Schwartz
Written by Larry Rhine & Al Schwartz
John Nolan .... Jim Douglas
Judd Laurance .... Director
Robbie Rist.. Oliver
Snag Werris .... Keystone Cop
Dick Winslow.. Truck Driver #1
Ralph Montgomery .... Truck Driver #2

Carol is bringing a new member of the family into the Brady residence. No, it's not a baby. Instead it's her eight-year-old nephew Oliver. His parents, Jack & Pauline, are gone on a trip to South America for an engineering project in a jungle area. There are no schools there so Oliver is staying with the Brady family. The kids welcome their cousin with open arms and involve him in their projects. But poor Oliver turns out to be a jinx. He ruins Jan's painting, splatters ketchup all over Greg, breaks some pots in the back yard, and tangles up Carol's knitting. The six Brady kids have had it up to here with Oliver and they let their feelings be known to each other. Unlucky Oliver happens to overhear their conversation. He's depressed and hides out in the doghouse. Carol discovers him there, finds out what's going on, and has Mike talk to Oliver. There is no such thing as a jinx, Mike says. Oliver is willing to forget the whole thing if the other kids are. The other kids are reluctant but agreeable. They take Oliver outside to play basketball. Oliver has the ball in his hands and tries to pass the ball to Greg. The ball is way overthrown and lands right on Marcia's ceramics project. Then it bounces inside through the sliding door in the kitchen and trips Mike who just so happens to be carrying a model of a building he designed. The model is destroyed and so is Oliver's confidence. The whole family is scheduled to go on a tour of Marathon Movie Studios that Saturday. Oliver is still feeling like a jinx and doesn't want to go. But Carol convinces him that he should go anyway. It turns out to be the best decision in Oliver's short life because he is the one millionth visitor to Marathon Studios! That means that he and everyone he came with get to appear in a movie as extras. They all dress up in early 20th Century clothing and have a big pie fight. Welcome to the family, Oliver.

TIKI TALK

The original draft of this script also included a scene where Bobby and Peter fight about in which bed Cousin Oliver will sleep. Both Bobby and Peter wanted the un-bunked bed.

#113 – Two Petes in a Pod
Airdate: February 8, 1974
Directed by Richard Michaels
Executive Producer Sherwood Schwartz
Produced by Howard Leeds and Lloyd Schwartz
Written by Sam Locke & Milton Pascal
Christopher Knight.................................... Arthur Owens
Robbie Rist.. Oliver
Denise Nickerson .... Pamela Phillips
Kathy O'Dare....................................... Michelle

Peter runs into a new kid in school who happens to look just like him. No, it's not his twin who was switched at birth; Arthur Owens is just a regular old doppelgänger who looks exactly like Pete but wears glasses. The two boys are immediately fascinated with each other and they want to pull a trick on their teachers. But first they test out their likenesses at Peter's house. Arthur goes into the Brady home pretending to be Peter to see if he can fool everyone. Indeed he does and the ruse is a success. But while Arthur is inside Mike asks him if he would entertain his boss's niece on Friday night. Arthur agrees. Unfortunately, the real Peter already has a date with Michelle for Friday. Now he's stuck with two dates, neither of whom he can disappoint. Then an idea comes to him. Arthur was the one who actually made the date with Pamela (the niece) so why doesn't *Arthur* keep it? Peter calls him up, tells him the plan, and Arthur agrees. When Friday night arrives, Peter arranges for all his siblings to be out of the house. Mike and Carol are going to the roast for Mr. Phillips' retirement party and the stage is set for Peter and Arthur's plan. The only problem is Arthur is running late. Pete is stuck with two girls in the house (one in the living room and one in the family room) and runs back and forth between each room entertaining the girls desperately trying not to blow his cover. To complicate matters, when he's with Pamela he has to be wearing jeans and a white shirt. When he's with Michelle (his real date), he is supposed to be in a Dracula costume for the party he will be going to with her. Pete has to effect quick costume changes in the kitchen every time he needs to enter a room with a girl in it. But soon Arthur does show up. Peter instructs him to go into the family room and entertain Pamela for a few hours until he gets back from his own date. Peter rushes upstairs to grab the tickets to the costume party. On the way down, he encounters his parents. Mike and Carol had to return because they forgot the notes for Mike's speech. They see who they thought was Peter in the living room with Pamela. Then they see Peter on the stairs and Michelle in the living room. Naturally, Peter's parents are completely baffled by their "double vision." Peter's ruse is found out and he and Arthur explain the whole thing to everybody involved. No one's feelings were hurt and it all works out for the better. Peter gets to stay with Michelle and Arthur with Pamela. Viewers never see Arthur Owens again.

#114 – Top Secret

Airdate: February 15, 1974
Directed by Bernard Wiesen
Executive Producer Sherwood Schwartz
Produced by Howard Leeds and Lloyd Schwartz
Written by Howard Ostroff

Allan Melvin	Sam
Lew Palter	Mr. Gronsky
Don Fenwick	Fred Sanders
Robbie Rist	Oliver

Bobby and Cousin Oliver meet a man from the F.B.I. who has to speak to Mike in his den about important business. Bobby and Oliver immediately assume the F.B.I. wants Mike for some sort of spy gig. Mike tries to quell the boys' imaginations by telling them the truth: that the man is just there to complete a routine security clearance background check on Mike. But what he doesn't tell them is that it's for a government building he's designing. The words "security clearance" only serve to heighten their fantasies. Next, they find out that Mike is developing some secret plans for Sam the butcher. Could Sam be involved with the F.B.I., too? Sure! Their theory is supported by what Alice tells them. She says that Sam used to be in the Army. Then Bobby and Oliver make a special trip to Sam's butcher shop to ask him about his history with the Army. Sam gives them some exaggerated story about stealing the enemy codebook. Now the boys are thoroughly convinced that Sam and Mike are up to some secret government business. A minute or two after they hear Sam's story, Mr. Gronsky walks into the butcher shop. He pulls Sam aside and asks him if he's gotten the plans from Brady yet. Their whispered conversation fuels the boys' minds and they now think that not only is Sam a spy for the F.B.I. but that he's a double-agent. They think Sam is going to steal some plans from Mike and sell them to this guy

Gronsky. The next day Sam stops by the Brady house to pick up the plans Mike created for him. Bobby and Oliver witness what they think is blatant thievery. They try to get a hold of Mike at work but he has already left…for Sam's butcher shop! Bobby and Oliver quickly pedal their way to the shop to stop Sam from selling Mike out and possibly hurting him in the process. They get there right before Mr. Brady does. Once the coast is clear, Oliver and Bobby shut Sam and Mr. Gronsky in the meat locker and wait for Mr. Brady to show up. When he does, he immediately releases Bobby and Oliver's captives. It turns out that, to no one's surprise but the boys', Mike's plans are for an addition to Sam's butcher shop. Mr. Gronsky is Sam's landlord; the plans have nothing to do with the F.B.I. whatsoever. Bobby and Oliver sheepishly apologize to Sam and Mr. Gronsky. They learn their lesson about jumping to conclusions.

#115 – The Snooperstar
Airdate: February 22, 1974
Directed by Bruce Bilson
Executive Producer Sherwood Schwartz
Produced by Howard Leeds and Lloyd Schwartz
Written by Harry Winkler
Natalie Schafer.................................... Penelope Fletcher
Robbie Rist.. Oliver

Mike has to design the Penelope Fletcher Cultural Center for none other than Ms. Penelope Fletcher herself. She is a demanding, rich old lady who drives Mike crazy every time she changes her mind about something. At home, Cindy is going crazy herself. She's thoroughly convinced that the family is keeping a secret about her. She asks everyone to fess up, but of course there really is no secret. So to get back at Cindy for snooping in her diary, Marcia and Jan concoct a plan for revenge. They write a fake entry in Marcia's diary that something wonderful is going to be happening for Cindy. Cindy reads the entry and can't wait to find out what the "wonderful thing" is. The next day, she sneaks a peek at Marcia's next entry. Marcia wrote that she submitted Cindy's picture to a movie contest to be the next Shirley Temple. She goes farther and says that a talent scout will be coming to the house anonymously within the next few days to check Cindy out. Cindy is instantly thrilled at the possibility of becoming the next curly top. She goes out and buys a record so that she can learn Shirley Temple songs. She gets a dress suitable for the 19th Century Alps and curls her hair up in anticipation of the anonymous visit. Meanwhile, Mike has finished the plans for the Cultural Center and Ms. Fletcher is due to stop by the house on Thursday to pick them up. Cindy catches wind of the visit and jumps to a conclusion of her own: Ms. Fletcher is the scout and she's really there to see her. She tells her theory to Marcia and Jan. Having been caught in a lie, Marcia and Jan tell Cindy that it was all a ploy to get back at her for snooping. There is no scout, so don't do anything stupid, they say. But Cindy doesn't believe them. She gets all dressed up and comes skipping down the stairs when Ms. Fletcher arrives. Cindy immediately begins a song and dance routine befitting a seven-year-old (Cindy's twelve), which charms the sour puss right off Ms. Fletcher's face. Within minutes Ms. Fletcher is totally taken by Cindy and ends up finishing the routine with her. Cindy's act is interrupted at the very end by Mike and Carol who ask her what she thinks she's doing. Cindy tells them the truth. Ms. Fletcher seems to think that the whole thing is very cute and she accepts Mike's architectural designs without a second thought. Cindy may have made a fool out of herself, but she got her dad the account.

#116 – The Hustler

Airdate: March 1, 1974
Directed by Michael J. Kane
Executive Producer Sherwood Schwartz
Produced by Howard Leeds and Lloyd Schwartz
Written by Bill Freedman & Ben Gershman

Jim Backus .... Harry Mathews
Dorothy Shay .... Frances Mathews
Charles Stewart .... Joe Sinclair
Leonard Breman .... Truck Driver
Jason Dunn .... Hank Thompson
Susan Quick .... Gloria Thompson
Grace Spence .... Muriel Sinclair

In return for a job well done on the Whitley Project, Mike's new boss Mr. Mathews sends him a pool table. Bobby immediately takes to the game and challenges his older brothers in a game of nine ball. Peter and Greg lose after Bobby sinks a ball on the break and sinks the other balls in sequence without even giving his brothers a chance. It turns out Bobby is a whiz at pool; he learned to play at his friend Steve's house and has become a regular hustler. Meanwhile, Mike and Carol decide to invite Mr. Mathews and his wife over for dinner and a game of pool in thanks for their gift. Mike had to invite two other couples, too. So, the Mathewses, the Thompsons, and the Sinclairs all come to the Brady house that Saturday. The men go out into the carport to play pool. They all slyly let Mr. Mathews win. Then Bobby comes outside. He asks Mike if he can play a game and Mr. Mathews takes him on. Bobby doesn't hold back and ends up whipping Mr. Mathews. Mathews bet on the game, too, and in the end he owes Bobby 256 packs of gum. Mr. Mathews woefully bemoans his own pool skills and even threatens to donate his own pool table that he keeps in his living room to charity. This makes *Mrs.* Mathews very happy; she's been waiting for ages to put her piano back in the living room. But after seeing how much time Bobby spent with the table instead of his homework, and because of a lack of space in their house, Mike decides that the pool table was perhaps too extravagant a gift and volunteers to give his table to charity instead. It's a deal and poor Mrs. Mathews must suffer more years with a pool table in her living room. In the end, Bobby gets his 256 packs of gum and the Bradys are rid of one big distraction.

#117 – The Hairbrained Scheme

Airdate: March 8, 1974
Directed by Jack Arnold
Executive Producer Sherwood Schwartz
Produced by Howard Leeds and Lloyd Schwartz
Written by Charles Stewart, Jr.

John Wheeler .... Second Man
Bern Hoffman .... Man
Brandy Carson .... Woman

Hope Sherwood...Gretchen
Barbara Bernstein...Suzanne
Robbie Rist..Oliver

Bobby is all set to become a millionaire. All he has to do is sell a million bottles of Neat and Natural Hair Tonic. Bobby recruits Oliver to be his assistant and together they go door-to-door peddling the Hair Tonic. The two boys strike out and Bobby considers himself a failure at twelve. Greg finds Bobby in his room feeling bad about himself. So, Greg takes pity on him (although he doesn't tell Bobby it's out of pity) and offers to buy a bottle of the Tonic. It's Greg's high school graduation tomorrow and Bobby wants him to look his best. Bobby offers to apply the Tonic personally and Greg agrees. They go into the bathroom and Bobby rubs the Tonic on Greg's brillowy head. To Bobby's dismay, Greg's hair turns orange! He quickly throws a towel on Greg's head and gets the heck out of Dodge. Greg soon discovers his new hair color and goes on the rampage looking for Bobby so he can clobber him. He finally finds Bobby hiding out in Mike's den. Carol has to intervene in order to protect Bobby. She calms the boys down, scorns Bobby for getting into a shady deal, and calls the Better Business Bureau to find out about the Tonic. It turns out that the FDA shut the Neat and Natural Company down. Fortunately, the tonic is not harmful, but that doesn't really help Greg out much. Carol has an idea, though. She asks Greg if he would be willing to go to a beauty parlor to have his hair dyed back to its original color. Greg agrees to the embarrassing procedure. It works and Greg comes home looking normal. He finds Bobby out on the service porch with Oliver and Cindy. Bobby is pouring out all the Tonic down the drain. When he sees Greg back to normal, he is very relieved, but accidentally spills some of the Tonic on Cindy's rabbits. Now the *rabbits* are orange. (Cindy had been hoping to earn her own million dollars by breeding rabbits, but she ended up with two male rabbits and the pet store wouldn't buy them back.) Poor Bobby can't seem to do anything right. Or can he? The kids get the idea to sell the orange rabbits back to the pet store and it works. Mr. Kirby buys back both bunnies as well as Bobby's whole supply of Hair Tonic. Cindy and Bobby have made their money back. Graduation Day arrives for Greg and he walks with full honors. The only thing that is missing is Mike; he was out of town on business through the whole escapade.

THE BRADY KIDS (cartoon series)
SEASON ONE, 1972
Saturdays 10:30-11:00am ET on ABC

Production notes: The Brady kids are animated! Like the Osmond Brothers and the Jackson Five, the powers that be decided that they were missing out on the young Saturday morning cartoon market. So Filmation in cooperation with Paramount and ABC-TV developed *The Brady Kids* in 1972. Much like the other two successful singing group cartoons, *The Brady Kids* included one song per episode. At this point the kids were just getting started in the music business. They had finished the "Meet the Brady Bunch" album, which was moderately successful. The producers wanted more songs and so, to keep viewers interested (and because Famous Music wanted them to keep recording), the kids recorded "The Kids from The Brady Bunch" album and featured a song from one of these two records in every episode.

Unlike the Jackson Five, the cartoon counterparts to the Brady kids were voiced by the actors themselves. (Michael J., Jermaine, and the others were too busy to lay down audio tracks for their cartoon.) The kids really enjoyed the work…until season two. (See Season Two for more details.)

The premise of the cartoon was that Greg, Marcia, Peter, Jan, Bobby, and Cindy really like to solve mysteries. They are aided by their talking magical mynah bird Marlon, the gibberish-speaking pandas Ping and Pong, and their non-verbal but no less intelligent dog Mop Top. Also helping them along the way are hippy friend Fleetwood and lady friend Babs. Their rival is Chuck. The kids spend most of their time in a big tree house. The Brady home of 4222 Clinton Way is nowhere to be seen. Also absent are Mike, Carol, and Alice. Guest stars are peppered in here and there as the kids work together to catch the bad guys.

Regulars =
Barry Williams .... Greg
Maureen McCormick .... Marcia
Christopher Knight .... Peter
Eve Plumb .... Jan
Michael Lookinland .... Bobby
Susan Olsen .... Cindy
Larry Storch .... Marlon, Fleetwood, Mop Top, and Chuck
Jane Webb .... Babs, Ping & Pong

#1 – The Jungle Bungle, Part I
Airdate: September 9, 1972
Directed by Hal Sutherland
Produced by Lou Scheimer and Norm Prescott
Written by Marc Richards

The kids enter a hot air balloon race against Fleetwood, Chuck, and Babs. Both balloons get punctured and everyone becomes stranded on a distant jungle island. The kids discover a magical talking mynah bird named Marlon in a cave and they become friends. Marlon tries his best to be a good magician, but usually his spells go badly. In the meantime, Chuck decides to try to have a little fun and scare the Brady kids. He hops around the island planting fake Bigfoot prints. But eventually he is caught and everyone works together to build a raft so that they can leave the island. Unfortunately, the raft is sabotaged and the gang is about to be attacked by giant crabs! To be continued....

#2 – The Jungle Bungle, Part II
Airdate: September 9, 1972
Directed by Hal Sutherland
Produced by Lou Scheimer and Norm Prescott
Written by Marc Richards

With a little help from Father Nature, Greg is able to ward off the giant crabs (which have since turned into alligators). The next thing to try is another method of escape, but first they want to eat. Marlon leads them to a giant egg with a 2500-pound canary on top. They get rid of the canary by spraying it with rubber from a rubber tree. When they attempt to crack the egg, two pandas named Ping and Pong emerge. The "egg" turns out to be a crashed space capsule and the panda bears are lost astro-pandas. Ping and Pong join the Brady kids as their friends. Chuck climbs into the capsule and starts pressing buttons at random. The capsule ends up stuck on the top of a mountain on the island. The kids make their way to Chuck and on the way up the mountain they encounter an abominable snowman. The snowman is angry because he's stuck on a tropical island. So Father Nature whips up a snow storm, which makes the snowman happy. He thinks that the space capsule is a snowball and hurls it from the top of the mountain all the way down to the beach. Then the pandas make the necessary repairs, they turn the capsule into a submarine and navigate back home.

#3 – Double Trouble

Airdate: September 23, 1972
Directed by Hal Sutherland
Produced by Lou Scheimer and Norm Prescott
Written by Marc Richards

Peter's heartthrob Nancy is in love with Clint Flint the movie star. Peter mumbles to himself that he wishes *he* looked like Clint Flint. Marlon hears his wish and performs a magic trick. Naturally, the trick backfires and Bobby turns into Clint instead of Peter. Now "Bobby" is being chased around town by girls and the real Clint is stuck inside Bobby's body. So the Brady kids all get into the movie studio set to find the real Clint. After a few mishaps, Marlon effectively changes Clint and Bobby back into their real selves. Greg asks Clint to come to the youth show that he's managing. He agrees and makes a personal appearance; the Brady kids perform a song at the show. Peter gets over Nancy but is in love with a girl named Peggy now. So he wishes he were a big football star. Marlon says a little magic and voila – Bobby becomes a football star.

#4 – Long Gone Silver

Airdate: September 30, 1972
Directed by Hal Sutherland
Produced by Lou Scheimer and Norm Prescott
Written by Marc Richards

Marlon accidentally makes Bobby's Lone Ranger silver pin change into Silver the horse. At the same time the Lone Ranger and Tonto appear on the streets looking for Silver. The Brady kids run into them on the street and reunite them with Silver. The city police force asks the Lone Ranger for help in capturing Dan and Ben and "The Masquerade Men" gang. The gang kidnaps the Brady kids' friends Fleetwood and Chuck and now it's up to them and the Lone Ranger to rescue the two. They find their friends in an abandoned mine and rescue them, but the Masquerade Men aren't there. They've dressed up as the Lone Ranger and Tonto and plan to go about town stealing everything for themselves. But they don't get away for long before the real Ranger, Tonto, and of course the Brady kids capture them and turn them in.

#5 – Cindy's Super Friends

Airdate: October 7, 1972
Directed by Hal Sutherland
Produced by Lou Scheimer and Norm Prescott
Written by Marc Richards

Mayor LaTrane has proclaimed this week to be "Paint Week." Volunteers are needed to help re-paint the downtown. The Brady kids all volunteer and Cindy recruits Clark Kent and Lois Lane, local television news anchors, to help out. Clark "brings" Superman to make the job go quickly. But Professor Too Loose LaTricks and his sidekick Igor have switched the real paint with delayed-action invisible paint. Ten minutes after the downtown is painted, it all disappears! The Professor and Igor plan to rob the bank when they and the building are invisible but Superman foils their plan with the help of the Brady kids.

#6 – Pop Goes the Mynah
Airdate: October 14, 1972
Directed by Hal Sutherland
Produced by Lou Scheimer and Norm Prescott
Written by Marc Richards

On a trip to a soda pop plant Marlon accidentally gets closed up inside a soda can. Marlon is packaged and shipped away on a truck and then a train. The Bradys put an ad in the local paper offering a $10 reward for any information leading to his safe return. The newspaper accidentally misprints the reward to be $1,000. An evil guy named Sleazy Sam and his henchman Knuckles find Marlon. They decide that instead of turning him in for the reward they will keep him and turn him into a novelty act so they can raise more than just $1,000. An act is advertised in the paper and the Brady kids go to the performance so they can get Marlon back. But Marlon is in a cage and they can't quite get him free. So they decide to sing for the crooks and hope that they take *them* on as an act instead of Marlon. Their ploy works as a distraction and they are able to free Marlon, Ping, Pong, and Mop Top (who were subsequently captured, too) and escape with their menagerie intact.

#7 – Who Was that Dog?
Airdate: October 21, 1972
Directed by Hal Sutherland
Produced by Lou Scheimer and Norm Prescott
Written by Marc Richards

Chuck is entering his dog Swifty into a pet contest. The winner of the contest gets admitted to the Pet Hall of Fame. So the Brady kids decide to enter Marlon, Mop Top, Ping, and Pong. Also participating are Babs and her dog, Fleetwood and his kangaroo, and the mayor and his dog. The kids are only entering their pets to teach Chuck a lesson about bragging. Marlon, however, refuses to demean himself to the level of a pet and doesn't want to enter the contest. So the kids dress up Mop Top, Ping, and Pong. But Marlon accidentally does a little dance for joy in front of the judges and they immediately pin him top pet.

#8 – It Ain't Necessarily Snow
Airdate: October 28, 1972
Directed by Hal Sutherland
Produced by Lou Scheimer and Norm Prescott
Written by Marc Richards

Greg is fed up with Chuck's bragging and challenges him to a ski race. They bet on who will win and the loser is supposed to do whatever the winner says for a week. Chuck secretly gets a replacement skier to finish the race for him. The replacement is an expert and wins the race. Marlon suspects Chuck of cheating, though. The bird discovers two sets of ski tracks behind the copse of trees where Chuck did his switch. So he tells Greg to stop doing chores for Chuck and challenge him to another race. This time the game is ice boat racing. Marlon and Greg teach Chuck a lesson by winning the race.

#9 – A Funny Thing Happened on the Way to the End Zone
Airdate: November 4, 1972
Directed by Hal Sutherland
Produced by Lou Scheimer and Norm Prescott
Written by Marc Richards

Greg is quarterback for the school football team. He practices in the park with his siblings and Fleetwood. During the practice a spaceship from Venus lands in the bushes. The ship is shaped and colored exactly like a football and the Brady kids switch it with their real football accidentally. The three tiny Venutians inside are whisked away to the Brady tree house. The next day Greg grabs the ship and brings it back to the park for further practice. Fleetwood kicks off the game and, since the ball is really a spaceship, the kick lands the ball all the way at the top of a nearby clock tower. The school's football coach immediately recruits Fleetwood as the kicker for their team. That evening the Brady kids discover the three tiny aliens sitting in their tree house. The aliens explain who they are. Greg and the kids are determined to find the real spaceship; they don't know it landed in the clock tower. So during the big game against the Tigers, Greg's team isn't doing very well. The score is tied 0-0 when a big wind blows the spaceship out from the clock tower and onto the playing field. Greg realizes it's the ship and manages, with the help of the other kids, to get it back to its rightful owners. The Venutians go back to Venus and Greg's team wins the game 7-0.

#10 – That Was No Worthy Opponent, That Was My Sister
Airdate: November 11, 1972
Directed by Hal Sutherland
Produced by Lou Scheimer and Norm Prescott
Written by Marc Richards

In a mirror to what happened on the original series, Greg and Marcia run against each other for Student Council Representative. A third candidate is Chuck. Marlon and the boys side with Greg; Ping, Pong, Mop Top and the girls side with Marcia. Greg and Marcia get the idea that the other is sabotaging their campaign. Really, Chuck is the saboteur. Marlon and the animals find out the truth about Chuck and make it known to the whole student body during the final campaign speeches. Marcia ends up winning the election by three votes…because Bobby, Peter, and Greg all voted for her.

#11 – You Took the Words Right Out of My Tape
Airdate: November 18, 1972
Directed by Hal Sutherland
Produced by Lou Scheimer and Norm Prescott
Written by Marc Richards

The Brady kids get their likenesses sculpted in wax for the local wax museum. Meanwhile, burglars Sam and Louis have their eyes on some jewels that will be on exhibit in City Hall soon. Also, Peter has been given a position of reporter at school and he carries around a tape recorder and keeps it on all the time. He records the thieves talking about stealing the Crown Jewels of Domania. The police don't believe the kids when they tell them about the thieves; they need more evidence than a recorded conversation. So when the jewels arrive at City Hall the kids are there to foil the robbers. They do just that. The jewels are safe but the robbers escape. The next planned heist is at the jewels' next exhibit: the wax museum. Thanks to Mop Top, the Brady kids find out that the thieves are still planning to steal the jewels. They are at the wax museum ready to capture them red handed. The kids take the places of their wax likenesses. When the thieves take the jewels they are so scared that the "wax" figures have come to life that they turn themselves in to the security guards.

#12 – Give Me a Home Where the Panda Bears Roam and the Dog and the Mynah Bird Play
Airdate: November 25, 1972
Directed by Hal Sutherland
Produced by Lou Scheimer and Norm Prescott
Written by Marc Richards

The Brady kids go to Fleetwood's Uncle Freddie's ranch to help out with his big cattle drive. It turns out that he only has one cow, but everyone stays at the ranch anyway. Fleetwood, Chuck, and Babs are there, too. They drive the cow on through the day and make camp. Then two old timey train robbers turned cattle rustlers break into the picture. They chase Chuck and the cow into a canyon with the Brady kids in hot pursuit. The rustlers back off and everyone drives the cow into an old ghost town. That night the rustlers show up again and capture Ping and Pong and take hold of the cow. It's up to the kids to rescue their panda friends and return the cow to Uncle Freddie. They succeed in stopping the rustlers and they find Ping and Pong at the bottom of an old well. They reel the pandas up in a bucket and everyone is safe and sound again.

#13 – It's All Greek to Me
Airdate: December 2, 1972
Directed by Hal Sutherland
Produced by Lou Scheimer and Norm Prescott
Written by Marc Richards

Miss Prince, the Administrative Assistant to the local university's Math Department is really Wonder Woman, but only Marlon seems to know the truth. When Miss Prince is talking to the Brady kids, Marlon accidentally casts them all back in time to ancient Greece. The first Olympic ceremonies are about to take place and Chuckonus challenges the Bradys to feats of athleticism. Jan scoffs at him and says that brains are more important than brawn, but the other kids take up the challenge. The kids try to qualify in various events but are sabotaged by Chuckonus's evil ways. Wonder Woman appears and helps the kids win in one event. She also turns Ping and Pong's Trojan Panda back into the Trojan Horse. But after the kids qualify for the marathon they realize that they really can't compete. They should not meddle in history and change the past. So they decide that they need to get back home to the present. Euclid the mathematician gives them a clue of where to find a magic spell. Miss Prince translates the ancient Greek into English, Marlon casts the spell, and everybody arrives back at the tree house safe and sound. Miss Prince tells them that the lesson here today is that a healthy mixture of brains and brawn is important.

TIKI TALK

This episode of *The Brady Kids* is the first ever television appearance of DC Comic's Wonder Woman. Her voice goes uncredited. It would be another year or so before the superheroine would grace the small screen again, this time in the series *Super Friends*.

#14 – The Big Time
Airdate: December 9, 1972
Directed by Hal Sutherland
Produced by Lou Scheimer and Norm Prescott
Written by Marc Richards

A national talent show is coming to town and the Brady kids want to audition their musical act. But one of Marlon's spells goes awry again and Cindy ends up with a deep, manly singing voice. Their act is ruined unless Marlon can save them. Chuck is sabotaging everyone's acts and the Brady kids won't be able to perform without Cindy. It's up to Marlon to fix things. He says a magic spell and Cindy's singing voice returns to normal. The Brady kids beat out everyone, except maybe for Mop Top.

#15 – Marlon's Birthday Party
Airdate: December 16, 1972
Directed by Hal Sutherland
Produced by Lou Scheimer and Norm Prescott
Written by Marc Richards

It's Marlon's birthday and he says that he always celebrates it with Merlin the magician. So Marlon casts a spell that sends him back to King Arthur's time. But as always, something goes terribly wrong. Merlin is simultaneously sent to the present time and appears in the Brady tree house. While in town, Merlin seems just as inept at magic as Marlon does and causes things to go wrong downtown. He turns a cable car into a horse and carriage and tries to get a horse to pull the Brady kids' jalopy only to conjure and elephant instead. Meanwhile Marlon is wreaking his own havoc on King Arthur's court. He also ends up sending quite a few historical figures to the tree house as he tries to find a way to get back to the Brady kids. But eventually Ping, Pong, and Mop Top find Merlin's book of magic spells and Merlin fixes everything.

#16 – The Richest Man in the World
Airdate: December 23, 1972
Directed by Hal Sutherland
Produced by Lou Scheimer and Norm Prescott
Written by Marc Richards

Nick L. Dime, the richest man in the world, has disappeared and it's up to the Brady kids to find him. But Dime makes it easy and befriends the kids. Bobby puts his detective skills to good use and figures out that their new friend – disguised as a vagrant – is none other than Nick L. Dime himself. The kids donate their reward for finding Dime to charity and in return Dime buys them a television set for their treehouse.

#17 – Wings
Airdate: December 30, 1972
Directed by Hal Sutherland
Produced by Lou Scheimer and Norm Prescott
Written by Marc Richards

The Brady kids and their animals are participating in a road race. Chuck, being Chuck, switches one of the directional signs on them and the kids end up at the farm of the Wrong brothers, Orville and Wilbur. Soon Chuck and Fleetwood arrive at the farm, too. The Wrong brothers steal parts off of the Brady car, Fleetwood's bicycle, and Chuck's car to help finish their airplanes when no one is looking. Many attempts at escape are thwarted by the wind and by the brothers. At one point their cars take flight instead of driving on the road. Finally, the kids are able to convince the brothers to give them their car parts back. They make repairs and get back on the road.

THE BRADY KIDS **(cartoon series)**
SEASON TWO, 1973
Saturdays 11:00-11:30am ET on ABC

Production Notes: The first season of *The Brady Kids* ran just in the fall of 1972 for 17 episodes. The folks at Filmation Studios wanted at least five more episodes to be produced so that the total number would be 22: the minimum required to go into syndication. But Filmation had a problem. The kids were being encouraged – rightly or wrongfully – by their manager to demand more money. Filmation did not want to pay up. In the end, Eve, Mike, and Susan stuck with the show, due mostly to the encouragement of their parents. Barry, Maureen, and Chris opted out. So the studio got three other voice talents (two of whom were the producer's children!) to be Greg, Marcia, and Peter for the remaining five episodes. After the 22nd episode was completed, the show was cancelled.

Barry, Maureen and Chris all cancelled their contracts with Filmation in July 1973. For the first season of *The Brady Kids* they had been paid $138 per episode plus a $127.65 bonus. That's not much considering the going rate for actors and voice actors at the time. So Barry and Chris sued Filmation in October 1973. As part of the suit they accused the studio of using their likenesses without their permission. The animated characters were drawn to look like the real-life actors, plus they were drawn to look like the characters of Greg and Peter as portrayed by Barry and Chris. Therefore, the plaintiffs alleged that Filmation was using them illegally and the two boys were suing for damages and equitable pay.

Case file WEC31008 was entered into the Los Angeles County Superior Court docket with 7 causes of action 115 paragraphs long. It would be five years before the case was finally settled in Barry and Chris' favor.

Regulars =
Lane Scheimer .... Greg
Erica Scheimer .... Marcia
David Smith .... Peter
Eve Plumb .... Jan
Michael Lookinland .... Bobby
Susan Olsen .... Cindy
Larry Storch .... Marlon, Chuck, Mop Top, and Fleetwood
Lola Fisher .... Ping and Pong, Babs

#18 – Frankincense
Airdate: September 8, 1973
Directed by Hal Sutherland
Produced by Lou Scheimer and Norm Prescott
Written by Marc Richards

There is a terrible storm and the kids are caught outside in the rain. They knock on the nearest door to ask for shelter. The door just so happens to be to a castle that belongs to Dr. Frankincense. The Doctor seems to be straight out of the book that Marcia is reading, <u>Frankenstein</u>, but this doctor is building a twenty-foot tall robot that plays card games. Marlon says a little magic to get the robot to come to life and the robot splits into twenty one-foot tall mini robots. The little bots subsist on jewels. They escape the castle and make their way to town, munching on any jewelry they happen upon. Naturally, there is a big jewel show at the mall. The Brady kids figure that that will be the next place the robots show up. But what they don't know is that the robots have been captured by a jewel thief who plans to use them to steal jewels for them. The thief and his feline cat burglar pull off the heist. They don't get far before the Brady kids capture them, call the cops, and return the jewels to their rightful owners.

#19 – Teacher's Pet
Airdate: September 15, 1973
Directed by Hal Sutherland
Produced by Lou Scheimer and Norm Prescott
Written by Marc Richards

Cindy's pet show is ruined when Marlon creates a mud puddle that her performing pets Mop Top, Ping, and Pong slip on. She says she wants a new, normal pet like a cat. So Marlon gets Tut-Tut the cat from his old magic teacher Miss Tickle. When he performs a spell on Tut-Tut, the cat turns into a hippo and is magicked away to Africa. Two poachers capture Tut-Tut. The Brady kids, Miss Tickle, and Marlon rescue her.

TIKI TALK

The characters of Miss Tickle and Tut-Tut were re-used for the Filmation cartoon series *Mission: Magic* with singer Rick Springfield. The show was kind of like *The Magic School Bus* of the 1970s.

#20 – Marcia's Lib
Airdate: September 22, 1973
Directed by Hal Sutherland
Produced by Lou Scheimer and Norm Prescott
Written by Marc Richards

Greg, Peter, Bobby, Chuck, and Fleetwood all belong to an exclusive club called the Bronco Backpackers. Their secret motto is "KTFFG" or "keep the forest for God." Marcia thinks it's unconstitutional that the Backpackers is for boys only so she forms her own group with Jan, Cindy, and Babs for members and calls it the Forest Phillies. *Their* motto is, "the forest is for everyone." The two groups go on campouts that weekend in the same forest. After some acts of sabotage by Chuck on the girls, the girls are left without equipment and tents and it starts to rain. So they are forced to join forces with the boys and everyone goes to a nearby cave for shelter. The boys' compass is lost during the night and all the kids have to find their way back to the cars to get out. They decide to work together. The boys and the girls come up with equally clever ways to navigate the terrain and they all learn a lesson about equality.

#21 – Ceiling Zero
Airdate: September 29, 1973
Directed by Hal Sutherland
Produced by Lou Scheimer and Norm Prescott
Written by Marc Richards

The Bradys visit the local art museum and are impressed with an original painting by Michael Angelglow. After the visit, Greg says that the tree house could use a new coat of paint. While the kids are at school the next day Marlon decides to surprise them by having Angelglow himself conjured up from the past to paint the tree house. Some crooks discover the paintings on the tree house and steal the tree, a painted fence, and kidnap Angelglow. The crooks plan to market Angelglow's work for hundreds of thousands of dollars. Never fear, the Brady kids find the crooks, rescue Angelglow, and have Marlon send him back to his own time.

#22 – Who Believes in Ghosts
Airdate: October 6, 1973
Directed by Hal Sutherland
Produced by Lou Scheimer and Norm Prescott
Written by Marc Richards

Colonel Useless Jones's old mansion is slated to be torn down by the city to make way for a new highway. The Brady kids want to save the house and petition the mayor to designate it as an historical monument. Loot and Thumbs are two crooks hiding out in the house. They've stored their ill-gotten gains in the attic. The Brady kids discover them, call the cops, and the reward money for the return of the stolen property is more than enough to pay to save the house from destruction.

When cartoons are made, one of the steps in creating the episode is to make story boards that outline the scenes and dialogue. This image is the first page of the story board for the final Brady Kids *episode. Courtesy of the ARTS Library and CBS Television Studios.*

THE BRADY BUNCH VARIETY HOUR (variety show) also known as **THE BRADY BUNCH HOUR**
SEASON ONE, 1976-1977
ABC airtimes varied: see specific episodes for details

Regulars =

Florence Henderson ....Carol Brady
Robert Reed ....Mike Brady
Ann B. Davis...Alice Nelson
Maureen McCormick ....Marcia Brady
Barry Williams.. Greg Brady
Geri Reischl ....Jan Brady
Chris Knight.. Peter Brady
Susan Olsen...Cindy Brady
Mike Lookinland..Bobby Brady

Production Notes:
In mid-1976, Sid and Marty Krofft of H.R. Pufnstuf fame decided that they would like to do a new variety show.
Already in existence were *Donny and Marie* and *Sonny and Cher*, both of which are extremely successful in
the ratings. The Kroffts saw Florence Henderson, Susan Olsen, Mike Lookinland, and Maureen McCormick
appear on an episode of *Donny and Marie* and enjoyed their performance. They also had had a positive

experience working with the Brady Kids on their televised special *Sid and Marty Krofft at the Hollywood Bowl* in 1973. Finally, they knew that *The Brady Bunch* was very successful in syndication. Add all these factors together and the Kroffts baked up an interesting variety hour idea.

They were eager for something new to hit the variety scene and so pitched the idea of a Brady variety show to ABC network executives. The studio bought the idea. Thus, *without* the permission of *Brady Bunch* creator Sherwood Schwartz, production began. All the principal actors agreed to join the project except Eve Plumb. Eve was persuaded by someone that the show would be a bad career choice for her. Plus, she was under contract to film *Alexander: the Other Side of Dawn*. Geri Reischl replaced Eve and later earned the infamous moniker "Fake Jan."

Filming began in November 1976 for the first special slated to air for the Thanksgiving Holiday. Needless to say that it was a very stressful schedule. On top of filming skits, the actors had to learn to sing and dance and learn to work around variety's newest innovation: a swimming pool. Thanks to a lot of hard work, the special was a ratings success. ABC ordered eight more specials to air for the Spring 1977 season. Unfortunately, the network was not as supportive as it could have been and they switched the timeslot around like a roulette. Viewers never caught on and the show was not renewed for the fall.

The premise: Bobby has the idea that the whole family move to Burbank and create a variety show. Mike has either quit his job or taken a leave of absence because he and Carol and all six kids make up the act. They move to a beach house in Burbank and put the show on from there. Greg calls singing and dancing "his life," Peter is in college majoring in girls (according to Carol), Jan keeps saying she'd rather be dead, Bobby has become the group leader, and Marcia and Cindy are more or less still themselves.

They end every episode except the pilot with a little song:

Carol: "There's nowhere in the world that I would rather be than with you, my love."
Mike: "And there's nothing in the world that I would rather see than your smile, my love."
Mike, Carol, and kids: "For united we stand, divided we fall, and if our backs should ever be against the wall we'll be together, together you and I."

#1
Airdate: Friday November 28, 1976, 7:00pm
Nielsen Rating: 21.6 HR, 31 HS, 1538 HP
Directed by Art Fisher
Executive Producers Sid and Marty Krofft
Produced by Lee Miller and Jerry McPhie
Writing Supervised by Carl Kleinschmitt
Arrangements by Sid Feller
Guests: Tony Randall, Donny & Marie Osmond, Ann B. Davis, the Krofftettes, and the Water Follies

Songs:

"Baby Face" "Love to Love You Baby" medley .... all
"Chorus Line" .... all
"Splish Splash" .... all plus Donny and Marie
"Gotta Find my Corner of the Sky" .... Greg
dramatic reading..Tony Randall
"Memories".. Carol
"Attitude Dancing," "Cheek to Cheek," "Dance with Me," "I Could Have Danced All Night," "The Hustle," and "(Shake, Shake, Shake) Shake Your Booty" medley......all plus Alice

The Brady family has their own television variety hour and they've dragged Mike to Burbank to participate. The Bradys are living in a beach house and Bobby is in charge of writing the scripts. The whole show is Bobby's idea. Unfortunately, after the opening act, Bobby is convinced that Mike has to go. He and the other kids feel that Mike didn't do very well. So Bobby starts thinking of other actors who could play his dad. Tony Randall rings the doorbell. He's the show's guest star this week and he comes by the beach house to pick up the script. Bobby tells him that the script isn't ready yet, but then he gets and idea. How would Tony like to play Mike Brady on the Show? Tony is seriously considering it when the real Mike comes down the stairs. Mike hears the whole thing and knows that his family – especially Bobby – wants to ditch him. Tony is embarrassed and leaves. Mike confronts his family: will they choose to keep him in the act or dump him? Bobby tells his dad that he loves him and thus apologizes and says that he'd like him to stay. Mike stays and the rest of the show continues as planned.

#2
Airdate: Sunday January 23, 1977, 7:00pm
Nielsen Rating: 19.5 HR, 31 HS, 1388 HP
Directed by Jack Regas
Executive Producers Sid and Marty Krofft
Produced by Lee Miller
Writing Supervised by Carl Kleinschmitt
Arrangements by Sid Feller & Van Alexander
Guests: Lee Majors, Farrah Fawcett-Majors, Rip Taylor, Kaptain Kool and the Kongs, Ann B. Davis, the Krofftettes, and the Water Follies.

Songs:

"Yankee Doodle Dandy".. all
"Razzle Dazzle" .... all
"Wicked Witch" "Workin at the Car Wash"................Alice, Marcia, Greg, Peter, and Merrill
"Your Song" ....Jan
"Send in the Clowns".. Carol

"Names" .... Kaptain Kool and the Kongs
"You Got to Have Heart," "Heart and Soul," "Heart of my Heart," "Don't Go Breakin my Heart," "How Do You Mend a Broken Heart?" "Heart Beat," medley...........all plus Alice, Merrill, and Kaptain Kool and the Kongs

The show is now on ABC once a month on Sunday nights and it has a new name *The Brady Bunch Hour*. To commemorate the new station, the Bradys decided to sell their house on Clinton Way and move into a permanent house on the beach in Burbank, California. Their mover Mr. Merrill is very inept and their furniture arrives a day later than expected. The day after that, Merrill shows up again saying that he allowed a couple to rent the beach house for the weekend before he realized that the Bradys already owned it. So, the Bradys are kind to the visiting couple and let them stay on their couches in the living room. The couple just so happens to be Lee Majors (the "6 Million Dollar Man") and his wife Farrah Fawcett-Majors (the blonde "Angel" from *Charlie's Angels*). The plot is broken up by a few musical numbers, including one where Alice dresses up as the Wicked Witch of the West, Peter as the Tin Man, Greg as the Scarecrow, Marcia as Dorothy, and Merrill as the Cowardly Lion.

#3
Airdate: Sunday February 27, 1977, 7:00pm
Nielsen Rating: 15.0 HR, 23 HS, 1068 HS
Directed by Jack Regas
Executive Producers Sid and Marty Krofft
Produced by Lee Miller
Writing Supervised by Carl Kleinschmitt
Arrangements by Sid Feller & Van Alexander
Guests: Milton Berle, Rip Taylor, Tina Turner, Ann B. Davis, the Krofftettes, and the Water Follies

Songs:
"Hooray for Hollywood" .... all
"Make 'Em Laugh"..... Mike, Carol, Greg, Peter, Marcia,
.... Alice, and Merrill
"Sing"........................... Peter and "Collette the Puppette"
"Hooray for Hollywood" .... all
"Rubber Band Man" .... Tina Turner
"Evergreen".. Carol
"Catch a Falling Star," "You Don't Have to be a Star," "You Are My Lucky Star," "Everybody is a Star," "Don't Let the Stars Get in Your Eyes," "Good Morning Starshine," "Shining Star" medley.....all plus Alice, Merrill, Milton Berle, and Tina Turner

Bobby is still trying to run the show. This time he gets Milton Berle to write and produce the second half of the show, but things don't go very well. Bobby and the other Bradys hired him because they (mostly Bobby) thought that the show has so far been boring and the jokes weren't funny. So they bring in "Uncle Milty" to raise the laughs. Berle has Mike dressed up in a fruit lady drag outfit (complete with lipstick and make-up!), Carol in a mustache, and the kids in crazy costumes. The jokes are silly and the family realizes they have to fire Milton Berle. Carol and Mike make Bobby do the firing since he is the one who did the hiring. Bobby does it gracefully and Milton takes it in stride.

#4

Airdate: Sunday March 4, 1977, 9:00pm
Nielsen Rating: 19.3 HR, 31 HS, 1374 HP
Directed by Jack Regas
Executive Producers Sid and Marty Krofft
Produced by Lee Miller
Writing Supervised by Carl Kleinschmitt
Arrangements by Sid Feller & Van Alexander
Guests: Vincent Price, Rip Taylor, H.R. Pufnstuf, Ann B. Davis, the Krofftettes, and the Water Follies

Songs:
"Sunny Side".. all
"It's Not Where You Start (It's Where You Finish)"..... all
"All By Myself"..Carol and Greg
"Let's Get on with Our Show"....................H.R. Pufnstuf
"Time in a Bottle"..Marcia
"I Want to be Happy," "You Make Me So Very Happy," "Make Someone Happy," "Happy Together," "Put on a Happy Face," "Happy Days," medley....................all plus Alice and Merrill

Greg is tired of living in the same house as all his siblings and his parents. So he gets family friend Mr. Merrill to find him an apartment and he moves out. The apartment is tiny, ugly, rundown, and the broken couch doubles as the bed. It's also haunted. Vincent Price stops by for a surprise visit and freaks Mr. Merrill and Greg out with his stories of Stella and Binky Beaumont, the former tenants. But Greg is determined to give the place a chance. He gets a phone (his number is 321-1321) and calls home to find out how everything is going. After a rendition of "All By Myself," Greg decides that he's had enough. Thirty-six hours in that decrepit place is all he can stand and he moves back home – much to the chagrin of Peter who wanted Greg's bedroom for himself. Alice and the family throw Greg a welcome home party and give him a key for his own bedroom.

#5

Airdate: Monday March 21, 1977, 8:00pm
Nielsen Rating: 18.5 HR, 29 HS, 1317 HP
Directed by Jack Regas
Executive Producers Sid and Marty Krofft
Produced by Lee Miller
Writing Supervised by Carl Kleinschmitt
Arrangements by Sid Feller, Van Alexander, & Claude Williamson

Guests: Charo, Rip Taylor, The Hudson Brothers, Ann B. Davis, the Krofftettes, and the Water Follies

Songs:
"Toot, Toot, Tootsie" .... all
guitar solo .... Charo
"Sorry Seems to be the Hardest Word" .... Carol
"I've Grown Accustomed to Her Face" .... Mike
"Strike Up the Band," "Seventy-Six Trombones" .....Greg, Carol, Mike, Peter, Marcia
"Disco Queen" .... The Hudson Brothers
"Chicago," "California Dreaming," "(Back Home Again in) Indiana," "Do You Know the Way to San Jose?"
"San Francisco," "Philadelphia Freedom," "America," "Big D," "America" medley ....all plus Charo, Merrill,
The Hudson Brothers, and Alice

The family thinks that Mike can't sing, so Mike goes off alone to practice and to try to teach himself the guitar. Charo runs into him in the studio and tells him that she will be his accompanist. She leans over his back and strums the guitar while Mike sings "I've Grown Accustomed to Your Face." Unfortunately, Merrill and Carol walk in on them and Carol is immediately jealous. Then Mike invites Charo to the house for dinner. Now Carol is *extremely* jealous and has a fit right in front of Charo. Mike tells Charo she'd better leave. Then he tries to make up with Carol. She accepts his apology for putting together a duet with the attractive and "unintelligible" woman. Mike and Carol are once again happy and the kids tell Mike they love him…even if he can't sing.

#6
Airdate: Monday March 28, 1977, 8:00pm
Nielsen Rating: 19.3 HR, 32 HS, 1374 HP
Directed by Jack Regas
Executive Producers Sid and Marty Krofft
Produced by Lee Miller
Writing Supervised by Carl Kleinschmitt
Arrangements by Sid Feller, Van Alexander, & Claude Williamson
Guests: Rich Little, Edgar Bergen, Rip Taylor, Melanie, Ann B. Davis, the Krofftettes, and the Water Follies

Songs:
"I Got the Music in Me" .... all
"Consider Yourself" .... all
"Cyclone" .... Melanie
"Beautiful Noise" .... Carol
"Ease on Down the Road" ....Peter, Alice, Greg, Merrill, and Marcia
"That's Entertainment," "Pinball Wizard," "Love Look at the Two of Us," "Pink Panther Theme," "Live and Let Die," "Supercalifragilisticexpialidocious," "Somewhere Over the Rainbow," "That's Entertainment" medley .... all plus Alice, Merrill, Melanie, and Rich Little

During a rehearsal for the show, Rich Little bumps into Cindy underwater. Their clash of heads leaves Rich with amnesia and Cindy feeling extremely guilty for the damage her thick skull caused. The Bradys have to bring Rich home with them because he can't remember where he lives. Rich tries out a whole slew of different personas from Carey Grant to Humphrey Bogart, but none of them seems quite right to him. The Bradys send him to bed hoping that a good night's sleep will cure his amnesia. The next morning, he wakes up and believes that he is Richie Brady, youngest son of Mike and Carol. Now Cindy really thinks she's done it. Merrill shows up pretending to be a psychologist, but of course he can't cure Rich. Then Rich suddenly remembers his underwater collision with Cindy. He rushes outside and into the ocean hoping that being underwater will jog his memory further. This time he crashes into Merrill, but the collision brings him back to his senses. He's Rich Little once again. Cindy is greatly relieved and the show can go on as planned.

#7

Airdate: Monday April 4, 1977, 8:00pm
Nielsen Rating: 16.2 HR, 25 HS, 1153 HP
Directed by Jack Regas
Executive Producers Sid and Marty Krofft
Produced by Lee Miller
Writing Supervised by Carl Kleinschmitt
Arrangements by Sid Feller, Van Alexander, & Claude Williamson
Guests: Robert Hegyes, The Ohio Players, Rip Taylor, Redd Foxx, Ann B. Davis, the Krofftettes, and the Water Follies

Songs:
"Celebrate".. all
"If My Friends Could See Me Now" .... all
"Southern Nights"..........................Greg, Marcia, and Jan
"Fire"... The Ohio Players
"How Lucky Can You Get" .... Carol
"April Showers," "Rose Garden," "Spring Will Be a Little Late This Year," "Paper Roses," "Tiptoe through the Tulips," "Stop and Smell the Roses," and "Laughter in the Rain" medley........all plus Alice and Merrill

Marcia is engaged? It's true! She brings home Winston Beaumont, a guy she met at a friend's party just one week ago. They hit it off and they're already engaged to be married, with or without Carol and Mike's blessing. The next day, though, Marcia decides on her own that she was being too hasty. She learns that Winston changes his personality for each girl he meets. For her he was behaving new agey; he said he was a vegetarian, he spoke about feelings, and called everyone "brother." This personality is not the real Winston. Marcia breaks off the engagement and tells Winston that if he ever figures out who he really is to give her a call. Meanwhile, Redd Foxx interrupts the show every now and then because he says he's getting tips for his own variety show scheduled to start next season. At the end of the Brady Bunch Hour he tells the audience that he's not going to do a variety show of his own; he can't smile for so long every week.

#8

Airdate: Monday April 25, 1977, 8:00pm

Nielsen Rating: 16.9 HR, 29 HS, 1203 HP

Directed by Jack Regas

Executive Producers Sid and Marty Krofft

Produced by Lee Miller

Writing Supervised by Carl Kleinschmitt

Arrangements by Sid Feller, Van Alexander, & Claude Williamson

Guests: The *What's Happening!!* Kids (Ernest Thomas, Haywood Nelson, Fred Berry, and Danielle Spencer), Rip Taylor, Rick Dees, Patty Maloney, Ann B. Davis, the Krofftettes, and the Water Follies

Songs:

"Get Ready" .... all

"Walk Right In," "Walking Happy"......................Carol, Mike, Greg, Peter, and Marcia

"Thank God I'm a Country Girl"..............................Alice

"Dis-Gorilla"..Rick Dees

"Maple Leaf Rag" on piano ....Bobby

"This Masquerade" .... Carol

"Turn the Beat Around," "Those Were the Days," "Enjoy Yourself," "Disco Duck," "Tangerine," "Dance Machine" "I Love Lucy Theme," "You Make Me Feel Like Dancing" medley.........all plus Alice, Merrill, Patty Maloney, Rick Dees, and the *What's Happening!!* Kids

Bobby, Cindy, Jan, and Peter are attending school at the studio (even though it was said in the first episode that Peter is in college now). The actors from *What's Happening!!* join them in the classroom this week. Peter tells them that he'd love for them to be guests on this week's *Brady Bunch Hour*. Everyone agrees and they all meet at the Brady beach house that evening. They discuss ideas for the show and everyone's excited about it. But then Mike and Carol come home and tell Peter and the other three kids that they already have guests booked for this week and the *What's Happening!!* kids can't come on the show. Peter has to break the news to them the next day and Ernest, Haywood, Fred, and Danielle aren't happy. So Peter tries to cover his tracks and tells them that he'll find some way to sneak them on. True to his word, the kids walk on stage to introduce Rick Dees and they also perform in the finale.

#9

Airdate: Wednesday May 25, 1977, 8:00pm

Nielsen Rating: 11.3 HR, 24 HS, 805 HP

Directed by Jack Regas

Executive Producers Sid and Marty Krofft

Produced by Lee Miller

Writing Supervised by Carl Kleinschmitt

Arrangements by Sid Feller, Van Alexander, & Claude Williamson

Guests: Paul Williams, Rip Taylor, Lynn Anderson, Ann B. Davis, the Krofftettes, and the Water Follies

Songs:
"I Got Love" .... all
"We Got Us" .... all except Mike
"Me and My Shadow" ....Peter and Merrill
"Right Time of the Night"........................Lynn Anderson
"The Hell of It" ....Paul Williams
"Born to Say Goodbye" .... Carol
"Music, Music, Music," "Look What They've Done to My Song," "The Sweetest Sounds," "Music is My Life," "Mr. Melody," "The Music Goes 'Round and Around," "Just an Old Fashioned Love Song," "Piano Man," "I Believe in Music" medley........................all plus Alice, Merrill, Paul Williams, and Lynn Anderson

Paul Williams loves Carol. At least that's what he tells her when he comes to the Brady beach house to discuss the show. Mike is right there when he professes his love for Carol and Mike almost ends up punching Paul out. But Mike contains himself and just throws Paul out of the house. It turns out that Paul tells this to all beautiful women he meets (he says the same thing to Lynn Anderson), so Mike feels a little better about him hitting on Carol. At the end of the show, the Bradys tell the audience not to worry. Paul is not crazy and it was only an act.

THE BRADY GIRLS GET MARRIED (television movie)
Fridays 8:30-9:00pm ET on NBC

Production Notes: The variety show notwithstanding, it had been over six years since America had seen an original *Brady Bunch* episode and Sherwood Schwartz and gang were getting lots of inquiries as to what the family was up to now. As Lloyd Schwartz explains, "We just thought there were more stories to tell and people were always curious about what happened when the bunch got older." A perfect way to reunite the family was to have a wedding. An even more perfect way was to have *two* weddings, and so the TV movie *The Brady Girls Get Married* was born. All the original actors came back for this movie, which was not an easy thing to accomplish. But it goes to show how important the original series had been in the actors' lives that they were willing to drop what they were currently doing and reunite. The Brady house was rebuilt and updated – at a cost of $200,000! – and the stage was set for grown-up Brady fun.

Airdates: February 6, 1981 (part I); February 13 (part II); February 20 (part III)
Directed by Peter Baldwin
Executive Producer Sherwood Schwartz
Produced by Lloyd J. Schwartz and John Thomas Lenox
Written by Sherwood Schwartz & Lloyd J. Schwartz
Robert Reed .... Mike Brady
Florence Henderson .... Carol Brady
Ann B. Davis... Alice Franklin
Barry Williams... Greg Brady
Maureen McCormick...................... Marcia Brady Logan
Christopher Knight.. Peter Brady
Eve Plumb.................................... Jan Brady Covington
Mike Lookinland..Bobby Brady
Susan Olsen...Cindy Brady
Ron Kuhlman................................Phillip Covington, III
Jerry Houser..Wally Logan
James Gallery... Mr. Logan
Carol Arthur ....Mrs. Logan
Ryan MacDonald .... Phillip Covington, Jr.
Jeane Byron...................................... Claudia Covington

114

Bill Erwin	Reverend
Hartley Silver	Wine Steward
Perla Walter	Mrs. Alvarez
Janice Darling	Debbie
Richard Brestoff	Ben Richards

Mike and Carol drop Cindy off at college and come home to an empty nest. The quiet of the house does not last long because Jan soon comes home with a big announcement. She is engaged! Her boyfriend of two years, Phillip Covington, III, proposed to her and she accepted. She and Phillip are home to ask Mike and Carol's permission and get their blessing. Mike and Carol stammer around for a bit and let it slip that they always expected Marcia to get married first. Jan is affronted at the mention of her older sister. (Remember "Marcia, Marcia, Marcia"?) Carol and Mike try to retract their statement and give Phillip and Jan their blessing, but Jan leaves disappointed.

TIKI TALK

WHERE ARE THE KIDS NOW?

Greg is a 25-year-old doctor fresh out of medical school. He appears to be doing a residency in obstetrics. Marcia is 24 and is a fashion designer at Casual Clothes. She is soon to be married to her boyfriend Wally Logan. Peter is 22 and has joined the Air Force as an Airman in order to figure out what he really wants to do with his life. Jan is 21 and must have finished college early. She is settled in a great apartment and is soon to be married to her boyfriend Phillip Covington, III. Bobby is 19 and attending college where he plays on the baseball team. Cindy is 18 and is just beginning her freshman year of college.

The next day Marcia is eating lunch in a cafeteria by herself. A guy named Wally Logan sits next to her. He can tell that she is bothered by something and tells her that sometimes it helps to confide your problems in a perfect stranger. Marcia takes him up on his offer and spills all her worries about Jan's relationship with their parents to Wally. Wally offers up a solution – Marcia should marry him before Jan marries Phillip and then there is no problem! Well, Marcia says Wally belongs in a loony bin and leaves. That evening when she gets home from work there is a huge bouquet of flowers waiting for her on her doorstep. Wally sent them and in the card he tells her to meet him at the same cafeteria tomorrow. And so their relationship begins. Seven days later Marcia agrees to his marriage proposal and the newly-engaged couple goes to the Brady house to tell Mike and Carol the good news. They make their announcement and Mike and Carol are quite surprised. But they've learned to be accepting of their children's choices now – they apologized to Jan not five minutes earlier – and give Wally and Marcia their blessing. Jan comes into the living room and hears Marcia's news and is very happy for her. Together the girls spontaneously decide to have their weddings on the same day in a double ceremony.

The family starts arrangements for the double wedding. Carol calls all the other kids (from work!) and tells them the good news. They all promise to be there. Soon Alice drops by the Brady house to help with the preparations; she's a welcome sight indeed. Alice has been married to Sam "the butcher" Franklin for almost four years now and no longer works for the Bradys. But she's back at the Brady house to help with the wedding. Marcia and Alice are in the family room trying out Marcia's dress design. Jan walks in and Alice gives her a fantastic greeting. Then Marcia tells Jan that she designed a dress for her, too. Unfortunately, Jan is not very keen on the design. She wants a traditional wedding and a traditional dress; Marcia wants a modern theme. Uh oh! The clash begins. Neither couple can seem to come to a compromise about the wedding theme and Wally and Phillip eventually even threaten to call the wedding off.

Phillip and Jan and Marcia and Wally decide to try to put their differences aside. They go to Phillip's favorite restaurant to talk things over. They manage to agree to agree on something, but they can't quite figure out what to agree on. Then Wally comes up with the idea: a twist on "spin the bottle." He takes the wine bottle, places it on the table, and spins it around. Whomever it points to when it's finished spinning gets to decide the theme for the wedding. The bottle stops halfway between Marcia and Jan. They all interpret that to mean that the wedding should be half-and-half. It'll be modern traditional or traditional modern. They call Mike and Carol from the restaurant and tell them that everything is back on schedule.

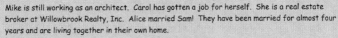

TIKI TALK

WHERE ARE MIKE, CAROL, AND ALICE NOW?

Mike is still working as an architect. Carol has gotten a job for herself. She is a real estate broker at Willowbrook Realty, Inc. Alice married Sam! They have been married for almost four years and are living together in their own home.

The wedding date is shifted up one week so that Peter can attend and all the preparations are being finished. The day of the wedding arrives. The ceremony is being held outside a nice hotel in City. Bobby, Peter, Greg, Mike, Carol, and Alice, Wally's parents, and Phillip's parents are all in attendance. Mike prepares to walk his two oldest girls down the aisle when a sudden downpour erupts and ruins the wedding. But Mike is a quick thinker and they move the whole thing to the Brady living room. The couples exchange vows. Jan and Phillip's are traditional while Marcia and Wally's are personal. Wally: "Marcia Brady, I love you with all my heart. And from this day forward everything I do will be with you, for you, and because of you." Marcia: "Wally Logan, I am proud to be your wife. I will try to make each day a part of our life to love, to remember, and to share. I love you." The rings are put on, kisses are had, and the reverend pronounces them man and wife and man and wife. Carol sings a brief rendition of "Because You Come to Me" and the ceremony is over.

The reception is in the living room, too, and the happy couples mill about talking to all their guests. A caterer brings out the cake and shows it to everyone. But Bobby is in the middle of a dramatic baseball story and accidentally knocks the caterer silly. He stumbles, Wally grabs the cake, then Phillip grabs the cake, then he accidentally rams the cake straight into Wally's face. It's just like Mike and Carol's wedding and everything has turned a perfect circle.

THE BRADY BRIDES (comedy)
SEASON ONE, 1981
Fridays 8:30-9:00pm ET on NBC

Production Notes: This is the first and only Brady series filmed before a live studio audience. The series was a quick follow-up to *The Brady Girls Get Married* and featured Marcia and Jan and their new husbands living together in the same household. The show got its start in a round-about way. Says a newspaper article from 1981: "The show's really the mating of 'The Brady Bunch' and another series [Sherwood] Schwartz has been trying to sell for six years. 'It was a show called "Full House" about two young couples who have to pool their resources and buy a house that they all share,' he said. 'I couldn't sell that until my son Lloyd, who now produces the series, came up with a solution. He said, "why don't we make the two girls who get married the two oldest Brady girls? Same show, but now you have the power of the old series behind you." So in a sense we gave the network what they wanted, a show with a built-in audience, and they gave us what we wanted.' "[6] The new series lasted only seven episodes.

Regulars =
Maureen McCormick ....Marcia Logan
Eve Plumb......................................Jan Brady Covington
Jerry Houser...Wally Logan
Ron Kuhlman.................................Phillip Covington, III
Florence Henderson ....Carol Brady
Ann B. Davis...Alice Franklin

#1 – Living Together
Airdate: March 6, 1981
Directed by Peter Baldwin
Executive Producer Sherwood Schwartz
Produced by Lloyd J. Schwartz and John Thomas Lenox
Written by Sherwood Schwartz & Lloyd J. Schwartz
Barbara Cason.......................... Miss Alverna Fritzsinger
Stuart Pankin...Frank
Bert Rosario ....Maxie
Steve Weldon ....Officer Dumont

It's right after the double wedding of Marcia & Wally and Jan & Phillip and both couples are looking for more suitable apartments for themselves. Carol just so happens to be working for Willowbrook Realty. Jan and Marcia meet her at one of her properties one day so that they can all go apartment hunting together. But the sisters are quite impressed with the house they're in. Both girls and their husbands cannot afford to buy a house on their own and Jan and Marcia have a brilliant idea: they *can* afford a house if they all live together. So the girls set about convincing their husbands to go in on the deal and they take the bait. Phillip warns them that it will be difficult – if not impossible – for two couples to live together but he nevertheless signs the paperwork. So all four move into this house, which is in Carol Brady and Alice Franklin's neighborhood. The house is at first stuffed with furniture from six different households, but they get that all sorted out. A neighbor of theirs, Miss Fritzsinger, drops by to welcome them to the neighborhood. When she finds out that both couples own the house, she is immediately wary. Young couples can be troublesome and loud, she thinks. That evening Marcia finds Wally up at two a.m. in the kitchen to get a glass of milk…in the buff. She's okay with Wally sleeping in the nude, but she's not so sure Phillip and Jan will appreciate him walking around the house like that. Their conversation wakes up Jan and Phillip who discover Wally in his birthday suit. Wally straps on an apron in order to confront the Covingtons about his choice of lifestyle. The couples argue about freedom of expression and Miss Fritzsinger drops by to tell them that they are too loud. She is chased away as soon as she sees Wally in the apron. They all go to bed, but the next morning the house is taped off with one side for each couple. Phillip argues that the tape is just like the border for a country: there's a reason countries have borders and it's so that everyone can get along. Marcia thinks it's childish. Then she starts complaining about the stink Phillip is raising…not from his words but from a science experiment he is conducting on his half of the living room. He has test tubes and beakers set up and is using stinky sulfur as part of the experiment. Then the pesky Miss Fritzsinger knocks on the door again but this time she is accompanied by a police officer. She complains that there is a suspicious stench coming from the house and as soon as she sees Phillip's setup, she says they're making drugs. Of course that's not true and the officer is familiar with Miss Fritzsinger's exaggerations. Nevertheless, he is compelled to ask Phillip what he's doing. Wally jumps to his rescue. He builds Phillip up to be a great scientist on the level with Jonas Salk. He says any interruption of Phillip's experiment will be like stopping the development of penicillin. The officer accepts the explanation and leaves. Miss Fritzsinger vows to catch them at something illegal. In response, Phillip drops his pants and sticks his derrière where Miss Fritzsinger can see it. She huffs off and all is well. After this display, the couples decide to remove the tape and get along.

#2 – Gorilla of My Dreams

Airdate: March 13, 1981
Directed by Peter Baldwin
Executive Producers Sherwood Schwartz and Lloyd Schwartz
Produced by John Thomas Lenox
Written by Sherwood Schwartz & Lloyd J. Schwartz
Keland Love .... Harry
Randy Stumpf .... Burglar
Byron Morrow .... Professor Thompson

As a toy salesman for Tyler Toys, sometimes Wally has to take his work home with him. This time it's an enormous stuffed gorilla named Phyllis. Wally is supposed to determine if his company should distribute the great ape. Wally needs the help of his business associate to determine the answer and invites him over. Harry is a young kid with an attitude and he rates the gorilla with an eight on a scale of ten. Harry's been working with Wally for quite a while and Wally trusts his opinions implicitly. After Harry leaves, Phillip informs the group that a professor is coming over tomorrow to talk about a grant possibility with Phillip. He insists to Wally that Phyllis has to go. Wally promises that Phyllis will be out of the living room in time. The next day arrives and Phillip comes home with Professor Thompson. Phillip checks the house and the coast seems to be clear of great apes. He offers to take the Professor's coat and opens the closet door to hang it up. Phyllis immediately falls out of the closet and appears to be attacking Phillip. Professor Thompson makes a bee line for the door and skedaddles; there goes Phillip's grant opportunity. Phillip is mad at Wally for ruining his chance at a grant. In the meantime, Carol comes over and practices self-defense with Jan and Marcia. There has been a rash of burglaries in the neighborhood and the neighborhood watch group is preparing a defense that includes karate. Carol teaches the girls how to smash a guy in the groin and how to flip an assailant. The girls seem well prepared, but everyone goes to bed that night still upset over the incident with Phyllis and Phillip. A burglar breaks in through the back door and encounters Phyllis, who growls loudly at him. The noise wakes up Wally and Marcia and they go into the living room to investigate. They see the burglar. He is armed and orders them to stand together in the living room. Wally's voice wakes up Phillip. Now he's held at gunpoint, too. Carol's self-defense techniques come in handy. Phillip disarms the burglar, which wakes Jan up. She comes rushing out of the bedroom and attacks the burglar, flipping him to the floor. They are all safe now. The story of the attempted robbery ends up in the local paper. Professor Thompson reads about Phillip's bravery and decides to offer him a second chance at a grant. This time, though, the grant is about home security. Wally and Phyllis are forgiven.

#3 – The Newlywed Game
Airdate: March 20, 1981 (pre-empted)
Directed by Peter Baldwin
Executive Producers Sherwood Schwartz and Lloyd Schwartz
Produced by John Thomas Lenox
Written by Warren Murray
Bob Eubanks .... Himself
Harvey Vernon .... Al Berg
Edith Fellows .... Sylvia Berg
Renee Jones...................................... Dorothea Anderson
Leonard Lightfoot .... Wayne Anderson
Johnny Jacobs .... Himself

Bob Eubanks' car breaks down in front of the Logan-Covington household. Marcia answers the door and offers for him to use their phone to call for roadside service. She recognizes him as the host of *The Newlywed Game* on television. She and Wally then not-so-surreptitiously "audition" for the show while they have the chance. Mr. Eubanks is impressed with their interactions and invites them to try out for the show. Success! Mr. Eubanks goes back outside to wait for the tow truck. In the meantime, Phillip, Jan, and Carol all arrive at the house. Marcia and Wally tell them their good news. Carol is especially excited and says that they should practice together for the show: Wally and Marcia versus Jan and Phillip. Carol acts as host and begins the practice round. Then there's a knock at the door again and Bob Eubanks is back. His battery is dead and he needs to call for help again. So they lead him to the phone and while he's on hold the couples and Carol begin the practice round. Mr. Eubanks is again impressed and asks Jan and Phillip to join the show as well. Now both couples will appear on television in the same episode of *The Newlywed Game*. The time for the show arrives and the Logans and Covingtons are pitted against the Bergs (an elderly couple) and the Andersons (a very passionate couple). It turns out that the Logans and Covingtons do not know each other quite as well as they thought they did. They end up tied for second place and lose to the Bergs. For their prize the Bergs win a home aquarium, which makes Phillip very jealous. The four go home feeling dejected. But then Phillip consoles them all by saying that it's okay that they don't know everything about each other already. This way there is something to look forward to discovering each and every day. Everyone is happy again.

EPISODE GUIDE

TIKI TALK

There was originally a tag at the end of this episode that went like this: Jan and Phillip are home in the living room. The doorbell rings. Phillip answers it and it's Monty Hall the gameshow host. Phillip then promptly slams the door in his face!

#4 – Cool Hand Phil

Airdate: April 10, 1981
Directed by Peter Baldwin
Executive Producers Sherwood Schwartz and Lloyd Schwartz
Produced by John Thomas Lenox
Written by Philip John Taylor

Keland Love	Harry
Alan Sues	Duke
Gloria Henry	Mrs. Marjorie Richardson
Bonnie Ebsen	Sunshine

Phillip comes home from work upset that he didn't receive any votes for popular professor at his college. His dull personality is getting him down so Wally offers to teach him a thing or two about being cool. But Phillip takes his new carefree personality too far and ends up ruining a lucrative architect deal for Jan. Now Jan and the other three roommates are all upset for one reason or another. Alice tries to reconcile Jan and Marcia and succeeds. But Wally and Phillip have to work their problems out for themselves. Wally finds Phillip sulking and drinking at a popular bar called Ken's Korral. He apologizes and gets drunk with Phillip. Then Wally and Phillip arrive back home to find Marcia, Jan, and Jan's client Mrs. Richardson trying to make amends and seal the architectural deal. But their inebriated demeanor almost scares Mrs. Richardson away again. The situation gets even crazier as a bunch of people from the bar come inside the house and start dancing. But Wally's quick on his feet and makes up an explanation that satisfies Mrs. Richardson. He says that this is all a demonstration for her benefit. He claims Jan wanted to go with a Western theme for Mrs. Richardson's summer home and they and everybody else are here in the house to give her a taste of Western life. Mrs. Richardson buys the explanation and tells Jan that she is a great architect. Problem solved. Phillip goes back to his old self having learned that you shouldn't pretend to be something you're not.

#5 – The Mom Who Came to Dinner
Airdate: March 27, 1981
Directed by Alan Myerson
Executive Producers Sherwood Schwartz and Lloyd Schwartz
Produced by John Thomas Lenox
Written by Mara Lideks
Keland Love..Harry
Donovan Womack... Policeman
Bruce Burton.. Paramedic
Joseph Sheen...Fireman

Mike Brady is out of town for a few days on a business trip and so Jan and Marcia invite Carol to spend the night at their house. Wally and Phillip think the night will be disastrous and they make a bet for $5 each against Marcia and Jan that something will go wrong. Carol shows up and they have a wonderful dinner together. Then it's time to go to sleep. Phillip volunteers to sleep in the living room on a cot while Carol bunks with Jan and Wally and Marcia stay together in their room. But soon Marcia convinces Wally that he should be the one on the cot. So everyone switches around. Wally can't sleep very well in the living room under the watchful eyes of Phillip's fish. Then the doorbell rings and Wally's young friend Harry drops in. He says his mother is working late and he doesn't want to spend the night in his house all alone. Can he sleep here? The doorbell woke everyone up and now they once again switch sleeping arrangements. Carol takes the cot, Marcia and Jan take Marcia's room, and Wally, Phillip, and Harry take Phillip's room. It's awkward for everyone and the only one who actually falls asleep is Harry. But the night isn't over yet. Alice drops by next because she has gotten locked out of her house. Carol lets her in and the two ladies decide that as long as they can't sleep they should play scrabble. Carol flips a light switch, which turns out to be a big mistake. Phillip wired the switch to a bunch of electronic devices in the house as well as to emergency services. All the lights and appliances start going crazy and then the cops show up. The firemen are next and the whole household (except Harry) has to explain to the emergency workers that there really is no emergency. Everyone goes back to their sleeping quarters. Then the paramedics burst through the front door, see Carol lying on the cot in the living room, assume she's a victim of some sort, and carry her out the front door. The night is indeed the disaster that Phillip and Wally predicted and they each end up five dollars richer.

#6 – The Siege
Airdate: April 3, 1981
Directed by Herbert Kenwith
Executive Producers Sherwood Schwartz and Lloyd Schwartz
Produced by John Thomas Lenox
Written by Hope Sherwood & Mark Esslinger
Keland Love..Harry
Joseph Campanella................................Inspector Rankin
Patrick Cronin ....Inspector Mann
Jacqui Evans..Beautiful Brunette

Phillip has yet another grant opportunity, this time with the government. He needs a government clearance to go forth with the application process. Wally, meanwhile, has accumulated $70 in parking tickets and has not paid them. He and Jan are home alone when there's a knock on the door. Wally opens it and it's a guy who has been staking out the house for the past hour. Wally assumes he's there to subpoena him for the parking tickets. In truth, he's an inspector with the government conducting Phillip's clearance. Wally is paranoid and at the spur of the moment decides to pretend to be Phillip so that the inspector will go away. The inspector, we later learn, now has his suspicions aroused because he knows what Phillip looks like and it's not like Wally. Inspector Mann comes to the house a second time to find out more. This time everyone is home, but Phillip can't very well tell him that he's the real Phillip with Wally standing right there. So Phillip and Marcia pretend to be George and Martha, traveling aquarium salesmen. Harry comes over with a toy ray gun and tells Inspector Mann that the gun is none of his business. Now the Inspector reports to his superior and fashions an elaborate, far-fetched theory as to what is going on in the Logan-Covington household. He thinks that Wally (aka Phillip) is a liar, that Harry is a mastermind arms dealer, and that "George and Martha" are accessories to whatever criminal activity "Phillip" is up to. Later that evening the inspectors conduct a raid on the unsuspecting roommates, Carol, and Harry. Wally thinks it's all for a few unpaid parking tickets, so he writes a check for $70 and throws it out the front door. The inspectors are not amused and they move in with their guns drawn. Finally, the misunderstanding is all cleared up. Phillip is awarded his federal clearance. Wally is subpoenaed the next day for his parking tickets – for real this time.

TIKI TALK

An alternate ending to this episode showed all cast members in the F.B.I. station sitting in a room. Above them are taped their mugshots. Harry asks if he can take his home with him.

#7 – A Pretty Boy Is like a Melody

Airdate: April 17, 1981
Directed by Tony Mordente
Executive Producers Sherwood Schwartz and Lloyd Schwartz
Produced by John Thomas Lenox
Written by Richard Gurman

Keland Love..Harry
Mr. Blackwell.. Himself
Tom Gagen.. Brandon
Tom Jordan... Lance

It's Marcia's turn to have her career put on the line by her roommates. She is scheduled to have some of her designs shown in a fashion show in front of Mr. Blackwell, a famous fashion critic. Two male models come over to the house to get measured for the clothes and Wally becomes insanely jealous. He threatens the models with bodily harm and the models storm off leaving Marcia without anyone to wear her clothes in the fashion show, which is tomorrow. Wally realizes that he was acting like a jerk and goes out and buys Marcia a huge display of flowers with a giant yellow happy face smacked right in the middle of them. Marcia finally forgives Wally for his behavior, but she is still out two male models. Wally volunteers himself for one of the positions. Now Marcia needs one more guy...Phillip is standing right there so why not him? At first he refuses but eventually he breaks down for the good of Jan and Marcia. The next day the fashion show is ready to go. Marcia gets Wally and Phillip dressed in their first outfits and the show begins. Phillip comes out in a fencing outfit, then Wally sports a scuba wetsuit. Then Phillip puts on a ski outfit and finally Wally is supposed to come on stage in small bathing trunks nicknamed "jungle fever." But Wally is unable to get out of his wetsuit and there's a last minute change in staging. Phillip is virtually forced into the tiny trunks and thrust on stage. He's very self-conscious but he goes out there in public anyway. The fashion show is a hit with the buyers and Mr. Blackwell pays Marcia a compliment.

A VERY BRADY CHRISTMAS (television movie)
Friday December 18, 1988; 8:00-10:00pm ET on NBC

Production Notes: The last time America saw the Brady family was in 1981, and that was just Marcia, Jan, Carol, & Alice. It is time again to give the public a Brady refresher. Says Lloyd Schwartz, "Sherwood feels there is nothing more American than Christmas and the Bradys. Why not put them together? It worked. Highest movie-of-the-week rating in two years." Yes, *A Very Brady Christmas* was the most successful post-original series endeavor. Families liked gathering around the television and watching the Bradys come together over the holiday table and wax nostalgic about the good old days while learning about the new additions to the ever-growing clan.

This NBC movie of the week was the second-highest rated television special of 1988, after *The Karen Carpenter Story*. The special won a Young Artist Award in 1989 for "Best Family TV Special." Jaclyn Bernstein was nominated for her own Young Artist Award that year for her performance as Jessica Logan, but did not win.

Airdate: December 18, 1988
Nielsen Rating: 25.1
Directed by Peter Baldwin
Executive Producer Sherwood Schwartz
Produced by Lloyd J. Schwartz and Barry Berg

125

Written by Sherwood Schwartz & Lloyd J. Schwartz

Robert Reed .... Mike Brady
Florence Henderson .... Carol Brady
Ann B. Davis.. Alice Franklin
Maureen McCormick .... Marcia Logan
Eve Plumb..................................... Jan Brady Covington
Jennifer Runyon .... Cindy Brady
Barry Williams .... Greg Brady
Christopher Knight...................................... Peter Brady
Michael Lookinland .... Bobby Brady
Jerry Houser... Wally Logan
Ron Kuhlman............................... Phillip Covington, III
Caryn Richman .... Nora Brady
Carol Huston .... Valerie Thomas
Jaclyn Bernstein... Jessica Logan
G. W. Lee .... Mickey Logan
Zachary Bostrom.. Kevin Brady
F.J. O'Neil.. Mr. Prescott
Barbara Mallory .... Mrs. Powell
Nick Toth.. Mr. Powell
Selma Archerd... Mrs. Crane
Tonya Lee Williams .... Belinda
Ines Pedroza... TV Announcer
Lewis Arquette .... Sam/Santa
Lenny Garner .... Howie
Doug Carfrae... Donald
Frances Louis Turner .... Nurse
Gerry Black... Police Chief
Patricia Mullins... Receptionist
Jack Kutcher.. Guard #1
Gilbert G. Garcia... Guard #2
Bart Braverman.. Mechanic
Phillip Richard Allen.................................... Ted Roberts

Christmas 1988 is just around the corner and Mike and Carol have decided to surprise each other with some very special gifts. Mike wants to spend Christmas in Japan and Carol would like to go to Greece. Their trips coincide, so they obviously can't go both places at one. The couple runs into each other at the travel agency where they each learn of their separate plans. They go home debating which place they'd like to go. Meanwhile, Alice has shown up at the Brady house crying on their front doorstep. Poor Alice – her husband Sam left her for another woman! Here's the note Sam wrote:

"Dear Alice,

I lied to you. I wasn't working nights plucking chickens; I met a younger woman. At first we just traded meatloaf recipes. Then one night she asked me over to season her rump roast. I guess I'm an old fool, but I fell for her like a pound of ground chuck."

TIKI TALK

The script to *A Very Brady Christmas* contains another line at the end of Sam's note: "I'll always love you, but I'm crazy about Bambi." Really, Sam? That's cold. Meat locker cold.

It's quite a blow to Alice and Mike and Carol invite her to stay at their house as long as she wants. She does just that. Later she, Mike, and Carol are discussing Christmas. Alice comes up with the idea that instead of going to Greece or Japan Mike and Carol should have Christmas at home with all the kids and their families. The Bradys think it's a great idea and they use their vacation fund to fly everyone in.

The kids, spouses, and grandchildren all arrive but they each come with their own set of personal problems. Greg had to come without his wife Nora because she decided to go to her own family's home instead. Greg does bring his son Kevin, though. Marcia's husband Wally has been laid off from Tyler Toys because of downsizing. Peter is afraid of commitment. He's dating his boss Valerie but can't work up the guts to ask her to marry him because she makes more money than he does. Jan and Phillip are having marital problems and Phillip is in the process of moving out of the house. Bobby quit business graduate school in order to become a racecar driver but he hasn't told his parents the truth yet. And finally, Cindy is feeling like she is still treated like a child. The "kids" have all hidden their problems from their parents, which perhaps is not the wisest thing to do in this family.

Mike and Carol are dealing with their own issue, too. Carol sold some land to a guy named Ted Roberts who subsequently hired Mike as the architect on his project "Roberts Plaza." Mike wants to make extra structural changes to Roberts' building: changes that would increase Roberts' budget by ten percent. Roberts does not appreciate Mike's recommendation and he takes it upon himself to call Carol up and tell her that she'd better change her husband's mind or else. Mike confronts Roberts on the job site the next day and quits. Presumably their troubles with Roberts are over.

Christmas Day arrives and Mike is giving a speech before dinner. One at a time, the kids interrupt his speech and confess their problems in front of everyone. Jan and Phillip made up that morning. Wally got a new job at Prescott Toys thanks to Mike's sly intervention that morning. Cindy tells the group that she's tired of being treated like a child; they had her sitting at the kids' table with Mickey, Jessica, and Kevin! Bobby confesses that he dropped out of school a year ago to become a racecar driver. Mike and Carol aren't too happy to hear his news, but they come around and tell him they'll support him if that's what he really wants to do. Peter and Valerie propose to each other. And Nora shows up at the door to spend Christmas Day with Greg and Kevin and the whole family.

All is well and Mike is getting ready to carve the turkey. Unfortunately, he is interrupted yet again, but this time it's because of a phone call. Ted Roberts is on the line and he is begging Mike to come to the build site because the building has collapsed and there are two security guards trapped inside. The architect who replaced Mike is out of town, so Mike is the guards' only hope…never mind the firefighters or other rescue workers…so it's Mike Brady to the rescue. Mike shows up at the job site where a crowd has gathered, including the local media. He enters the rubble to see what the situation is. And then the building collapses even further and now *Mike* is trapped inside! The Safety Commission shows up and says that it's not safe for anyone to enter the building. Thus it's up to the people who are trapped to rescue themselves. The whole Brady family is present now, too. They've been notified about Mike's accident and they're all there waiting anxiously to see if he will make it out. A lot of time passes and finally the two security guards emerge, dirty and shaken but okay. But where's Mike? He still hasn't come out. So Cindy pulls Carol aside to lift up her hopes by reminding her that miracles do happen. Carol starts to sing "O Come, All Ye Faithful" and the whole crowd joins in. The song acts like a lasso and ropes Mike Brady, giving him the extra energy he needs to free himself. He's pulled right out the rubble by their singing and indeed it is a miracle. He's a-okay! The reporter on the scene makes a note that the miracle happened on 34th Street; the Bradys have made their own mark in history now. Everyone goes home happy.

There's one more loose end to tie up and that's with Alice and Sam. The doorbell rings during the re-heated dinner and it's Santa Claus. Santa is really Sam dressed up in a costume and he appeals to Alice for forgiveness saying he'll never do anything like that again. Alice takes him back. Now, finally, everything is perfect and the Bradys can celebrate the rest of the season in peace and harmony.

EPISODE GUIDE

TIKI TALK

WHERE ARE THEY NOW?

It's 1988 and you know what that means: big hair, mustaches, and shoulder pads. It's been about seven years since the Brady family was last seen in a new episode on television. Here's what they're doing now.

Mike is still working as an architect and Carol is still a realtor, although she is now working for Advantage Properties instead of Willowbrook. Alice is still married to Sam "the butcher," but her marriage is on the rocks after Sam cheats on her and leaves her crying into a note written on butcher paper.

Greg is married now to a woman named Nora. They have a son Kevin who looks to be *at least* seven years old. How can that be? Kevin didn't exist in 1981 – in fact, Greg was even married seven years ago. (The actor, Zachary Bostrom, was born in January 1981.) It's a mystery. Perhaps the character Kevin is younger than he really looks.

Peter has severed ties with the Air Force and now works in an office as a businessman. He becomes engaged to his boss Valerie Thomas at the end of the movie.

Bobby has quit graduate school to become a racecar driver.

Marcia and Wally are still together and they have two children, Jessica and Mickey. Jessica, too, looks too old to have been conceived after April 1981 when *The Brady Brides* was cancelled. The mystery of the rapidly aging kids continues....

Jan is having marital trouble and Phillip is moving out. Luckily, they work out their differences at Christmastime and make up.

Finally, Cindy is still in college. Yes, her parents dropped her off at school in early 1981 and she's finally graduating in December 1988. Seven years' of study...perhaps she was a quintuple major?

THE BRADYS (drama)
SEASON ONE, 1990
Fridays 8:00-9:00pm ET on CBS

Buoyed from the success of *A Very Brady Christmas*, the Brady family makes one more stab at television ratings. Lloyd Schwartz says: "[*The Bradys* was] never supposed to be a series. After the huge rating of *A Very Brady Christmas*, CBS bought three more movies-of-the-week, but the network felt they needed a series more. We really didn't want to do it. We felt that the Brady franchise would be better served with a movie every six months or so, but studios and network are built on series, and our opinion didn't matter. We also felt that our stories were more adult and would be better served to be on at 9:00. The network put the series on at 8:00 against *Full House,* which had kids. We lost." Unfortunately for the Schwartzes and all else involved, the series was a flop. Rick Marin from The Washington Times said, "The desperate strategy behind CBS' two-hour premiere of 'The Bradys,' tonight at 8 on Channels 9 and 11, is to hit the yuppie demographic where it lives: its Achilles' heel for junk-culture nostalgia. Everybody watched 'The Brady Bunch,' right? Everybody watches 'thirtysomething.' So why not 'bradysomething'? Watch tonight's mawkish, laughably unfunny hugfest and you'll see why not."[7]

America could not handle the Bradys in their new dramatic roles. It was just too much for fans of the time-won original series and viewers chose not to watch Marcia become a drunk, Bobby get in a racing accident, and Peter reveal the fact he's been engaged four times. As Marin succinctly states, "Just because people wanted to watch 'America's favorite family' when they were growing up doesn't mean we want to live our adult life with them, too."

"Conceptually it made sense. They were calling it 'Brady Something' kind of like 'Thirty Something,'" says Susan Olsen. "They thought that we could transition to a serious format, but the critics called it 'Brady Nothing.'" "Even if it had been done really, really well I still don't think the public would have liked it."[8]

All the original cast reprised their roles save for Maureen McCormick who was replaced by Leah Ayers.

Regulars =

Robert Reed .... Mike Brady
Florence Henderson .... Carol Brady
Leah Ayres.. Marcia Logan
Eve Plumb.. Jan Covington
Susan Olsen.. Cindy Brady
Barry Williams... Greg Brady
Christopher Knight....................................... Peter Brady
Mike Lookinland.. Bobby Brady
Ann B. Davis.. Alice Franklin
Jerry Houser .... Wally Logan
Ron Kuhlman............................... Phillip Covington, III
Caryn Richman .... Nora Brady
Martha Quinn... Tracy Brady
Ken Michelman.. Gary Greenberg
Jaclyn Bernstein .... Jessica Logan
Michael Melby .... Mickey Logan
Jonathan Weiss... Kevin Brady
Valerie Ick .... Patty Covington

#1 – The Brady 500 or Start Your Engines (Part I) and Here We Grow Again (Part II)
Airdate: February 9, 1990
Directed by Bruce Bilson
Executive Producers Sherwood Schwartz & Lloyd J. Schwartz
Produced by Barry Berg
Written by Sherwood Schwartz & Lloyd J. Schwartz
Mary Cadorette .... Valerie Thomas
Lennie Garner .... Howie
Richard Heckert .... Dr. Stevens
Sheila Shaw.. Maxine
Hope Juber .... Erica Hopkins
Jack Stauffer.. Track Paramedic
Greg Collins.. Track Security Guard
John Wheeler.. Joe Fletcher
Kim Maxwell .... Lisa

131

Darcy De Moss ....Donna
Dinah Lenney...Laura
Jeffrey J. Nowinski .... Steve
Barbara Mallory ....Mrs. Powell
Nick Toth..Mr. George Powell
Leonard Ross ....Man
Stu Nahan.. Track Announcer
Dabbs Greer .... The Minister

Bobby won the Riverdale 200 and is set to race in the Nashville 500. The whole family is excited about Bobby's success and Mike, Carol, and Cindy make the trip to Nashville to watch the race live and in person. Everyone else watches it on television. After the race is underway for a while, Bobby's car is in trouble. It stalls at the top of the track and rolls down toward the bottom, Bobby helpless to control it. Bobby gets T-boned at close to 200mph. The family anxiously has to await news from Bobby's doctor to see if he's going to be okay or not. The rest of the family immediately flies to Tennessee to support Bobby. Doctor Greg has to give them the bad news. "Several vertebrae have been compressed, causing his spinal cord severe trauma…Bobby's paralyzed from the waist down. He can't walk." It's devastating news.

Bobby tries to keep his spirits up and undergoes rehab in Nashville until he is stable enough to come home. Wally, Marcia, Mickey, and Jessica are now living at the Brady house because Wally has lost his job and then their house. Additionally, Alice and Peter arrive at the Brady residence to welcome Bobby home. He arrives and coasts down a ramp Wally built for him into the living room. Carol is having a hard time seeing Bobby in a wheelchair but the young Brady is determined not to bring everybody down.

Meanwhile, the other Brady kids are having problems of their own. Jan and Phillip desperately want a baby but can't conceive. Peter quit his job and broke up with his fiancée Valerie. She put work over her relationship with Peter and he therefore ended it. In light of Bobby's injury, Greg is debating whether or not to switch specialties from obstetrics to orthopedics. Finally, Cindy doesn't know whether she should start dating her boss at work; he's an older man with two kids ages 15 and 12. So, Peter moves back home and is immediately on the rebound, shuffling girls around his schedule like a deck of cards. Wally is offered a job as an insurance salesman, which he immediately takes. Bobby, on the other hand, is getting more and more depressed. He can't seem to make progress fast enough. Carol is pressing him to call his ex-girlfriend Tracy because she has been trying to reach him ever since the accident. Bobby refuses because he's still sore that she broke up with him. But a few days later Peter brings a surprise home with him: Tracy. Bobby is at first upset with Peter for doing this and he tells Tracy that it's over. Carol overhears his conversation and admonishes Bobby for being so rude. He's really only denying Tracy because he's in a wheelchair and feels sorry for himself. But deep down he still loves her and she loves him. After Carol's stern pep talk, Bobby and Tracy go to their favorite lake and talk things over. Bobby proposes to her right then and there.

Wedding bells are in the air and the Brady family rushes to put the ceremony on while Tracy's sister and parents are still in town. They get the same reverend who officiated over Mike and Carol's wedding to perform Bobby and Tracy's. The wedding takes place in the Brady living room, just like Marcia and Jan's. It's a nice ceremony and Bobby heroically stands on his own two feet when he says his vows. They kiss, the knot is tied, and Tracy's sister gives birth to a baby boy upstairs in the Brady house during the end of the ceremony.

#2 – A Moving Experience
Airdate: February 16, 1990
Directed by Bob Sweeney
Executive Producers Sherwood Schwartz & Lloyd J. Schwartz
Produced by Barry Berg
Written by Sherwood Schwartz & Lloyd J. Schwartz

Anne Haney	Mrs. Abrogast
Phillip Glasser	Jake Greenberg
Jennifer Kolchier	Carly Greenberg
Jerry Hauck	Borden
Pat Crawford Brown	Mabel
Aaron Lustig	Fred Meadows
Dyana Ortelli	Lisa Wallach
Patricia Mullins	Secretary
Herbert Edelman	Gene Dickinson

Mike and Carol get a certified letter in the mail telling them that they have six months to vacate their property because the city is building a freeway off-ramp through their neighborhood. The house has so many memories for them that they will do anything in their power to save it. Unfortunately, protesting to their district representative and to City Council is not enough. The city plans to go through with the freeway no matter how many homes stand in their way. The only thing left in the Bradys' arsenal is to physically move the house to a new location. That's exactly what they do. No longer is the Brady residence located at 4222 Clinton Way! The house is moved eleven blocks to an unnamed street. During the month-long process to get the house moved, Carol, Mike, Marcia, Wally, Jessica, and Mickey all have to live in a two-bedroom rental property right under the flight path of a major airport. It's crowded, to say the least. Peter temporarily moves in with Bobby and Tracy who are now in a place of their own. And, Greg accepts a new job as Head of Obstetrics at Tower General Hospital in City. He, Nora, and Kevin are moving to the city; Nora will work as a nurse in the same hospital. Meanwhile, Cindy's relationship with her boss Gary is becoming more complicated when he introduces her to his children Carly and Jake. The kids don't take to the idea of their father dating and storm out of Gary's office in a huff. All this time Mike is being asked by a local community group (the Committee of Concerned Citizens) if he would run for City Council next term. He thinks about it and after getting a lot of pressure from his family to run, he calls them up and tells them they've got themselves a candidate.

#3 – Hat in the Ring
Airdate: February 23, 1990
Directed by Nancy Malone
Executive Producers Sherwood Schwartz & Lloyd J. Schwartz

Produced by Barry Berg
Written by Sherwood Schwartz & Lloyd J. Schwartz
Charlie Spradling .... Teri Dickinson
Fran Ryan .... Housewife
Aaron Lustig .... Fred Meadows
Dyana Ortelli .... Lisa Wallach
Jerry Hauck .... Borden
Joe Lucas .... Delivery Man
Frank DeVol .... Man #2
David Sage .... Glen Martinson
Charles Dougherty .... Dennis
Fred Holliday .... Leo Barwell
Jay Arlen Jones .... Foreman
Herbert Edelman .... Gene Dickinson

Wally loses his job as an insurance salesman because he beats his boss Joe Fletcher in golf and then accidentally hits him with the golf cart, sending him flying into a water hazard. But there's a job waiting for him at home as public relations manager for Mike Brady's City Council campaign. Wally eagerly accepts the position and Peter falls in as Mike's campaign manager (he takes a leave of absence from his job at People for a Better Planet). Mike's opponent is Gene Dickinson, the current City Council Representative. (Rep. Dickinson previously ignored the Bradys' and their neighbor's plea to get the city to move the freeway they were planning. As a consequence, the Bradys had their entire house moved eleven blocks away from Clinton Way.) So Mike, Wally, and Peter hit the campaign trail. A few days before the actual election, Mike gets a piece of blackmail. It's a fake newspaper article with a picture of Mike holding a stack of money in his hands accusing him of taking bribes. Naturally, Mike never did anything like that. It turns out that Dickinson's campaign manager Leo Barwell is the one who is trying to set Mike up for scandal. Dickinson fires Barwell and the article is never printed. Election Day arrives and the votes are in: Brady 13,119, Dickinson 12, 871. Michael Thomas Brady is elected the new Representative of the 4th District to City Council.

#4 – Bottoms Up
Airdate: March 2, 1990
Directed by Bruce Bilson
Executive Producers Sherwood Schwartz & Lloyd J. Schwartz
Produced by Barry Berg
Written by Sandra K. Siegel
Bill Cort .... Morty St. James
John Terrence .... Jordan Armstrong

Marcia is feeling left out and unwanted. She isn't working, Wally is constantly losing jobs, and Carol is taking over the parenting of Mickey and Jessica. Marcia tries applying for a fashion job with Home of St. James, but Mr. St. James turns her down quite brutally. She tries to find comfort through Wally, but he's not listening. All

134

he's concerned about is getting Jordan Armstrong (aka the Condo King of Northern California) to make a deal with Mike. Mr. Armstrong wants Mike to "waive" some property zoning laws so that he can build new condos, strip malls, and parking lots. Mike doesn't want to compromise his own principles and turns Mr. Armstrong down. Meanwhile, Greg, Nora, Bobby, and Jan are appealing to Mike – as Councilman – to help fund a new Trauma Center. The Center will coordinate emergency medicine communications so that emergency patients are delivered to the appropriate hospital and care as swiftly as possible. They need the City's funding or else the funding from a private donation. Wally has an idea on how to get the funding. He asks Mr. Armstrong if he will fund the Center in exchange for Mike allowing him to build the condos. Armstrong comes up with the donation for the Trauma Center and Mike names the Center after him: the Armstrong Trauma Center. Little does Mike know that he's now in an awkward position. When he finds out, he has no choice but to fire Wally. Cindy is experiencing her own troubles with her boss Gary. Cindy's been offered a great new job as co-host for "LA Tomorrow," a local television program. But that means she will have to leave KBLA…and Gary…if she accepts the offer. After a little fight, Gary comes through and says that he is putting Cindy before "Cindy at Sunrise." He gives her a small pay raise and a new format for her show that includes some time to talk about issues with local fans. During this whole time, Marcia has been hitting the booze heavily. With no one in whom to confide her troubles, she picks up the bottle and doesn't stop. She almost drives the kids in the car while drunk and she shows up to the ground breaking ceremony for the Armstrong Trauma Center raucously drunk. Finally, the family realizes that Marcia has a problem. Marcia, too, comes to terms with her alcohol dependency. She talks things over with Carol and Wally. Then she decides to be one of Cindy's first guests on her new radio talk show so that she can share her experiences with the public in the hope of helping someone else out there who has the same problem. Marcia will get the help she needs.

#5 – The Party Girls
Airdate: March 9, 1990
Directed by Dick Martin
Executive Producers Sherwood Schwartz & Lloyd J. Schwartz
Produced by Barry Berg
Written by Ed Scharlach
Gerard Maguire..Graham Riley
Alison Rockwell... Party Guest
Bob Garon.. Party Guest

After being fired by Mike, poor Wally is out another job. But the Brady girls have an idea. Nora, Marcia, and Tracy all band together to propose starting a catering business together called The Party Girls. Wally thinks that he should be a PR man and he bravely and humbly approaches Mike for a loan to start his own PR business. Not long after, Marcia, Nora, and Tracy approach Mike and Carol with their own idea and ask for a $30,000 loan to cover start-up costs. Mike and Carol think it over and come back the next morning with an offer. They will give the girls the money if they can hire someone to do the PR for them. Enter Wally. Wally likes the idea of working to advertise The Party Girls and he joins the company. The girls get started and purchase the lease to Sam's Butcher Shop from Alice. Sam is retiring and is putting his building lease up for sale. The girls move in right away and things get going thanks to Wally's public relations skills. Meanwhile, the Brady boys

Greg and Peter are at odds with each other this week. Greg forgot that he committed to seeing a Lakers game with Peter one weekend. When Pete shows up, Greg bails on him because he would rather go with Nora and Kevin to Kevin's teachers' conferences. Peter is angry at his older brother's betrayal. The two fuss and feud and things go from bad to worse. Greg ends up telling Peter, "From now on, pal, you don't even exist." Peter retorts, "That's the best news I've had all day." Things are getting ugly between the two brothers and Nora tries to conceive of a way for them to make up. There is a party the Party Girls are catering at the Brady house soon. Their waiters are already booked at another party that night, so Nora asks Peter and Greg if they would fill in. They both say yes, unaware that the other will be there. When they find each other at the party, they do their best to ignore one another. But then it happens. Peter chokes on an hors d'oeuvre and can't breathe. Greg rushes over and tries the Heimlich maneuver, but to no avail. Pete passes out and Greg has to conduct pulmonary resuscitation on his brother: he gives him mouth to mouth! Greg successfully dislodges the food and Peter comes to saying, "I didn't know you cared." The brothers make up and the party is a success. The Party Girls end up having to move to a bigger place because Sam's old shop is too small. That's great news to Alice because Sam has been driving her crazy ever since he retired. The Girls move, Sam goes back to work in his old digs, and all is well.

BONUS EPISODES!

There was a lot of drama going on behind the scenes in *The Bradys*. It was getting to be a very difficult set to work on, and everyone was on tenterhooks. Some of the cast didn't like the storylines, CBS and Paramount were unsure of them as well, and Sherwood Schwartz decided that he had had enough of Robert Reed. (For more background, read the Schwartzes' book Brady, Brady, Brady and Barry Williams' book Growing Up Brady.) So he decided to commission a script that kills off the character of Mike Brady.

It's true. Beloved TV dad Mike Brady was scripted to die in a helicopter crash. The American Radio and Television Script (ARTS) Library has this never-filmed script. The script was written by Lloyd Schwartz himself. In a nutshell, here's what happens.

"Changes"
Written by Lloyd J. Schwartz
Script dated February 16, 1990

Gary decides he wants to marry Cindy, but his children Jake and Carly want nothing to do with her and Cindy is uncomfortable with that.

Jan finds out she's pregnant.

Local television news channels announce that a helicopter in which Mike Brady is flying has crashed. It's unknown who survived.

Soon, the audience follows the Brady family to the hospital where they learn that the pilot of the copter survived, but Mike Brady did not. Greg says, "The pilot is here. They never even found Dad. Nothing."[9]

Carol Brady sings, "You'll Never Walk Alone" at Mike's funeral. Jan says she'll name her baby Michael if it's a boy (and Katy if it's a girl).

Another follow-up episode was written, but also never filmed:

"Where Do We Go from Here?"
Written by Sandra Kay Siegel
Script dated February 8, 1990

This episode takes place after Mike Brady has died and deals primarily with how Carol Brady is reacting to her husband's death. It's not good. At one point, Carol is looking at a picture of Mike and exclaims, "Damn you, Mike! Why?! If you really loved me, you wouldn't have done this to me!"[10] We all say things we don't mean in our bereavement, but this seems unfair. It's not like Mike died on purpose. Soon, Carol can't take things anymore and runs away to a ski lodge where she and Mike once went when they were young. But, Cindy and Gary track her down and take her back home.

Also, Peter replaces his father as Councilman.

Finally, it's revealed that Carol has an aunt named Bridget. (The Brady "kids" consult great-aunt Bridget when they try to find the name of the lodge Carol ran away to.) Then Bridget comes to a big family dinner with the whole Brady clan, including Gary, Jake, and Carly. Bridget reveals herself to be a staunch Anti-Semite and Carol kicks her out.

So that's where *The Bradys* would have gone had it not been cancelled. As Paul Harvey used to say, now you know the rest of the story.

The Unrealized Spin-offs

This chapter has taken readers through the original series of *The Brady Bunch* and its six spin-offs: the cartoon, variety show, two TV movies, sitcom, and dramatic series. But those are just the spin-offs that were actually filmed. There are several more that never saw the light of day. Here they are, some for the first time ever.

Idea #1: "Kelly's Kids"

Remember *The Brady Bunch* episode in season five featuring the Bradys' friends the Kellys and their three newly-adopted sons? Well, this episode was originally written with the intent of turning it into a series. The Kellys appeared on *The Brady Bunch* in order to get viewers to swing over to the show.

On June 3, 1975 Sherwood Schwartz wrote a letter to the FCC asking if the new series *Kelly's Kids* would qualify for the children's programming exception to the new primetime broadcasting rule. The FCC wrote back and said it didn't know because it didn't know enough about the series.

Based on that letter, we know that Sherwood was still thinking about this series a year after *The Brady Bunch* had been cancelled. Alas, it never came to fruition and all that remains is the single episode that aired on *The Brady Bunch*.

Idea #2: "The Brand New Brady Bunch" aka "Brady House":

In 1983, Sherwood penned a new series proposal for the Brady family. This would have taken place about two years after *The Brady Brides* was cancelled and five years before *A Very Brady Christmas*. Here's the premise.

Mike is now semi-retired and working as a part-time lecturer on architecture. One day, Carol is out shopping, and her purse is stolen by a kid. Carol goes to court to identify the kid as a twelve-year-old boy named Johnny. She learns that Johnny is a street kid and feels sorry for him. So she asks the court to release him into her custody and the court complies. She talks things over with Mike, and they decide to adopt Johnny. So they do.

Then, their hearts swell even bigger when they learn that there is an epidemic of unwanted older children in this county. So they adopt three more children. Their biological kids are all grown, but the house feels too empty without them, so now there are four more children in the Brady home. In addition to Johnny, there is Chi Lin, an eight-year-old Vietnamese girl, Louella, a fourteen-year-old black girl with a leg brace, and Ryan, a six-year-old deaf boy.

Says Sherwood: "Basically, kids are kids. They need love; they need to be heard; and they need to be respected."[11]

Idea #3: "Brady Time" aka "Brady Machine"

It's now 1990 and all the "real" spin-offs have been filmed. Sherwood decides to pitch the idea of his own Brady-related cartoon series to networks. This one is different than *The Brady Kids* that aired back in the 1970s.

Brady Time is proposed as an animated show featuring all nine main cast members of the original series as cartoon characters. The family has a time machine that can transport them back in time and all across the world. The kicker is that when they go back in time they have to blend in with the locals. "When the Brady family is in Japan, they look Japanese; when they're in Egypt, they look Egyptian; when they're in Brazil, the look South American," Sherwood writes.[12]

When they are in the past, the Bradys attempt to live like the locals. Hence, the series is intended to be educational. Sherwood pitched the idea to DIC Entertainment along with another cartoon – this one a feature film or television movie – called *The Shadow That Ran Away*. DIC is the company that gave us *Inspector Gadget* and *The Super Mario Brothers*. They must have passed on Sherwood's shows.

Idea #4: "Brady House"

Although the title is the same as the series pitched in 1983, the plot of this 1995 newer spin-off is quite different. This *Brady House* is a joint effort from Sherwood and Lloyd Schwartz. Here's what happens.

Mike has passed away (Robert Reed has been dead for 3 years at this point). Carol wants to sell the house, but changes her mind when random college students start coming by thinking that she advertised a room for rent. She didn't – it was a mix-up with the address in the paper – but the kids' presence gives her an idea. She talks it over with Alice (who is again abandoned by Sam for another woman). The two ladies decide that they can live together in the Brady home with six college students. They choose six from the flock waiting below and that's how the show starts.

The sitcom would have been filmed before a live audience and the six Brady children and their families would have had the opportunity to make guest appearances.

Idea #5: A Bobby Brady Show

It has been 22 years since viewers last saw the Brady Bunch on scripted television. In July 2012, actor and producer Vince Vaughn announces that he is working with CBS to create a new Brady spin-off. The show is to be about a grown Bobby Brady and his family. Bobby is now a divorcee with kids who remarries a woman with kids of her own. Additionally, they have their own child. Sound familiar? History repeats itself, it seems. Mike Mariano was slated to write for the series and Peter Billingsley (of *A Christmas Story* fame) was also to be involved. However, CBS ultimately rejected the series idea and nothing was ever filmed.

The details of the show are somewhat mysterious, including its title and whether or not Vaughn and company had gone so far as to cast any actors. Mike Lookinland – the original Bobby Brady – says that he found out about the show the same way everybody else did: from the Internet. He was never asked anything about it by CBS, let alone whether or not he would reprise his role.

EPISODE GUIDE

THE SPOOFS & TRIBUTES

Finally, there are the many spoofs, parodies, tributes and homages made to and of *The Brady Bunch*. When something is as successful as *The Brady Bunch*, it is ripe for the picking and fodder for snarky talk show hosts, other television series to make fun of, and even for feature films to be developed around the show.

The Brady Bunch has been parodied on *The Simpsons, Saturday Night Live*, and *That '70s Show*. The "characters" have appeared on shows like *Day by Day, The Love Boat*, and *Hi, Honey, I'm Home*. A tribute even appeared on the sci-fi drama *The X-Files*. There was a play called "The Real Live Brady Bunch" and another called "A Very Brady Musical." A television movie based on Barry Williams' book *Growing Up Brady* aired in 2000. Snickers premiered a *Brady* commercial during the 2015 Super Bowl of all things. There are many, many more instances: too many to list here.

Most well-known are the three 1990s parodies, two of which were highly successful feature films. *The Brady Bunch Movie, A Very Brady Sequel*, and *The Brady Bunch in the Whitehouse* (a television movie) were all spoofs cum homages to the original series. They cast the Brady family in contemporary times with all the trappings of their 1970s fake naïveté and absurd positivity. There was even a fourth parody film idea called *The Brady Bunch Meets the Mob*, written by Sherwood Schwartz that never got made. (See inset.)

Ultimately, one can conclude that the *Brady* franchise is vast, lucrative, and popular.

TIKI TALK

The unrealized film *The Brady Bunch Meets the Mob* began life in 1992 (well before the first feature film) as a script called *Gone. Gone* originally had nothing to do with *The Brady Bunch*. It was the story of a middle-class black family who witnesses an act of arson by two young members of the Italian mob and then later gets taken captive by the mobsters. It was intended as a comedy. Apparently, *Gone* didn't sell, so Sherwood replaced the Morse family with the Bradys. It was re-titled *Bradys on the Go*. Two months later, it became *Where, Oh Where, Is The Brady Bunch?* followed by *The Brady Bunch Meets the Mob*. The idea made the papers in 1993 but ultimately was never filmed. Instead, Paramount went forward with what would become *The Brady Bunch Movie*.

By 2000, the Schwartzes – now son Lloyd was involved – re-upped their efforts to sell the script. The mob family's name became the Altos: a nod to HBO's Soprano family. In December 2001, the show was re-titled *The Brady Bunch vs. The Mob* and was pitched as a movie of the week.

[1]Kramer, Carol. "Brady Bunch Star Serves Up 'Pudding' On Show Business." Chicago Tribune. April 13, 1970, p. 11 section 1A.

[2]Witbeck, Charles. "'Brady Bunch' Hangs On for New Season." Toledo Blade. August 11, 1970, p. 18.

[3]16 SPEC. No. 33. November 1971, p. 48.

[4]Schwartz, Sherwood. The Bradleys. Series Proposal. 1967, p. 4.

[5]AP. "Robert Reed, 'Brady Bunch' Father, Has Trouble with Cooking, Travel." Sarasota Herald-Tribune. September 28, 1973, p. 5-B.

[6]AP. "Producer Seems to be an Expert at Recycling." Park City Daily News. April 3, 1981, p. 5-B.

[7]Marin, Rick. "'Bradys' is Schlock Full of Causes." The Washington Times. February 9, 1990, p. E1.

[8]On Screen and Beyond. "Susan Olsen Interview." August 31, 2009. Episode 72. Online. http://onscreenandbeyond.com/podcast/osb072Olsen.mp3

[9]Schwartz, Lloyd. Changes. February 16, 1990, p. 29.

[10]Siegel, Sandra Kay. Where Do We Go from Here? February 8, 1990, p. 15.

[11]Schwartz, Sherwood. Brady House. Series Proposal. September 14, 1983, p. 3.

[12]Schwartz, Sherwood. Brady Time. Series Proposal. December 14, 1990, p. 2.

CHAPTER 2: CHARACTER ENCYCLOPEDIA

HOW TO READ THIS CHAPTER

Most entries will appear alphabetically. Entries are from *The Brady Bunch* as well as all the spin-off series. The entries are arranged by character or item. For actors, look under the character's name.

ABBREVIATIONS
AVBC = *A Very Brady Christmas*
BB = *The Brady Brides*
BGGM = *The Brady Girls Get Married*
BK = *The Brady Kids*
OS = The "Original Series," *The Brady Bunch*
TB = *The Bradys*
VH = *The Brady Bunch Variety Hour* and *The Brady Bunch Hour*

Mrs. Abrogast (Anne Haney*)
Appearance: TB #2
Mrs. Abrogast lives in the apartment building shared by Mike, Carol, Wally, Marcia, Jessica, and Mickey for the month when the Brady house is being moved to a new location. She walks in on Mike's birthday party and asks him to sign a petition to get the airport flight path moved from over their neighborhood.
Anne Haney is a prominent actress who has performed on many, many television shows and movies. She was very good friends with Robert Reed.

Advantage Properties
Appearance: AVBC; TB #1
Advantage Properties is the second real estate office Carol Brady works for. Their slogan is, "a customer isn't a customer unless the customer is a satisfied customer" and the phone number is 555-6021.

Alan
Appearance: OS #30
Alan is Marcia's boyfriend, but we are not told if he is the same Alan she dated previously: Alan Anthony.

Alan Anthony (Mike Robertson)
Appearance: OS #20
Alan is Marcia's first date. She waffles on whether or not she will go with him to the school dance, but

eventually decides that she will. Her reservations stemmed from her braces, but when Alan proves his like for her, she agrees to go. Right before the dance Alan falls off his bike and has to get braces, too.

Allen, Ross and Wife
Appearance: OS #94
The Allens are invited to Mike and Carol's barbeque/Mexican dinner/smorgasbord.

Amy
Appearance: OS #80
Greg asks Amy to meet up with him at the Charity Ho-Down. Her family is going and so is his. Amy has groovy red hair.

Amy
Appearance: AVBC
Amy is a nurse at the hospital where Greg Brady works.

Anderson, Dorothea (Renee Jones)
Appearance: BB #3
Dorothea and her husband Wayne are contestants on Bob Eubanks' show *The Newlywed Game*.

Anderson, Lynn (herself)
Appearance: VH #9
Lynn Anderson is a musical guest on an episode of *The Brady Bunch Variety Hour*. She sings "Right Time of the Night." She's Jan's idol; Lynn is a country singer.

Anderson, Wayne (Leonard Lightfoot)
Appearance: BB #3
Wayne and his wife Dorothea are contestants on Bob Eubanks' show *The Newlywed Game*. They quit the game before the show is even over.

Armstrong, Jordan (John Terrence)
TB #4
Jordan Armstrong is a local business mogul who lives in City. He donates funds for the City to set up a Trauma Center to coordinate emergency medicine. He also wants to conduct some shady deals with Mike Brady (who is serving as City Councilman), but Mike doesn't go for that kind of thing.

Arnaz, Desi, Jr. (himself*)
Appearance: OS #22
Marcia has a wild crush on Desi Arnaz, Jr., a popular teen idol at the time. Alice is acquainted with Desi's mother's housekeeper, so they work together to arrange a meeting between Desi and Marcia. Desi comes to the

Brady residence and ends up giving Marcia a kiss on the cheek. Marcia swears she will never wash her cheek again.

Desi Arnaz, Jr. is the son of Lucille Ball and Desi Arnaz, Sr.

Arnold, Benedict
Appearances: OS #7, 47, 54, 72, 79, 84, 96

Benedict Arnold is an historical figure who betrayed the American colonies during the Revolutionary War to the British. He is referred to in seven Brady episodes, all as allusions to one of the kids, Mike, or Carol being a traitor. In episode #84, Peter plays Benedict Arnold in his school play.

Arnold, Peggy (Barbara Bernstein*)
Appearance: OS #84

Peggy Arnold is the wife of Benedict Arnold. She is a character in Peter and Jan's school play about George Washington and Benedict Arnold. Peter plays the traitorous Benedict.

Barbara is the real-life daughter of Florence Henderson, aka Carol Brady. She makes three separate appearances in different episodes throughout the run of the original series. She is billed as "Barbara Henderson" once and "Barbara Bernstein" (her real name) twice.

Aunt Jenny (Imogene Coca*)
Appearance: OS #66

This is Carol Brady's aunt. She is a world-traveler and is acquainted with all sorts of famous people. She knows Harry Houdini, Wilt Chamberlin, Golda Maier, Indira Gandhi, Peggy Fleming, Paul Newman, Sir Edmund Hilary, and many more. She owns a llama and a zebra. She gets a marriage proposal from a US Senator named Lester, but turns it down claiming she's too young to settle down now (she's at least 53!). Aunt Jenny looked just like Jan when she was a young girl. Jan writes to her when she discovers their similarities and Aunt Jenny comes to City to pay her "soul sister" a visit.

Imogene Coca is a famous actress most well known for her role opposite Sid Cesar in Your Show of Shows. Younger viewers might remember her as Aunt Edna in National Lampoon's Vacation. Mrs. Coca died in 2001 at the age of 92.

Aunt Martha
Appearance: OS #25

This is Carol Brady's aunt. Carol suspects her of sending a locket to Jan and forgetting to enclose a card. Although she didn't send the locket, she did send the family a totem pole from Alaska! Aunt Martha is very forgetful. One time she drove home in a black sedan and didn't realize it wasn't her own tan station wagon until she got in her garage. Aunt Martha lives in the same city as the Bradys, yet she is never seen.

Aunt Mary
Appearance: OS #19

This is another of Carol Brady's aunts. Carol goes to visit her once to help her recover from an illness.

CHARACTER ENCYCLOPEDIA

Axelrod, Harold (Randy Case)

Appearance: OS #56

Harold plays Romeo in Fillmore Junior High's production of "Romeo and Juliet." Harold is nearsighted and has a squeaky voice.

Babs (Lola Fisher, Jane Webb)

Appearances: BK #1-3, 5, 7, 10, 12, 14, 20

Babs is constantly fawning over cartoon Greg. She likes to hang out with the Brady kids but most of the time she is associated with Chuck and Fleetwood. She is kind of a ditz and Greg doesn't return her advances. She has a pet poodle named Beaucoup.

Miss Bailey (Sara Seegar)

Appearance: OS #84

Miss Bailey is the director of Fillmore Junior High's production of a play about George Washington. She casts Peter Brady as Benedict Arnold and puts Jan Brady in charge of sets and scenery.

Bailey, Alfred (Robert Nadder*)

Appearance: OS #88

Alfred "Alfie" Bailey runs a counter at a department store. He sells the Brady kids the silver platter they bought for their parents' fourth anniversary. There's no indication he's related to "Miss Bailey."

Robert Nadder also plays Gregory Gaylord in the original series.

The Banana Convention

Appearance: OS #39

This is a high school rock group that Greg belongs to. They play at Stephen Decatur High and really bend the gig out of shape. Other members of the band are Tommy Johnson, Phil, and Johnny.

Barbara

Appearance: OS #97

Barbara is a friend of Cindy's. Her brother is Bobby's friend Eric.

Barbara

Appearance: OS #103

Barbara is a girlfriend of Peter's. She invites Peter to a party but he says he can't go because something much more important came up…shining Bobby's shoes.

Barton, Hal (Jeff Davis)

Appearance: OS #96

Hal Barton has a local television show called *Hal Barton's Talent Review*. He signs the Brady kids to perform on his show. They sing "Good Time Music" for the show.

Barwell, Leo (Fred Holliday)

Appearance: TB #3

Leo is the campaign manager for Gene Dickinson's bid for City Council. Leo is unscrupulous and tries to blackmail Mike Brady – Dickinson's opponent – into dropping out of the race. Dickinson finds out what he did and fires him.

The Bear (L. Jeffrey Schwartz*)

Appearance: OS #106

This guy is an animal – a red bear – at King's Island Amusement Park in Cincinnati, Ohio. The Bradys visit the Park and Greg rents the bear suit in order to chase a girl named Marge.

This is Lloyd Schwartz, Sherwood Schwartz's son. He worked with his father as producer on the original series and is involved in most of the spin-offs. In this case he makes a cameo as "the bear" at King's Island. His sister Hope (Sherwood) Juber can also be seen in various roles on the original series.

Beaumont, Winston (Robert Hegyes*)

Appearance: VH #7

Winston is a new age kind of guy who says a lot of "rights," "hey, brothers," and spouts crazy lines about feelings. He is a vegetarian, but most importantly he is engaged to Marcia Brady for two days. Yes, before Marcia married Wally she was engaged to Winston. The couple met at a party one week before they were engaged. But it didn't last long because Marcia realized that Winston is a phony and puts on different personae just to impress girls. He's really not a vegetarian nor is he really into new age. Marcia tells him he needs to find out who he really is and sends him on his way.

Robert Hegyes was well known for his role as Juan Epstein in Welcome Back, Kotter *at the time this variety show episode was filmed.*

Belinda (Tonya Lee Williams*)

Appearance: AVBC

Belinda is Cindy's roommate at U of A. She is planning a skiing trip for Christmas vacation.

You might recognize Tonya as Olivia from TV's The Young and the Restless.

The Bellfields

Appearance: OS #82

The Bellfields moved in down the block from the Bradys. Mr. Bellfield is a doctor. His kids invited Bobby and Cindy to go swimming in their pool – in the nude!

Benji

Appearance: OS #69

This is a friend of Bobby's. He loans Bobby and Cindy his pet mouse Goliath for a day.

Berg, Al (Harvey Vernon)
Appearance: BB #3
Al and his wife Sylvia appear on *The Newlywed Game* with the Logans and Covingtons.

Berg, Sylvia (Edith Fellows)
Appearance: BB #3
Sylvia and her husband Al appear on *The Newlywed Game* with the Logans and Covingtons. Al and Sylvia win the game and are awarded a collection of fish tanks.

Bergen, Edgar (himself*)
Appearance: VH #6
Edgar Bergen is a funny man and ventriloquist. He does his act on *The Brady Bunch Variety Hour* and tries briefly to teach Cindy and Bobby how to throw their voices.
Edgar Bergen was a well-respected ventriloquist of his time. He is father of actress Candice Bergen. He died just one and a half years after filming this episode.

Berle, Milton (himself*)
Appearance: VH #3
On *The Brady Bunch Variety Hour*, Milton Berle is brought in by Bobby to help make the show and the acts funnier. He does a good job but Bobby ends up letting him go because his brand of humor just isn't compatible with the Bradys.
Milton Berle is a very well known, very well respected comedian. He's nicknamed "Uncle Miltie."

The Bernsteins
Appearance: OS #94
The Bernsteins are invited to Mike and Carol's barbeque/Mexican dinner/smorgasbord.

Berry, Sue
Appearance: OS #41
Sue says that Bobby sounds like a frog when he sings.

Bessie
Appearances: OS #50, 51
Bessie is Zaccariah T. Brown's mule. She is very stubborn and won't help Jan, Marcia, and Alice carve out the word "help" in the ground with her plough.

Big Hit Management Company
Appearance: OS #96
The Company employs Tammy Cutler and Buddy Burkman as musical agents. Greg is signed with them for a short time as Johnny Bravo.

Mr. Binkley (George D. Wallace*)

Appearance: OS #101

Mr. Binkley is the boys' Vice Principal at Westdale High School. He catches Greg with Coolidge High's mascot, Raquel the goat. As punishment Mr. Binkley assigns Greg a 5,000-word essay on the evils of mascot stealing. Mr. Binkley himself was caught stealing a rival's mascot when he was in high school. His punishment was suspension for one month.

George D. Wallace is a very prolific actor who has appeared on television shows all the way from 1951-2004. He died in 2005 at the age of 88.

Mr. Blackwell (himself)

Appearance: BB #7

Mr. Blackwell is a real-life fashion critic who puts out the ten best and ten worst lists for clothes. He gives Marcia's potential as a fashion designer a thumb's up after watching her fashion show with Casual Clothes; Phillip and Wally served as her models.

Mr. Borden (Jerry Hauck)

Appearances: TB #2, 3

Borden is a member of the Committee of Concerned Citizens in City. He and his cohorts convince Mike Brady to run for City Council.

Mrs. Brady (uncredited*)

Appearances: OS #1, 4

This is Mike Brady's first wife, who is the biological mother of Greg, Peter, and Bobby Brady. Mrs. Brady died but we do not know exactly when or how. Even though Mike tells Bobby in the pilot episode "I don't want you to forget your mother and neither does Carol," she is never mentioned after the fourth episode of the original series. But if we're clever and listen to the context clues, we can make some inferences about when the original Mrs. Brady died. In episode #4, Alice said she started working for Mr. Brady 7 years, 4 months, 13 days, and 9½ hours ago. That episode aired in October 1969. In the same episode, Alice is talking to her sister Myrtle on the phone. "Now that Mr. Brady's married I'm just not needed anymore," she says. Given that statement, we can further infer Alice did not work for Mr. Brady while the original Mrs. Brady was still alive. He must have needed her when he was single again. All that taken into account, the best guess is that Mrs. Brady died in July or August 1962 when the boys were still quite young. A remark in episode 10 by Alice to Bobby ("I've known you since the day you were born") throws a slight wrench in the cog. Bobby is eight years old in the first season, not seven. But still, Alice could have *known* Bobby when he was born, but still not have been hired by Mike until a few months or a year afterward.

There is a rumor (perpetrated in part by a Pop-Up Brady episode on Nick-At-Nite) that this photograph is of an actress who was a contender for the part of Carol Brady. A reliable source says that that rumor is unfounded.

Brady, Carol Ann (Tyler) (Martin) (Florence Henderson*)

Appearances: OS #1-117; VH #1-9; BGGM; BB #1-3, 5-7; AVBC; TB #1-5

Education = Westdale High School; State University

Nickname = "Twinkles"
Occupation = housewife, mother of six, and later a real estate agent

Carol Brady (née Tyler, née Martin) married Mike Brady in a small ceremony in her parents' backyard in 1969. Her first husband – known only as Mr. Martin – is no longer with her. Viewers are not told if he divorced Carol or if he died. Sherwood Schwartz, creator of *The Brady Bunch*, wanted Carol to be divorced, but the network would not support that; thus, the fate of her first husband remains undisclosed. Carol had three beautiful blonde daughters by Mr. Martin: Marcia, Jan, and Cindy. With her marriage to Mike, her girls become step-sisters to Mike's three boys Greg, Peter, and Bobby. A new family life begins when she and her girls move into Mike's house after the wedding.

TIKI TALK

Little known fact: before Carol married Mike and after her marriage with Mr. Martin, Carol was engaged to a guy named Thomas Patrick O'Malley. Viewers learn in an episode of *The Bradys* that she broke it off with Thomas because he wanted her to wear green all the time. She wanted someone who loved her for her, so she married Mike instead of Thomas.

Carol is a housewife who is fond of needlepoint, sculpting (she won 3rd place in a sculpture contest with a bust of Mike's head), singing, and shopping. She and her housekeeper Alice keep the nine-person household running like clockwork. Carol is always around when one of the kids has a problem. She and Mike are masters at patching things up for their kids.

Sometimes Carol can be a bit helpless around the house, though. Every time that Alice is gone (it happens three times), she hires a replacement. The first time Alice is gone for a week and Mrs. Brady brings in Alice's cousin Emma to hold down the fort. The second time Alice leaves, Carol immediately brings in Kay to take care of the house: also for just one week. The third time Alice is about to leave – when Carol thinks she's eloping with Sam – she immediately calls in a replacement maid from Alice's service. Carol finally takes sole responsibility for her household *after* the kids are all gone and Alice has married Sam.

That said, Carol is savvy and beautiful, musical and loving. As far as her musical talents go, she sang at church on Christmas Day once, she performed a song from "Gypsy" with Marcia for Westdale's Family Night Frolics, and she sang at Jan and Marcia's double wedding. She loves to be with her family and always makes time for

Mike and the kids. She hosts the entire brood for Christmas dinner in 1988, a dinner that includes three of her grandchildren.

Later in life – after all the kids left home – Carol gets a job as a real estate agent for Willowbrook Realty, Inc. Through this agency she sells a house in 1981 to Marcia and her husband Wally and Jan and her husband Phillip. By the time 1988 rolls around she is working for a different realty company: Advantage Properties.

Carol can be summed up as a doting wife, mother, and grandmother. She loves life, loves her family, and they love her.
(See the Biography chapter)

Brady, Cynthia "Cindy" (Martin) (Susan Olsen*) (Jennifer Runyon**)
Appearances: OS #1-117; BK 1-22; VH #1-9; BGGM; AVBC; TB #1-5
Education = Dixie Canyon, Clinton Avenue Elementary/Grammar School, U of A (college)
Boyfriends = Tommy Jamison, Gary Greenberg

Cindy Brady is the youngest of the six Brady children. She isn't a very bright child; she's constantly asking obvious questions and she shows signs of dyslexia, too. Notes she's written read "Vtoe fro Mriaca" and "Makr Maldrill," when they're supposed to say "Vote for Marcia" and "Mark Millard." Her innocence lasts quite a while but by the time she is ten or eleven Cindy is at the top of her class. She beats Bobby out for a chance to appear on a television quiz show called *Question the Kids* because she scored the highest in her class on an exam.

Cindy is as cute as a button. She can warm your heart with her big blue eyes and cute platinum curls. When she is young Cindy is very attached to a doll named Kitty Karry-all. She also wants to be like her older sisters; she dresses up in Carol's clothes, puts on lipstick, and wants to go on dates like Jan and Marcia do. Cindy's hobbies and school activities include ballet dancing, playing jacks, and acting in school plays.

Cindy grows up and goes to college at "U of A." She starts school in 1981 and doesn't graduate until December 1988; it took her over seven years! At any rate, Cindy does eventually graduate and goes on to become a disc jockey. She has her own radio show on KBLA called "Cindy at Sunrise." Her boss at the station is Gary Greenberg. Cindy has an on-and-off relationship with Gary. He is older than she is and has two children, which complicates their relationship a bit. But they are determined to make it work and Gary even gives her a raise and a new format for her show just so that she'll stay with the radio station instead of going to a more glamorous job in television. How their relationship turned out remains unknown because *The Bradys* was cancelled before

any decisions (either breaking up or getting married) were made.
(See the Biography chapter)
**Jennifer Runyon played Cindy in* A Very Brady Christmas.

Brady, Gregory "Greg" (Barry Williams*) (Lane Scheimer**)
Appearances: OS #1-117; BK #1-22; VH #1-9; BGGM; AVBC; TB #1-5
Education = Fillmore Junior High, Westdale High School, and enough
higher education to become an obstetrician.

Girlfriends = Randy Peterson, Kathy Lawrence, Linette Carter, Rachel,
Amy, Jennifer Nichols, back to Rachel, Sandra Martin, and finally to his
wife Nora.
Occupations = delivery boy at Mike's architectural firm; delivery boy for
Sam's Butcher Shop for $1.50 an hour; obstetrician.
Nicknames = "Casanova of Clinton Avenue" & "Old Silver Tongue."

Greg is the eldest of the six Brady kids and acts as their leader. He is the
one, along with Marcia, who organizes them into action as a group when
the situation calls for it. As a youngster Greg was involved in baseball
and other sports. He took baseball very seriously and even got to meet
two pro players: Don Drysdale and Wes Parker. A year or two later Greg is on the football team (against his
mother's objections) and surfing. Greg is also intelligent and is elected President of the Student Body during
his final year at Fillmore Junior High. He's popular and attractive.

Greg is a ladies' man. He had at least seven girlfriends while in high school. He's a pretty cool cat and folks in
the music biz think so, too. Greg started singing and playing in a band during his freshman year of high school.
He also sang with his family on two local televised talent shows and later in the variety show. His talents were
noted by an agent for Big Hit Management Company and he briefly put on the persona of "Johnny Bravo," a
musical star. However, his musical career didn't last and Greg went on to become a successful obstetrician.

After high school and the variety show, Greg completes medical school. He meets and marries a nurse named
Nora and together they have one son named Kevin.
(See the Biography chapter)
**Lane Scheimer is the voice of Greg Brady during Season Two of* The Brady Kids. *Lane is the producer's son.*

Brady, Henry "Hank" (Robert Reed)
Appearance: OS #93
Judge Hank Brady is Mike Brady's grandfather. He is very conservative and served as a judge for forty years.
He is fond of spouting quotes in Latin and admonishing the Brady kids for using terms such as "far out" and
"groovy." The Judge ends up marrying Carol Brady's grandmother, Connie Hutchins.

Brady, Jan see **Covington, Jan**

Brady, Kevin (Zachary Bostrom*) (Jonathan Weiss**)
Appearances: AVBC; TB #1-5
Kevin is Greg and Nora Brady's son. He's a little nerdy, but super cute. His cousin Mickey Logan frequently taunts him and calls him "the slug." Kevin is very well behaved, especially compared to Mickey. The character is named for Lloyd Schwartz's son Elliot Kevin.
*Zachary played Kevin in A Very Brady Christmas. *He went on to play Ernie Henderson in* Harry and the Hendersons *and won a Young Artist Award for his work on that show. Zachary is still an active actor.*
**We know Jonathan Weiss better through his stage name Jonathan Taylor Thomas. He played Kevin in the short-lived The Bradys. *"JTT" was made famous in his role as Randy Taylor in TV's* Home Improvement. *He has been nominated for eleven awards and won four of them.*
Apparently it's good luck to play Kevin Brady!

Brady, Marcia see **Logan, Marcia**

Brady, Michael "Mike" Paul (Thomas? Andrew?) (Robert Reed*)
Appearances: OS #1-81, 83-116; VH #1-9; BGGM; AVBC; TB #1-5
Education: Freemont High School & Norton College (he was a member of the drama club in college).
Mike's favorite dish: tuna salad with chopped eggs and pickle relish.
Nicknames: Checker Camp of Chestnut Avenue and Hot Lips.
Occupation: architect.
Activities: member of the National Guard, golfer, scout master for the Frontier Scouts.

Mike's first wife died sometime when the boys were very young and he has been living with his three sons and housekeeper Alice alone ever since…that is until 1969. He meets a woman with lovely hair of gold and marries her after dating her for only two months. In addition to herself, Carol (Martin) Brady brings Mike three new daughters. Mike gladly adds them all to his household and is determined that everyone get along.

Mike is a very fair parent to his six children and always makes sure that order is maintained through a regimen of lectures and lessons. He's such a good father, in fact, that The Daily Chronicle newspaper honors him as Father of the Year. All the kids adore him and go to him for advice on life. Mike's number one as far as they and Carol are concerned.

Mike Brady is an architect for a living. He closes some very lucrative deals for his firm and is awarded with even more prestigious projects. He designs factories, buildings, houses, and even the new city courthouse. His talents are well-known in City. He keeps his scruples about him, too, quitting jobs that he doesn't think are safe or worthwhile…jobs such as the one that got him trapped inside a fallen building in 1988.

TIKI TALK

WHAT IS MIKE BRADY'S MIDDLE NAME?

Over the course of time, Mike Brady's middle name changes two times. Originally, it is **Paul** as we hear in the pilot episode when he and Carol get married. Then in an episode of *The Bradys*, Peter refers to him as Michael **Thomas** Brady. There is also a third middle name assigned to Mike. This third name is revealed for the first time in Bradypedia: **Andrew.**

If you look closely at Mike Brady's college diploma on the wall in his office, you can see that it lists a first, middle, and last name. That middle name just happens to be Andrew.

So maybe Mike's full name is Michael Paul Andrew Thomas Brady?

Mike Brady is a model husband, father, and employee. Everyone loves him. His bright blue eyes draw a person in and convey a high level of intelligence and fairness. He's an all-American, one for all kind of guy.
* *(see the Biography chapter)*

Brady, Nora (Caryn Richman)
Appearances: AVBC; TB #1-5
Nora is married to Greg Brady and together they have one son Kevin. She is a nurse where Greg works and presumably that's how they met. Nora comes from a very traditional family that always tries to celebrate holidays together. This poses a slight problem when Greg's family wants all *their* kids home for Christmas '88. Her sibling is either Tom or Tricia and they have five kids: Trent, Tim, Terry, Tina, and Tony. She also has an Aunt Frances.

Brady, Peter (Christopher Knight*) (David Smith**)
Appearances: OS #1-34, 36-117; BK #1-22; VH #1-9; BGGM; AVBC; TB #1-5
Activities: baseball, football, glee club, and science club.
Girlfriends: Kerry Hathaway, Linda, Barbara, Michelle, Linda (a different one than before), Mary Agnes MacLeod, Sandy, Debbie, Conchita, Valerie Thomas, Lisa, Donna, Evonne Blaise, Terry Dickinson.
Occupations: 3 days as a bicycle repairman for Mr. Martinelli's Bicycle Shop; 3 days at Haskell's Ice Cream Hut; pizza delivery boy at Leaning Tower of Pizza Parlor; Airman in the US Air Force; businessman; aid worker for People for a Better Planet; campaign worker for Mike Brady.

Peter is the middle boy and one year older than his sister Jan, the middle girl. He has some adventures as a kid including saving a girl from a falling wall of shelves in a toy store. That act of valor earned him toys from the girl's mother, a story in the local paper, and the Outstanding Citizenship Award. He likes baseball and football and plays basketball in the driveway with his brothers. Pete has bad luck with his first few jobs as a kid; he only lasts three days in each of his first two jobs.

Peter tries to follow in his older brother Greg's footsteps when it comes to girls. He gets Greg to coach him on his first date with Linda and he also uses Greg in a plot right out of <u>Cyrano de Bergerac</u> to court Kerry Hathaway. As a junior high school kid, Peter is very nice and conscientious around his dates. When he gets older, though, things change.

Peter goes to college and majors in girls (according to Carol). He tries to go on a date with a girl named Mary Agnes while he's already dating someone else. After college he does a short stint in the Air Force. Sometime after the Air Force (1981) and before his job as a businessman (1988), Peter gets engaged three times! All we know about the girls are their first names: Sandy, Debbie, and Conchita. Apparently Peter didn't really love them and so he broke it off with each of them in turn.

It seems like Peter would never settle down. But sometime around 1988 he meets and falls in love with his boss Valerie Thomas. Valerie seems to be a great, wonderful woman who loves Peter. They propose to each other at the Brady dinner table during Christmas dinner 1988. All seems well until two years later when we learn that Valerie won't put Peter and his family ahead of her job. So Peter breaks off his engagement with Valerie. This time was the hardest for him, he says, because he really loved Valerie. Now Peter is single again and it takes a lot of girls for him to rebound.

Peter is a little tragic as an adult, but as a kid he was great. He loved acting in plays and shadowing his big brother around. He participated in all his siblings' musical schemes. In fact, he was the one who came up with the idea for the six Brady kids to become a singing group in the first place. Then his voice changed, but big brother Greg worked out a way for Peter to sing with the group anyway. Pete loves his family and they all wish the best for him.

(See the Biography chapter):

**David Smith is the voice of Peter Brady in* The Brady Kids *Season Two (episodes 18-22).*

155

Brady, Robert "Bobby" (Mike Lookinland*)
Appearances: OS #1-41, 43-117; BK #1-22; VH #1-9; BGGM;
AVBC; TB #1-5
Favorite dessert: strawberry shortcake.
Girlfriends: Millicent, Tracy Wagner.
Education: Clinton Avenue Elementary School (and presumably
Fillmore Junior High and Westdale High Schools), college, and
some graduate school.

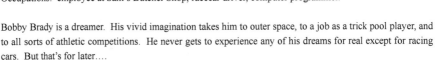

Activities: singing, playing the kazoo, drums, and organ/piano, baseball, and auto racing.
Occupations: employee at Sam's Butcher Shop, racecar driver, computer programmer.

Bobby Brady is a dreamer. His vivid imagination takes him to outer space, to a job as a trick pool player, and to all sorts of athletic competitions. He never gets to experience any of his dreams for real except for racing cars. But that's for later....

Bobby's chief activities as a kid include playing with Tiger the dog, tagging along with his older brothers, trying to set a world's record, and trying his hardest to grow taller. One time he attempted to stretch himself by hanging from the swing set. Every time the family goes on vacation, Bobby ends up in trouble. On the trip to the Grand Canyon, he and Cindy were lost. Then the next year in Hawaii, Bobby, Greg, and Peter were all three captured by a crazy archaeologist and held hostage at spear point. But Bobby is a trooper and came through these experiences unfazed. The only things that really seem to affect him as a youngster are adjusting to a new step-mother and spraining his ankle and becoming afraid of heights. Both of these experiences turned out a-okay, though.

In college Bobby plays baseball. His team does quite well. This is also the time in which he meets his future wife, Tracy Wagner. Bobby attends graduate school in business for a while but he drops out before he finishes his degree. He'd prefer a career racing cars. He and his friend Howie tour the racing circuit for two years before Bobby finally hits it big. In 1990 he gets a spot in the Nashville 500 (Brady world's equivalent of the Indy 500). But then tragedy strikes. Bobby's car stalls on the tracks and is hit sidelong by another racer. He's injured and the doctors tell him and the Brady family that his vertebrae have damaged his spinal cord and that he is paralyzed below the waist. It's devastating news to him and his family.

Bobby is in a wheelchair for an undetermined amount of time. But after Tracy Wagner re-enters his life he is determined to walk again. Bobby marries Tracy in a small, private ceremony right in the Brady living room. The reverend who officiates is the same one who married Mike and Carol. The wedding is very nice and Bobby manages to stand up when he says his vows to Tracy. Physical therapy seems to be doing its job and every week Bobby is getting a little bit stronger.

Now that Bobby is temporarily confined to a wheelchair he has to find other means of employment. He puts his computer skills to work and develops a centralized communication system for City's emergency programs. He's a smart guy and with the help of Peter, Greg, Tracy, Wally, and Mike the communication center is funded.

Bobby Brady is adventurous and a dreamer. He has an iron will and for that his family loves him.
(see the Biography chapter)

Brady, Tracy (Wagner) (Martha Quinn)
Appearances: TB #1-5
Tracy Wagner marries Bobby Brady in 1990 shortly after Bobby's auto racing accident. He and Tracy were college sweethearts, broke up after college, and got back together after his accident. Tracy has one sister. Tracy forms a catering company with Marcia and Nora Brady called The Party Girls.

Brandon (Tom Gagen)
Appearance: BB #7
Brandon is a male model who works for Marcia's company Casual Clothes.

Bravo, Johnny (Greg Brady)
Appearance: OS #96
Greg takes the stage name Johnny Bravo when he signs with Bit Hit Management Company. The agents Tammy Cutler and Buddy Burkman convince him that he will be a great solo act…that is until Greg realizes that they're using some electronic sleight of hand to manipulate his voice and that Tammy and Buddy only liked him because he fit in the Johnny Bravo suit. Then Greg says "adios" to Johnny Bravo.

Mr. Brenner
Appearance: OS #62
Mr. Brenner works at the playground. He calls Mr. Brady to tell him that Jan stole a bicycle.

Brother
Appearance: OS #65
Carol Brady says that she has a brother. We don't know if this is Jack (see "Cousin Oliver" entry) or not because she doesn't say his name. At any rate, when he was growing up his voice changed and when it did he sounded just like their mother Mrs. Tyler.

Brown, Chester
Appearance: OS #10
Chester used to pick on Bobby, but stopped after Bobby told him that Mike is twice as big as Chester's father.

Brown, Felix
Appearance: OS #11, 14
A creep who is twice accused of having the hots for Marcia.

Brown, Zaccariah T. (Jim Backus*)
Appearances: OS #50, 51
Old Zaccariah T. is a prospector based near Cactus Creek Ghost Town. He meets the Bradys when they are

camping out at Cactus Creek. He takes them prisoner by locking them in the town's jail. Then he steals their station wagon and camper and leaves them high and dry. Pretty soon he has a change of heart and drives back to town to give them their car back. He figured they didn't really want to claim his gold after all.

Jim Backus played Thurston Howell, III on Sherwood Schwartz's Gilligan's Island. *You can also look for him in the roll of Harry Mathews in Season Five of* The Brady Bunch.

Bryan, Eddie
Appearance: OS #85
Eddie wants to take Marcia on a bowling date but Marcia tells Greg (Eddie's go-between) that she's not interested because he's too immature. But, she sets up the date anyway only to cancel it a few days later in favor of babysitting for Dr. Vogel.

Burglar (Randy Stumpf)
Appearance: BB #2
This burglar tries to rob the Logan-Covington household. He is unsuccessful. Phillip gets his gun away from him and Jan knocks him to the floor.

The Burkes
Appearance: OS #94
The Burkes are invited to Mike and Carol's barbeque/Mexican dinner/smorgasbord.

Burkman, Buddy (Paul Cavonis)
Appearance: OS #96
Buddy is partners with Tammy Cutler at Big Hit Management Company. Together he and Tammy try to sign Greg as "Johnny Bravo," but after Greg hears that they're going to electronically manipulate his voice on all the records he forfeits the deal.

Cactus Creek
Appearances: OS #50, 51
Cactus Creek is a ghost town where the Bradys plan to spend the night on their way to the Grand Canyon. When they get there, they meet up with trouble in the form of Zaccariah T. Brown. Cactus Creek is really the set for television's *Gunsmoke*.

Calderon, Juan (Paul Fierro)
Appearance: OS #100
Mr. Calderon is a businessman from Mexico City. He and his wife are visiting City to close a deal with Mike and his firm.

Calderon, Maria (Alma Beltran)
Appearance: OS #100
Maria is Juan's wife. She and her husband both speak English. When visiting City they want to taste an

authentic American dish: pizza. So Mike and Carol take the couple out to a restaurant where they catch two girls necking with Peter.

Dr. Cameron (Herbert Anderson*)
Appearance: OS #13
Dr. Cameron is Greg, Peter, and Bobby's pediatrician. After he meets Dr. Catherine Porter, the girls' doctor, he and Dr. Porter decide to combine their practice. Now the Brady children can see a woman or a man doctor whenever they need.
You'll most likely remember Herbert Anderson as Dennis the Menace's father Henry Mitchell in the 1959-1963 television series.

The Campbells
Appearance: OS #49
They are an acquaintance of the Bradys'. Carol was introduced to Mr. Delafield at their party.

Carter, Elizabeth aka "Dear Libby" (Jo deWinter)
Appearance: OS #2
Marcia finds a letter to Dear Libby in her local paper. The letter is written by someone who has just remarried who called him/herself "Harried and Hopeless." This person has three kids of his/her own and the new spouse also has three children. Dear Libby is the columnist who answers Harried and Hopeless' letter. She comes to the rescue of the Brady children after she receives seven letters from the same address begging her to reveal the true identity of the letter-writer. It turns out the letter is from someone in Indiana and the kids and Alice (the 7th letter-writer from the Brady household) are very relieved. The Dear Libby character is a fictional version of real-life columnist Dear Abby.

Carter, Hank (Chris Beaumont*)
Appearance: OS #95
Hank is a friend of Greg's who is a year older than he is. Hank is away at college and he invites Greg to be his roommate. Mike and Carol say no to Greg and give him the attic instead.
Chris Beaumont played three different characters in three different episodes of The Brady Bunch. The others are Jerry Rogers and Eddie.

Carter, Linette (Elvera Roussel)
Appearance: OS #60
Linette is a cheerleader at Westdale. Greg dates her for a while and takes pictures of her doing her cheers.

Carter, Myrna (Bonnie Boland)
Appearance: OS #57
Myrna is a bad actress who Mike and Carol recruit to teach them about acting. When the Bradys are asked to film a commercial for Safe Laundry Soap, Myrna comes over and tells them they need to "motivate."

Casual Clothes
Appearances: BB #1, 7
This is the company that Marcia works for as a fashion designer. Some of her clothes are exhibited in a fashion show and Wally and Phillip are recruited as her models.

Charley (Stuart Getz*)
Appearance: OS #90
Charley is Marcia's boyfriend for a time. He is clumsy but really nice and understanding. He works at his father's wallpaper and paint shop and helps Mike and Carol pick a new paint color for their bedroom. While dating Marcia, he discovers that she tried to see Doug Simpson at the same time. When Doug starts taunting Marcia in the pizza shop, Charley belts him and gives him a swollen nose.
*Stuart Goetz [spelling is correct] was nominated for a Daytime Emmy in 1990 for his work as sound editor for TV's The Wizard of Oz. He has worked on many television movies and shows as music editor.

Charlie
Appearance: OS #95
Charlie is a friend of Peter's.

Charo (herself)
Appearance: VH #5
Charo appears on The Brady Bunch Hour and makes Carol very jealous because of her closeness to Mike and willingness to help him with his solo. Charo plays a beautiful guitar solo herself on the show. She is a well-known figure from the '70s and '80s, famous for her thick Spanish accent, her comedic talents, her musical talents, her looks, and her trademark phrase, "Cuchi, cuchi."

Checkered Trading Stamps Corporation
Appearance: OS #15
This company issues trading stamps at grocery stores. The Brady girls redeem 94 books of stamps for a color television set for the family living room.

Cheryl
Appearance: BBVH #1
Cheryl is a friend of Marcia's.

Chief Eagle Cloud (Jay Silverheels*)
Appearance: OS #52
The Chief is the grandfather of Jimmy Pakaya, who ran away from home. The Bradys help reunite the pair and in return, Chief Eagle Cloud invites the whole family to his village where he makes them members of his tribe and gives them Indian names.

You might know Jay Silverheels after you hear the famous words he uttered as Tonto on The Lone Ranger: *"You are alone now. Last man. You are lone ranger." He is a Mohawk from Canada and his birth name is Harold Smith.*

Chuck
Appearance: OS #42
A friend of Bobby's.

"City"
We're never told the name of the city in which the Brady family lives; it is simply referred to in writing as "City." Here is a list of some of "City's" amenities:
Best food = Candlelight Room at the Royal Hotel
Best pizza joint = Marioni's
At least nine used book stores
Forest Printing @ 12th and Sunset
Movie theatres = The Elite and The Cornet
Lloyd's Stereo Center
Zap-it Exterminator Company
The King's Lodge = fancy restaurant
Parks = Highland Park and Woodland Park and Glenville Park
Schultz's Delicatessen
Royal Towers Hotel where Davy Jones stayed
Atlas Records where Davy Jones cuts an album
High Schools = Westdale (where Carol, Alice, Greg, and Marcia went), Freemont (where Mike went), Tower, Stephen Decatur, Fairview, and presumably Evander (where Alice went for a short time) and an all girls' high school (also where Alice went for a short time), Coolidge.
The Golden Spoon, located at 4th and Oak
Winston's Savings and Loan = "The friendly bank always at your service"
The "Rock Bottom" establishment – concerts
Woodside Grammar School

Miss Clairette (Judy Landon)
Appearance: OS #105
Miss Clairette is Jan, Marcia, and Cindy's ballet teacher. She chooses Marcia and Cindy to participate in her school's recital, but not Jan.

The Clarks
Appearance: OS #94
The Clarks are invited to Mike and Carol's barbeque/Mexican dinner/smorgasbord.

Sidebar: CHARACTER ENCYCLOPEDIA

Clinton Avenue Elementary/Grammar School
Appearance: OS #86, 94
Bobby is Safety Monitor at this school.

Coach (Bart LaRue)
Appearances: OS #41, 60
This is Peter's football coach in junior high and Greg's coach the next year in high school. He is friends with Deacon Jones.

Collette the Puppette
Appearance: VH #3
Collette is a puppet of Sid and Marty Krofft's creation. She appears on one episode of *The Brady Bunch Hour* and sings a duet with Peter. Collette is quite the coquette.

Collins, Jethroe (Burt Mustin*)
Appearance: OS #89
Mr. Collins visits the Brady household to tell Bobby about the real Jesse James. Mr. Collins' father was killed by Jesse James and he tries to get the message across to Bobby that his hero was a real bad guy. It works. Bobby has a nightmare and afterward gives up Jesse and cap guns for good.
Burt Mustin's résumé includes over 150 television appearances spanning the 1950s through the 1970s. He was born in 1884.

Conway, Pat (Rita Wilson*)
Appearance: OS #83
Pat Conway is a contestant for head cheerleader at Westdale. Greg is on the selection committee and votes for Pat over his own girlfriend Jennifer Nichols and his own sister Marcia.
This is Rita Wilson's first television appearance. She is still an active actress as is her famous husband Tom Hanks.

Corset, Dick (John Reilly*)
Appearance: OS #76
Dick is a friend of Greg's from Westdale High School. Marcia embarrasses herself by acting stupid in front of him on her first day of school.
Not to be confused with John C. Reilly!

Cousin Clara
Appearance: OS #107
This is Sam Franklin's cousin. She elopes and Sam is best man and Alice serves as maid of honor.

Cousin Emma (Ann B. Davis)
Appearance: OS #69

Emma is Alice's look-alike cousin. She is assigned to help the Bradys out for one week while Alice is on vacation. Emma is a Master Sergeant in the Army and runs a mess hall for a whole company. She received the General Hagerty Award for her campaign "Make Your Barracks Beautiful." After twenty years in the Army, she can't quite let go of the routine of calisthenics at 06:00 hours, of Army-regulation hospital corners on beds, and smartly arranged dishes in the kitchen. She gets the whole Brady family up at 6:00 in the morning for exercises during the week she is in charge.

Cousin Gertrude
Appearance: OS #63
This is Carol's cousin. She finally gets married this year; apparently she was turning into an old maid. Mike, Carol, Marcia, Jan, Greg, and Peter all attend her wedding. Carol buys her a silver frog (for flowers) for her wedding present.

Cousin Oliver (Robbie Rist*)
Appearances: OS #112-117
Oliver is Carol Brady's nephew and cousin to the six Brady kids. He is eight years old when his parents Jack and Pauline leave him to stay at the Brady house for an undetermined amount of time. Jack is an engineer and will be working on a job in South America. The job site is so remote that there are no schools nearby; that's why they leave Oliver with the Brady family. Oliver is smart, but when he first gets to the Brady house he thinks he's a jinx. It takes some good luck to turn his attitude around. He spends most of his time with Bobby and Cindy. Oliver is the only one who ever says the word "sex" on the Original Series and he has the very last line in the very last episode.
See the Biography chapter for info on Robbie.

TIKI TALK

What is Oliver's last name? Well, Oliver is the son of Carol's sibling, but we do not know if it's Oliver's father Jack or his mother Pauline who is the sibling. If it's Jack, then Oliver's surname is Tyler. If it's Pauline, then his name could be anything.

Many references will give "Martin" as Oliver's surname, but that is incorrect. Martin is Carol's first husband's name, so it is unlikely that a sister also married a Martin. Unless, of course, Oliver is her ex's blood relation and not hers! Stranger things have happened.

CHARACTER ENCYCLOPEDIA

Covington, Claudia (Jeane Byron)
Appearance: BGGM
This is Phillip Covington, III's mother. She is very weepy and cried throughout Phillip and Jan's whole wedding ceremony.

Covington, Jan Brady (Martin) (Eve Plumb*) (Geri Reischl**)
Appearances: OS #1-117; BK #1-22; VH #1-9; BGGM; BB #1-7; AVBC; TB #1-5
Education: Fillmore Junior High, presumably Westdale High School, and college
Boyfriends: Clark Tyson, Stevie, Phillip Covington, III
Occupations: worker at Haskell's Ice Cream Hut; architect.

Jan Brady Covington is the middle child from the Brady family and she occasionally suffers from middle child syndrome. She doesn't feel special because she's not the oldest and not the youngest. But Alice the housekeeper gives her a special locket that once belonged to her. Alice's aunt gave it to her when she was Jan's age because Alice was a middle girl, too. Alice passes it along to Jan who says that as long as she has the locket she will always feel like she is someone special.

Nevertheless, Jan still has a few issues to overcome. She tries her hardest to escape from Marcia's shadow and utters the famous line, "Marcia, Marcia, Marcia!" She even makes up a fake boyfriend named George Glass so that she can fit in with the other kids. Three years later she says, "I do have confidence; I'm confident that I'm a no talent loser." Poor Jan finally hits her stride after high school when she goes to college to become an architect. (This time she's in her father's shadow, which is apparently a much more comfortable place to be than Marcia's.)

Jan finishes college early and at the age of twenty-one marries Phillip Covington, III. She and Phillip had been dating for two years. Phillip is a science professor at a local community college. When Jan tells Mike and Carol about her engagement they insinuate that they always expected Marcia to get married first. There's that shadow again! The next day Marcia meets a guy of her own, Wally Logan, and one week later they're engaged, too. Now she and Jan plan a double wedding. The wedding takes place in the Brady living room. Afterward, Jan, Phillip, Marcia, and Wally all move into a house together.

The house is in City and Mike, Carol, and Alice are just a few streets away. The two newly-married couples experience differences of opinions in nearly everything they do, but they learn to appreciate each other. By 1988 the couples are in their own houses. Unfortunately, Jan's marriage is in trouble. She and Phillip are separated because Jan doesn't feel appreciated anymore and Phillip doesn't think that Jan loves him. But a trip back home for Christmas heals their wounds and they kiss and make up. Two years later they're trying desperately to have a baby, but they can't conceive. They adopt a little girl instead. Patty is Korean and Jan and Phillip love their new roles as parents.

Jan Brady Covington is a blonde beauty with a dynamic personality. She was easy to love as a kid and is great at her architect's job as an adult. (She even ends up running Mike's architectural business after he is elected City Councilman.) Everyone really digs her and it's not hard to see why.
(See the Biography chapter)
**Geri Reischl played Jan in* The Brady Bunch (Variety) Hour.

Covington, Patty (Valerie Ick)
Appearances: TB #1-5
Patty is Phillip and Jan's adopted daughter. She was born in Korea, but moved to the US before she was adopted and speaks English. She is at first shy, but then learns to socialize with her cousins. She still remembers a lot of Korean customs, so she probably has not been in the US for very long before she joined the Covington family.

Covington, Phillip, Jr. (Ryan MacDonald)
Appearance: BGGM
This is Phillip Covington, III's father.

Covington, Phillip, III (Ron Kuhlman*)
Appearance: BGGM; BB #1-7; AVBC; TB #1-5
Phillip Covington, III is Jan Brady Covington's husband. He is a professor of science at a junior college. As of 1981 he had been teaching for three years. Seven years after that he's already made the rank of full professor, which is considerably faster than what it normally takes in the "real world." He is always very precise, analytical, and never spontaneous. He and Jan adopt a daughter together they name Patty.
Ron was a well-known Broadway performer when he joined the Brady family. He was Don in the original 1975 Broadway cast of "A Chorus Line."

Mrs. Crane (Selma Archerd*)
Appearance: AVBC
Mrs. Crane is a travel agent for Here 'N There Travel. She doesn't believe that Carol Brady is who she says she is.
Selma had a recurring role as Nurse Amy on Melrose Place.

Mr. Crawford (Howard Culver)
Appearance: OS #9
Mr. Crawford is a multi-millionaire for whom Mike is planning a factory complex. He is surprised when he learns that Mike is calling him from a payphone in the Brady house. He follows Mike's example and installs a payphone in his own home for his three teenagers to use. The factory deal goes through because of Mike's clever phone idea.

Mrs. Crawford
Appearance: OS #68
This is Marcia's gym teacher. She makes a puppet of Mrs. Crawford for Fillmore Junior High's Jamboree Night.

Cub Scouts
Appearance: OS #47
Yes, the Cub Scouts exists in Brady World, but the Boy Scouts, as far as we know, have been replaced by the Frontier Scouts. Bobby is a member of the Cub Scouts and skips going to the zoo with them in order to pass out petitions to save Woodland Park.

The Cunninghams
Appearance: OS #92
The Cunninghams were at the costume party that Mike and Carol attended. The Cunninghams won first prize dressed as Sherlock Holmes and Watson. Mike and Carol were dressed as Antony and Cleopatra.

Cutler, Tammy (Claudia Jennings*)
Appearance: OS #96
Ms. Cutler is Tammy Cutler of Big Hit Management Company. She is a music agent and wants to sign Greg Brady to be "Johnny Bravo." She spies him at a musical audition for the Hal Barton Talent Show and takes him away from his siblings' group. But Greg finds out that she only wanted him for the Johnny Bravo suit and he takes a walk on the deal.
*Claudia was 1970's Playmate of the Year. She died tragically in a car accident at the age of twenty-nine (she was just twenty-three in this Brady episode).

The Daily Chronicle
Appearances: OS #2, 3, 10, 14-16, 24, 26, 31, 32, 54, 57, 59, 61, 63, 79, 81, 90, 110, 113, 116; TB #3
This is the local newspaper for the city the Bradys live in. At one point, Peter gets in the paper for saving a girl from a falling wall in Driscoll's Toy Store. Mike is named Father of the Year. Later on, Bobby and Cindy's pictures are in the paper for attempting to break the world record for teeter-tottering. The Chronicle sells for ten cents an issue.

Dalrymple, Willy
Appearance: OS #25
An admirer of Jan's.

Mrs. Danhoff
Appearance: OS #62
Jan's teacher. She writes to Carol and Mike and tells them that Jan is having trouble in class. It turns out Jan needs glasses.

Danny

Appearance: OS #30

Danny is Marcia's third boyfriend after Harvey Klinger. Marcia breaks up with him because he is a "drip."

David (Patrick Adiarte)

Appearances: OS #73, 74

David is an employee of Kipula Construction Company. Mike designed the building that the Company is erecting. David picks up the Brady family at the airport and shows them around Honolulu. He is the judge in a surfing contest that Greg enters and wipes out in. David tells the Bradys about old island superstitions but does not believe them himself.

Debbie (Marcia Brady)

Appearance: OS #77

"Debbie" is an invention of Marcia and Greg's. Marcia dresses up in a wig and sunglasses in order to convince someone she's never met – Kerry Hathaway – that she is Greg's "other woman" and that Greg is a dirty rat. They do this so that Kerry will break up with Greg and realize what a great person Peter is compared to his brother.

Dees, Rick (himself*)

Appearance: VH #8

Rick Dees is a disco singer and is a musical guest on *The Brady Bunch Hour*. He sings "Dis-Gorilla" and "Disco Duck:" two wacky disco songs.

Rick Dees later became a radio host.

Mr. Delafield (Richard Simmons*)

Appearance: OS #49

Mr. Delafield is the editor of <u>Tomorrow's Woman Magazine</u>. Carol writes a story for the magazine about the Brady family. Mr. Delafield at first rejects it, then accepts a revised rosy version, then goes back and finally prints the original version that tells the truth.

Richard has been in close to 100 different television shows and movies. He starred as Sergeant Preston in Sergeant Preston of the Yukon *from 1955-1958.*

Mr. Dempsey

Appearance: OS #106

Mr. Dempsey works at King's Island Amusement Park. He reviews some plans that Mike drew up for a Park expansion and approves them. His colleague is Mr. Remington.

Mrs. Denton

Appearances: OS #28, 35

Mrs. Denton is Marcia's teacher. Marcia does a drawing of George Washington, but her friend Paula Tardy wrote a caption to the picture, "Mrs. Denton? Or a hippopotamus?" The remarks on the drawing get Marcia a week's detention.

Diane (Angela Satterwhite)
Appearance: OS #68
Diane goes to Peter's school. Pete writes a flattering column about what a good singer she is. Because of the column, Diane gets invited to sing a solo at the Junior High Jamboree Night. Diane invited Peter to a party to say thanks.

Mr. Dickens (Martin Ashe)
Appearance: OS #11
Member of the Fillmore Junior High faculty (and presumably the principal) who moderated Marcia and Greg's campaign speeches for president of the student body.

Dickinson, Gene (Herbert Edelman*)
Appearance: TB #2, 3
Mr. Dickinson is the Councilman of the Fourth District in City where the Bradys live. The Bradys and their neighbors appeal to him to change the plans to build a freeway off ramp through their neighborhood. He says no and so Mike Brady decides to run against him in the next election. Mike wins.
Herbert Edelman was nominated twice for Emmy Awards for his role as Stan in The Golden Girls.

Dickinson, Teri (Charlie Spradling)
Appearance: TB #3
Teri is Gene's daughter. Peter is dating her until she finds out that Mike is running against her father for City Council. She only wants to make up with him when she thinks her father has won the election. It turns out that Mike actually won, so Teri throws some water in Pete's face.

Mr. Dimsdale (John Wheeler)
Appearance: OS #65
Mr. Dimsdale owns Dimsdale Recorders, a music recording studio. He charges $150 for a recording session. He is the one who records the Brady kids singing "Time to Change." Greg says that Dimsdale Recorders is the best recording studio in town.

Dimsdale, Johnny
Appearance: OS #65
Johnny is in Peter's class in school. His father is Mr. Dimsdale.

Mr. Dittmeyer (uncredited)
Appearances: OS #42, 95
Mr. Dittmeyer is the Bradys' neighbor. His house is over the fence behind the Bradys' driveway. He is the only Dittmeyer we ever see on screen. Carol accidentally hooks him with her fishing line. The Dittmeyers also

participate in a charity bazaar with the Bradys; their junk doesn't bring in as much money as the Bradys'. The Dittmeyer family name was commandeered by the movie spoof *A Very Brady Movie*.

Dittmeyer, Carla
Appearance: OS #10
One of the Dittmeyer children from next door to the Brady house.

Dittmeyer, Mary
Appearance: OS #3
Another of the Dittmeyer children. Cindy beat out Mary Dittmeyer for the part of the fairy princess in her school play.

Dittmeyer, Nancy
Appearance: OS #10
A third Dittmeyer child. Nancy and Carla are closer to Jan and Marcia's ages than Cindy's.

Dixie Canyon
Appearance: OS #3
Cindy attends Dixie Canyon Grammar School in the beginning of OS Season 1. This is the school where she plays the fairy princess in the school play.

Donald (Doug Carfrae)
Appearance: AVBC
Donald works at Here 'N There Travel. He is Mike Brady's travel agent.

Donna
Appearance: OS #80
Donna is a friend of Jan's who is an only child. Jan envies her.

Donna (Angela B. Satterwhite)
Appearance: OS #84
Donna plays the narrator in Peter and Jan's junior high school play about George Washington and Benedict Arnold. We don't know if this is the same Donna from four episodes previous.

Donna (Darcy De Moss)
Appearance: TB #1
Donna volunteers at People for a Better Planet. She dates Peter.

Doreen (Tina Andrews*)
Appearance: OS #61
Doreen is a friend of Marcia's who is serving with her and Laura on the Fillmore Junior High Senior Prom

Entertainment Committee. Doreen doubts that Marcia can get Davy Jones to sing at their prom.
Tina won a Writers Guild of America Award for her teleplay Sally Hemmings: An American Scandal.

Mr. Driscoll (Pitt Herbert)
Appearances: OS #7, 21
Mr. Driscoll owns Driscoll's Toy Shop, which was featured in two episodes during the Original Series. First, Bobby visits the store to buy a replacement Kitty Karry-all doll for Cindy. Then, Peter is in the shop when a giant bookshelf falls and almost crushes a little girl. Peter saves the girl just in time. In later episodes throughout the whole series, you can see boxes labeled "Driscoll" in the Brady garage.

Drysdale, Don (himself)
Appearance: OS #26
Don Drysdale is a former pitcher for the Los Angeles Dodgers. Mike Brady designs a house for him and while Don is at the Brady home, he encourages Greg to pursue baseball. This is the second major Dodger player that Greg has met; the first was Wes Parker.

Duane (Joe Ross)
Appearance: OS #16
Duane is Beebe Gallini's secretary.

Duke (Alan Sues*)
Appearance: BB #4
Duke is a local drunkard that Phillip meets at Ken's Korral.
Alan played Uncle Al the Kiddies' Pal on Rowan and Martin's Laugh In.

Duggan, Harry (Jackie Coogan*)
Appearance: OS #72
Harry Duggan accuses Carol Brady of backing into his car at the supermarket. He has an itemized list of damage that he wants the Bradys to pay for, totaling $295.11. When Carol says that it is his fault and not hers, he takes her to small claims court. Mr. Duggan shows up in court with a neck brace, claiming he has whiplash. The judge is not impressed with Mr. Duggan and rules in favor of Carol.
Jackie Coogan is a famous child star. He went on to appear in many films as a teenager and adult. He's most well-known as an adult for his role as Uncle Fester in The Addams Family. *He appears in one other* Brady *episode.*

Mr. Duncan
Appearance: OS #47
Mr. Duncan is a Park Director in City.

Eddie (John Daniels)
Appearance: OS #20

Alice bribes Eddie the delivery boy to ask Marcia to the school dance. Marcia will have nothing to do with him after she learns that he was bribed. Instead, she ends up going with Alan Anthony, the boy she originally planned on going with.

Eddie (Chris Beaumont)
Appearances: OS #53, 64, 72
This Eddie is a friend of Greg's. He sells Greg his car for $100. Greg gets ripped off because the car turns out to be a lemon. Later, Eddie gives Greg a tip about a surfboard for sale.

Eddie
Appearance: OS #68
Eddie is a friend of Peter's. Pete asks him if he has any ideas for his newspaper column "The Whole Truth."

Edith (Cheryl Beth Jacobs)
Appearance: OS #84
Edith is a classmate of Peter's who derides him for playing the part of Benedict Arnold in their school's play.

Edwards, Ted
Appearance: OS #92
Ted calls Marcia at home and Jan thinks he sounds cute. Marcia describes him as "tall, blond, handsome… nothing special." She apparently has very high standards.

The Elf (Brian Forster*)
Appearance: OS #3
The Elf is the only other onscreen speaking role in Cindy's school play, "The Fairy Princess," aside from the Fairy Princess herself: Cindy Brady.
*Brian was cast as Chris Partridge in The Partridge Family: the Bradys' "rival" singing family.

Ellie
Appearances: OS #42, 49
A friend of Carol's.

Englebert, Danny (uncredited)
Appearances: OS #49, 63
This photographer appears here and there in City. He accompanies the people from Tomorrow's Woman Magazine to take pictures of Carol and the Brady family. He also comes along with Mark Winters from The Daily Chronicle newspaper to take pictures of Bobby and Cindy.

Mrs. Engstrom (Marjorie Stapp)
Appearance: OS #3
Mrs. Engstrom is the director of Cindy's school play, "The Fairy Princess."

Ernie
Appearance: OS #103
Ernie is a friend of Peter's.

Eubanks, Bob (himself)
Appearance: BB #3
Bob Eubanks' car breaks down in front of the Logan-Covington household. He uses their telephone to call for a repair truck and in the process invites Marcia, Wally, Jan, and Phillip all to appear on *The Newlywed Game*. Bob Eubanks is the host of the show in real life and in Brady world.

Family Night Frolics
Appearance: OS #79
Westdale High School puts on an annual show called "Family Night Frolics" to raise money for school equipment. Carol and Marcia perform a duet at the Frolics and Mike and Greg do a dramatic, but comedic, reading of a poem.

FAMILY TREE

The Brady family tree expands with every spin-off. It is complicated to begin with because of Mike and Carol's previous marriages and it only grows from there. It also looks like Carol and Mike might be related to each other because their grandparents are married, but they weren't married until 1973, long after Mike and Carol were born. Other relatives not shown on the chart include:

Carol's other relatives:
Grandmother who won four blue ribbons for her strawberry preserves, Cousin Gertrude, Aunt Jenny, Aunt Mary, Aunt Martha, and a great-grandmother who was arrested for indecent exposure.

Mike's other relative:
An aunt in Albuquerque.

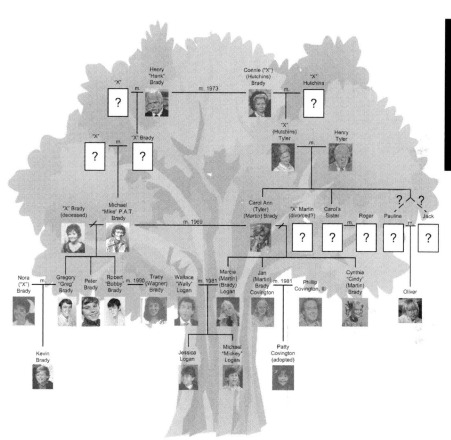

The Brady Family Tree

Farnum, Skip (Paul Winchell*)
Appearance: OS #57
Skip is the owner of Skip Farnum Film Enterprises, a company that films television commercials. He drafts the Brady family for a commercial he is filming about Safe Laundry Soap. He wants a real, natural family, but ends up firing the Bradys because their acting is horribly fake.
Do you recognize Paul Winchell's voice? If you do, you might know that he is the voice of Tigger from Winnie the Pooh. *Woo hoo hooo! He also voiced Gargamel on* The Smurfs. *Moreover, Paul is a famed ventriloquist from the 1940s through 1960s.*

Father (Frank DeVol*)
Appearance: OS #79
The father is part of a father-daughter duet in the Family Night Frolics at Westdale High School.
Frank DeVol is The Brady Bunch's *musician, composer, and editor. He makes a cameo appearance here on the barry sax.*

Fawcett-Majors, Farrah (herself*)
Appearance: VH #2
Farrah Fawcett-Majors is married to Lee Majors at the time the couple appears on *The Brady Bunch Hour*. They come to the Brady house because of a mix-up. Mr. Merrill had promised them the house for the weekend but the Bradys were already living there. So Farrah and Lee end up sleeping on the living room couches.
Farrah Fawcett divorced Lee Majors in 1980. When they appeared on the Hour *together Farrah was starring in* Charlie's Angels. *Farrah succumbed to cancer in 2009.*

Mrs. Ferguson (Ruth Anson)
Appearance: OS #105
Mrs. Ferguson is directing Fillmore Junior High's production of "An American Girl in Paris." She is also an art teacher and she recruits Jan for her art class after Jan bombs out auditioning for the play.

Ferrellville
Appearance: OS #63
Two college boys from Ferrellville try to break the world's teeter-totter record.

Fillmore Junior High
Appearances: OS #11, 44, 45, 54, 59, 61, 68, 71, 76, 77, 84, 105, 108, 113
This is the school where Greg and Marcia go for a time and Peter and Jan followed. School newspaper = Fillmore Flyer (#76).

Mr. Fisk
Appearance: OS #98
Mr. Fisk owns a theatre in town.

The Five Monroes

Appearance: OS #65

This singing group is a guaranteed gold record according to Mr. Dimsdale. The group is recording a song in his studio and Peter gets the idea to form The Brady Six after watching The Five Monroes.

Flathead

Appearance: OS #67

Flathead is a high school classmate of Mike Brady's.

Fleetwood (Larry Storch*)

Appearances: BK #1-5, 7-10, 12, 14-15, 17, 20

Fleetwood is the Brady kids' hippy friend. He speaks like a stereotypical hippy from the era using lots of "man," "cool," "cat" and other words and phrases. Fleetwood sometimes works against the Brady kids when he teams up with their rival Chuck White.

*Larry Storch is a noted vaudeville performer and voice actor. He also had his own variety show in 1953 called The Larry Storch Show.

Fletcher, Joe (John Wheeler)

Appearances: TB #1-2

Joe is an insurance agent who offers Wally Logan a job as an insurance salesman. He fires Wally not long afterward because Wally runs him over with a golf cart.

Fletcher, Penelope (Natalie Schafer*)

Appearance: OS #115

Ms. Fletcher is a rich client of Mike's firm. She wants Mike's boss Mr. Matthews to design her Penelope Fletcher Cultural Center instead of Mike, but Matthews is out of town so she has to settle for Mr. Brady. She comes to the Brady house to pick up Mike's plans and is entertained by a misled Cindy who thinks she's auditioning to be the next Shirley Temple.

*Natalie is the second Gilligan's Island star to guest star on The Brady Bunch (after Jim Backus). She played Mrs. Howell on the show.

Floor plan to the Brady home

FLOOR PLAN:
THE BRADY RESIDENCE
Address = 4222 Clinton Way, City
Phone Number = 762-0799 (OS #34); **555-6161** (OS #97)

The Brady home is one of the most recognizable fictional television sets in American television history. But if you pay attention to its floorplan, the home doesn't make sense architecturally.

If you match up the two floors and the attic on the plan above, you will realize that there is no way that the exterior of the Brady house matches the interior. Moreover, the attic is left hanging over almost nothing, and part of the second level also hangs over nothing. Alice's room fits in the same space as the landing and mystery bathroom.

But all these "mistakes" are okay. We can use our imaginations to fit everything cozily inside the Brady residence. Mike is, after all, a dazzling architect; he is the architect who designed and built the house so of course everything fits just perfectly, right? Right.

The cardinal directions on the floorplan above were derived from a remark Peter made in OS #111. He and Bobby were in the backyard and Peter told Bobby to watch the east sky while he watches the west for UFOs.

Floor Plan: Alice's Room
Appearances: OS #4, 18, 19, 23, 48, 70
Alice's room connects to the service porch and occupies the same space "north" of the living room staircase. We only see her room a few times in the series. In OS #113, Alice says she'll be watching TV in her room. There is no television in there in OS #70 (the last time we saw the room), so it must have been added sometime after 70 and before 113.

Floor Plan: Attic
We first get a good look at the attic in episode #78 when the kids are trying to scare each other. Prior to that, it was mentioned in the episode where Aunt Jenny comes to visit and in "Our Son, the Man." In the latter episode, Mike says the attic would work as a bedroom only if Greg were two and a half feet tall. Clearly, the attic is much larger than that in later episodes. Greg moves into the attic in the last episode of season four. It becomes his bedroom and he hangs beads from the ceiling and decorates it the way he wants to.

Floor Plan: Backyard
The Brady backyard is full of kid-friendly activities. There is a teeter-totter that was featured in the episode "The Teeter-Totter Caper." The swing set has two swings and a glider. It has been used as a means for Bobby to stretch himself and also as a place for Greg and Bobby to hold a chin-up contest. The arbor is large with a big wooden floor, stone walls, and wooden beams for the ceiling. The arbor was put to good use in "Snow White and the Seven Bradys" for a staging of "Snow White" starring the Brady family. The Astroturf lawn is a great place for the kids to play games of catch. But there are elements of the Brady backyard that appear and disappear. Take for instance the ping pong table. Sometimes it's there, sometimes it's not. Then there are

CHARACTER ENCYCLOPEDIA

the boys' and girls' clubhouses which exist for just one episode and then mysteriously disappear. The family restores an old boat they call the S.S. Brady and it's never seen again either. At one point the family borrows a trampoline, but at least we have an explanation of where the trampoline went, considering it was borrowed and not bought. Finally, Tiger's doghouse is an ever-present fixture even after the pooch himself disappears.

Floor Plan: Boys' Room

This is Greg, Peter, and Bobby's room for seasons one through four of the original series. The north and east walls are wood paneling and the south and west walls are wallpapered. The boys get a small portable television set in their room in OS #55. In OS #97 the boys' room gets new wallpaper and a yellow closet door. The bathroom door and main door are painted yellow in OS #108. In the very last episode of season four Greg moves out of the room and into the attic. So now it's just Peter and Bobby's room and the beds are unbunked. But then Cousin Oliver comes to stay in OS #112 and the bunk beds are put back in place with Oliver on top, Bobby on bottom, and Peter in the single bed. In *A Very Brady Christmas* the boys' room is converted into an office for Carol and her real estate paraphernalia. Mike and Carol put a rented double bed in the room for Phillip and Jan to sleep on.

Floor Plan: Carport

The carport is a wide open structure not quite long enough to fully cover one of the Bradys' massively long '70s era vehicles. The Bradys use it to store their camping equipment and bicycles. The carport is mainly used to store stuff and not cars. It's amazing they're never robbed because the carport is so open. There are barn door-like doors at the far end of the carport that are never open; perhaps that is where the Brady family is able to lock away some of its more valuable stuff. The carport served as a place for the Bradys to put their pool table (that they had for just one episode), and Bobby has also used it as a place to practice his drums in season one and to practice the organ in season five. There is a basketball hoop on the outside of the carport that the kids play with. Their neighbors the Dittmeyers are over the fence that adjoins the carport.

Floor Plan: Dining Room

The dining room seats eight people and it is where the Brady family has dinner every night. Alice never eats with the family; in fact, we never see Alice eating a meal outside of an occasional snack. One wall of the dining room is a large sliding glass door that leads to the patio.

Floor Plan: Entry Hall

The entry hall is floored with bricks. It's where the main doors to the house are and also where the coat closet is. There is a partition through which people can see the living room.

Floor Plan: Family Room

The family room stays much the same throughout the original series. The wall hangings change from season one's duck prints to season two's girl Indians. Shelves and a hi-fi stereo appear to the west of the first couch. Other than that, the same checkered couches/daybeds remain in the room as does the TV. The small red, round table appears in season two and stays for the duration.

Floor Plan: Girls' Room

In the beginning, the girls' room goes through a change. At first, just the west wall is covered in pink and blue flowered wallpaper. Then in the third episode to air, the other three walls in the room go from solid pink paint to being covered in the flowered wallpaper halfway through the episode…and then back to solid pink again! The solid pink walls stay on through episode #8 where the whole room becomes wallpapered in flowers again. The flowers disappear at the start of the third season, episode #50. Now all the walls are painted pink and the closet and doors are beige. In OS #103 the family wallpapers the girls' room in a yellow flower pattern. The girls get new shag carpet and new bedspreads to boot. The room flip-flops back to pink walls in episode #104 and then back to the new yellow wallpaper in #105, which is how it remains through the end of the series. The room itself also appears to change shape on occasion. For the first season, it's mostly square with an angled entrance. Then it seems that the whole wall where Cindy's bed sits is angled.

Floor Plan: Kids' Bathroom

The kids' bathroom is upstairs right between the two bedrooms. The bathroom has three points of entry. It is famous for its lack of a toilet. That's right, we never ever see a toilet in the Brady house: not in this bathroom, Mike and Carol's bathroom, or the mystery bathroom downstairs.

Floor Plan: Kitchen

The heart of any home is the kitchen. This is primarily Alice and Carol's domain, but the kids and Mike are in the kitchen quite often. Breakfast takes place in the kitchen and so does lunch. (Dinner is held in the dining room.) The kitchen has a double oven, a double sink plus a single, narrow sink, a fridge, and a stove, but no dishwasher. The Bradys get a new stove (it's yellow) in #110. The kitchen is totally remodeled for *A Very Brady Christmas*; it gets white cabinetry with glass doors and a window is installed above the single sink that has a sill for some plants.

Floor Plan: Landing

For lack of a better word, we'll call the brick area "south" of the staircase the landing. This area is seldom used in a Brady plot, but we do see a kid or two hiding behind the staircase once and Tiger utilizes the area as a jumping point (over the flowers and the horse statue) to get into the living room. The south wall of the landing is two stories high. The wall has geometric shapes on the left side and a geometric, colored stained-glass window on the right. In *A Very Brady Christmas* the window is changed to a series of glass blocks; the stained glass is gone.

Floor Plan: Living Room

The living room is the biggest room in the house. It is separated into two main sections: the seating area and the "empty" area. The seating area contains a large, wide coffee table flanked by a couch and two chairs. The empty area behind the two chairs contains the space between the living room and dining room and leads to the stairs. The empty space is versatile and has served as a dining area, a sleepover room, a place to practice the ho-down and the Charleston, and a place for Mike to practice his golf putts.

Floor Plan: Mike and Carol's Bedroom

The couple's second closet plays the vanishing and reappearing act during the first season. We see the second closet (the one closest to the bathroom) in episode #2 for the first time. It's gone, however, in episodes #4, 6, and 8. It reappears permanently in episode #9. The walls are painted a light blue color for most of the time, and in OS #90 they are re-painted more or less the same color. In OS #114, the walls turn green. There is a mysterious area of the room that we never get to see; it's the area directly behind Mike and Carol's bed behind the screen. But if you're very clever, you can catch glimpses of the hidden area in Carol's vanity mirror. It's from the reflection that we can see that there is a chair and a cabinet against the far wall. Mike and Carol's bathroom is also never seen beyond the sink and its lower cabinets. We are told that there is a tub in there; Carol uses it in OS #24.

Floor Plan: Mike's Den

Mike's den is off limits to the kids, although they sometimes disobey that rule. Mike spends a lot of time in here working on his architectural designs. He has his own phone line at one point. The den is also used as a private place where Mike and Carol lecture the kids when they've done something wrong. In OS #43 Greg converts the den into his own groovy bedroom complete with lava lamps and a couple crazy lamp shades. But he decides that he'd rather be back in his own room upstairs with Peter and Bobby; thus, the "funky" bedroom only lasts one episode. In *A Very Brady Christmas* the den is used as a bedroom for Valerie and Cindy.

Floor Plan: Mystery Bathroom

This is the bathroom on the first floor that was introduced in *A Very Brady Christmas*. Previously, there was no bathroom on the ground floor. We are not shown what it looks like inside, unfortunately. Mickey and Kevin are the only Bradys to ever use it.

Floor Plan: Mystery Closet

This is the closet at the top of the stairs. (It's indicated in the floorplan above by a question mark.) Perhaps this is where the water heater and furnace are housed, since we never see those utilities anywhere else in the house, including the service porch. During almost every episode of *The Bradys* the door to the mystery closet is kept open. All we can see is that the walls are white; we can't see inside, unfortunately.

Floor Plan: Patio

The patio is concrete and is on the south side of the house. It leads to a brick patio, which leads to the driveway and the backyard. The Bradys eat out here once and Mike cleans the barbeque once. Peter builds a model volcano on the patio.

Floor Plan: Service Porch

The service porch is the Brady family laundry room. It contains a washer and dryer and a sink. The shape of the service porch changes virtually every time we see it. Its design in the floor plan above is taken from the first season. Later, the washer and dryer are moved to the "south" wall and the walls become angled. In season five the washer and dryer are moved to the "north" wall and then back again. There is a door to the outside in the service porch. The service porch flooded twice during the original series: once when Jan was doing the laundry when Alice sprained her ankle, and again when Bobby was washing his own suit and put in a whole box of Safe laundry soap.

Floor Plan: Walk-in Closet
This closet is upstairs between the kids' bathroom and the girls' room. The closet holds towels and other sundries, but it also includes an air vent that links up to Greg's room in the attic. Various members of the Brady family have eavesdropped on Greg by way of this vent.

CHARACTER ENCYCLOPEDIA

TIKI TALK

Ever wondered what happened to the Brady house set after the show was cancelled in 1974? Well, right before it was dismantled, horror movie producer William Castle used it in his 1975 flick *Bug*, a Paramount production. A bunch of creepy, fire-starting cockroaches invade a sleepy California town and some of them find their way to the Brady house! In the movie, the house belongs to the main character Professor Parmeter and his wife. His wife bites the dust in the house when a bug starts a fire in her hair.

The set also appears in a few episodes of *Mannix* (a show Robert Reed was a major part of), one of *Mission: Impossible*, and a few others.

Fluffy the Cat see "Pets, Fluffy"

Mr. Foster (Snag Werris*)
Appearance: OS #82
Mr. Foster is the owner of the Golden Spoon Café. Alice briefly worked there as a waitress. Mr. Foster is very demanding of his staff.
*Snag Werris is a guest on The Brady Bunch *four different times, each time as a new character.*

Mr. and Mrs. Foster
Appearance: OS #84
A couple for whom Mike designed a dream house. There's no indication that this Mr. Foster is the same who owns the Golden Spoon.

Foxx, Redd (himself*)
Appearance: VH #7

Redd Foxx, a noted comedian of the time, appears on *The Brady Bunch Hour* supposedly so he can check out the workings of a variety show to get ideas for his own show for next season. By the end of the show he decides that singing, dancing, and smiling are not part of his repertoire.

*Redd Foxx is best known for his portrayal of Fred Sanford on Sanford and Son. *He died in 1991 at the age of 68.*

Frank (Stuart Pankin*)
Appearance: BB#1
Frank is a mover who, with a guy named Maxie, moves Marcia, Jan, Phillip, and Wally's furniture into their new house.
*Stuart Pankin won a Cable ACE Award for Not Necessarily the News.

Franklin, Alice (Nelson) (Ann B. Davis*)
Appearances: OS #1-117; VH #1-9; BGGM; BB #2, 4, 5, 7; AVBC; TB #1-5
Education: Evander High School where she was a cheerleader, Westdale High School where she won a dance competition, and an unnamed all girls' school as a senior where she played Julius Caesar in the school play.
Boyfriends: Sam Franklin and Mark Millard
Occupations: housekeeper, waitress

Alice joined Mr. Brady as their live-in housekeeper 7 years, 4 months, 13 days, and 9½ hours prior to October 17, 1969 (from episode #4). She knew Bobby when he was born and watched the boys grow up. When Mike Brady re-marries, Alice continues her position and helps out Carol Brady with the chores while Carol manages the six children. Alice is always there when the Bradys need her to do work or look after the kids. She is extremely reliable. There are two moments when she contemplates leaving the Bradys and she actually does leave them once for about a week because the kids are giving her a hard time. The first time Mike says, "We can't make her stay. Abraham Lincoln put a stop to that." He effectively calls her a slave!! She stays then, but the second time she threatens to leave she actually does. However, the kids soon find her at her new job as a waitress at the Golden Spoon and they ask her to come back. She does just that and never leaves again until the kids are grown and she marries Sam.

Sam "the butcher" Franklin is Alice's longtime boyfriend. It's not easy for him to make a commitment. The couple is dating all the way through the five seasons of *The Brady Bunch*. Mostly they go bowling together. Alice's patience with Sam finally pays off, though. We learn in 1981 that they did actually get married; they had been married for almost four years at that point, so we can assume they tied the knot in 1977. It must have been right after the variety show was cancelled (also in 1977) because she was not married during that time period.

Alice can usually always be seen wearing her blue and white maid's uniform. Many Brady fans will tell you that it's rare for her to be seen out of uniform, but in fact she is wearing something else in thirty-nine different episodes during the original series: #1, 2, 4, 8, 9, 14, 16, 19, 23, 26, 27, 29, 35, 37, 48, 50, 51, 52, 57, 62, 65, 69, 73, 74, 75, 77, 78, 82, 85, 86, 92, 93, 96, 102, 107, 109, 112, 113, and 117. Nevertheless, she is so fond of her uniform that she dons it long after she stops working for the Bradys. When she visits them in 1988 for Christmas, Alice pops into her favorite duds for old time's sake.

The Bradys consider Alice part of their family. She lives with them throughout the boys' entire childhood and most of the girls'. She helps out with Jan and Marcia's wedding and she is always quick to lend a hand. Although Alice does have two sisters of her own (Emily and Myrtle), she rarely interacts with her own family, preferring to stay with the Bradys for the holidays. She's got a great personality and sense of humor and she's always willing to go along with the kids on their projects. There's never a moment when Alice says "no" to helping anyone out.

Alice is the most hard working, funniest member of the Brady family. She will do anything for them and they will do anything for her.

(See the Biography Chapter)

Franklin, Sam (Allan Melvin*) (Lewis Arquette**)
Appearances: OS #9, 19, 48, 64, 79, 98, 107, and 114; AVBC.
Mentioned in: OS #16, 17, 27, 35, 40, 42, 49, 61, 65, 69, 78, 85, 99, 108, and 110; BGGM; TB #1-2, 5
Occupation: butcher.

Sam "the butcher" Franklin is Alice Nelson's longtime boyfriend. He has a butcher shop in City (called either "Sam's Quality Meats," (OS #98) "Sam's Fine Meats," (OS #114) or "Sam's Butcher Shop") and will occasionally give the Bradys their meat wholesale. He's got a boisterous personality and loves to go bowling. In fact, he sometimes puts bowling before Alice. Sam was in the Army at one point in his life and Bobby Brady and Cousin Oliver think that he is working as a spy against the F.B.I., which of course is not true. Anyway, Sam can be a little hard to handle at times, but he does love Alice. He and Alice get married in mid- to late-1977. They even go bowling on their wedding night! Their marriage is happy until one day in 1988 when Sam decides to leave Alice for another – younger – woman. Alice is, of course, very upset. But Sam comes crawling back to her on Christmas Day dressed as Santa Claus and asks her if she will take him back. She agrees, saying that he'd better not do such a stupid thing again. Sam promises not to and he and Alice stay together.

(See the Biography Chapter)

**Lewis played Sam in* A Very Brady Christmas.

Fred

Appearance: OS #100

Fred is a friend of Greg's who turns down the chance to go out with Sandra Martin's cousin Linda.

Fred

Appearance: OS #103

Fred is a friend of Peter's.

Freddie (Jimmy Bracken*)

Appearance: OS #84

Freddie plays Major Andre in Fillmore Junior High's play about George Washington and Benedict Arnold. Freddie gives Peter a bloody nose after Peter insinuates that Freddie's character should be the traitor, not Benedict.

Jimmy Bracken appears three times on The Brady Bunch.

Freddy

Appearance: OS #42

An acquaintance of Greg's.

Friend in Need Society

Appearance: OS #22

The Society takes donations from citizens to be given to the needy. They also take donations of books that they in turn give to used book stores to be sold. The Bradys donated several boxes of books to the Society once, but Marcia's diary got mixed up in the donation by mistake. Cindy and Carol find the diary at a used book store and return it to its rightful owner.

Fritzsinger, Alverna (Barbara Cason*)

Appearance: BB #1

Miss Fritzsinger is Jan, Phillip, Marcia, and Wally's conservative neighbor. She calls the cops on the two couples because she smells sulfur coming from the house; the sulfur is part of a science experiment Phillip is conducting.

Barbara Cason played Ruth Shandling on The Garry Shandling Show.

Fritzsinger, Charles

Appearance: BB #1

Charles is Alverna's brother. The brother and sister live together next to the Logan-Covington household.

Frontier Scouts

Appearance: OS #44

This is City's equivalent of Boy Scouts. Greg belongs to Troop #2 when he is a freshman in high school. Mike serves as his scout master along with a man named Stan Jacobsen. Marcia decides to join the Frontier Scouts in order to prove to Greg that girls can do anything that boys can do. She makes it through the field initiation tests but then decides not to join; she just wanted to prove she was capable. The initiation tests included mouth-to-mouth resuscitation, leg splints, the fireman's carry, digging a hole, tending to a concussion, starting a fire, putting up a tent, and following a marked trail.

Gallini, Beebe (Abbe Lane*)
Appearance: OS #16
Beebe Gallini is a famous cosmetologist who asks Mike to design a factory for Beebe Cosmetics, Inc. She is very eccentric and insists that her factory be "Beebe pink." She is constantly changing her demands with Mike and in the end fires him because he will not design a factory that has a flip-top lid like a makeup compact.
Abbe Lane was a sexy Italian actress in the 1950s and 1960s. She was married at one point to Xavier Cugat (the same man who later married Charo, who also made an appearance on a Brady show) and was a regular on his show.

Garst, Billy
Appearance: OS #108
Billy is Most Popular Boy at Fillmore Junior High the same year that Jan is Most Popular Girl. Billy doesn't want to take Jan to the dance, though, and takes her rival Kathy Williams instead.

Gates, Tank (Denny Miller*)
Appearance: OS #104
"Tank" Gates is an old high school sweetheart of Carol Brady's. She dated him during her senior year at Westdale. Tank was an all-around athlete and participated in all sports. He went pro after college in football and lasted a few years. He comes back to City to watch the Fairview-Westdale League Championship game and drops in on Carol, aka "Twinkles."
Denny played Duke Shannon on Wagon Train. He also played Tarzan in the 1959 film Tarzan, the Ape Man.

Gaylord, Gregory (Robert Nadder)
Appearance: OS #62
Gregory Gaylord is a photographer. He's very forgetful and a bit "out there." He takes a picture of the six Brady kids so that Mike can surprise Carol with a photograph for their third wedding anniversary.

George
Appearance: OS #41
A classmate of Bobby's who switches his bugle for Bobby's drums.

George
Appearance: OS #46
George is a golfing buddy of Mike's. Mike cons him into buying a magazine subscription from Bobby.

CHARACTER ENCYCLOPEDIA

George

Appearance: OS #100

Mike completed some designs for George.

Gilbert, David

Appearance: BGGM

David is a friend of Wally's who is invited to his wedding. Mrs. Brady places David at the same table as Julie Sullivan.

Glass, George

Appearance: OS #34

George is a figment of Jan's imagination. She invented him to be her boyfriend so that she wouldn't have to explain to her family that boys don't like her. As soon as Clark Tyson, a real boy, notices her George disappears as quickly as he came.

Gloria

Appearance: OS #27

Jan's longwinded friend.

Gloria

Appearance: OS #47

Gloria is a member of the Women's Club and appoints Carol Brady to be the Vice Chairwoman.

Gondola Gourmet

Appearance: OS #63

The Gondola Gourmet is a radio personality in City who gives "housewives everywhere" great Italian recipes over the radio. Alice listens to the Gourmet.

Mrs. Gonzales

Appearance: OS #116

Mrs. Gonzales gives Alice a recipe for Swedish meatballs.

Mr. Goodbody (Harold Peary*)

Appearance: OS #88

Mr. Goodbody is a loan officer at Winston Savings and Loan Bank. He denies Bobby and Cindy a loan because of their age but rewards their efforts by presenting them each with a bank and a dime.

*Harold Peary is known for his comedy character Throckmorton Gildersleeve, and his wicked laugh, on the radio show The Great Gildersleeve.

Miss Goodwin (Lois Newman)

Appearance: OS #56

Miss Goodwin is the director of Fillmore Junior High's production of "Romeo and Juliet."

Dr. Gordon

Appearance: OS #85

Dr. Gordon is the Brady kids' dentist. He is partners with Dr. Vogel.

Gordy

Appearances: OS #4, 10, 47

Gordy is a friend of Greg and Peter's.

Mrs. Gould (Sandra Gould*)

Appearance: OS #101

Mrs. Gould is a member of the P.T.A. for Westdale High School. She is accidentally shut in a closet with Raquel the goat.

Sandra Gould is best known for her role as the nosy Gladys Kravitz on Bewitched.

"The Great Earring Caper"

Appearance: OS #92

"The Great Earring Caper" is the nickname that Peter assigns his detective case. Peter and Cindy are trying to find out what happened to a pair of earrings that Cindy "borrowed" from Carol. The earrings are clip-on, gold, and dangly. They were given to Carol by her mother, Mrs. Tyler. Mike ends up solving the case instead of Peter.

Great-Grandmother

Appearance: OS #66

This is Carol's great-grandmother and Marcia, Jan, and Cindy's great-great-grandmother. She was arrested for indecent exposure because she wore a bathing suit that showed her knees.

Greenberg, Carly (Jennifer Kolchier)

Appearance: TB #2

Carly is fifteen years old in 1990. She is the one who recommends to her father that Cindy Brady be hired by KBLA. She adores Cindy and her radio program, "Cindy at Sunrise." That is until she meets Cindy in person and learns that she's dating her father Gary. Then Carly gets really upset and storms out of the room.

Greenberg, Gary (Ken Michelman)

Appearances: TB #1-5

Gary's first wife Leslie was killed in 1987 by a drunk driver. He has two kids by her, Carly and Jake. Gary is Cindy Brady's boss at radio station KBLA. He goes out with Cindy and they go back and forth about how much they like each other. By TB #4 they've settled on liking each other a lot; Gary gives Cindy a raise and a new platform for her show in order to keep her from going into television.

Greenberg, Jake (Phillip Glasser*)

Appearance: TB #2

Jake is Gary's twelve-year-old son (12 in 1990). He likes to listen to "Cindy at Sunrise."

Phillip won a Young Artist Award for his voice performance as Fievel the mouse in An American Tale.

Gretchen (Hope Sherwood*)

Appearance: OS #117

Gretchen is a classmate of Greg's. She and her friend Suzanne are getting their hair done at the beauty parlor and they run into Greg. Greg is there to get his orange hair dyed back to its natural color but he lies to Gretchen and Suzie and tells him that he's there to help Mrs. Brady with her wig.

Hope Sherwood (aka Hope Schwartz aka Hope Juber) is Sherwood Schwartz's real-life daughter. She makes four appearances on The Brady Bunch, *writes for* The Brady Brides, *and has a guest appearance in* The Bradys *as well. Hope also wrote the script for* The Brady Bunch in the White House, *the third in a series of spoofs. She married Laurence Juber who became the musical editor for* The Bradys *series and for* The Brady Bunch in the White House.

Mr. Gronsky (Lew Palter)

Appearance: OS #114

Mr. Gronsky is the landlord for Sam Franklin's butcher shop. He offers Sam the chance to buy the building next door to the shop in order to expand his own. Bobby and Oliver get the wrong idea that Mr. Gronsky is an enemy spy and lock him and Sam in the freezer.

Grossman, Bert (Lindsay Workman*)

Appearance: OS #23

Mr. Grossman is a real estate man who represents the Bradys when they decide to put their house up for sale. The Bradys change their mind about selling when Mike and Carol realize the kids are willing to go to great lengths ("haunting" the house) to keep it.

Lindsay appeared in four Brady Bunch *episodes.*

Mr. Gunther

Appearance: OS #98

Mr. Gunther owns a theatre in town.

Gus

Appearance: OS #48

Gus is a fruit vendor at the supermarket.

"Hal Barton's Talent Review"

Appearance: OS #96

This is an amateur show much like "The Pete Sterne Amateur Hour." The Brady kids audition for the show with "You've Got to be in Love to Love a Love Song" and sing "Good Time Music" on the show. The "Talent Review" appears on TV station KBEX and seems to have replaced the "Amateur Hour."

Hamner, Tom (Eric Woods)
Appearance: OS #97
Tom is a friend of Bobby's. Tom doubts Bobby's story about knowing Joe Namath. But he gets to meet the great quarterback himself at the Bradys' after he comes for a visit.

Mr. Hanalei (David "Lippy" Espinada)
Appearances: OS #73, 74, 75
Mr. Hanalei is a construction worker for Kipula Construction Company, the company that is building a building in Hawaii that Mike Brady designed. Mr. Hanalei is superstitious and tells the Brady boys about an old idol superstition. Bobby's tiki idol is taboo and Mr. Hanalei directs the boys to the burial ground of the first king so that they can return the idol to its proper resting ground and not have to worry about bad luck anymore.

Hank Colman Show
Appearance: OS #61
The Hank Colman Show airs at 4:00-4:30pm daily in City. Davy Jones and the head of the sanitation department are guests that we know about. The Show is a talk show.

Harris, Gladys (Bella Bruck)
Appearance: OS #107
Gladys works for the same agency that Alice does. Carol briefly considers hiring her for a week when she thinks that Alice is eloping with Sam. However, Sam and Alice are not eloping and therefore Gladys' services are not required.

Harry (Keland Love)
Appearances: BB #2, 4, 5-7
Harry is Wally Logan's young business associate. Harry gets to test out toys that are going into production by Tyler Toy Company. Wally pays Harry for his advice on the toys with McDonald's gift certificates.

Harvey
Appearance: OS #9
Greg's friend who he is trying to convince to trade a bicycle for Greg's baseball mitt, an autographed picture of Raquel Welch, and his pet white rabbit.

Harvey (Bobby Riha*)
Appearance: OS #68
Harvey goes to Peter's school. Pete writes a flattering column about him in the school paper saying what a good dancer he is. Now Harvey has girls falling all over him. As thanks for the column, Harvey gives Pete a box of

CHARACTER ENCYCLOPEDIA

candy bars.

*Bobby played Bruce Landers in The Debbie Reynolds Show.

Harvey (Michael Barbera)

Appearance: OS #84

Harvey is a classmate of Peter's who calls Peter a traitor for playing the part of Benedict Arnold in the school play.

Harvey

Appearance: OS #88

Harvey owes Greg $5. We don't know if this is the same Harvey from Episode 9 or not.

Mr. Haskell (Henry Cordon*)

Appearance: OS #102

Mr. Haskell is the owner of Haskell's Ice Cream Hut. He employs Marcia Brady. Then Peter is hired, but Marcia fires him for being lazy, and then Jan is hired to replace Peter. Mr. Haskell was taking afternoons off to relax but soon realizes that the only thing that relaxed him was work. So he goes back to working afternoons which means he has to let go either Marcia or Jan. He chooses to lay Marcia off and keep Jan because she is a slightly better worker.

*Henry Corden took over as the voice of Fred Flintstone in 1977. He has over 180 shows on his résumé.

Hathaway, Kerry (Kym Karath*)

Appearances: OS #77, 96

Peter has a wild crush on Kerry and concocts a scene right out of Cyrano de Bergerac in order to court her. The scene backfires and Kerry falls for Greg instead of Pete. After it's all said and done, Kerry ends up with Peter because she realizes what a swell guy he is. Peter met Kerry because she is Jan's friend.

*Kym played Gretl, the youngest Von Trapp child, in the movie The Sound of Music.

Hazel

Appearance: OS #66

This is Aunt Jenny's secretary.

Helen

Appearance: OS #103

Helen is a friend of Marcia's. Marcia, Jan, and Cindy spend the night at Helen's house while their room is being wallpapered.

Herman (Darryl Seman)

Appearance: OS #108

Herman is a classmate of Jan's. He is flunking algebra and Jan promises him that Greg will help him out. Greg says no and then Herman is mad at Jan for breaking her promise.

Hesselroff, Irene
Appearance: OS #67
Irene was Mike Brady's girlfriend his senior year at Freemont High. Mike called her "Bobo."

Mr. Hillary (Richard Carlyle)
Appearance: OS #89
Mr. Hillary is the principal for Clinton Avenue Elementary School. He speaks to Mike and Carol about Bobby's infatuation with Jesse James.

Mrs. Hinton (Ceil Cabot)
Appearance: OS #33
This is Buddy Hinton's mother. She does whatever her husband Ralph tells her to do.

Hinton, Buddy (Russell Schulman)
Appearances: OS #33, 49
Buddy is a bully who teases Cindy because she lisps. He gives Peter a black eye for trying to defend his sister. Peter gets his revenge, though, and knocks Buddy's front tooth loose so that he ends up lisping just like Cindy. He apologizes and asks to borrow Cindy's tongue twister book to practice his "s." A few episodes later, Buddy is up to his old tricks and gives Peter another black eye.

Hinton, Ralph (Paul Sorensen)
Appearance: OS #33
Ralph is Buddy Hinton's father. He's very much like a bully himself and doesn't care if his son picks on little girls or picks fights.

Ho, Don (himself)
Appearance: OS #73
Don Ho is a famous Hawaiian musician. He encounters Cindy and Bobby outside their hotel. Bobby is trying to learn to play the ukulele and Don Ho offers to play a song for him. Don is accompanied by his friend Sam Kapu who sings with him at the Polynesian Palace in Honolulu.

Hobart, Patty
Appearance: OS #71
Patty Hobart is the most popular girl in Marcia's senior class at Fillmore Junior High School.

Hoffsteader, Freddy
Appearance: OS #64
Freddy is the smallest kid in Bobby's class, but only because he got a haircut. Bobby is the second smallest.

CHARACTER ENCYCLOPEDIA

Hope
Appearance: OS #17
Hope is a friend of Marcia's.

Hopkins, Earl (Dave Morick)
Appearance: OS #21
Earl works for The Daily Chronicle as a reporter. He writes the story about Peter being a hero when he saves a girl from a falling wall of toys.

Hopkins, Erica (Hope Juber)
Appearance: TB #1
Erica is the physical therapist hired by the Brady family for Bobby Brady after he suffers his spinal cord injury.
Recognize Erica? She's played by Hope Juber aka Hope Sherwood, Sherwood Schwartz's daughter. See the "Gretchen" entry for more information.

Houston, Joe
Appearance: OS #86
Joe owns a marina. Mike designs some plans for an addition to his marina and while there he takes a rundown old boat off Joe's hands and brings it home for the family to fix up.

Dr. Howard (John Howard*)
Appearances: OS #42, 76
Dr. Howard is the doctor who recommends that Cindy and Carol's tonsils have to come out. He makes house calls. Apparently the Bradys are through with Drs. Cameron and Porter, who were their family doctors in season one. Dr. Howard makes a second house call on Marcia's first day of high school. He diagnoses her with a case of the nerves.
John Howard has a star on the Hollywood Walk of Fame. He starred in movies and television.

Howie (Lenny Garner*)
Appearance: AVBC; TB #1
Howie is Bobby's buddy and mechanic from the racetrack. He follows Bobby all the way to the Nashville 500 where Bobby has his accident and is paralyzed.
Lenny Garner is now a successful director.

H.R. Pufnstuf
Appearance: VH #4
H.R. Pufnstuf is a singing dragon from the world of Sid and Marty Krofft. He and his fellows appear on the *The Brady Bunch Variety Hour* and sing a song.

The Hudson Brothers (themselves*)

Appearance: VH #5

The Hudson Brothers are a musical group from the '70s. They are Brett, Bill, and Mark and their music was usually accompanied by comedy.

Bill Hudson's daughter is actress Kate Hudson.

Mrs. Hunsaker (Fran Ryan*)

Appearance: OS #23

Mrs. Hunsaker is a prospective buyer of the Brady residence. She is almost scared away by "ghosts" until Mike reveals that it's really the kids who are haunting the house. The deal is off and Mrs. Hunsaker must find a new home elsewhere.

Fran Ryan's acting career spanned four decades: the 1960s through the 1990s.

Hutchins, Connie (Florence Henderson)

Appearance: OS #93

Connie Hutchins is Carol Brady's grandmother and therefore great-grandmother to the six Brady kids. Mrs. Hutchins hails from Owensboro, Kentucky, which just happens to be where Florence Henderson went to high school. Hutchins is full of spunk and spirit, exercises every day, and likes her share of liquor. She ends up eloping with Judge Hank Brady who happens to be Mike Brady's grandfather. The couple elopes in Las Vegas and goes waterskiing soon afterward.

Huxley, Tommy

Appearance: OS #64

Tommy was acting like a big-shot, so Bobby starts a fight with him. Tommy gives Bobby a black eye.

Injuries

The Brady kids suffer their share of injuries over the years. Most were minor, except for a few broken ribs on Greg and spinal cord injury to Bobby. Here's how they break down.

Alice: Alice sprains her ankle when she trips over the kids' Chinese checkers game. Her injury prevents her from going to the Meat Cutters Ball with Sam (OS #19).

Bobby: Bobby had a scraped knee from slipping on a banana while riding his bike (OS #4). When he was younger, he got a big lump on his head when the antenna lead fell on him (OS #23). He sprains his ankle by falling from a climb to a tree house (OS #36). Tommy Huxley gives him a black eye when he is 10 (OS #64). He suffers compressed vertebrae after a high-speed car accident that causes him to be temporarily paralyzed in 1990 (TB #1).

Carol: She's injury-free, although she did have a tonsillectomy.

Cindy: She's injury-free, although she did have a tonsillectomy.

Greg: Greg broke three ribs when he fell off the garage roof and onto Mike's car when he was younger (OS #23). He suffers a hairline fracture of another rib playing for his high school football team (OS #60). Greg goes surfing in Hawaii and gets a bump on his head and a skinned neck (OS #73/74).

Jan: Jan sprains her ankle in gym class and couldn't be Peter's assistant for his magic show tryouts (OS #45).

Marcia: Marcia gets a swollen nose after being hit in the face with Peter's badly-thrown football (OS #90).

Mike: He's injury-free, even after a building crumbles down around him in *A Very Brady Christmas*.

Peter: Back in the day, Pete got four stitches in his nose when he ran into the bathroom door. He says the dent is still there (in the door) (OS #23). Also, he cut his foot once when he was diving for abalone (OS #27). He gets a black eye from a lucky punch thrown by Buddy Hinton (OS #33). Buddy clocks him again, which results in a second black eye in OS #49. A third fight leaves Peter with a bloody nose, but this time a kid named Freddie is his opponent. In 1990 Peter chokes on an hors d'oeuvre and loses consciousness. Greg has to bring him back by giving him mouth-to-mouth and blowing the obstruction out of his airway (TB #5).

Inspector Mann (Patrick Cronin*)
Appearance: BB #6
The Inspector works for the U.S. Government. He is conducting a background check on Phillip Covington, III but makes some silly leaps in logic and ends up thinking that Wally is Phillip, that Harry is an evil mastermind, and that Wally is some sort of criminal.
Patrick played Sparky in six episodes of Home Improvement *and had spots on lots and lots of other shows over the years.*

Inspector Rankin (Joseph Campanella*)
Appearance: BB #6
Inspector Rankin is Inspector Mann's boss. Together the two inspectors conduct a raid on the Logan-Covington house.
Joseph has been nominated for both a Daytime Emmy and an Emmy.

Iris (Jennifer Reilly)
Appearance: OS #68
Iris is in Peter's class at Fillmore Junior High. Pete writes a complimentary column about her. As thanks for the flattering column, Iris takes Peter out for a malt, her treat.

Jacobs, Johnny (himself)
Appearance: BB #3
Johnny Jacobs is the announcer for *The Newlywed Game*. Marcia, Wally, Jan, and Phillip are contestants on the Game.

Jacobsen, Stan (Ken Sansom*)
Appearance: OS #44
Stan is a scout master for the Frontier Scouts. He shares the responsibility with Mike. He helps oversee the field initiation tests for Marcia when she attempts to join the scouts.
Ken is yet another talented voice actor to appear on The Brady Bunch. *He is the voice of Rabbit from* Winnie the Pooh *and Hound from* Transformers.

James, Jesse (Gordon DeVol)
Appearances: OS #50, 89

194

Jesse James is Bobby Brady's hero until Bobby finds out what a truly bad guy he was. Bobby has a dream that Jesse shoots his whole family. In real life, Jesse James shot many people and died at the age of 34.

Jamison, Tommy (Eric Shea*)

Appearance: OS #70

Bobby bribes Tommy to pretend to be Cindy's secret admirer with a Kennedy Half Dollar. Tommy takes the deal but ends up liking Cindy enough to return the Half Dollar to Bobby, no strings attached. He is fond of lizards and gives a lizard to Cindy as a present. Tommy is Cindy's first boyfriend.

Eric played Phillip in the film Yours, Mine and Ours. *Remember the importance of that film from the introduction to this book? He also had a major role in* The Poseidon Adventure.

Jane

Appearance: OS #55

Jane is a friend of Peter's. At her party, Peter is told that he has no personality.

Jason (Iler Rasmussen)

Appearance: OS #21

Jason is one of Peter's friends. He makes up an excuse of having to go to a piano lesson rather than attend the party Peter is throwing for himself celebrating the fact that he is a hero.

Jeff (Michael Gray*)

Appearance: OS #102

Jeff is Marcia's boyfriend. He gets disappointed every time Marcia turns him down because she's working. Then he gets a new girlfriend to make Marcia jealous. Marcia squirts him and his new girl with whipped cream at the Ice Cream Hut where she works. But then Jeff calls Marcia to tell her that he was only seeing someone else to make her jealous. The couple gets back together because Marcia is no longer working.

Michael Gray was a teen heartthrob at this point in his career. He was well-known at the time for a role in TV's The Little People.

Jennifer

Appearance: OS #27

Jennifer is a kid Greg and Marcia's age who does babysitting. Greg and Marcia convince their parents that they no longer need a babysitter because, after all, kids their age *are* babysitters.

Jenny (Susan Joyce)

Appearance: OS #21

Jenny is one of Peter's friends. She makes up an excuse that she has to visit her grandmother rather than attend the party Peter is throwing for himself celebrating the fact that he is a hero.

CHARACTER ENCYCLOPEDIA

Jeremy
Appearance: OS #45
Jeremy has a birthday party that includes a magician. Cindy and Peter go to the party.

Jerry
Appearance: OS #48
The Bradys' milkman. Sam accuses Alice of two-timing him with Jerry, but it's not true. She's two-timing him with Mark Millard instead!

Jerry
Appearance: OS #70
Jerry asks Marcia out for a soda. He's number 10 in a long list of boyfriends.

Jill (Shawn Schepps*)
Appearance: OS #86
Jill is a girl in Bobby's class. Her cat Pandora is trapped in an abandoned house and she asks Bobby to rescue the cat. Even though Bobby knows it's trespassing to go inside, he does it for the sake of Jill and Pandora.
Shawn is now a successful film and television writer.

Jimmy (Jimmy Bracken*)
Appearance: OS #36
Jimmy is a friend of Peter's. He gives Bobby a hard time for chickening out on a second climb to their tree house.
See "Freddie."

Jimmy
Appearance: OS #89
Jimmy is a classmate and friend of Bobby's. Jimmy writes about Robin Hood as his hero whereas Bobby writes about Jesse James.

Joanne
Appearance: OS #103
Joanne is a lady friend of Greg's.

Joey
Appearance: OS #32
Joey is a friend of Peter's. His dad is a lawyer and Peter asks him for information on what the law says about getting money from a lost wallet.

Johnny (Michael Lerner*)

Appearance: OS #10

A bike salesman.

*Michael Lerner was nominated for an Oscar for his performance in the Coen Brothers' film Barton Fink.

Johnny (Bobby Kramer)

Appearance: OS #39

Johnny is a friend of Greg's and a member of his band The Banana Convention.

Mrs. Johnson (Marie Denn)

Appearance: OS #39

Mrs. Johnson is Tommy Johnson's mother. She is the chair of the anti-smoking campaign for Westdale High School. Carol Brady joins the campaign after Greg is caught smoking. Mrs. Johnson falsely accuses Greg of continuing to smoke when a pack of cigarettes falls out of his letter jacket. In actuality, the cigarettes belong to her own son.

Johnson, Tommy (Craig Hundley)

Appearance: OS #39

Tommy is the drummer for the band The Banana Convention. He, Phil, Johnny, and Greg Brady make up the group. Tommy smokes, which gets Greg into trouble.

Jon (Jon Hayes)

Appearance: OS #86

Jon is a classmate of Bobby's. Bobby, acting as Safety Monitor, turns Jon in for disorderly conduct. Jon and another kid were playing "monkey in the middle" with a third kid's books.

Jones, David "Davy" (himself*)

Appearance: OS #61

If you're a celebrity and your name is David Jones, you very well might end up on *The Brady Bunch*. Both this Davy Jones and "Deacon" David Jones (see below) guest starred on the show. Marcia Brady is the president of his Fillmore Junior High Fan Club. When Davy Jones shows up in City, he is flooded by all kinds of admirers. Marcia finally breaks through the crowd and finds Davy at a recording session at Atlas Records. There, Davy overhears Marcia's plea to his manager that he sing at her prom. Davy makes a personal appearance at the Brady house and tells Marcia that he will gladly sing at her prom if she will go with him as his date. Who could resist such an offer? Marcia gives him two pecks on the cheek.

*Davy Jones is a famous teen rock idol from the late 60s and the 1970s. He was a member of the band "Monkees."

Jones, David "Deacon" (himself)

Appearance: OS #41

Deacon Jones comes to Peter's football practice twice to give his team some pointers. Deacon is a friend of Peter's coach. In real life, he played football for the Rams.

Jones, Ken (himself)
Appearance: OS #44
Ken Jones is a real-life California television news man. In City, he works for WKS station and interviews Marcia and Judy Winters about the women's liberation movement.

Judge (Robert Emhardt)
Appearance: OS #72
The Judge is in charge of a small claims court that sees "Duggan vs. Brady." Harry Duggan accuses Carol Brady of backing into his car at the supermarket, and Carol contends the opposite. The Judge rules in Carol's favor.

Judy (Margie DeMeyer)
Appearance: OS #55
Judy is a friend of Peter's. Peter invites her to a party and Judy ends up trying to convince him that he isn't dull.

The Kaplutians (Frank and Sadie Delfino*)
Appearance: OS #111
The Kaplutians are part of a dream that Bobby has. After seeing what he thought was a real UFO in his backyard, Bobby dreams that aliens have landed. The two aliens are from the planet called "Kaplutus" and they are little people with orange hair and grayish skin. They offer to take Bobby back to their home planet with them and Bobby agrees.
Frank and Sadie were the stand-ins for four of the Brady kids throughout the original series.

Kapu, Sam (himself)
Appearance: OS #73
Sam Kapu is a musical partner to Don Ho. Bobby and Cindy get to meet them both when their family vacations in Hawaii. Sam and Don sing "Sweet Someone" for Bobby and Cindy.

Kaptain Kool and the Kongs
Appearance: VH #2
The musical group is the guest musical act in an episode of *The Brady Bunch Variety Hour*. They sing their song, "Names." The group started on Sid and Marty Krofft's show *The Krofft Supershow*.

Karen (Carolyn Reed*)
Appearance: OS #28
Karen is one of Marcia's friends who attends a slumber party at the Brady household. Karen discovers a fake spider hidden in her sleeping bag by the Brady boys.
Carolyn Reed is the real-life daughter of Robert Reed. Her actual name at this time was Karen Rietz, but she chose a stage name like her father's. She appears in this episode along with Florence Henderson's daughter Barbara and Sherwood Schwartz's daughter Hope.

Kartoon King (Hal Smith*)

Appearances: OS #46, 63

The Kartoon King is a local celebrity in City and has his own cartoon show. Bobby and Cindy like to watch the show. Bobby enters an ice cream eating contest on the show once, but he doesn't win. The phone number for the Kartoon King Show is 555-6161. Does this phone number look familiar? It should. It was also the number for the Brady residence in Episode #97!

*Hal Smith played Otis the drunk on The Andy Griffith Show. He is also the third member of the Brady cast to work as a voice on Winnie the Pooh; Hal was the voice of Owl.

Kathy

Appearance: OS #46

Kathy is a friend of Carol's. Carol cons her into buying a magazine subscription from Bobby.

Kathy

Appearance: OS #85

Kathy is a friend of Jan's.

Katie

Appearance: OS #95

A friend of Marcia's.

The Kauffmans

Appearance: OS #94

The Kauffmans are invited to Mike and Carol's barbeque/Mexican dinner/smorgasbord.

Kay (Mary Treen*)

Appearances: OS #82, 88

Kay is a good friend of Alice's who also happens to be a housekeeper. Kay substitutes for Alice at the Brady household after Alice leaves the family for other employment. Her absence only lasts one week, however, and soon Alice is back and Kay is out of the Brady house. Later on, Kay loans Alice some money so she can pay her insurance premium.

*Mary Treen's acting career spans all the way from the 1930s to the 1980s.

KBEX

Appearances: OS #88, 96, 111; AVBC

KBEX is a television station. The Brady kids appear in the Pete Sterne Amateur Hour contest on this station. First prize is $100, but the Bradys come in third and are awarded a plaque for their efforts. The next year KBEX has a different talent show called Hal Barton's Talent Review. The Bradys audition for this show as well and make it on television. We aren't told if it's a competition, though. Station KBEX interviews Jim McDivitt the astronaut in January 1974.

KBLA
Appearances: TB #1-5
KBLA is the radio station for which Cindy Brady and Gary Greenberg work. Gary is Cindy's boss at the station and Cindy's show is called "Cindy at Sunrise."

Keller, Herb (Tim Herbert)
Appearance: OS #97
Herb Keller is Joe Namath's manager in Brady world.

Kelly, Dwayne (William Attmore, II*)
Appearance: OS #109
Dwayne is Kathy and Ken Kelly's adopted son. He has two adopted brothers, Matt and Steve. Dwayne and Steve decide to run away from the Kellys their first night because they think they're causing their new parents too much trouble.
*William was a Disney Mouseketeer where he had the nickname Billy "Pop" Attmore.

Kelly, Kathy (Brooke Bundy)
Appearance: OS #109
Kathy is married to Ken. Together the couple adopts three eight-year-old boys: Dwayne, Matt, and Steve. She is friends with Carol Brady and she and Ken go to the Bradys for advice on their new sons. They live in the same neighborhood.

Kelly, Ken (Ken Berry*)
Appearance: OS #109
Ken is the new father to three adopted boys: Matt, Dwayne, and Steve. Ken works as a singer and dancer at a nightclub in City. He starts trying to teach his new kids how to do a soft shoe dance.
*Ken has appeared in numerous television shows, most notably F-Troop, Mayberry R.F.D., and Mama's Family. He has a background in the military and in dancing.

Kelly, Matt (Todd Lookinland*)
Appearance: OS #109
Kathy and Ken Kelly adopt Matthew from the Terrace Adoption Home in City. He is eight years old. His best friends at the Home were Dwayne and Steve. So, one week later the Kellys adopt Dwayne and Steve so that Matt won't be lonely anymore.
*(See the Bonus Biographies Chapter)

Kelly, Steve (Carey Wong)
Appearance: OS #109
Steve is Kathy and Ken Kelly's adopted son. He makes up number three of the "Three Musketeers" with his adopted brothers Dwayne and Matt.

Ken's Korral
Appearance: BB #4
This is a bar with a western theme. It's supposedly one of the hippest places in City.

Kevin
Appearance: OS #102
Kevin is a friend of Peter's.

Kim (Vickie Cos)
Appearance: OS #76
Kim is the leader of the Westdale Boosters, an exclusive club for girls at the high school. The rules for the Boosters are very strict – they only accept three freshmen each year and all members of the club are allowed to date only certain boys and they all have to dress nicely at all times.

King's Island Amusement Park
Appearance: OS #106
King's Island is a real park located outside Cincinnati, Ohio. The Park had been open for just one year before the Bradys visited it. Mike worked on some plans for expanding the Park that were accepted by the Park's director, Mr. Remington.

Kipula Construction Company
Appearances: OS #73, 74, 75
The Kipula Construction Company is constructing a building that Mike designed. They are based in Hawaii. Employees of the Company include Mr. Hanalei and David.

Mr. Kirby
Mr. Kirby owns Mr. Kirby's Pet Shop where Cindy buys two rabbits she names Romeo and Juliet. The rabbits both turn out to be boys but Cindy is able to sell them back to Mr. Kirby when Bobby accidentally dyes their fur orange.

Kitty Karry-all*
Appearances: OS #2, 3, 5, 7, 10, 12, 14, 16, 17, 19, 21, 22, 23, 25, 26, 35, 40, 42, 70, and 110.
This is Cindy's doll. Cindy is very attached to Kitty Karry-all and is quite distraught when the doll goes missing once. Cindy blames Bobby for its disappearance, but it turns out that Tiger swiped her and put her in his doghouse.
The doll was a real toy available in toy stores at the time. See the "Memorabilia Chapter" for more.

Klinger, Harvey (Billy Corcoran*)
Appearance: OS #30
Marcia has a crush on Harvey, who does not know that Marcia exists. Greg thinks Harvey is an, "all-time,

all-American, grade-A creep besides being a jerk, a goof, and a double-dingbat," but Marcia is willing to do anything to get him to notice her. After she studies entomology, Marcia finally gets Harvey's attention. The two of them decide to go steady. Soon afterward, Marcia dumps him for a boy named Danny. Harvey is Marcia's second boyfriend after Alan Anthony.

Billy, aka Bill, Corcoran is a successful television director.

Kramer, Doug
Appearance: OS #36
Mr. Kramer is the father of an unnamed friend of Peter's. He is taking Peter, his son, and another boy or two camping overnight.

The Krofftette Dancers
Appearances: VH #1-9
The Krofftette Dancers are so named because of the variety show's creators Sid and Marty Krofft. They appear in every episode of the variety hour. They are back up dancers in the show. There are eight of them (although the first show had ten). The ladies double as the Water Follies.

KTRY
Appearance: OS #14
KTRY is a local television station. They film the presentation of Mike Brady's Father of the Year Award.

Kyle (Monica Ramirez)
Appearance: OS #55
Kyle is a friend of Peter's. When she attends Peter's party, she tries to convince him that he isn't dull.

Lance (Tom Jordan)
Appearance: BB #7
Lance is a male model who works for Marcia's company Casual Clothes.

Laura (Kimberly Beck*)
Appearance: OS #61
Laura is a friend of Marcia's. She, Marcia, and Doreen are on the Entertainment Committee for the Fillmore Junior High Senior Prom. The Committee – well, Marcia, really – picks Davy Jones as their entertainer. Laura is a doubting Thomas at first, but then Marcia comes through.

Among other roles, Kimberly Beck played one of the North children in the movie Yours, Mine, and Ours, *a movie with a plot similar to* The Brady Bunch.

Laura (Dinah Lenney)
Appearance: OS #1
Laura is Tracy (Wagner) Brady's sister. She gives birth to a baby boy during Tracy and Bobby's wedding ceremony.

Lawrence, Kathy (Sheri Cowart)
Appearance: OS #54, 55
Kathy beats Marcia out for head cheerleader at Fillmore Junior High and Marcia considers her public enemy number one. Greg asks Kathy out in order to get back at Marcia for dating his enemy, Warren Mulaney. In the next episode, Kathy and Marcia are friends. We must assume they patched things up with each other.

Ledbetter, Polly
Appearance: OS #77
Mike had a crush on Polly when he was Peter's age.

Leeds, Lloyd
Appearance: OS #56
Lloyd is in Greg's English class and he thinks Marcia is groovy.

Len (Bill Miller)
Appearance: OS #100
Len is a friend of Greg's. He turns down a chance to date Sandra Martin's cousin Linda.

Lester (Rory Stevens)
Appearance: OS #30
Lester is Marcia's fifth boyfriend. He comes after Alan, who came after Danny, Harvey Klinger, and Alan Anthony.

Lester
Appearance: OS #82
Lester is a classmate of Greg's. Someone (maybe Greg himself) filled his shoes with shaving cream as a joke.

Lewis, Daisy
Appearance: OS #49
An editorial assistant for <u>Tomorrow's Woman Magazine</u>.

Linda (Teresa Warder)
Appearance: OS #17
Linda is a friend of Marcia's who just moved to town from Seattle. Mrs. Brady thinks that she is the Linda that Greg has a crush on, but she isn't.

Linda
Appearance: OS #41
Linda is a friend of Jan and Cindy's who is in the Glee Club with them.

Linda

Appearance: OS #95

Linda is a friend of Marcia's. We don't know if this is the same Linda from OS #17.

Linda (Kathie Gibboney*)

Appearance: OS #100

Linda is Sandra Martin's cousin. She has a blind date with Peter when he is pretending to be a boy named Phil Packer. Linda realizes that Peter/Phil is younger than he's pretending to be and she and Sandra plot revenge on Pete and Greg.

Kathie won a Soap Opera Digest Award for her work as Gina Capwell on Santa Barbara.

Lisa (Kim Maxwell)

Appearance: TB #1

Lisa volunteers at People for a Better Planet. She dates Peter.

Mr. & Mrs. Liston

Appearances: OS #35, 36

The Listons are neighbors of the Bradys'. They add a room onto their house and Cindy overhears Mr. Liston say that Mrs. Liston's mother will never have an excuse to leave now when she visits.

Little, Rich (himself*)

Appearance: VH #6

Rich Little is rehearsing a scene in the swimming pool on the set of *The Brady Bunch Variety Hour* when he knocks into Cindy headfirst underwater. He temporarily loses his memory and Cindy feels very guilty about the accident. After going through a whole bunch of different personalities, Rich remembers who he really is.

Rich Little was known as "The Man of A Thousand Voices," and was renowned for his impressions at the time of this episode.

Liz

Appearance: OS #110

Liz is an acquaintance of Carol Brady's.

Mr. Logan (James Gallery)

Appearance: BGGM

Mr. Logan is Wally Logan's father. He has a wacky sense of humor just like Wally's.

Mrs. Logan (Carol Arthur*)

Appearance: BGGM

Mrs. Logan is Wally Logan's mother.

Carol is actor Dom DeLuise's wife.

Logan, Jessica (Jaclyn Bernstein*)
Appearances: AVBC; TB #1-5
Jessica is Wally and Marcia Logan's oldest child of two. She is prim and proper and very supportive of her parents. Her little brother Mickey frequently torments her, but she always tries to quell him and restore order.
Jaclyn was nominated for a Young Artist Award for her portrayal of Jessica in A Very Brady Christmas. *She didn't win that time, but she did win two other Young Artist Awards for a* Twilight Zone *episode and for a TV movie* A Fight for Jenny.

Logan, Marcia (Martin) (Brady) (Maureen McCormick*) (Erica Scheimer**) (Leah Ayres***)
Appearances: OS #1-35, 37-117; BK #1-22; VH #1-9; BGGM; BB #1-7; AVBC; TB #1-5
Education: Fillmore Junior High, Westdale High School, and college
Marcia's boyfriends: Alan Anthony, Harvey Klinger, Danny, Alan (we're not told if it's the same Alan again), Lester, Gordon, Tommy, Warren Mulaney, Doug Williams, Jerry, Dr. Stanley Vogel (sort-of), Eddie Bryan, Charley, Doug Simpson, Jeff, Jerry Rogers, Winston Beaumont. She marries her last boyfriend Wally Logan in 1981.
Activities: ballet, drum majorette, cheerleader, swimming, and lots of others.
Occupations: worker at Haskell's Ice Cream Hut, fashion designer, stay-at-home mom, and caterer.

CHARACTER ENCYCLOPEDIA

Marcia is the only Brady for whom we have vital statistics; that is, we know when she was born and therefore how old she is. During the episode where Marcia receives her driver's license, we get a brief glimpse of her temporary license. It says that Marcia Brady was born on August 5, 1956 (which is Maureen McCormick's birthday), she's 17 years old at the time, she is 5'3", weighs 96 pounds, and received her license on January 15, 1974. Despite being 17 Marcia is just a sophomore in high school. For some reason she started out the series as one year younger than Greg but ended up two years behind him in school. At any rate, it is nice to have some solid facts on one of the Bradys.

As a child, Marcia could be called an over-achiever. She participates in many different school activities, including drama, student council, and the art club. At one point during her freshman year of high school she is a member of thirteen different clubs at once! She's desperate to be popular and will try anything once to achieve popularity. But Marcia is also sensible. She learns that people will like her for who she is and not for what she pretends to be. She drops all her clubs except one (ceramics) and returns to a normal life.

Marcia is the oldest Brady girl and as such is a mentor to Jan and Cindy. She and Jan become very close as

205

teenagers and Marcia even shares the contents of her diary with Jan. She has a long series of boyfriends (even longer than Greg's list of girlfriends) and never really seems to have a problem getting a date.

Marcia is also self-conscious. She worries about her nose after it is swollen from being hit with a football, she worries about her appearance when she gets braces and again when she starts high school, but she also has a tendency to let things go to her head such as the time she had the lead in "Romeo and Juliet."

Marcia's teen years are filled with boys and school activities. As a young adult, she is also still very deep in the dating game. In 1977 when she's only 20 (even though she says she's 19), Marcia becomes engaged to a guy named Winston Beaumont, a boy she's only known for one week. Winston is a laid back dude who refers to Marcia's parents – even Carol – as "brother." But Marcia is quick to realize that Winston isn't the guy for her and they break it off a few days later.

In 1981 she meets Wally Logan, a charismatic toy salesman for Tyler Toys. Marcia's quick decision-making is still in effect and after only one week of dating she and Wally decide to get married. They tie the knot in a double ceremony with her sister Jan and her husband Phillip Covington, III. Both couples live together in the same house for a period of time and they adjust to married life in often funny and awkward ways.

By the time 1988 rolls around, Marcia and Wally have two children: Jessica and Mickey. Jessica is a pretty dark-haired girl who is kind and serious. Mickey has a mop of flaming red hair (that soon turns to brown!) and a personality to match. He's wild, quick to say whatever pops into his head, and often uncontrollable. But Marcia and Wally love their kids.

Unfortunately Wally has trouble keeping jobs and he, Marcia, and the kids move in with Mike and Carol in 1990. The move doesn't go that well. Marcia spends too much time with the bottle and becomes a drunk. Her family rallies around her after they realize what is wrong, and soon she's back on her feet again. To get her own family back on the right track, Marcia forms a catering company called The Party Girls with her sisters-in-law Tracy and Nora. The Party Girls is a huge success and things are finally going well for the Logans.

Marcia (Brady) Logan is a high-achieving, lovely, family-oriented girl and woman.
(see the Biography chapter)
**Erica Scheimer played Marcia in Season Two of* The Brady Kids. *Erica is the producer's daughter.*
***Leah Ayers played Marcia in* The Bradys.

Logan, Michael "Mickey" (G.W. Lee*) (Michael Melby**)
Appearances: AVBC; TB #1-5
Mickey is a trouble-maker and a loudmouth. He is Marcia and Wally Logan's son, younger brother to Jessica. He's always underfoot and getting into other people's business, but he has a good heart.
**G.W. Lee played Mickey in* A Very Brady Christmas.
***Michael Melby played Mickey in* The Bradys.

Logan, Wallace "Wally" (Jerry Houser*)

Appearances: BGGM; BB #1-7; AVBC; TB #1-5

Wally is Marcia (Brady) Logan's husband. He's very funny and charismatic. He asks Marcia to marry him on the very day he meets her. One week later she says yes and soon they're married and living together with Jan and Phillip Covington. Wally is a salesman. He works for Tyler Toys from about 1978 through 1988. He has a young associate named Harry who helps him rate the toys for the company. Unfortunately, in 1988 the company downsizes him right out of his job, even though he's their star salesman. He then gets a job working for Prescott Toys, but that doesn't last long either. By 1990 he's going through a series of jobs as an insurance salesman, as a campaign worker for Mike Brady, and finally as the PR guy for Marcia's catering company The Party Girls. Wally never gives up, never loses his sense of humor, loves Marcia with all his heart, and takes good care of his kids.

Jerry Houser has a long list of films and television appearances under his belt. He also does a significant amount of voiceover work, including a Keebler Elf, on G.I. Joe, and Danger Ranger.

Lorraine

Appearance: BGGM

Lorraine is a fashion model with Marcia's company.

Machado, Mario (himself*)

Appearance: OS #111

Mario is the host of a local KBEX talk show that interviews Brigadier General Jim McDivitt. Mario asks him about the experience he had aboard Gemini 4 when he encountered a UFO.

The real-life Mario has been nominated for ten Emmys and won eight of them for his work as a newscaster.

The MacIntyre House

Appearance: OS #23

This house is haunted and has been for sale for years. Alice knows the former cook who claimed that there were voices in the night, that chains rattled, and lights went off and on.

Mahakian, Carl

Appearance: OS #117

Carl Mahakian is a quitter, according to Carol. In real life, though, Carl is the post-production coordinator for *The Brady Bunch*. They use his name in the last episode of the series.

Majors, Lee (himself*)

Appearance: VH #2

Lee Majors and his then wife Farrah Fawcett-Majors appeared on *The Brady Bunch Variety Hour* as themselves. They spend the night at the Brady house.

Lee Majors was well-known for his role as Steve Austin in The Six Million Dollar Man *at the time of his appearance on the* Hour. *Three years later, he and his wife were divorced.*

CHARACTER ENCYCLOPEDIA

Malcolm
Appearance: OS #79
Sam accuses Alice of dating Malcolm after Jan and Cindy lead him to believe that Alice is cheating on him. Malcolm is a fruit vendor.

Maloney, Patty (herself)
Appearance: VH #8
Patty Maloney is a little person actress and stand-in from the '70s. In the variety hour show in which she appears, she plays herself. A security guard at the studio mistakes her for one of the Brady kids.

Manager (Britt Leach)
Appearance: OS #61
Davy Jones's manager doesn't get a name, but he has a lot of things to say to Marcia. First, he tells Marcia (while she is in disguise as a boy!) that Davy Jones is making a recording down at Atlas Records. Then when she gets there, he tells her basically to go away: no fans allowed. In the end, he promises her a copy of Davy's latest record, which Davy Jones delivers to her personally.

Mandy (Cris Callow)
Appearance: OS #74
Mandy is a mainlander vacationing in Hawaii. Greg wants to pick her up and feeds her the line that he is an island native in order to get close to her and put sun block on her. Bobby and Peter spoil his advances.

Marge (Hilary Thompson)
Appearance: OS #106
Marge works at King's Island Amusement Park at a football-throwing booth. Greg hits on her and she agrees later to have lunch with him. Her brother works at the Park in an animal suit.

Marlon (Larry Storch*)
Appearances: BK #1-22
Marlon is a talking mynah bird who knows magic…or at least pretends he does. The Brady kids discover him on a tropical island and bring him home with them. Most of his magic spells go awry and he is constantly making things difficult for the Brady kids. Marlon is very old; he's been around for centuries and has met many great historical figures.
*See "Fleetwood" entry.

Miss Marlowe (Tracy Reed)
Appearance: OS #3
Miss Marlowe is the co-director of Cindy's school play, "The Fairy Princess."

Marshall, Howie
Appearance: OS #87
Howie is a friend of Greg's.

Marshall, Monty (Edward Knight*)
Appearance: OS #94
Monty is the host of KBEX's *Question the Kids* show. Cindy appears on the show representing Clinton Grammar School.
**(See the Bonus Biographies chapter).*

Martin, Sandra (Cindi Crosby)
Appearance: OS #100
Sandra is Greg's girlfriend. She gets her visiting cousin a blind date with Peter (aka "Phil Packer") and they double-date together. Sandra and Linda play a joke on Greg and Peter after they discover that Peter is really Greg's brother and not the older, swinging guy he claims to be.

Mr. Martinelli (Jay Novello*)
Appearance: OS #91
Mr. Martinelli is the owner of Martinelli's Bicycle Shop. He hires Peter Brady to work as a repairman but fires him after three days. He says Pete's not mechanically inclined and thinks he would do better elsewhere.
**Jay Novello started his career on the stage in Chicago and eventually made his way to LA. Most of his parts had him playing Italian, Spanish, or Greek Americans and he was a specialist in dialects. His most memorable role is Major Lugato in* McHale's Navy.

Mathews, Frances (Dorothy Shay)
Appearance: OS #116
Frances is Harry Mathews' wife.

Mathews, Harry (Jim Backus*)
Appearances: OS #115, 116
Mr. Mathews takes over as president of Mike's architectural firm when Mr. Phillips retires in OS #113. He sends Mike a pool table, which the Bradys put in the carport. Bobby is a really good player and ends up beating Mr. Mathews in a game of nine ball. Mr. Mathews bets on the game and owes Bobby 256 packs of gum when it's over.
**See "Brown, Zaccariah T." entry.*

Maude
Appearance: OS #27
Maude is a friend of Alice's.

Maxie (Bert Rosario)
Appearance: BB#1
Maxie is a mover who, with Frank, moves Marcia, Jan, Phillip, and Wally's furniture into their new house.

Maxine
Appearance: OS #115
Maxine is a friend (maybe a girlfriend?) of Greg's.

Maxine (Sheila Shaw)
Appearance: TB #1
Maxine is a rehab nurse at the hospital in Nashville where Bobby is being treated for his spinal cord injury.

Maynard, Nora (Elaine Swann)
Appearance: OS #49
Nora runs a syndicated literary column. She reviews Carol Brady's article for Tomorrow's Woman Magazine and tells Carol that she should "tell it like it is."

Captain McCartney (James Flavin*)
Appearance: OS #111
Captain McCartney works for the local police force. He comes to the Brady house to investigate an alleged sighting of an alleged UFO. He's two years from retirement and he ends up being fooled by the same UFO trick Greg pulled on Bobby and Peter.
James Flavin has made hundreds of television appearances.

Brigadier General James A. McDivitt (himself*)
Appearance: OS #111
Former astronaut Jim McDivitt appears of television station KBEX in City. He talks about a UFO he saw on Gemini 4 in June 1965. Mario asks him, "Do you believe that life exists elsewhere in the universe?" General McDivitt replies, "Yes, Mario, I really do. I think it would be very naïve and really super egotistical on our part to believe that we're the only form of life in all this vast, vast universe in which we live."
James McDivitt served on the Gemini 4 and Apollo 9 missions. He served as manager for Apollo missions 12-16.

McGwyer, Bernie
Appearance: OS #62
Jan likes Bernie, but she doesn't want him to see her with glasses on.

Meadows, Fred (Aaron Lustig*)
Appearances: TB #2, 3
Fred is a member of the Committee of Concerned Citizens in City. He and his cohorts convince Mike Brady to run for City Council.

Aaron was nominated once for a Daytime Emmy.

Melanie (herself)
Appearance: VH #6
Melanie was the musical guest on episode #6 of *The Brady Bunch Variety Hour*. She sang "Cyclone."

Merrill, Jack (Rip Taylor*)
Appearances: VH #2-9
Mr. Merrill is constantly hanging around the Brady beach house. He starts out as their very inept mover, then goes through several other jobs including real estate broker, teacher, psychiatrist, and magician. He tries to go out on a date with Alice, but she turns him down. He often gets to perform during the *Hour* with the Bradys and is always paired with Alice. The Bradys have no reservations when it comes to making fun of his mustache and toupee.
Rip Taylor is an expressive comedian known for throwing confetti, for his outrageous toupees, and his big handlebar mustache. He has been a headliner in Las Vegas, has appeared on The Ed Sullivan Show *and many other venues.*

Metzger, Don and Wife
Appearance: OS #94
The Metzgers are invited to Mike and Carol's barbeque/Mexican dinner/smorgasbord.

Michelle (Kathy O'Dare)
Appearance: OS #113
Michelle is Peter's girlfriend. He takes her to a costume party. Michelle breaks a date with another guy just so that she can go out with Peter instead. Michelle goes to the party as Little Bo Peep and Peter is Dracula.

Michelson, Joey (Brian Nash*)
Appearance: OS #20
Joey is a friend of Greg's. Greg bribes him to go out with Marcia in exchange for tutoring Joey so that he can pass physics. Marcia is hip to Greg's plan, though, and will have nothing to do with Joey or the other two boys her family has bribed to go out with her.
Brian had one of the starring roles on the 1965-1967 television series Please Don't Eat the Daisies; *he played Joel Nash.*

Millard, Mark (Steve Dunne)
Appearance: OS #48
Mark Millard is an old high school flame of Alice's. He calls her up one day and courts her. He's a conman, an incessant gambler, and has had six wives. Poor Alice is snowed over by him until Mike and Carol come to her rescue just as she is about to hand him over a bunch of money. Alice is two-timing Sam when she dates Mark!

CHARACTER ENCYCLOPEDIA

Miss Miller

Appearance: OS #85

Miss Miller is the receptionist for Drs. Gordon and Vogel's dentistry practice.

Miller, Steve

Appearance: OS #18

Greg's friend who calls to let the Bradys know that he has seen their lost dog Tiger.

Millicent (Melissa Anderson*)

Appearance: OS #99

Millicent is Bobby's first girlfriend and first kiss. She kisses him because he stopped a boy at school from teasing her. Then a few days later Bobby kisses her. Unfortunately this time Millicent might have the mumps and Bobby has been exposed. Never fear, the doctor says she isn't sick and Bobby runs right over to her house to spend time with her.

*Melissa is known for her role as young Mary Ingalls on Little House on the Prairie.

Minkis, Billy

Appearances: OS #20, 41

Billy is a classmate of Peter's who can make bird noises through his braces. He also says Bobby couldn't carry a tune even if it had a handle on it.

Mop Top (Larry Storch*)

Appearances: BK #1-22

Mop Top is the Brady kids' pet dog. He goes along with Ping and Pong the pandas on all the kids' adventures. Unlike Marlon, Ping, and Pong, Mop Top can't talk. He is very imaginative, though, and tries to communicate with people by gestures.

*See "Fleetwood" entry.

Mr. Morton

Appearance: OS #85

Bobby and Peter got an old lawn mower engine from Mr. Morton that they used to build a go-cart.

Mount Claymore

Appearances: OS #36, 43

This is a local mountain where the Bradys like to go camping, climbing, and hiking.

Mulaney, Warren (Gary Rist)

Appearance: OS #54

Warren is Greg's #1 enemy. He beat Greg out for Student Council President and got on the first string basketball team in place of Greg. Warren asks Marcia out for a date and Greg is unhappy when he finds out.

Murdoch, Sam
Appearance: OS #83
Sam is a golfing buddy of Mike Brady's.

Muriel (Karen Foulkes)
Appearance: OS #79
Muriel is a look-alike to Margie Wimple (they're played by the same actress). Margie had a crush on Peter and Muriel does, too. Muriel blackmails Peter into going out with him in exchange for the sale of some tickets to the Family Night Frolics at Westdale High.

Myron the Mouse see **"Pets, Myron"**

Namath, Joe (himself*)
Appearance: OS #97
Joe Namath is a famous quarterback who played for the New York Jets. He is a hero of Bobby's and Bobby tells his friends that he knows Mr. Namath and that he has dinner at the Brady house every time he's in town, which will be next week for an exhibition game. Of course this is a lie. But Cindy concocts a scheme to get Joe to the Brady house to visit Bobby. Joe comes and ends up throwing passes to Bobby and all his friends. He's a real stand-up guy.
**Joe Namath was quarterback for the New York Jets from 1965-1976. All together he was in the NFL for thirteen years. He brought the Jets to victory in the 1969 Super Bowl.*

Naylor, Billy (Darryl Seman)
Appearance: OS #105
Billy is trying out for the part of the landlord in Fillmore Junior High's production of "An American Girl in Paris." He tries out opposite Jan, who ends up spilling paint all over his shirt.

Nelson, Alice see **Franklin, Alice**

Nelson, Emily
Appearance: OS #25
Alice's older sister.

Nelson, Joe
Appearance: OS #83
Joe Nelson is a golfing opponent of Mike Brady's. He has an "overgrown" son and Mike and Greg are supposed to compete against them as pairs.

Nelson, Myrtle
Appearances: OS #4, 25
Alice's younger sister.

CHARACTER ENCYCLOPEDIA

Nichols, Jennifer (Tannis G. Montgomery)

Appearance: OS #83

Jennifer is a contestant for head cheerleader at Westdale. She courts Greg Brady with her wily feminine ways and the two of them go surfing together and to a movie. Greg discovers after the contest is over that she was only using him in order to become head cheerleader. Greg was chairman of the selection committee and voted for Pat Conway instead of Jennifer. Jennifer's phone number is 814-9031.

Officer Dumont (Steve Weldon)

Appearance: BB #1

The Officer is called to the Logan-Covington residence by their pesky neighbor, Miss Fritzsinger, to investigate a mysterious smell.

O'Hara, Linda (Gigi Perreau*)

Appearance: OS #17

Miss O'Hara is Greg's math teacher. Greg has a crush on her and is flunking math because he cannot concentrate in class. Miss O'Hara is engaged to Wes Parker.

Gigi won a Young Artist Award: Former Child Star Lifetime Achievement Award.

The Ohio Players (themselves)

Appearance: VH #7

The Ohio Players are a guest musical act on *The Brady Bunch Variety Hour*. They sing "Fire," which is still a popular song today (it appears on the movie soundtrack for *Ladder 49* and many other films). They are introduced on the show by Redd Foxx.

Oliver

Appearances: OS #74, 75

Oliver is a big Hawaiian tiki that resides in a cave. Professor Whitehead, an archaeologist, discovers it, names it "Oliver," and commences talking to it as if it were alive.

Oliver, Cousin see **Cousin Oliver**

Operation Alice

Appearance: OS #4

This is the scheme Mike invents for the kids, Carol and himself to convince Alice that she should stay in employment as their housekeeper. Alice had decided to leave after the boys were comfortable with Carol; she thought she was no longer needed. The Operation, of course, is successful and Alice stays.

Operation Bounce Back

Appearance: OS #36

The plan is for Bobby to get over his fear of heights, so the Bradys borrow a trampoline. Some of the kids and

Alice try jumping on it and enticing Bobby down from his room. This Operation is a failure; Bobby is still scared of heights.

Operation Wipeout
Appearance: OS #104
Operation Wipeout is the plan that Greg, Peter, and Bobby put into effect to trap Jerry Rogers. They place a phony playbook in the family room as bait. The plan is to find out if Jerry is interested in Marcia or interested in stealing the playbook. The Operation is a success because now they have proof that Jerry is a fink: he stole the book.

Osborn, Dave
Appearance: OS #99
Dave lends Greg some records for the Roaring 20's Party the Bradys are attending.

Osmond, Donny and Marie (themselves*)
Appearance: VH #1
Donny and Marie appear on the first variety hour show. They participate in a 1950s roller rink skit with the Brady family. Donny plays Donnzie and Marie is Marie. Before *The Brady Bunch Hour* ever aired, the Bradys appeared as guests on Donny and Marie's show. This gave them the opportunity to return the favor.
Donnie and Marie Osmond have been famous singing and acting stars their whole lives. At this point in time they had their own variety show.

"Our Pilgrim Fathers or Through Hardship to Freedom" Written, produced, and directed by Gregory Brady
Appearance: OS #29
This is the film that Greg makes for his history class. He writes it about the Pilgrims and makes a movie with Mike's 8mm camera.

The Players:
Peter = John Alden & Samoset
Bobby = Miles Standish & Squanto
Jan = Priscilla
Mike = Pilgrim & Captain Jones
Alice = Pilgrim & John Carver
Carol = Pilgrim
Cindy = Pilgrim
Marcia = Pilgrim

The Narration (as read by Greg Brady):
It was September the 16th in the year 1620 that the Pilgrims set sail from England for Virginia. They missed Virginia because in the middle of the Atlantic they ran into storms. But they persevered and sailed on and finally they made it to the New World, and on a stormy day they first set foot on Plymouth Rock. December came and

CHARACTER ENCYCLOPEDIA

it was very cold and they didn't have much shelter so they got sick. Then came a terrible snow storm and they got even sicker, and sicker, and sicker, and sicker, and sicker. Finally spring came and so did the Indians...so did the Indians. The Indians amazed the Pilgrims by speaking some English and the Pilgrims made friends with the Indians and invited them to a feast. First they gave thanks for safely reaching the New World. Then they ate, and ate, and ate, and ate, and ate, and ate. Then one day it was time for the Mayflower to sail back to England. Captain Jones asked the Pilgrims who had survived if any wanted to go back with him. Not one of them did. He reminded them of the storms and the Indians, but they wouldn't go. So he split and the Mayflower sailed leaving the Pilgrims to build a new country, which they did.
Greg turns in his project to his teacher and gets an A!

Owens, Arthur (Christopher Knight)
Appearance: OS #113
Arthur is Peter's doppelgänger; he's a look-alike who just transferred to Fillmore Junior High. He and Peter run into each other in the hallway and hatch a plan to fool each other's family members. Arthur goes to the Brady house to see if he can pass as Peter. He does, which gives Peter the idea to get Arthur to go out with Mike's boss's niece in his place. The "twins" are discovered by Mike and Carol, though, and Peter's plan is uncovered. Arthur is never seen again.

Packer, Phil (Peter Brady)
Appearance: OS #100
Phil is Peter's alter ego. He assumes this identity to go out on a date with an older woman, Linda. Phil is a swinging guy from another high school. The ladies can't resist him! But Linda and her cousin soon find out that Phil is really Peter and the jig is up.

Page (Whitney Rydbeck*)
Appearance: OS #61
The Page works at the Hank Colman Show. He tells Marcia and Mike that they are 24 hours too late to catch Davy Jones. They are currently filming tomorrow's episode, which will be an interview with the head of the Sanitation Department in City.
Whitney also appears in the movie A Very Brady Sequel *as an auctioneer.*

Pakaya, Jimmy (Michele Campo)
Appearances: OS #51, 52
Jimmy is a Navajo boy who is running away from home. Bobby and Cindy encounter him at the Grand Canyon and Jimmy helps them find their way back to camp. In return, Bobby and Cindy bring him some food to eat for dinner. Jimmy is running away because he is afraid that his grandfather will not understand that he wants to become an astronaut. After a good talk with Mike Brady, Jimmy comes to the realization that all he has to do is talk to his grandfather Chief Eagle Cloud and they are reunited.

Parker, Eric (Kerry MacLane)
Appearance: OS #97

Eric is a friend of Bobby's. He doubts Bobby's story that the Bradys know Joe Namath. In the end he gets to meet the famous quarterback himself and never doubts Bobby again.

Parker, Wes (himself)
Appearance: OS #17
Wes Parker is a first baseman for the Los Angeles Dodgers and he won a Golden Glove. His character is engaged to Miss O'Hara, Greg's math teacher in school. Wes tells Greg that if he gets an A in math, he can trade in his autograph for two tickets to the season opener.

Pauline
Appearance: OS #92
Carol Brady borrows a black wig from Pauline for her Cleopatra costume.

Mrs. Payne (Molly Dodd)
Appearance: OS #109
Mrs. Payne is aptly named because she serves as a royal pain in Mr. and Mrs. Kelly's sides. She is their neighbor and tells the Kellys she's none too happy about their newly-adopted children. She makes a bigot of herself when talking about Dwayne and Steve Kelly.

Mrs. Pearson
Appearances: OS #26, 29
Greg's freshman history teacher. Mrs. Pearson calls Mike and Carol to tell them that she is worried about Greg's falling grades. Three episodes later, she is Greg's favorite teacher because of the history assignment on the Pilgrims she gives. Greg makes a movie about the Pilgrims for the project called, "Our Pilgrim Fathers."

Peggy
Appearance: OS #55
Peggy is a friend of Peter's.

Penny
Appearance: OS #88
Penny is acquainted with Marcia Brady. Marcia tries to sell her her watch, but Penny doesn't buy it.

Miss Perry (Ruth Anson)
Appearance: OS #89
Miss Perry is a librarian in City.

Mr. Peterson (Bob Peoples)
Appearance: OS #31
This is Randy Peterson's father.

Peterson, Randy (Annette Ferra)

Appearance: OS #31

Randy is Greg's first girlfriend. Greg tries to impress her by talking about the car he's going to buy when he gets his license and by talking about all the buildings he's going to design as an architect. Randy takes after school drama lessons at Campus Drama School.

Peterson, Tom (Kelly Flynn)

Appearance: OS #76

Tom is a friend of Greg's. Greg introduces Marcia to Tom on Marcia's first day of school. She promptly makes a fool out of herself. There is no indication that Tom is related to Randy Peterson or her father.

Pets: The Brady Bunch owned a few pets you might know about: Tiger the dog, Fluffy the cat, and "Bird." But did you know that during the original series the Bunch had an astonishing *twenty-three* animals? It's true! The pets ranged from a parakeet to frogs, rabbits, goldfish, and a hamster. Unfortunately for the animals, the Bradys did not seem to take very good care of them...no pet except one (Tiger) lasted for more than one episode. We'll never know what really happened to the pets, but it must not have been very lucky to be a Brady pet. Each of the Bradys' animals (and some non-pet animals) is described below.

Pets: Fluffy the Cat

Appearance: OS #1

Pet Tally = 1

Owned by the Brady girls Marcia, Jan, and Cindy, Fluffy appears in the pilot episode, "The Honeymoon." Fluffy is the first of the Brady pets to be here one minute and gone the next. Perhaps Fluffy stayed behind at Grandma and Grandpa's house after Carol moved in with Mike, but we never hear any sort of explanation on the show.

Pets: Goldfish

Appearance: OS #54

Pet Tally = 2

Mike Brady won a goldfish at the kids' school carnival.

Pets: Goldfish #2

Appearance: BB #5

Pet Tally = 2

Carol mentions that when the girls were little, Marcia had some pet goldfish. Jan felt sorry for them because they swam all day long, so she took them out of the bowl, dried them off, and put them on her pillow so they could sleep one night. Obviously, Jan's idea was flawed and the poor fishies ended up dead. (These fish don't count toward the pet tally because they were pets before the Bradys became the Brady Bunch.)

Pets: Goliath

Appearance: OS #69

Pet Tally = 2

Goliath is a pet mouse that belongs to Bobby's friend Benji, so he doesn't count as a Brady pet. Nevertheless, he is an animal worth mentioning.

Pets: Guppy

Appearance: OS #35

Pet Tally = 3

After the cap for the salt shaker falls off on Mike's breakfast, Cindy says, "Peter was using the top to strain a guppy out of the fish tank." "Strain a guppy out of his fish tank?" Carol asks. Apparently, the guppy is Peter's. We never see the guppy or the fish tank on screen.

Pets: Henrietta the Hamster

Appearance: OS #92

Pet Tally = 4

Bobby is giving his hamster a treat. The day before was Henrietta's birthday and Bobby brings her sunflower seeds.

Pets: Herman the Goldfish

Appearance: OS #115

Pet Tally = 5

When Cindy and Oliver ask Alice if she has any secrets to reveal she says, "One of my goldfish is an expectant mother...the mother-to-be is named Herman." She apparently has more than one goldfish (note she says, "one" of my), but without knowing the full total we will just count Herman.

Pets: Herman the Turtle

Appearance: OS #3

Pet Tally = 6

Bobby has a pet turtle named Herman. He is on screen for about 10 seconds altogether during the episode. We never see Herman again.

Pets: Henry the Bullfrog

Appearance: OS #10

Pet Tally = 7

Cindy is sad when her bullfrog Henry does not turn into a prince after she kisses him two times.

Pets: Lizard

Appearance: OS #70

Pet Tally = 8

Cindy's secret admirer Tommy Jamison gives her a lizard. The lizard escapes from the shoe box where it's kept and ends up in the kitchen, frightening Alice.

Pets: Myron the Mouse

Appearance: OS #38

Pet Tally = 8

Myron is technically not a pet because he is Greg's science project. Greg must teach him to run a maze over the weekend. During his short time in the Brady household, he causes quite an uproar. After filming for the episode was over, Eve Plumb took Myron home with her and made a pet out of him!

Pets: The Mystery Cat

Appearance: OS #3

Pet Tally = 8

During the same episode we see Herman the turtle, there is a mysterious black-and-white cat sitting on a lawn chair on the Brady patio. It's not Fluffy; Fluffy was orange. So whose is it? Where did it come from? Is it the Bradys' cat or a neighborhood stray? Or, could she be Guinevere, the neighbor's cat mentioned by Greg in episode #38? (Greg was afraid his mouse Myron would be eaten by Guinevere.) The most likely theory is that it was a stray that wandered onto the set. Apparently Paramount Studios had a stray cat problem at the time. Since the Mystery Cat's origins are dubious, it does not count toward the pet tally.

Pets: Parakeet

Appearance: OS #36

Pet Tally = 9

After Bobby falls from a climb to a tree house, Mike buys him a parakeet to cheer him up and keep him busy while he's confined to his bed with a sprained ankle. Peter quips, "Wow, a parakeet just for a sprained ankle. Can I get an alligator if I broke my leg?" No such luck, Peter. The parakeet never gets a name because the Bradys do not know if it is a boy or girl bird. This type of parakeet is very popular in the United States and is called a budgerigar or "budgie." Budgies are native to Australia.

Pets: Rabbit and Canary

Appearance: OS #45

Pet Tally = 11

Peter auditions for his school's vaudeville show as a magician. Jan is supposed to be his assistant, but she has sprained her ankle and cannot come to the audition. Peter tells the judges that he could do some neat tricks, if only he had his assistant to help him out. He says, "I've got an even better trick. It's really terrific with a rope, a rabbit, and a canary. But I can't do that one either without my assistant." The rope, rabbit, and canary are curiously absent from the stage. But if Pete says he has them, they must be there somewhere. Eventually Cindy shows up to save the day and performs the disappearing lady trick for the judges. We never see the canary/rabbit/rope trick.

Pets: Raquel the Goat

Appearance: OS #101

Pet Tally = 11

Raquel is another one of those Brady animals who is here for a short time, but is not technically a pet and therefore does not count toward the tally. Raquel is Greg's rival high school's (Coolidge High School) mascot. Greg steals her in retaliation for some Coolidge guys who took Westdale's bear cub. Greg gets caught, of course, and must write a 5,000-word essay on "the evils of mascot stealing" as punishment. If you consider a typical hand-written page (Greg probably wouldn't have typed it) to be 250 words, that's a twenty-page essay Greg has to write!

Pets: Romeo and Juliet the Rabbits
Appearance: OS #117
Pet Tally = 13
Cindy and Cousin Oliver buy two white rabbits so they can breed them, sell the babies, and make a million dollars. Their scheme goes awry when they discover that Juliet is really a male rabbit. However, they are able to sell their rabbits back to the pet store after Bobby accidentally spills hair tonic on the rabbits that turns their fur orange. Since this is the last episode of *The Brady Bunch*, Romeo and Juliet get the honor of being the last Brady pets.

Pets: Spunker, Old Croaker, Herman, Flash, and 3 Unnamed Frogs
Appearance: OS #87
Pet Tally = 20
Spunker is Bobby's entrant in a frog jumping contest. Spunker is a store-bought frog that Bobby thinks can beat any old pond frog. Peter decides to join Bobby's adventure and gets Old Croaker from Burke's Pond. Peter and Bobby hold their own jump-off and Spunker loses. This prompts Bobby to go to the Pond and pick up his own wild frog. He grabs 5 new frogs. Two of them are named Herman (or possibly Hermit) and Flash; the other three aren't named. Greg drives Bobby, Peter, and their frogs to the jumping contest. Peter's frog comes in 35th and Bobby's is 49th. When Greg drops the boys off back home, he goes on a date with Rachel. But the frogs are still in the car and end up jumping on poor Rachel's head.

| *Chip* | *Rupert* | *Tiger* |

Pets: Tiger the Dog
Appearances: OS #1, 5, 7, 10, 15, 18, 35, 36, 38
Pet Tally = 21

Tiger is the most well-known of the Brady pets. Tiger makes his first appearance in the pilot episode, "The Honeymoon." He is a mutt and is owned by the Brady boys Greg, Peter, and Bobby. The boys and Mike had Tiger even before they had Bobby, so he had been around with the family for quite some time before Mike married Carol. After the wedding, Tiger becomes the family pet for the whole blooming Brady bunch.

Tiger appears in 9 episodes altogether and has feature stories in episodes 5 and 18. In "Katchoo," the family fears that Jan is allergic to Tiger and that they must get rid of the dog. Fortunately, it turns out that Jan is allergic to Tiger's flea powder, and the dog stays. The day is saved! In "Tiger! Tiger!" Tiger runs away and Bobby is very forlorn. The family soon discovers that Tiger is cavorting with a neighborhood dog and is the father of a litter of three puppies.

Tiger appears in several episodes during the first season, but mysteriously disappears after episode #38 in season 2. What happened? Well, the real Tiger was struck by a car during the first season. Then they got a replacement Tiger but the second dog wasn't a reliable actor so they canned him. There is never an explanation on the show as to where Tiger went. Even more strange, Tiger's dog house stays in the backyard long after Tiger himself disappears from the scene. The dog house is seen as late as episode #114 (out of 117).

Tiger was actually played by three different dogs: Chip (episode #1) had a whitish muzzle, Rupert (#5, 7, 15) had a dark muzzle, and Tiger* (#10, 18, 35, 36, 38) had a very shaggy brown muzzle. Rupert is the one who was hit by a car. Tiger was the bad actor who once had to be tied down to the floor so that he wouldn't move! (Don't worry, he wasn't hurt.)

*Tiger eventually learned how to act and co-starred in a 1975 kinky science fiction film A Boy and His Dog for which he won a Patsy Award for best animal performance.

Pets: Turtle
Appearance: OS #60
Pet Tally = 22
Cindy tells Alice her sandwiches always get the best trades. Once she traded a peanut butter & jelly sandwich for a turtle.

Pets: White Rabbit
Appearance: OS #9
Pet Tally = 23
When Greg is on the phone bartering with his friend Harv, Greg offers him "my baseball mitt, my autographed picture of Raquel Welch, and my pet white rabbit" in exchange for Harv's bike. When Mike interrupts his phone call, Greg tells him, "If I don't unload that rabbit in a hurry, we're going to have dozens of them." Apparently the rabbit is a pregnant female. We never see the rabbit on screen, and this is the only mention of the bunny. Thus, we can assume that Greg's deal went through. Is it any coincidence that the rabbit is "invisible" and Greg's friend's name is Harvey? You be the judge.

Phil (Gary Marsh)
Appearance: OS #39
Phil is a friend of Greg's and is a member of their rock group called The Banana Convention.

Phillips, Ed (or Harry) (Jack Collins)
Appearance: OS #31, 42, 47, 73, 81, 88, 106, 113
This is Mike's boss at his architectural firm; Mr. Phillips is president. In OS #47, his name changes from "Ed" to "Harry R. Phillips." Then in #113 it goes back to Ed! He invites the whole Brady family to go deep sea fishing with him and his wife. He also threatens to fire Mike a few episodes later because his family is protesting against his firm building a new courthouse on their favorite park's land. Mr. Phillips is both benevolent and stern.

Phillips, Jane (Jackie Joseph*)
Appearance: OS #109
Miss Phillips works at the Terrace Adoption Home. She helps Mr. and Mrs. Kelly adopt a boy named Matt. Later she lets them adopt two more boys, Dwayne and Steve, after only one week's worth of paperwork. She has a paperweight on her desk that Matt made.
Interestingly, Jackie Joseph was married to Ken Berry, the man who plays Ken Kelly in "Kelly's Kids." They adopted two children of their own in real life before they divorced.

Phillips, Pamela (Denise Nickerson)
Appearance: OS #113
Pamela is Ed/Harry Phillips's niece. She is supposed to be on a date with Peter Brady, but Pete gets his look-alike Arthur Owens to stay at home with her instead.
Denise played Violet in Willy Wonka and the Chocolate Factory.

Pierce, Lance (Bill Mullikin)
Appearance: OS #14
Mr. Pierce works for television station KTRY in City. He and his crew film the presentation of the Father of the Year Award to Mike Brady.

Ping and Pong (Lola Fisher, Jane Webb)
Appearances: BK #2-22
Ping and Pong are pandas from China. They were sent into space but crash landed on a deserted island where the Brady kids find them. They join the kids in all their adventures. The pandas speak some sort of Chinese-like gibberish.

Policeman (Elvenn Havard)
Appearance: OS #98
This policeman stops Sam and tells him that he's parked in a red zone. It doesn't matter much, though, because

CHARACTER ENCYCLOPEDIA

Sam and Mike Brady are only there temporarily. They stopped at the supermarket to buy an apple. Since we don't know what city the Bradys live in, the policeman's arm badge simply says "municipal police."

Porky
Appearance: OS #67
Porky is a high school classmate of Mike Brady's.

Dr. Catherine Porter (Marion Ross*)
Appearance: OS #13
Dr. Porter is Marcia, Jan, and Cindy's pediatrician. She combines practices with Dr. Cameron to ease her workload. Both doctors still make house calls!
Marion Ross is, of course, Marion Cunningham on Happy Days. She is still acting today.

Mr. & Mrs. George Powell (Nick Toth) and (Barbara Mallory*)
Appearances: AVBC; TB #1
Mrs. Powell is having a baby and Greg delivers it. Two years later we learn the baby was a boy whom they named Andrew. The Powells are back to deliver a second child with Greg in 1990.
Barbara is Lloyd J. Schwartz's wife. In addition to appearing as Mrs. Powell, Barbara played Mrs. Whitfield in Growing Up Brady and Carol Brady in the stage production A Very Brady Musical.

Prescott, Leonard (F.J. O'Neil)
Appearance: AVBC
He owns Prescott Toys. He hires Wally Logan to be his new salesman after Wally loses his job at Tyler Toys.

Mr. Price (Milton Parsons)
Appearance: OS #68
This is Peter's science teacher at Fillmore Junior High. Greg and Marcia also had him when they were in Junior High. Mr. Price is notoriously difficult. Pete ends up getting a C in his class. Marcia made a puppet figure of Mr. Price for the Junior High's Jamboree Night.

Price, Vincent (himself*)
Appearance: VH #4
Mr. Price walks in on Greg when he and Merrill are in Greg's new apartment. Mr. Price is there because he's heard it's haunted and he wants to research the ghosts. He is kind of scary and Merrill runs away as hastily as possible, leaving Greg to find out about the ghosts on his own.
You'll remember Vincent Price from the Original Series in his role in the Hawaiian episodes as Professor Whitehead. Vincent Price is a renowned actor most well-known for his roles in horror films. He died in 1993 at the age of 82.

Prince Victor

Appearance: OS #3

Prince Victor is a character in the play where Cindy plays the fairy princess. The Prince is turned into a frog by the Wicked Witch.

Pringle, Mr. (James Millhollin)

Appearance: OS #1

Mr. Pringle is the stuck-up hotel owner where Mike and Carol spend their honeymoon. He "obviously does not dig the modern generation" when he learns that the newlyweds already have children.

Rachel (Hope Sherwood*)

Appearances: OS #67, 87

Rachel is Greg's girlfriend. She has two bad luck dates with him. On the first date to the drive-in Bobby tags along and ruins it. On the second date, Bobby and Peter's frog ends up jumping on her head at the drive-in. Poor Rachel put up with a lot to see Greg.

*See "Gretchen" entry.

Ralph

Appearance: OS #79

Ralph owns a fish market. Sam accuses Alice of cheating on him with Ralph.

Rand, Katy (Julie Reese)

Appearance: OS #59

Katy is a friend of Jan's who also has a big sister whose shadow is hard to escape. Katy and Jan both try out for the Pom-Pom Girls and Katy makes it but Jan doesn't.

Randall, Tony (himself*)

Appearance: VH #1

Tony Randall is the first guest on *The Brady Bunch Hour*. He is asked to take over the role of Mike Brady for the show because the kids think the real Mike stinks. But they soon withdraw their offer and give the job back to their real dad. Mr. Randall does a dramatic…well, it's more aptly described as comedic…recitation of Dame Edith Sitwell's poem, "Polka" set to music by Sir William Walton.

*Tony Randall won an Emmy for his performance on The Odd Couple. He has been nominated five other times for Emmys and six times for Golden Globes.

Randi

Appearances: OS #17, 28

Randi is a friend of Marcia's. This is a different Randi than the one Greg dates later.

Randolph, J.D. (E.G. Marshall*)

Appearance: OS #28

Mr. Randolph is the principal of Fillmore Junior High. He sentences Marcia to a week's detention when he discovers a drawing she did in class. The drawing was of George Washington, but another classmate of Marcia's added the words, "Mrs. Denton? Or a Hippopotamus?" to the drawing and Marcia got blamed for it.

E.G. Marshall won two Emmys for his performance in The Defenders, a show in which Robert Reed was co-star before The Brady Bunch.

Raquel the Goat see **"Pets, Raquel"**

Raymond, Jim

Appearance: OS #49

Head of the promotional department for Tomorrow's Woman Magazine.

Mr. Remington

Appearance: OS #106

Mr. Remington owns and directs King's Island Amusement Park. He reviews some plans that Mike drew up for a Park expansion and approves them. His colleague is Mr. Dempsey.

Reverend (Dabbs Greer*)

Appearance: OS #1; TB #1

This is the reverend who married Mike and Carol Brady in episode #1 of *The Brady Bunch.* He reprises his role in *The Bradys* to marry Bobby Brady and Tracy Wagner.

Dabbs Greer has a distinguished career as a character actor.

Reverend Melbourne (Byron Webster)

Appearance: OS #107

The Reverend is officiating at Sam's cousin Clara's elopement.

Reynolds, Harold (Jerry Levreau)

Appearance: OS #20

Mike and Carol call Harold and bribe him to be Marcia's date to the school dance. Harold is very shy and can only mutter, "I, uh, I, uh," when he sees Marcia. Marcia figures out her parents' plan very quickly and will have nothing to do with Harold or the other two boys her family members have bribed to go out with her.

Rich (Don Carter)

Appearance: OS #104

Rich is a football player for Fairview High.

Richards, Ben (Richard Brestoff)
Appearance: BGGM
Mr. Richards is Carol Brady's boss at Willowbrook Realty.

Richardson, Marjorie (Gloria Henry*)
Appearance: BB #4
Mrs. Richardson is very rich and employs Jan Brady to design a summer home for her. Jan almost loses her business because of Phillip and Wally's outlandish behavior, but she ends up getting it back along with Mrs. Richardson's praise.
Gloria Henry played Alice Mitchell (Dennis's mother) in TV's Dennis the Menace.

Richie
Appearance: OS #108
Richie is an acquaintance of Greg's.

Riley, Graham (Gerard Maguire)
Appearance: TB #5
Mr. Riley is visiting City from Australia on business. Mike plays host and throws a party for him. Because of a misunderstood phone call, the party has an Austrian theme instead of Australian. But that's just fine with Riley; he and his wife have heard enough "G'day, mates" from Americans to last them a lifetime.

Roberts, Ted (Phillip Richard Allen)
Appearance: AVBC
Mr. Roberts bought some property from Advantage Properties with Carol Brady as the realtor. Carol recommends Mike to be Ted's architect on a new plaza he's constructing. But Mr. Roberts wants to skimp on a higher margin of safety and his building ends up collapsing. Mike quit the job but he's called back on emergency when the building caves in. The collapse traps two security guards and Mike inside, but they all come out okay.

The Rockets
Appearance: OS #3
This is the baseball team for which Greg and Peter play. Later, Greg joins the Tigers as a pitcher.

Rogers, Jerry (Chris Beaumont)
Appearance: OS #104
Jerry plays quarterback for Fairview High School, Westdale's rival. He pretends to like Marcia in order to swipe Greg's football playbook. He succeeds in swiping the book, but only after Marcia learns that he is using her. He gets benched during the League Championship game because his coach found out that he stole Westdale's playbook, even if it was phony.

Ronnie (Charlie Martin Smith*)
Appearance: OS #53
Ronnie is a friend of Greg's. Greg tries to get him to buy his broken-down car for $100. In the end, Greg has a change of heart and lets Ronnie the sucker off the hook.
*Charlie played Terry "The Toad" Fields in American Graffiti.

Dr. Ruskin
Appearance: OS #20
This is the dentist who puts braces on Marcia.

Rusty (Stephen Liss)
Appearance: OS #11
Rusty is Greg's campaign manager while he runs for president of the Fillmore Junior High student body. Greg fires Rusty after he proposes to start a nasty rumor about Marcia, who is Greg's opponent in the race.

Ruthie (Barbara Henderson*)
Appearance: OS #28
Ruthie is Marcia's friend who attends a sleepover party at the Brady household. Ruthie is asked a truth or dare question and takes the dare – she has to go upstairs to see what Marcia's brothers are doing. When she and Marcia get to the top of the stairs, Greg jumps out in a Halloween mask and scares them.
*See "Arnold, Peggy" entry.

Safe
Appearances: OS #57, 84, 86
The new and improved Safe Laundry Soap is featured in an episode where the Bradys are invited to film a television commercial for the product. The Bradys are paid 2,000 boxes of Safe soap when they drop out of the commercial. In future episodes, one can see boxes of Safe lying around in the Brady service porch.

Sally
Appearance: OS #30
Marcia's friend.

Sam
Appearance: OS #66
Sam is Aunt Jenny's limo driver.

Sam the Butcher see **Franklin, Sam**

Samuels, Hamilton (Oliver McGowan)
Appearance: OS #14

Mr. Samuels is the publisher of The Daily Chronicle, the newspaper for the city in which the Bradys live. Mr. Samuels personally delivers the Father of the Year Award to Mike Brady.

Mrs. Sanders
Appearance: OS #68
Mrs. Sanders is Marcia's English teacher at Fillmore Junior High. Marcia makes a puppet figure of Mrs. Sanders for Jamboree Night.

Sanders, Fred (Don Fenwick)
Appearance: OS #114
Fred Sanders works for the F.B.I. He comes to the Brady house to complete a background check on Mike. Mike is the architect for a confidential government building and the F.B.I. is there to get him security clearance. Bobby and Oliver get the idea that Mike is some sort of spy after they see Mr. Sanders come and go.

Mr. Schultz
Appearance: OS #116
Mr. Schultz owns a supermarket.

Scott (Casey Morgan)
Appearance: OS #11
Scott is Greg's second campaign manager while he runs for president of the Fillmore Junior High student body.

Scott
Appearance: OS #87
Scott is a friend of Greg's who's trying to get rock concert tickets. We don't know if this Scott is the same as the one who was Greg's campaign manager three years earlier.

Sheldon, Martha
Appearance: OS #9, 16, 54, 60
Martha is Carol's quirky friend who needs advice on hemming a dress and who believes in horoscopes. Carol agrees with Mike that Martha is a "fruitcake."

Shirley (Jerelyn Fields)
Appearance: OS #108
Shirley is a friend of Jan's. Jan promises her that she will babysit for Shirley's little brother sometime, but when Shirley asks her to one day, Jan says she can't.

"The Silver Platters"
Appearance: OS #88
This is the name that the six Brady kids assign themselves when they perform on *The Pete Sterne Amateur Hour* on TV. The name comes from the gift they plan to give their parents for their fourth wedding anniversary:

CHARACTER ENCYCLOPEDIA

an engraved silver platter. Under the guise of "The Silver Platters" the kids audition for the show by singing "Sunshine Day" and perform "Keep On" in the competition. The Silver Platters place third and are awarded a plaque for their efforts.

Mrs. Simpson (Maggie Malooly)
Appearance: OS #18
Mrs. Simpson owns the female dog that Tiger has puppies with.

Simpson, Doug (Nicholas Hammond*)
Appearance: OS #80
Doug Simpson is the star of the football team and the big man on campus at Westdale High. He asks Marcia for a date but breaks it off after he sees her with a swollen nose. He's the stereotypical shallow jock. After Marcia is healed he asks her out again but she declines by saying, "something suddenly came up." Doug himself gets a swollen nose after Marcia's boyfriend Charley punches him for teasing Marcia.
*Nicholas is the first of two actors from The Sound of Music to appear in a Brady episode. (Nicholas played Friedrich in the movie and the actress who played Gretl appears in a season five episode.) He is also very well known for his role as Peter Parker / Spider-Man in the 1978-79 series The Amazing Spider-Man.

Sinclair, Joe (Charles Stewart)
Appearance: OS #116
Joe works in the blueprints department of Mike's architectural firm. He comes to the Brady house for dinner and an evening of pool.

Sinclair, Muriel (Grace Spence)
Appearance: OS #116
Muriel is Joe Sinclair's wife.

Smasher Duran
Appearance: OS #67
Smasher is a high school classmate of Mike Brady's.

Snoozie Suzie
Appearance: BGGM
Tyler Toy Company created the Snoozie Suzie doll. Marcia says she had one as a kid. First it sings a chorus of lullabies, then one of Suzie's eyes closes, then the other.

Mrs. Spencer (Dani Nolan)
Appearance: OS #21
Mrs. Spencer is the mother of Tina Spencer, the little girl whom Peter saves from a falling wall in Driscoll's Toy Store.

Spencer, Tina (Melanie Baker)
Appearance: OS #21
When Tina climbs up some shelves in Driscoll's Toy Store, the structure begins to wobble. Peter Brady saves her just in time from being crushed by the wall.

St. James, Morty (Bill Cort)
Appearance: TB #4
Morty is the owner of House of St. James, a fashion company. He turns Marcia down when she applies for a job. He thinks Marcia's out of touch with modern styles.

Stephen Decatur High
Appearance: OS #39
This is a high school in City. None of the kids attend the school, but Greg and his band The Banana Convention play a gig there. Stephen Decatur, Jr. was a naval officer who fought in the Barbary Wars.

Mrs. Stephens
Appearance: OS #64
Mrs. Stephens orders a porter house steak and some veal from Sam's Butcher Shop. Greg is supposed to deliver them to her at 231 Elm Street, but Sam ends up making the delivery himself.

Sterne, Pete (Steve Dunn*)
Appearance: OS #88
Pete Sterne is the host of *The Pete Sterne Amateur Hour* on television station KBEX. He hosts the Brady kids when they sing "Sunshine Day" and "Keep On." The kids win third prize (a plaque) for the week's competition.
**Steve also played Mark Millard.*

Steve (Randy Lane)
Appearance: OS #21
Steve is Peter's friend. He makes up an excuse for not going to Peter's party celebrating his being a hero.

Steve (Harlen Carraher)
Appearance: OS #86
Steve is a classmate of Bobby's. Bobby, acting as Safety Monitor, turns him in for chewing gum in the hallway.

Steve
Appearance: OS #103, 116
Steve is a friend of Bobby's who invites him to a ballgame. Steve is pitching against the Woodland Wolves. Steve has a pool table in his house where Bobby learns to be a regular hustler.

Dr. Stevens (Richard Heckert)
Appearance: TB #1
Dr. Stevens is Bobby Brady's doctor in Nashville.

Stevens, Burt (Larry Michaels)
Appearance: OS #97
Burt is a friend of Bobby's. Burt doubts Bobby's story about knowing Joe Namath. But he gets to meet the great quarterback himself at the Bradys' after he comes for a visit.

Stevie
Appearance: OS #66
Stevie is a friend of Jan's. He asks her to go to a party with him.

Mr. Stokey (Fred Pinkard)
Appearance: OS #4
Mr. Stokey is the mailman who delivers the boys' telescope.

Mr. Stoner (Victor Killian*)
Appearance: OS #32
Mr. Stoner is the owner of the wallet the Brady boys found while playing football in a vacant lot. He lost $1,100 and gives the boys $20 for a reward.
Victor Kilian (correct spelling) appeared in dozens of westerns and other films in the 1930s, 40s, and 50s. He continued acting through his death in 1979 when he was brutally murdered by burglars at the age of 88.

TIKI TALK

According to the Bureau of Labor and Statistics' online inflation calculator, $1,100 in 1970 is equivalent to $6,810.81 in 2016! Maybe Mr. Stoner and his "missus" were on their way home from a lucrative trip to Vegas.

Stuart (Sean Kelly)
Appearance: OS #84
Stuart is a classmate of Peter's who calls Peter a traitor for playing the part of Benedict Arnold in the school play.

Sue
Appearance: OS #42
A friend of Marcia's.

Sullivan, Julie
Appearance: BGGM
Julie is a friend of Wally's who is invited to his wedding. Mrs. Brady places Julie at the same table as David Gilbert.

Sundale
Appearance: OS #89
A town not far from City. Jethroe Collins lives here.

Sunflower Girls
Appearance: OS #44
The Sunflower Girls are the equivalent of the Girl Scouts. They even sell cookies for a dollar a box. Marcia has many badges with them: her Water Fun Badge, Foot Travelers Badge, Gypsy Badge, Daniel Boone Badge, Cooking Badge, and Sewing Badge. The Sunflower Girls motto is: "I am a little sunflower, sunny, brave, and true. From tiny bud to blossom, I do good deeds for you." Peter is conned into joining the Sunflower Girls in retaliation for Marcia joining the Frontier Scouts. Poor Pete has to go door-to-door reciting the motto and selling cookies.

Sunshine (Bonnie Ebsen*)
Appearance: BB #4
Sunshine is a barmaid at Ken's Korral.
Bonnie is Buddy Ebsen's daughter.

Suzanne (Barbara Bernstein*)
Appearance: OS #117
Suzanne is a classmate of Greg's. She is graduating with him and she and her friend Gretchen run into Greg at the beauty parlor.
See "Arnold, Peggy" entry.

Suzie (Karen Peters)
Appearance: OS #55
Suzie is a friend of Peter's. Peter invites her to a party and Suzie ends up trying to convince him that he isn't dull.

Suzie
Appearance: OS #95
Suzie is a friend of Marcia's.

Swanson, Chuck and Wife
Appearance: OS #94
The Swansons are invited to Mike and Carol's barbeque/Mexican dinner/smorgasbord.

Tardy, Paula (Chris Charney*)

Appearances: OS #28, 35

Paula is Marcia's friend who is invited to the Brady house for a sleepover. Marcia finds out that Paula is the one who wrote some offensive remarks about their teacher on a drawing that Marcia did. Marcia had been blamed for the remarks and was sentenced to a week's detention at school. In a later episode, Paula is told by her teacher Mrs. Denton to wash off her mascara.

**It may be a little hard to recognize her, but Chris Charney is none other than actress and comedienne Christine Baranski, winner of an Emmy and nominee for many other prestigious awards.*

Teen Time Romance Magazine

Appearance: OS #85

Jan reads this magazine. She read an article in there that stated it's good for women to date and marry men who are ten to twelve years older than they are.

Terrace Adoption Home

Appearance: OS #109

This is the Home where Mr. and Mrs. Kelly adopt their three new sons Matt, Dwayne, and Steve. The names of other kids living at the home are Joe, Julie, Hope, Wendy, Paul, Margaret, Randy, Barbara, Jeannie, Tommy, and Karen Martin. Karen bit Matt once, so he doesn't like her too much.

Thomas, Valerie (Carol Huston*) (Mary Cadorette**)

Appearances: AVBC; TB #1

Valerie is Peter Brady's fiancée and boss. Peter proposes to her in front of his whole family at Christmas dinner 1988 and Valerie proposes to him at the exact same time. Unfortunately, Valerie turns out to value her job more than Peter and he breaks it off with her in early 1990.

**Carol plays Valerie in* A Very Brady Christmas.

***Mary plays Valerie in* The Bradys. *She also played Vicky Bradford in* Three's a Crowd, *the spin-off sequel to* Three's Company.

Professor Thompson (Byron Morrow*)

Appearance: BB #2

The Professor is considering Phillip Covington, III for a grant.

**Byron Morrow has an extensive résumé going back to the 1950s and even father back for radio.*

Thompson, George

Appearance: OS #87

George lends Greg his car so that Greg can go downtown to the stadium and pick up some rock concert tickets. Greg is supposed to be grounded at the time.

Thompson, Gloria (Susan Quick)
Appearance: OS #116
Gloria is Hank Thompson's wife.

Thompson, Hank (Jason Dunn)
Appearance: OS #116
Hank is an engineer with Mike Brady's architectural firm. He comes to the Brady house for an evening of pool.

Thompson, Jenny (Gracia Lee)
Appearance: OS #87
Jenny is George Thompson's mother. She tells Carol that Greg borrowed George's car. That revelation gets Greg into trouble.

Tiger the Dog see **"Pets, Tiger"**

The Tigers
Appearance: OS #26
Greg plays for the Tigers during his freshman year of high school. The team is in the baseball pony leagues and Greg is a pitcher. His uniform is #53. The Tigers' uniforms are made by Embrey Dress, Inc.

Tiki
Appearances: OS #73, 74, 75
Bobby finds this tiki at a construction site in Hawaii. The idol is an old Hawaiian taboo that brings bad luck to anyone who touches it. At first, Bobby thinks it's a good luck charm but later he learns the truth. When the idol was in the possession of the Brady boys, Bobby almost had a heavy wall hanging bang him on the head, Greg suffered an unfortunate wipeout during a surfing contest, and Peter had a giant, hairy spider crawl on his chest. Alice possessed the tiki for a brief moment, too, and during that time she threw her back out doing the hula. The tiki is eventually returned to its rightful place.

Tim (Sean Kelly)
Appearance: OS #36
Tim is a friend of Peter's. He taunts Bobby and calls him a chicken when Bobby is afraid to climb up to their tree house after falling the first time.

Tina
Appearance: OS #40
Tina is a friend of Cindy's. They swapped hair ribbons once.

Tina
Appearance: OS #56

Tina is Marcia's understudy for the part of Juliet in the school play. Tina gets to play Juliet because Marcia gets kicked out of the play.

Tom
Appearance: OS #100
Tom is a friend of Greg's who turns down the chance to go out with Sandra Martin's cousin Linda.

Tommy (Brian Tochi*)
Appearance: OS #36
Tommy is a friend of Peter's. He, Peter, and two other boys formed a tree house club.
*Brian has appeared in many television series and films, including the Revenge of the Nerds and Teenage Mutant Ninja Turtles franchises.

Tomorrow's Woman Magazine
Appearance: OS #49
This magazine is edited by Mr. Delafield. Carol writes a story about the Brady family for the magazine and it gets published after revisions.

Turner, Tina (herself)
Appearance: VH #3
Tina Turner was the musical guest on The Brady Bunch Variety Hour once. She is a very well-known singer. On the show she sang "Rubber Band Man" and joined the Bradys in their finale.

Mrs. Tuttle (Barbara Morrison)
Appearance: OS #79
Mrs. Tuttle works at Westdale High School. She is in charge of putting together the Family Night Frolics where Marcia, Carol, Greg, and Mike all do performances.

Tyler, Henry (J. Pat O'Malley*)
Appearance: OS #1
Mr. Tyler is seen in episode #1 of the original series. He is Carol Brady's father and has a great sense of humor. When Cindy asks her grandfather if he is going to visit her after the wedding, Mr. Tyler replies, "Of course we are!" Carol confirms when she says, "Mike's house is only 20 minutes away." Nevertheless, Mr. and Mrs. Tyler are not seen on screen again.
*J. Pat O'Malley has appeared in over 100 different television series.

Tyler, Mrs. (Joan Tompkins)
Appearance: OS #1
Mrs. Tyler is Carol Brady's mother. She is not given a first name and is not seen on screen beyond the first The Brady Bunch episode.

Tyson, Clark (Mark Gruner)

Appearance: OS #34

Clark is Jan's first boyfriend. At first he has a crush on Marcia, but after Jan behaves more womanly and starts wearing dresses, Clark thinks she's real cool.

Uncle Winston

Appearance: OS #82

This is Alice's uncle. He owns a dress shop and Alice quits her housekeeping job at the Bradys' to go work for him. But it only lasts a week or so and then she's back home where she belongs.

Van Owen, April

Appearance: BGGM

April is a friend of Phillip and Jan's who is invited to their wedding.

Vehicles

The Bradys own several vehicles from a blue Chevy convertible to a camper they took to the Grand Canyon. The Bradys really like to switch out their vehicles; there are four different blue cars, two different tan station wagons, and two different maroon convertibles! Here they are in order of appearance.

Vehicle #1 = blue 1966-68 Dodge Polara convertible, license plate = unknown. Appearances: OS #1 and 21.

Vehicle #2 = tan 1968 Plymouth Satellite station wagon. License plate = Y18 078 (Episode 8) or 748 AEH (Episode 18) or JOP 745 (Episodes 41 & 48). Appearances: OS #3, 7, 8, 11, 14, 15, 18, 19, 21, 22, 24, 35, 38, 39, 41, 42, 43, 46, 47, 48, 58, 60, 62, 63, 64, 66, 68, 72, 77, 80, 81, 85, 88, 90, and 94.

Vehicle #3 = blue 1968-70 Plymouth Fury III convertible with blue interior. License plate = unknown. Appearances: OS #7, 8, 13, 14, 22, 23, 26, 27, 31, 33, 34, 36, 41, 43, 45, 46, 47, 53, 57, 60, 66, 73, 90, and 94. This model replaces the blue convertible seen in the pilot episode of the original series.

Vehicle #4 = tan 1971-2 Plymouth Satellite station wagon. License plate = 268 DMD (Episode 51) or 953 EJC (Episode 72). Appearances: OS #50, 51, 52, 53, 54, 57, 58, 62, 65, 70, 72, 77, 80, 82, 83, 86, 87, 95, 98, 99, 103, 109, 110, and 112. The car is in a fender-bender when Mrs. Brady is backing out of a parking space at the supermarket. A small claims court rules in her favor.

Vehicle #5 – The blue Brady convertible is swapped for yet another model in episode #53. This time it's a 1971 Plymouth Barracuda convertible. License plate = 200 DIR (Episodes 58, 59, 72). Appearances: OS #53, 55, 58, 59, 60, 62, 63, 67, and 72. Bobby opens up an umbrella from the inside of the car and rips a hole through the white soft top. Mike and Greg estimate that it will cost $150 to replace the top.

Vehicle #6 = Camping Trailer. License Plate = (xx) 9139. Appearances: OS #50, 51, 52. This is the camper that the Brady family takes on a trip to the Grand Canyon. They use it just this once and it is never seen again: kind of like a Brady pet!

Vehicle #7 = 1956 Chevrolet Bel Air. License plate = (xxx) 157. Appearance: OS #53. Greg buys this car from his friend Eddie for $100. It turns out to be a lemon, and Greg is forced to sell it to a junk yard for $50. Today this car in prime condition is worth about $25,000.

Vehicle #8 = blue 1971-2 Chevrolet Impala 400 convertible with black interior, license unknown. Appearances: OS #76, 81, 87, 88, and 94.

Vehicle #9 = not really a car at all, but a go-cart. Bobby, Peter, and Greg build this cart. Appearance: OS #85. Peter also builds a go-cart in episode #26 and starts building yet another one for Bobby in episode #103.

Vehicle #10 = "S.S. Brady" sailboat. Appearance: OS #86. Mike salvages this boat from the marina and the family restores it. Perhaps it sank because it lasts only this one episode.

Vehicle #11 = maroon 1974 Chevrolet Impala convertible with white interior, license unknown. Appearances: OS #96, 98, 100, 101, and 102

Vehicle #12 = maroon 1975 Chevrolet Impala convertible with black interior. License Plate = TEL 635 (#110). Appearances: OS #110, 112, and 117.

Vehicle #13 = silver 1988 Chrysler LeBaron convertible. License Plate = California 2FNY734. Appearance: AVBC

Vehicle #14 = 1980-1 Oldsmobile Vista Cruiser station wagon, license unknown. Appearances: TB #3 and 4 This is a family car by every definition. First Peter is seen driving it with Bobby in the passenger seat. Then in the next episode Marcia almost drives it drunk with Mickey and Jessica as passengers (but she doesn't).

Vicki (Lisa Eilbacher)
Appearance: OS #90
Vicki is an acquaintance of Marcia's who shares her liking of the big man on campus Doug Simpson.

Vinten, Joey
Appearance: OS #85
Eleven-year-old Cindy Brady has a crush on twelve-year-old Joey.

Vogel, Dr. Stanley (Don Brit Reid*)
Appearance: OS #85
Dr. Vogel is a dentist. Marcia has a crush on him and he asks her to baby sit for his three-year-old. Marcia misunderstands the message and thinks that Dr. Vogel is asking her for a date.

Don Played Dr. Willis in TV's Silent Number *(1974-1976).*

Wallach, Lisa (Dyana Ortelli)
Appearances: TB #2, 3
Lisa is a member of the Committee of Concerned Citizens in City. She and her cohorts convince Mike Brady to run for City Council.

Warren (Joseph Tatner)
Appearance: OS #45
Warren tries out for Fillmore Junior High's Vaudeville Show with his accordion.

Water Follies
Appearances: VH #1-9
The Water Follies accompany the Bradys on their opening and closing numbers on the variety show and sometimes perform in other minor acts as well. The set is graced by a swimming pool and underwater and above-water cameras are ready to capture the action. Essentially, the Water Follies are eight girls who perform underwater; they synchronize swim, dive, and do acrobatics underwater. They are the same eight girls who serve as the Krofftette Dancers on the show.

Mr. Watkins (Lindsay Workman*)
Appearance: OS #71
Mr. Watkins serves as the faculty chair for the Senior Banquet Night Hostess Selection Committee when Marcia and Molly Webber are running for Hostess.
See "Grossman, Bert" entry.

Mrs. Watson (Gwen Van Dam)
Appearance: OS #59
Mrs. Watson is Jan's teacher. She presents the Honor Society Essay Contest Award. Mrs. Watson thinks Marcia was a really great student and expects Jan to be just as great.

The Watsons
Appearance: OS #94
The Watsons have a grill cleaner that can eat the rust off of any old grill. Unfortunately it eats the grill, too.

Webber, Molly (Debi Storm)
Appearance: OS #71
Molly is an awkward, gawkish girl in Marcia's senior class. Her classmates nominate her for Hostess of Senior Banquet Night as a joke. Marcia is very upset at her classmates and takes Molly on as her personal project. She gets Molly a new look and a new attitude. When it turns out that Marcia will be running against Molly, Molly becomes snobbish and challenges Marcia to the contest. Molly ends up winning, but later confesses to

the principal that she won because of a speech that Marcia wrote for her. She and Marcia become co-hostesses for the Banquet.

Wendy

Appearance: OS #99

Peter mentions that he's going to Wendy's house because he likes her.

Westdale High School

Appearances: OS #43, 54, 60, 76, 83, 90, 100, 101, 104

This is the high school where Greg and Marcia go. Mascot = the bears. Alice and Carol also attended Westdale, and presumably each of the other Brady kids will go there in turn.

What's Happening!! Kids (Ernest Thomas*, Haywood Nelson**, Fred Berry***, and Danielle Spencer****)

Appearance: VH #8

The stars of TV's *What's Happening!!* join the Bradys onstage in one of the variety shows. They attend studio class one day with the four youngest Bradys, who invite them to be on their upcoming show.

**Ernest Thomas played Roger on* What's Happening!!. *He is an active actor today, most recently playing the role of Mr. Omar in* Everybody Hates Chris.

***Haywood played Dwayne Nelson on the show.*

****Fred played "Rerun" on the show.*

*****Finally, Danielle was Dee on the show.*

White, Chuck (Larry Storch)

Appearances: BK #1-5, 7, 8, 10, 12, 14, 15, 17, 20

Chuck is out to cause trouble for the Brady kids. He is always in their hair, challenging them, and bullying them. Chuck has a sidekick named Fleetwood who is sometimes a good guy and sometimes in cahoots with Chuck. Despite Chuck's irksome ways, the Brady kids always end up getting the better of him.

Whitehead, Professor Hubert (Vincent Price*)

Appearances: OS #74, 75

Professor Whitehead is an eccentric archaeologist working a cave site in Hawaii. Greg, Peter, and Bobby stumble across the cave when they intend to return a tiki idol to the first king. The Professor takes them hostage and demands to know the location where the idol was found. The boys tell him the truth (Honolulu) but he doesn't believe them. He chooses to listen to an old man-sized tiki named "Oliver" that he talks to. The Professor may be crazy but after Mike and Carol rescue the boys, Mike tells him that he will support his claim as the person who found the cave. The Professor is pleased and the mayor throws him and the Bradys a luau. Professor Whitehead even gets a new wing to the museum named after him and is appointed curator.

**See "Price, Vincent" entry.*

Mrs. Whitfield

Appearance: OS #88

Mrs. Whitfield borrows $100,000 at an eight percent interest rate from Winston Savings and Loan Bank. Mr. Goodbody is the lending agent.

Mrs. Whitfield (Frances Whitfield*)
Appearance: OS #98
Mrs. Whitfield is Cindy's teacher. She has had Marcia, Jan, and Carol in class, too, and they all think of her as their favorite. Because Mrs. Whitfield is retiring, Cindy and the other Bradys put on a play of "Snow White" for her and present her with some first edition books.
Frances Whitfield was the real-life studio teacher for the six Brady kid actors on the show. They all loved her.

Whitfield, Col. Dick (William Wellman, Jr.*)
Appearance: OS #71
Col. Whitfield is an astronaut. He is the most famous graduate of Fillmore Junior High. He is the host for Senior Banquet Night where Marcia Brady and Molly Webber serve as co-hostesses.
William is an Emmy-winner, but he is not an astronaut.

Whittaker, Andrew
Appearance: OS #58
Marcia says she's in love with him.

Wig Saleswoman (Marcia Wallace*)
Appearance: OS #40
The woman sells Jan the wig she wears when she becomes "The New Jan Brady."
This is Marcia's first of two appearances on The Brady Bunch. *She had a co-starring role on* The Bob Newhart Show. *More recently, people know her as the voice of teacher Edna Krabappel on* The Simpsons. *Wallace passed away in 2013.*

Mr. Williams
Appearance: OS #91
Mr. Williams is a customer of Martinelli's Bicycle Shop. Peter is supposed to be fixing his bike but he is taking too long. Mr. Martinelli has to fire Peter and finish the bike himself.

Williams, Doug
Appearance: OS #70
Doug is Marcia's date for the school dance.

Williams, Kathy
Appearance: OS #108
Kathy Williams is running against Jan for Most Popular Girl. Kathy is beautiful, brainy, and built.

Williams, Paul (himself*)

Appearance: VH #9

Paul Williams is a famous musician, singer, and songwriter. He appears on *The Brady Bunch Variety Hour* as himself and pretends to be in love with Carol Brady. He sings "The Hell of It" on the show. He makes a lot of short jokes about himself on the show and the Bradys join in later with jokes of their own. (He's 5'2".)

Mr. Williams wrote such songs as "Just an Old Fashioned Love Song," "Rainbow Connection," and "Rainy Days and Mondays."

Willy

Appearance: OS #93

Willy is a friend of Peter's. He has a sprained ankle and Peter and Bobby go to visit him to cheer him up.

Wilmore, Jenny

Appearance: OS #34

Jenny walks home with Peter and Clark Tyson one day. Peter thinks she's really cool.

Wilton, Jenny (Hope Sherwood*)

Appearance: OS #28

Jenny is Marcia's best friend. Marcia falsely accuses her of writing some offensive remarks on a drawing she did of George Washington. Marcia got in trouble at school for the remarks about their unfortunate teacher Mrs. Denton and "uninvited" Jenny to her slumber party. After Marcia realizes her mistake, she asks Jenny to come over for the party.

See "Gretchen" entry.

Wimple, Margie (Karen Foulkes)

Appearance: OS #40

Margie has a crush on Peter and clings to him whenever they're in the same room together. Peter can't stand her and contemplates skipping a birthday party just so he won't have to deal with her. Margie has a brother who is Bobby's age.

Winters, Judy (Claire Wilcox)

Appearance: OS #44

We don't know if Judy and Lucy Winters are related, but we do know that Judy has a brother. She is a friend of Marcia's who is interviewed by Ken Jones about the women's liberation movement.

Winters, Lucy (Pamelyn Ferdin)

Appearance: OS #40

Lucy is a friend of Jan and Peter's. She invites both of them to her birthday party and Jan wears a brunette wig to make a big entrance. Lucy and the other kids tease Jan until they realize the wig was not intended to be a joke.

Winters, Mark (Dick Winslow*)
Appearance: OS #63
Mark is a reporter for The Daily Chronicle. He writes a story about Bobby and Cindy and their attempt to break the world's teeter-totter record of 124 straight hours. There is no evidence that Mark is related to Judy and Lucy Winters.
Dick Winslow has close to 150 television appearances on his résumé.

Witherspoon, Wally (Jonathan Hole)
Appearance: OS #49
A reviewer for The Daily Chronicle. He has a column called "Wake up with Witherspoon."
Jonathan Hole has close to 150 television appearances on his résumé.

WKS
Appearance: OS #44
This is a local television station in City. Ken Jones works there; he is the reporter who interviews Marcia Brady about the women's lib movement.

The Women's Club
Appearance: OS #47
The Club organizes Operation Clean Sweep for the City Council, they get work groups to clean up the parks when the maintenance budget is cut, and they stop the building of a new courthouse on the Woodland Park land. Carol Brady is not only the Vice Chairwoman of the Women's Club but also the Chair of the Save Woodland Park Committee.

CHARACTER ENCYCLOPEDIA

CHAPTER 3: BIOGRAPHIES

This chapter will help you get to know the actors who brought the Bradys to life. In addition to brief biographies, their complete filmographies are included. Please note that the filmographies do not include Brady episodes, theatre, commercials, or instances where the actors appeared as him/herself (as in talk shows, reality shows, etc.).

Ann B. Davis

Birth: May 3, 1926; Schenectady, New York
Birth Name: Ann Bradford Davis
Death: June 1, 2014; San Antonio, Texas
Siblings: She and her twin are the third and fourth children of four
Marital Status: Single
Kids: None
Favorite Brady Episode: unknown

Ann B. Davis is one of the lucky one out of one hundred who got to grow up as a twin. She and her identical twin sister Harriet had a great time as children, as most twins do. They had similar interests in acting. They started out with their own puppet show (which earned them two whole dollars!) and it just grew from there. The Davis twins came from a dramatic family; their mother Marguerite was a dancer and stage actress. Their older brother Evans was also a dancer and he appeared on Broadway. During their teenage years Harriet and Ann B. starred in plays at Strong Vincent High School. They even went to the same university together – The University of Michigan – and

Ann B. and her twin Harriet.
Can you guess who is who?

studied acting (although Ann B. started as a pre-med major). But during their junior year Harriet fell in love and soon married. That left Ann B. to take up the theatrical reigns all by herself. After graduation she trained at the Erie, Pennsylvania Playhouse, but soon she was gripped with an eagerness for something bigger and moved to California. She got her first on-screen role in 1955 with a small part in the feature film *A Man Called Peter.*

Then luck struck big-time and Ann B. was cast as Charmaine "Schultzy" Schultz in the television comedy *The Bob Cummings Show*. Also up for the role was Jane Withers. In a 1958 interview, Ann B. says she got the role over Miss Withers because, "'I was so cheap, so willing, so available!'"[1] This character would be her defining role for many years. She was a fantastic comedienne and played well off Cummings' often lusty antics. Ann B. was nominated for *four* Emmys during the run of the show! She won two Best Supporting Actress Emmys for her hilarious performances. Ann B. is the only *Brady* actor/actress to ever have won an Emmy (Robert Reed was nominated three times but never won).

By the time Sherwood Schwartz was looking for a funny lady to be foil to Mrs. Brady, Ann B. had created quite an impressive résumé. She had racked up several television appearances, theatre appearances, and even the chance at another TV pilot for a show called *R.B. and Myrnaline* (the show was not picked up). Ann B. was comfortable playing the sidekick-type role and fell more or less comfortably into the role of Alice. She says, "'I like what I do. Ingénue parts are the best parts in the world. Besides, do you know how much fun it is to dust the furniture and find a way to make people interested?'"[2] She has also faithfully returned to every *Brady* reunion and thinks highly of her co-stars.

After *The Brady Bunch* ended in 1974, Ann B. decided to take things a little more slowly. Mostly she did theatre work, but did manage a few guest spots on television. Soon, though, she moved to Colorado where she joined an Episcopal congregation. After Colorado she lived in Pennsylvania and Texas and dedicated much of her time to religion. Ann B. wrote a book in 1994 called Alice's Brady Bunch Cookbook that contains over 100 recipes and neat *Brady Bunch* history and photographs. She passed away in Texas in 2014.

Filmography

Pre-Brady
1. *A Man Called Peter* – feature film – Ruby Coleman – April 1955
2. *Matinee Theatre* – "Belong to Me" – Peg Miller – July 31, 1956
3. *Lux Video Theatre* – "The Wayward Saint" – Miss Killicat – August 30, 1956
4. *The Best Things in Life Are Free* – feature film – Hattie Stewart – September 28, 1956
5. *The Bob Cummings Show* aka *Love That Bob* – all 106 episodes – Charmaine "Schultzy" Schultz – January 25, 1955-July 7, 1959
6. *Wagon Train* – "The Countess Baranof Story" – Mrs. Foster – May 11, 1960
7. *Pepe* – feature film – Ann B. "Schultzy" Davis – December 21, 1960
8. *All Hands On Deck* – feature film – Nobby – March 30, 1961
9. *R.B. and Myrnaline* – "Pilot" – unknown character – filmed in December 1961
10. *Lover Come Back* – feature film – Millie – March 3, 1962
11. *The New Breed* – "Wherefore Art Thou, Romeo?" – Elizabeth MacBaine – May 15, 1962
12. *McKeever & the Colonel* – "Too Many Sergeants" – Sergeant Gruber – January 6, 1963
13. *The Keefe Brasselle Show* – unknown episodes – unknown characters
14. *Bob Hope Presents the Chrysler Theatre* – "Wake Up, Darling" – Martha – February 21, 1964
15. *The John Forsythe Show* – multiple episodes – Miss Wilson – 1965-1966

16. *The Pruitts of Southampton* aka *The Phyllis Diller Show* – "Phyllis Takes a Letter" – Mrs. Derwin – September 27, 1966
17. *Insight* – "The Late Great God" – Pat – 1968

Concurrent Brady

1. *Love, American Style* – "Love and the Fur Coat/Love and the Trip" – Vi – November 13, 1970
2. *Big Fish, Little Fish* – TV movie – Hilda Rose – January 5, 1971
3. *Love, American Style* – "Love and the Clinical Problem/Love and the Eat's Cafe/Love and the Last Joke/Love and the Persistent Assistant/Love and the Unsteady Steady" – unknown character – November 9, 1973

Post-Brady

1. *Only with Married Men* – TV movie – Mola – December 4, 1974
2. *The Love Boat* – "Invisible Maniac/September Song/Peekaboo" – Agnes – April 19, 1980
3. *Day by Day* – "A Very Brady Episode" – Alice Nelson – February 5, 1989
4. *Hi, Honey, I'm Home* – "SRP" – Alice Nelson – August 23, 1991
5. *Naked Gun 33 1/3: The Final Insult* – feature film – Ann B. Davis – March 18, 1994
6. *The Brady Bunch Movie* – feature film – Schultzy – February 17, 1995
7. *Something So Right* – "Something About Inter-Ex-Spousal Relations" – Maxine – April 29, 1997

Robert Reed

Birth: October 19, 1932; Highland Park, Illinois
Birth Name: John Robert Rietz
Death: May 12, 1992; Pasadena, California
Siblings: He's an only child
Kid: Karen
Favorite Brady Episode: unknown

Robert Reed, aka John Robert Rietz, grew up on farms in Illinois, Missouri and Oklahoma. His parents raised mink for a brief time, probably in Missouri ("Bobby" adopted one as a pet that he named Charlie), and in Oklahoma the family farm focused on cattle and turkeys. He was a member of the local 4-H Club in Oklahoma and proudly showed off his Herefords. It was in high school that Bob got his first taste of the performing arts. He had a radio show on his local high school station and also acted in school plays. He loved acting and went to college at Northwestern University and majored in drama. Right after graduation he married his girlfriend Marilyn Rosenberg. Together they moved to England where Bob attended the Royal Academy of Dramatic Arts and studied theatre and Shakespeare. He took his art very seriously and was lucky enough to perform Shakespeare with some of the best actors of the day in London. After he finished his studies, the couple moved back to the U.S. and Marilyn gave birth to their daughter Karen. By this time Bob had begun using the pseudonym Robert Reed, a name that he told reporters he disliked. The only reason he changed his name – although never legally – was to please the people in the television and theatre industry who thought Rietz sounded too ethnic. Bob was able to land parts in several productions in New York and Chicago, including more Shakespeare.

Although his professional life was taking off, Robert's personal life was making a downturn. After only five years of marriage, he and Marilyn divorced in 1959. He moved to Hollywood and there he was able to get a guest role on TV's *Father Knows Best*. He played a lawyer and although the part was only a one-time gig, it opened the door for a continuing series called *The Defenders*. The producers of this soon-to-be hit law drama saw Bob on *Father Knows Best* and thought that he would be perfect for the part of Kenneth Preston, a young lawyer learning the ropes under the tutelage of his father. His screen test went well and soon he was filming the pilot episode with experienced actor E.G. Marshall as his character's father.

The Defenders began in 1961 and lasted four seasons. Bob and E.G. formed a professional friendship. The show was filmed in New York and the two actors lived close enough to the studio that they both bought bicycles and sometimes pedaled to work together. But Bob

Reed in The Defenders *(1961-1965)*

kept his personal life to himself and instead focused on the art and craft of acting. In a TV Guide article, Marshall said of his co-star: "He's the sort of person who just doesn't like to talk about himself."[3] But Bob very much enjoyed his time on *The Defenders*. When the show was cancelled, he moved back to California and bought a house in Pasadena. Between 1965 and 1969 he kept busy with several television and theatre appearances.

Bob Reed had always been a serious person, which is why *The Brady Bunch* seemed like such an unlikely next step. Bob tried out for the role more or less because it was a potential job. He filmed the pilot episode and thought the show would immediately flop. He was wrong! The show continued for five seasons and during that time he had many disagreements with Sherwood Schwartz about the scripts and the direction of the show. In 1970 he said, "I thought the show was going to be something else – that it was going to be more realistic, that we would be real humans. The pilot turned out to be *Gilligan's Island* with kids – full of gags and gimmicks."[3] Despite his objections to plot lines and the believability of the scripts, Bob stayed on for the full run of the series. Those close to him say this is because he was strongly attached to the kids on the show. He seemed to adopt them in his own way and they in turn relished the attention and respect he showed them. He gave them presents at Christmastime and even took them on a once-in-a-lifetime trip to New York and London.

But as it goes in television, all good things must come to an end. *The Brady Bunch* was cancelled in 1974. Bob had been working on other television shows during the time the show was on the air, namely *Mannix* in which he played a recurring character, and therefore had a vast and varied résumé for producers of future shows to see. His determination to work, work, work paid off and there wasn't a single year between 1974 and the year of his death 1992 in which he did not appear on television. During his post-Brady career, Bob was nominated for three Emmy Awards. Although he never won, he was still honored and kept hard at work. He had many notable roles, including *Medical Center*, *Roots*, and *Nurse*. A few series came his way such as *The Runaways* and the aforementioned *Nurse*. And he appeared in every *Brady Bunch* reunion show. The cast says that he wouldn't ever let anybody else be the father to his "kids."

We all know that Robert Reed died an untimely death. He was just 59 years old when he succumbed to cancer and complications from HIV. But those of us who are *Brady Bunch* and Robert Reed fans will always remember him as the kind and caring Mike Brady.

Filmography

Pre-Brady

1. *Pal Joey* – feature film – boyfriend – October 25, 1957
2. *The Hunters* – feature film – Jackson – September 1958
3. *Torpedo Run* – feature film – Woolsey – October 24, 1958
4. *Make Room for Daddy* – "Terry Comes Home" – airline pilot – October 5, 1959
5. *Father Knows Best* – "The Impostor" – Tom Cameron – October 26, 1959
6. *Men Into Space* – "Earthbound" – Russell Smith – January 27, 1960
7. *Bronco* – "Volunteers from Aberdeen" – Tom Fuller – February 9, 1960
8. *Lawman* – "Left Hand of the Law" – Jim Malone – March 27, 1960
9. *Tallahassee 7000* – "The Hostage" – unknown character – 1961
10. *Bloodlust!* – feature film – Johnny Randall – 1961
11. *The Defenders* – TV series, 132 episodes – Kenneth Preston – September 13, 1961-May 13, 1965
12. *Dr. Kildare* – TV series, 6 episodes – Judd Morrison – October 26-November 16, 1965
13. *Bob Hope Presents the Chrysler Theatre* – "The Admiral" – Lt. Chris Callahan – December 29, 1965
14. *Preview Tonight* – "Somewhere in Italy...Company B" – Lt. John Leahy – August 21, 1966
15. *Operation Razzle-Dazzle* – feature film – Lt. John Leahy – August 21, 1966
16. *Family Affair* – "Think Deep" – Julian Hill – December 26, 1966
17. *Hurry Sundown* – feature film – Lars Finchley – February 9, 1967
18. *Li'l Abner* – TV pilot – Senator Cod – September 5, 1967
19. *Hondo* – "Hondo and the Superstition Massacre" – Frank Davis – September 29, 1967
20. *Ironside* – "Light at the End of the Journey" – Jerry Pearson – November 9, 1967
21. *Journey into the Unknown* – "The New People" – Hank Prentiss – 1968, re-aired on April 14, 1969 as *Journey into Darkness*
22. *Star!* – feature film – Charles Fraser – October 29, 1968
23. *The Maltese Bippy* – feature film – Lt. Tim Crane – 1969

Concurrent Brady

1. *Love, American Style* – "Love and the Burglar/Love and the Roommate/Love and the Wild Party" – Ira Skutch – November 17, 1969

2. *Love, American Style* – "Love and the Big Game/Love and the Nutsy Girl/Love and the Vampire" – Wayne – January 29, 1971

3. *The City* – TV movie – Sealy Graham – May 17, 1971

4. *Love, American Style* – "Love and the Lovesick Sailor/Love and the Mistress/Love and the Reincarnation/ Love and the Sexy Survey" – Nick – October 29, 1971

5. *Assignment Munich* – TV movie - Doug "Mitch" Mitchell – April 30, 1972

6. *The Mod Squad* – "The Connection" – Jerry Silver – September 14, 1972

7. *Haunts of the Very Rich* – TV movie – Reverend John Fellows – September 20, 1972

8. *Mission: Impossible* – "Hit" – Arthur Reynolds – November 11, 1972

9. *Snatched* – TV movie – Frank McCloy – January 31, 1973

10. *Owen Marshall: Counselor At Law* – "They've Got to Blame Somebody" – Ken Harker – February 14, 1973

11. *Intertect* – TV movie – Blake Hollister – March 13, 1973

12. *The Man Who Could Talk to Kids* – TV movie – Tom Lassiter – October 17, 1973

13. *Pray for the Wildcats* – TV movie – Paul McIlvian – January 23, 1974

14. *Chase* – "Remote Control" – Dr. Playter – February 27, 1974

15. *Mannix* – 22 episodes – Sgt./Lt. Adam Tobias – February 1, 1969-March 24, 1974

Post-Brady

1. *Harry O* – "Accounts Balanced" – Paul Virdon – December 26, 1974

2. *The Secret Night Caller* – TV movie – Freddy Durant – February 18, 1975

3. *Medical Center* – "The Fourth Sex Part I and Part II" – Dr. Pat Caddison – September 8 & 15, 1975

4. *McCloud* – "Fire!" – Jason Carter – November 16, 1975

5. *Rich Man, Poor Man* – TV miniseries – Teddy Boylan – February-March 1976

6. *Jigsaw John* – "Promise to Kill" – Alan Bellamy – February 2, 1976

7. *Law and Order* – TV movie – Aaron Levine – May 6, 1976

8. *Lannigan's Rabbi* aka *Friday the Rabbi Slept Late* – TV movie – Morton Galen – June 17, 1976

9. *The Streets of San Francisco* – "The Honorable Profession" – multiple characters – August 5, 1976

10. *Nightmare in Badham County* – TV movie – Superintendent Dancer – November 5, 1976

11. *The Boy in the Plastic Bubble* – TV movie – Johnny Lubitch – November 12, 1976

12. *Revenge for a Rape* – TV movie – Sheriff Paley – November 19, 1976

13. *Wonder Woman* – "The Pluto File" – The Falcon – December 25, 1976

14. *Disneyland* – "Kit Carson and the Mountain Men, Part I & II" – Captain John C. Fremont – January 9 & 16, 1977

15. *The Love Boat II* – TV movie – Stephen Palmer – January 21, 1977

16. *Roots* – TV miniseries; Parts II-IV – Dr. William Reynolds – January-February 1977

17. *SST: Death Flight* aka *SST: Disaster in the Sky* – TV movie – Captain Jim Walsh – February 25, 1977

18. *Barnaby Jones* – "Death Beat" – DeWitt Robinson – September 15, 1977

19. *The Love Boat* – "Ex Plus Y/Golden Agers/Graham and Kelly" – Barney Mason – October 8, 1977

20. *The Hunted Lady* – TV movie – Dr. Arthur Sills – November 28, 1977

21. *The Runaways* – TV series, Season 1 (4 episodes) – Dr. David McKay – April 27-May 18, 1978

22. *The Love Boat* – "The Kissing Bandit/Mike and Ike/Witness" – Frank McLean – October 21, 1978
23. *Thou Shalt Not Commit Adultery* – TV movie – Jack Kimball – November 1, 1978
24. *Vega$* – "The Pageant" – Mike Logan – November 15, 1978
25. *Bud and Lou* – TV movie – Alan Randall – November 15, 1978
26. *Fantasy Island* – "Vampire/The Lady and the Longhorn" – Leo Drake – December 16, 1978
27. *Hawaii Five-O* – "The Mieghan Conspiracy" – Matthew Mieghan – January 18, 1979
28. *Mandrake* – TV movie – Arkadian – January 24, 1979
29. *The Paper Chase* – "Once More with Feeling" – Professor Howard – February 27, 1979
30. *Love's Savage Fury* – TV movie – Colonel Marston – May 20, 1979
31. *Vega$* – "The Usurper" – Johnny "J.T. Rodmore" Roth – September 26, 1979
32. *Hawaii Five-O* – "Though the Heavens Fall" – Richard Slade – October 18, 1979
33. *The Seekers* – TV movie – Daniel Clapper – December 3-4, 1979
34. *Galactica 1980* – "Galactica Discovers Earth, Parts I-III" – Dr. Donald Mortinson – January 27, February 3 & 10, 1980
35. *Scruples* – TV miniseries – Josh Hillman – February 1980
36. *Nurse* – TV movie – Dr. Kenneth Rose – April 9, 1980 (see also #39 below)
37. *Charlie's Angels* – "One Love...Two Angels, Parts I & II" – Glenn Stanley – April 30-May 7, 1980
38. *Casino* – TV movie – Darius – August 1, 1980
39. *Nurse* – TV series, all episodes – Dr. Adam Rose – April 2, 1981-May 21, 1982
40. *Death of a Centerfold: The Dorothy Stratten Story* – TV movie – David Palmer – November 1, 1981
41. *ABC Afterschool Specials* – "Between Two Loves" – Henry Forbes – October 27, 1982
42. *Fantasy Island* – "The Tallowed Image/Room and Bard" – Shakespeare – January 29, 1983
43. *Hotel* – "Secrets" – Phil Jamison – October 26, 1983
44. *The Love Boat* – "Friend of the Family/Affair on Demand/Just Another Pretty Face" – Jack – October 29, 1983
45. *The Mississippi* – "Abigail" – Tyler Marshall – February 7, 1984
46. *The Love Boat* – "And One to Grow On/Seems Like Old Times/I'll Never Forget What's Her Name" – Larry Peters – October 27, 1984
47. *Hotel* – "Transitions" – Larry Dawson – November 14, 1984
48. *Matt Houston* – "Stolen" – Bradley Denholm – December 21, 1984
49. *Cover Up* – "A Subtle Seduction" – Martin Dunbar – December 29, 1984
50. *Finder of Lost Loves* – "From the Heart" – Tim Sanderson – February 9, 1985
51. *Murder, She Wrote* – "Footnote to Murder" – Adrian Winslow – March 10, 1985
52. *International Airport* – TV movie – Carl Roberts – May 25, 1985
53. *The Love Boat* – "Your Money or Your Wife/Joint Custody/The Temptations" – Carl Gerra – October 5, 1985
54. *Glitter* – "Suddenly Innocent" – unknown character – December 27, 1985
55. *Crazy Like A Fox* – "Just Another Fox in the Crowd" – unknown character – February 26, 1986
56. *Search for Tomorrow* – two episodes – Lloyd Kendall – December 16, 1986 & February 26, 1986
57. *Hotel* – "Restless Nights" – Jason Beck – December 10, 1986
58. *The Love Boat* – "Who Killed Maxwell Thorn?" – Mike Brady – February 27, 1987

59. *Jake and the Fatman* – "Happy Days Are Here Again" – Kyle Williams – September 26, 1987

60. *Hunter* – "City of Passion, Parts I-III" – Judge Warren Unger – November 7, 14, & 21, 1987

61. *Duet* – "I Never Played for My Father, Parts I-II" – Jim Phillips – November 15 & 22, 1987

62. *The Law of Harry McGraw* – "Beware the Ides of May" – unknown character – January 20, 1988

63. *Murder, She Wrote* – "Murder through the Looking Glass" – Jackson – February 21, 1988

64. *Day By Day* – "A Very Brady Episode" – Mike Brady – February 5, 1989

65. *Free Spirit* – "The New Secretary" – Albert Stillman – December 10, 1989

66. *Murder, She Wrote* – "See You in Court, Baby" – Truman Calloway, Esq. – September 30, 1990

67. *Prime Target* – feature film – Agent Harrington – September 27, 1991

68. *Jake and the Fatman* – "Ain't Misbehavin'" – Alexander Baldwin – April 8, 1992

Florence Henderson

<u>Birth</u>: *February 14, 1934; Dale, Indiana*
<u>Birth Name</u>: *Florence Agnes Henderson*
<u>Death</u>: *November 24, 2016; Los Angeles, California*
<u>Siblings</u>: *She's the youngest of ten*
<u>Marital Status</u>: *Divorced once and widowed once*
<u>Kids</u>: *Barbara, Joseph, Robert, & Elizabeth*
<u>Favorite Brady Episode</u>: *The Grand Canyon trilogy*

Florence as she appeared in The Brady Bunch Variety Hour

Florence Henderson grew up in a large family of ten children in Kentucky. Florence was a natural singer and performer and would sometimes even sing outside the local grocery store as a child for change. By the time she was two she had 50 songs memorized! She was lucky enough to find support in many ways from a family friend who gave her enough money when she was 17 to go to New York to the Academy of Dramatic Arts. Young Florence studied there for two years. At age 19, she won a part in the chorus for the Broadway show "Wish You Were Here." Soon she caught the eye of Rodgers & Hammerstein who cast her as the lead in "Oklahoma!" Sadly, two days before she was to go on tour for "Oklahoma!" her 82-year-old father died, but Florence was obligated to complete the tour. She became the darling of Broadway with her next role in "Fanny" and landed parts in several Broadway shows through the 1950s and 1960s. The shows included "The Sound of Music," "South Pacific," and "The Girl Who Came to Supper." During these two decades she also appeared on several television talk shows and music-oriented shows such as *Toast of the Town, Dean Martin,* and *The Oldsmobile Music Theatre*. She was also one of the original *Today Show* "girls." Her voice was heard on several Broadway records as well as her own 1959 LP (see "Music" chapter for more).

When she was in her early 20s, Florence married Broadway producer Ira Bernstein. Together they had four children and Florence continued to work through it all, but she yearned for a steady television comedy job. In a 1967 interview she complained, "I would like to persuade Hollywood that a woman who has proved she can sing, can also be a pretty good actress. I wonder what I have to do to get a chance?"[4] As we know, her chance came in 1969 when *The Brady Bunch* premiered with her in the lead female adult role.

Florence remained Carol Brady through all five seasons and in every spin-off. During the years the show was being filmed, she lived half the week (when they were filming) in California and the other half (non-filming days) in New York with her family. Youngest children Robert & Lizzy would often travel with her to California, but the older two kids had to stay in New York and attend school. Her oldest child, Barbara, did manage to squeeze into a guest role on *The Brady Bunch* thanks in part to Maureen McCormick's persuasive powers with Sherwood Schwartz. Florence said that Barbara and Maureen had formed a fast friendship during the first season of filming and during the summer hiatus between the first and second seasons. All four of her children have done a little something professional with their mother.

After *Brady*, Florence and her husband of nearly thirty years were divorced. A few years later she remarried. Her new husband, John Kappas, was a hypnotherapist and Florence learned the craft herself. She continued to perform in musical theater and perform and act on television. In 1985 – the same year she was divorced from Bernstein – Florence landed her own cooking show on The Nashville Network. The show was called *Country Kitchen* and she provided small talk and cooked by herself or with guests. As a result of the show, Florence wrote a book in 1988 called A Little Cooking, A Little Talking and A Whole Lot of Fun. The show lasted eight years. During this time, she served as spokeswoman for Wesson Cooking Oil, Polident, and others. From 1995-1996 she and her daughter Barbara co-hosted a show on The Faith and Values Network called *Our Generation*. But Florence couldn't stay away from the kitchen for long and in 1998 she was back on screen cooking for a delighted audience. This time the show was *Short Cut Cooking*. Again she was inspired to write another cookbook, the title of which is the same as the show.

Florence penned a few other books, such as One-Minute Bible Stories and Speaking of Women's Health: The Book. She was an advocate for women's health and often spoke out in order to raise money for the cause. She also founded The FloH Club, which helped senior citizens learn to use current technology like digital television and computers. The business closed in 2010.

Recently Florence was still on the airwaves with *The Florence Henderson Show* on RLTV. She still also made it onto the Broadway stage (which she shared briefly with Eve Plumb in March 2010) and was frequently interviewed by late-night television hosts. In 2011, her autobiography called Life Is Not a Stage was released. The book is a good read for those interested in more of Florence's personal life.

She appeared on ABC's *Dancing with the Stars* in its 2010 season at the age of 76. Maureen McCormick appeared a few years later and Florence was there to root her on. It was at the end of Maureen's season that Florence suffered a sudden heart attack on Thanksgiving Day 2016 and passed away at the age of 82.

Filmography

Pre-Brady

1. *General Foods 25th Anniversary Show: A Salute to Rodgers and Hammerstein* – TV special – Laurie – March 28, 1954
2. *I Spy* – "The Abbey and the Nymph" – unknown character – c1955
3. *The United States Steel Hour* – "The Adventures of Huckleberry Finn" – Mary Jane Wilk – November 20, 1957
4. *The United States Steel Hour* – "A Family Alliance" – Gladys Pratt – June 4, 1958
5. *Little Women* – TV movie – Meg March – October 16, 1958
6. *Sing Along* – unknown episodes – 1958

Concurrent Brady

1. *Song of Norway* – TV movie – Nina Grieg – November 4, 1970

Post-Brady

1. *Medical Center* – "Torment" – Jenny Delaney – September 22, 1975
2. *Good Heavens* – "See Jane Run" – Jane/Julia Grey – March 29, 1976
3. *The Love Boat* – TV movie – Monica Richardson – September 17, 1976
4. *3 Girls 3* – Episode 1.1 – unknown character – March 30, 1977
5. *The Love Boat* – "Lonely at the Top/Divorce Me, Please/Silent Night" – Audrey Baynes – December 10, 1977
6. *The Love Boat* – "Folks from Home/The Captain's Cup/Legal Eagle" – Diane DiMarzo – December 2, 1978
7. *Fantasy Island* – "Pentagram/A Little Ball/The Casting Director" – Jane Garwood – February 17, 1979
8. *The Love Boat* – "The Captain's Ne'er-Do-Well Brother/The Perfect Match/Remake" – Christine Frank – February 2, 1980
9. *The Love Boat* – "Isaac's Teacher/Seal of Approval/The Successor" – Harriett Rogers – January 10, 1981
10. *The Love Boat* – "Country Cousin Blues/Daddy's Little Girl/Jackpot" – Annabelle Folker – October 31, 1981
11. *Hart to Hart* – "Hartland Express" – Violet Casper – November 3, 1981
12. *Fantasy Island* – "A Very Strange Affair/The Sailor" – Laura Myles – January 2, 1982
13. *Police Squad!* – "Rendezvous at Big Gulch/Terror in the Neighborhood" – Shot Woman – July 1, 1982
14. *The Love Boat* – "Hits and Misses/Return of Annabelle/Just Plain Folks Medicine/Caught in the Act/The Real Thing/Do Not Disturb/(Country Music Jamboree Part 1 & 2)" – Annabelle Folker – April 23 & 30, 1983
15. *The Love Boat* – "Friend of the Family/Affair on Demand/Just Another Pretty Face" – Anita – October 29, 1983
16. *Alice* – "It Had to be Me" – Sarah James – October 30, 1983
17. *Fantasy Island* – "Random Choices/My Mother, the Swinger" – Ellen Ashley – December 3, 1983
18. *Glitter* – "A Minor Miracle" – Vivian – December 18, 1984
19. *Finder of Lost Loves* – "Forgotten Melodies" – Lyla Armstrong – December 22, 1984

20. *The Love Boat* – "The Ace Takes a Holiday/The Runaway/Courier" – Irene Patton – February 9, 1985

21. *Cover Up* – "Healthy, Wealthy and Dead" – Penelope Reinhart – February 23, 1985

22. *Murder, She Wrote* – "Death Stalks the Big Top Part I & II" – Maria Morgana – September 28 & October 5, 1986

23. *The Love Boat* – "Who Killed Maxwell Thorn?" – Carol Brady – February 27, 1987

24. *ABC Afterschool Specials* – "Just A Regular Kid: An AIDS Story" – Ellen Casio – September 9, 1987

25. *Day by Day* – "A Very Brady Episode" – Carol Brady – February 9, 1989

26. *Free Spirit* – "The New Secretary" – Blanche Stillman – December 10, 1989

27. *Murder, She Wrote* – "Ballad for a Blue Lady" – Patty Sue Diamond – December 2, 1990

28. *Out of This World* – "My Mom, and Why I Love Her" – Florence – February 9, 1991

29. *Shakes the Clown* – feature film – The Unknown Woman – March 13, 1992

30. *For Goodness Sake* – short film – unknown character – 1993

31. *Dave's World* – "Death and Mom Take a Holiday" – Maggie Colby – November 22, 1993

32. *Roseanne* – "Suck Up or Shut Up" – Flo Anderson – January 4, 1994

33. *The Mommies* – "Mommies Day" – Peggy, Caryl's Mom – February 7, 1994

34. *Dave's World* – "The Funeral" – Maggie Colby – March 28, 1994

35. *Dave's World* – "How Long Has This Been Going On?" – Maggie Colby – November 28, 1994

36. *ABC Weekend Specials* – "Fudge-A-Mania" – Muriel Hatcher – January 7, 1995

37. *The Brady Bunch Movie* – feature film – Grandma – February 17, 1995

38. *Dave's World* – "The Mommies" – Maggie Colby – May 8, 1995

39. *Night Stand* – "Salute to Getting Off Easy" – Florence – 1995

40. *For Goodness Sake II* – feature film – Video Store Customer – 1996

41. *Bad Hair Day: The Videos* – straight-to-video – Amish Wife – June 4, 1996

42. *Ellen* – "Joe's Kept Secret" – Madeline – January 15, 1997

43. *Hercules* – "Hercules and the King for a Day" – Demeter (voice) – October 24, 1998

44. *Ally McBeal* – "Two's a Crowd" – Dr. Shirley Grouper – November 6, 2000

45. *The King of Queens* – "Dark Meet" – Lily – November 20, 2000

46. *Legend of the Candy Cane* – TV movie – Thelma (voice) – June 1, 2001

47. *Mom's on Strike* – TV movie – Betty – March 17, 2002

48. *"Weird Al" Yankovic: The Ultimate Video Collection* – straight-to-video – Amish Wife – November 4, 2003

49. *Loonatics Unleashed* – "The Menace of Mastermind" – Mallory Casey/Mallory Mastermind (voice) – February 18, 2006

50. *Loonatics Unleashed* – "Acmegeddon Part I & II" – Mallory Casey/Mallory Mastermind (voice) – May 6 & 13, 2006

51. *For Heaven's Sake* – feature film – Sarah Miller – September 23, 2008

52. *Ladies of the House* – TV movie – Rose Olmstead – October 18, 2008

53. *Venus & Vegas* – feature film – unknown character – February 2009

54. *The Christmas Bunny* aka *Just Where I Belong* – feature film – Betsy Ross – 2010

55. *Scooby Doo!: Mystery Incorporated* – "Dead Justice" – Ruby Stone (voice) – May 28, 2011

56. *The Cleveland Show* – "The Men in Me" – White Woman/Nanny Barbara (voice) – March 25, 2012

BIOGRAPHIES

57. *Handy Manny* – "Handy Manny and the Seven Tools" – Aunt Ginny (voice) – April 13, 2012

58. *Matchmaker Santa* – TV movie – Peggy Montgomery/Pegasus – November 17, 2012

59. *Happily Divorced* – "Meet the Parents" – Elizabeth – December 5, 2012

60. *30 Rock* – "My Whole Life is Thunder" – Florence Henderson – December 6, 2012

61. *Trophy Wife* – "The Wedding: Part Two" – Frances Harrison – March 18, 2014

62. *Instant Mom* – "Not Your Mother's Day" – Carol Brady – May 8, 2014

63. *Fifty Shades of Black* – feature film – Mrs. Robinson – January 29, 2016

64. *The Eleventh* – streaming TV series – all episodes – Regina – first episode May 5, 2016

65. *Sofia the First* – "Best in Air Show" – Queen Mum (voice) – May 6, 2016

66. *K.C. Undercover* – "Dance Like No One's Watching" – Irma – May 22, 2016

67. *Grandmothers Murder Club* – feature film – Mimi – expected 2017

Barry Williams

Birth: September 30, 1954; Santa Monica, California
Birth Name: Barry William Blenkhorn
Siblings: He's the youngest of three
Marital Status: Divorced twice, currently engaged
Kids: Brandon and Samantha
Favorite Brady Episode: "Adios, Johnny Bravo"

Barry William Blenkhorn was born to parents Doris and Frank as the youngest of three children (all boys) and the only one in his family with acting aspirations. By the time he was four he was telling his parents that he wanted to be on television. They were able put their son's pleas off until he was eleven years old when they finally gave into his persistent requests. Barry took acting classes and then got an agent, headshots, and the works.

Barry's first headshot.
Courtesy of Barry Williams.

Doris Blenkhorn explains that during his earliest jobs, Barry's agent thought that the last name Blenkhorn was "too difficult." Thus, the agent suggested that he use his middle name William his last and add an "s." At first, "Barry Williams" was just a stage name but later on it got to be more trouble than it was worth having two names and Barry and his parents had it legally changed when he was still a child. Barry's first acting job came in the form of an educational reel-to-reel film called *Why Johnny Can Read*. The film, an answer to the popular 1955 book <u>Why Johnny Can't Read</u>, was distributed to local elementary schools. Soon afterward, Barry made some commercials and got his first role in a feature film as Young Max in *Wild in the Streets*.

Next Barry did a rather long spat of guest work on television shows (see his filmography) and finally in 1968 he auditioned for Greg Brady in *The Brady Bunch*. Close to his fourteenth birthday he received a telegram telling him that he got the part. Mrs. Blenkhorn says that it was the proudest moment for her in her son's career and no doubt Barry was very excited himself. Filming began soon afterward and from there he continued the role of Greg for five years and for the subsequent spin-offs. Barry was popular while he was on the show and received thousands of fan letters each week at the height of his stardom. There was an official Barry Williams Fan Club in 1971 and later a Brady Bunch Fan Club (see the Memorabilia chapter). His photo was featured in teen magazines from 1970-1974 in color pin-ups and there were countless articles about him and his fellow actors in these same publications. As part of *The Brady Bunch* cast, he signed autographs at various venues including Lion Country Safari in Irvine, Knotts Berry Farm, record stores, and during the kids' singing tour in the summer of 1973.

Barry was also a singer and musician (for more on this see the Music chapter). It was this musical talent that brought him to the next stage in his career after *The Brady Bunch* ended in 1974. Right afterward he signed on with a traveling Broadway production to appear as the lead in "Pippin." He received good reviews for the show and stayed with the role for over a year. Then came *The Brady Bunch Variety Hour*. After that, Barry did more musical theatre.

Barry's career has stayed in show business. Throughout the 1980s, 1990s, and 2000s he traveled the country doing talks at colleges promoting *The Brady Bunch*, singing and acting in all kinds of stage shows, and doing occasional guest spots on a television series. For many years he maintained a blog called The Greg Brady Project at www.thegregbradyproject.com that was updated with pop culture tidbits, Brady stories, and Barry's current activities. He had a son in 2003. When asked whether or not he would let his son become an actor, Barry said maybe "after college."[5] Most recently, he signed on with the Yakov Theatre in Branson, Missouri to do a recurring show he calls "Brady Brunch." The show was put on in the morning and Barry sang and told stories of his time with the Bradys while the audience enjoyed munching on brunch. The brunch idea didn't last long, and soon the show morphed into a celebration of the 1970s. Now Barry is in his own theatre and he has backup singers and dancers as well as a reality television series profiling the show. In 2012 he became a father again by his then-girlfriend Elizabeth Kennedy.

Filmography

Pre-Brady

1. *Why Johnny Can Read* – educational film – Johnny – 1965
2. *Run for Your Life* – "The Company of Scoundrels" – Stanley – October 18, 1967
3. *Dragnet '67* – "The Christmas Story" – John Heffernan – December 21, 1967
4. *The F.B.I.* – "The Messenger" – Boy – March 10, 1968
5. *The Invaders* – "The Pursued" – Boy on Bike – March 12, 1968
6. *Wild in the Streets* – feature film – young Max – May 29, 1968
7. *Lancer* – "Blood Rock" – Ben Price – October 1, 1968
8. *That Girl* – "7 1/4 Part 2" – Fan – October 24, 1968
9. *Gomer Pyle, U.S.M.C.* – "A Star Is Not Born" – Boy #1 – November 22, 1968
10. *The Mod Squad* – "The Guru" – newspaper boy – December 13, 1968
11. *Short-Story Showcase: Bartleby* – Encyclopedia Britannica film – Ginger Nut – 1969

12. *Here Come the Brides* – "A Kiss for Just So" – Peter – January 29, 1969

13. *It Takes A Thief* – "A Matter of Grey Matter Part I and Part II" – Herbie DuBois – February 4 & 11, 1969

14. *Adam-12* – "Log 152: A Dead Cop Can't Help Anyone" – Johnny Grant – March 8, 1969

15. *General Hospital* – unnamed episode – Jack Larson – April 10, 1969

Concurrent Brady

1. *Marcus Welby, M.D.* – "The Chemistry of Hope" – Pancho McGurney – December 16, 1969

2. *The Shameful Secrets of Hastings Corner* – "Pilot" – Junior Fandango – January 14, 1970

3. *Mission: Impossible* – "Gitano" – King Victor – February 1, 1970

4. *Goodnight Jackie* aka *Games Guys Play* – feature film – Barry – 1973

Post-Brady

1. *Police Woman* – "Generation of Evil" – Steve – February 10, 1976

2. *Greatest Heroes of the Bible* – "Jacob's Challenge" – Jacob – March 18, 1979

3. *Three's Company* – "Up In the Air" – David Winthrop – May 4, 1982

4. *General Hospital* – unknown episode(s) – Hannibal – 1984

5. *Highway to Heaven* – "A Song for Jason Part I and Part II" – Miki Winner – September 18 & 25, 1985

6. *Murder, She Wrote* – "Night of the Headless Horseman" – Nate Findley – January 4, 1987

7. *Kids Incorporated* – "Breaking Up Is Hard To Do" – Ana's Dad – 1991

8. *Summertime Switch* – TV movie – Frederick Egan, II – October 8, 1994

9. *Full House* – "Making Out Is Hard To Do" – himself/member of The Rippers – October 11, 1994

10. *The Brady Bunch Movie* – feature film – music agent – February 17, 1995

11. *Perversions of Science* – "People's Choice" – Neighbor – July 23, 1997

12. *S-Club 7 in Hollywood* – 13 episodes – Dean Strickland – September 15, 2001-March 2002

13. *According to Jim* – "Sex Ed Fred" – Ben – January 10, 2006

14. *That '70's Show* – "We Will Rock You" – Jeff – May 4, 2006

15. *Mega Piranha* – TV movie – Bob Grady – April 10, 2010

16. *A.N.T. Farm* – "America Needs TalANT" – Gameshow Host – November 25, 2011

17. *You'll Never Amount to Anything* – feature film – Bob Sandusky/Reporter – expected 2011, but never released

18. *Bigfoot* – TV movie – Simon Quinn – June 30, 2012

19. *The Comeback Kids* – "Child Star Support Group Part Two" – Barry – 2015

20. *Flea* – TV movie – Marsh Man – January 8, 2016

Christopher Knight

Birth: November 7, 1957; New York, New York
Birth Name: Christopher Anton Knight
Siblings: He's the second of four
Marital Status: In his fourth marriage after three divorces
Kids: None
Favorite Brady Episode: The Hawaii episodes

Born in New York, Chris's family moved when he was young to sunnier skies in California. Chris's father Edward Knight was the first in the family to enter show business. Edward was a stage actor, but he also appeared on TV starting in 1960 and continuing through the 1970s. (See the next chapter for Edward's biography.) The Knight children were all encouraged to go into acting and each of them did; however, Chris was the only one who landed a television series. His first commercial was for Purex Bleach when he was 8 years old. Chris's big success came in late 1968 when he signed on to the part of Peter Brady on _The Brady Bunch_. He was only ten years old. Viewers watched the cute child grow up to be a handsome teenager over the next five years. Chris was perhaps the most popular of the Brady kids in terms of number of fan letters received and articles and pictures in teen magazines of the day. That's not to

_Chris from Season 1
of_ The Brady Bunch.

say the others weren't popular: just that Chris was a boy and most fans and magazine readers tended to be girls. Many of the articles featured Chris surrounded by his pets. At the time, he and his family owned a dog, several cats, a bunch of fish, and even a whole flock of pigeons. Chris and his brother Mark entered the pigeons in shows, and the boys frequently came home with blue ribbons.

Chris greatly enjoyed acting and loved going to the _Brady_ set every day to be with his "second family." After the show ended he finished high school and did a few guest roles. Chris became a professional computer technician in 1988. He worked for several companies, including Martec, Inc., New Image Industry, and Visual Software. At New Image he served as Vice President. Then in 1995 he founded Kidwise Learningware where he developed, among other programs, a geography program called "Bradys Across America" featuring the characters of _The Brady Bunch_. The company was sold off after one year and the Brady program was never released. Chris continued working in the computer industry for the next eight years.

In the mid-2000s, Chris got back into television. He ekes out Barry for Brady family poster boy of modern reality television shows. His first foray into the "real" world was in 2004 when he appeared on Discovery Health Channel's _Body Challenge: Hollywood_. (The show also featured fellow Brady Susan Olsen.) The next year Chris participated in the infamous 2004-5 season of _The Surreal Life_ on VH1. On the show he met and fell in love with Adrianne Curry, the winner of 2004's _America's Next Top Model_. The network was so enamored with the dating couple that they gave them their own reality show the following season in fall 2005. *My Fair Brady* premiered in September. The premise was to follow Chris and Adrianne in their romantic endeavors in the hope they would become engaged and then married. Sure enough, season two under the subtitle "We're Getting Married!" featured Chris and Adrianne's wedding. They were married on May 29, 2006 with fellow Bradys Barry Williams, Mike Lookinland, and Susan Olsen in attendance. Season three was titled "Maybe Baby," which, naturally, followed the newlyweds as they contemplated having a child. Next for Chris, it was onto a one-time show on NBC called *Celebrity Circus*. He had to do some demanding acts, including one with fire, but had to leave the show because of a broken arm. But Chris wasn't off the airwaves for long. The fall of 2008 saw him as host of the daytime game show *Trivial Pursuit: America Plays*, which lasted through part of 2009. Finally, he hosted a lottery game show in Michigan called *Make Me Rich*. Chris and Adrianne divorced in 2012. In the late fall of that year, Chris launched his own line of furniture called Christopher Knight Home. There are hundreds of pieces to choose from, and they are all delivered directly to your home. Browse the selection at http://christopherknighthome.com.

TIKI TALK

Now you know that both Robert Reed and Barry Williams are not the actors' real birth names. But did you know that Christopher Knight might not have been named "Knight" if it weren't for his father? Chris' dad, Edward, was born with the name Edward Kozumplik! He had it legally changed in 1951 to Knight. Without that change, our Chris would have been Chris Kozumplik. Imagine that.

Filmography

Pre-Brady:
1. *Mannix* – "Coffin for a Clown" – Josh – November 25, 1967
2. *Gunsmoke* – "The Miracle Man" – boy – December 2, 1968
3. *Bonanza* – unknown episode – unknown date

Concurrent Brady:
None known. Although many filmography sites – and even magazine articles of the day – will list Chris as having appeared in a movie called *Cotter* (aka *The Narrow Chute*), he was actually not in it. Curiously, though, the name "Christopher Knight" appears in the opening credits. So either his scenes were entirely cut or it's a different Christopher Knight altogether, perhaps the one who played Studs Lonigan.

Post-Brady:

1. *ABC Afterschool Specials* – "Summer of the Swans" aka "Sara's Summer of the Swans" – Joe – October 2, 1974

2. *One Day at a Time* – "Barbara's Emergence" – Pete – October 26, 1976

3. *Bigfoot and Wildboy* – "White Wolf" – White Wolf – October 1977

4. *The Bionic Woman* – "Max" – Bobby – December 3, 1977

5. *Happy Days* – "Be My Valentine" – Binky Hodges – February 14, 1978

6. *CHiPs* – "Family Crisis" – Wes Miller – September 30, 1978

7. *Just You and Me, Kid* – feature film – Roy – July 13, 1979

8. *Diary of a Teenage Hitchhiker* – TV movie – Nick – September 21, 1979

9. *Joe's World* – TV series, 11 episodes – Steve Wabash – December 29, 1979-July 19, 1980

10. *Valentine Magic on Love Island* – TV movie – Jimmy – February 15, 1980

11. *Another World* – TV soap opera – Leigh Hodges or Hobson – unknown episodes, 1980-1982

12. *Masquerade* – "Oil" – unknown character – January 26, 1984

13. *The Love Boat* – "Paying the Piper/Baby Sister/Help Wanted" – Peter Barkan – December 1, 1984

14. *Day by Day* – "A Very Brady Episode" – Peter Brady – February 5, 1989

15. *Curfew* – feature film – Sam – June 1989

16. *Good Girls Don't* – feature film – Montana – 1993

17. *The Brady Bunch Movie* – feature film – coach – February 17, 1995

18. *The Doom Generation* – feature film – TV anchorman – October 27, 1995

19. *Nowhere* – feature film – Mr. Sighvatssohn – May 9, 1997

20. *Family Jewels* – feature film – the guru – February 6, 2003

21. *Less Than Perfect* – "Claude the Expert" – waiter – April 15, 2005

22. *That '70's Show* – "We Will Rock You" – Josh – May 4, 2006

23. *L.A. Dicks* – feature film – Bernie Taylor – April 10, 2007

24. *Fallen Angels* – feature film – Belmont – October 5, 2007

25. *Light Years Away* – feature film – David Sommers – 2007 & 2015

26. *Spring Breakdown* – direct to video – celebrity judge – 2009

27. *American Pie Presents: The Book of Love* – feature film – Alumnus Guy #3 – December 22, 2009

28. *The Bold and the Beautiful* – Episode #1.5901 – Dr. Andrews – September 15, 2010

29. *CSI: Crime Scene Investigation* – "Malice in Wonderland" – Pastor – March 12, 2012

30. *Letting Go* – feature film – The Boss – October 2, 2012

31. *The Lords of Salem* – feature film – Keith "Lobster Joe" Williams (scenes deleted) – April 19, 2013

32. *Heartbreakers* – TV miniseries – Hurley Fontenot – August 13, 2014

33. *Guardian Angel* – feature film – Brian Casey – September 1, 2014

34. *Prisoner* – short film – Brad – April 1, 2016

35. *Where the Fast Lane Ends* – feature film – Cooley Swindell – expected 2017

BIOGRAPHIES

Mike LookinlanD

Birth: December 19, 1960; Mount Pleasant, Utah
Birth Name: Michael Paul Lookinland
Siblings: He's the middle of three
Marital Status: Married
Kids: Scott & Joseph
Favorite Brady Episode: "The Un-Underground Movie"

Mike Lookinland on The Jonathan Winters Show

The third Brady boy got his start in the acting world at a very young age. A talent agent saw his photograph on his father Paul's desk at work and said that Mike ought to be in show business. He filmed his first commercial when he was just seven years old. He completed approximately thirty by the time he was cast as Bobby Brady in *The Brady Bunch*. Mike's first non-commercial television appearance was on *The Jonathan Winters Show*. Then he auditioned for *The Courtship of Eddie's Father* and *The Brady Bunch* in 1968. Mike was offered <u>both</u> roles and chose the *Brady* show because his parents liked the idea of having more kids on the set for him to play with (he would have been the only one on *Eddie*; that role instead went to Brandon Cruz).

Sherwood Schwartz liked young Mike so much that he would have been Bobby Brady no matter if the boys were blond or dark-haired. So brownish/reddish-headed Mike's hair was dyed black when dark-haired Robert Reed was cast as the series' father and off went Mike's career. He was sought-after during the run of *The Brady Bunch* and starred in a Disney TV movie, educational films for Encyclopedia Britannica, another television movie, and a handful of other roles (see "Filmography" below). After *The Brady Bunch* ended in 1974, Mike was cast with a dazzling array of stars to appear in the blockbuster film *The Towering Inferno*, which was 1974's top-grossing film. Soon afterward he auditioned for and was offered the role as Franz Robinson in the 1975 television series *The Swiss Family Robinson*. But Mike declined the role, deciding instead that he wanted to be a regular kid and attend high school. (The role went to Willie Aames who later starred in *Eight Is Enough*.)

Later he went to college at the University of Utah but dropped out before graduating to become a production assistant and cameraman. He liked being behind the scenes of television and movies and in fact that is where he met his wife Kelly. The two hit it off and were married in 1987. That year they were production assistants together for *Halloween 4*, and in 1988 worked together on *Stranger On My Land* and *Halloween V*. In 1990, Kelly gave birth to their first son Scott. Three years later Joe was born. The family lived happily in Utah.

In 2000, Barry Williams was working on a television movie of *Growing Up Brady*. Mike joined the production as a cameraman (and in a cameo as...a cameraman), but more significantly Scott Lookinland was cast to play none other than his very own father at age ten. Scott was the spitting image of his dad right down to the mannerisms and there couldn't have been a better choice for the "character" of Michael Lookinland. But Scott isn't the only other Lookinland who became involved in acting. Check out the next chapter called "Bonus Biographies."

Today Mike works as a concrete countertop craftsman in Utah. The Lookinland family is very talented and we look forward to more to come from them!

Filmography

Pre-Brady:
1. *The Jonathan Winters Show* – two unknown episodes, one of which possibly aired in November or December 1968 (speculation based on the date of the photograph above, which was 11-25-1968, but no episode actually aired on that day)

Concurrent Brady:
1. *The Point* – TV movie – Oblio (voice) – 1971
2. *Germs and the Space Visitors* – Encyclopedia Britannica educational film – boy – 1971
3. *Disneyland* – "The Boy from Dead Man's Bayou" aka "Bayou Boy" – TV Movie – Claude – February 7 & 14, 1971
4. *Funny Face* – "A Crush on Sandy" – Richie – December 4, 1971
5. *Dead Men Tell No Tales* – TV movie – Bud Riley – December 17, 1971

Post-Brady:
1. *The Towering Inferno* – feature film – Phillip Allbright – December 14, 1974
2. *Isis* aka *The Secret of Isis* – "How to Find a Friend" – Tom Anderson – October 25, 1975
3. *Little House on the Prairie* – "Times of Change" – Patrick – September 19, 1977
4. *Day by Day* – "A Very Brady Episode" – Bobby Brady – February 5, 1989
5. *The Stand* – TV miniseries episode #4 – Sentry #1 – May 12, 1994
6. *Gambler V: Playing for Keeps* – 2-part TV movie – Bosun – October 2, 1994
7. *The Brady Bunch Movie* – feature film – cop #3 (scene deleted) – February 17, 1995
8. *Growing Up Brady* – TV movie – cameraman – May 21, 2000

Maureen McCormick

Birth: August 5, 1956; Los Angeles, California
Birth Name: Maureen Denise McCormick
Siblings: She's youngest of four
Marital Status: Married
Kid: Natalie
Favorite Brady Episode: "The Show Must Go On??"

Maureen started acting at a young age and had an impressive list of television and theatrical appearances by the time she became Marcia Brady. Her first major acting gig was a part in a La Jolla Playhouse play called "Wind It Up and It Breaks" that starred Mike Connors and ran in late summer of 1964. From there she made several television appearances and an amazing *fifty* television commercials, nearly half of which were for Mattel. She provided voices for dolls like Chatty Cathy and was also once the voice of Peppermint Patty for a Peanuts commercial. Then she had guest spots on television shows from the mid- to late-1960s. Midway through her first year on *The Brady Bunch* she was chosen with

Maureen in Season One of The Brady Bunch

three other child stars to appear on a television news show hosted by Art Linkletter called *A Kid's Eye View of Washington* and got to interview Richard Nixon, tour Washington, D.C., and dress up in Eighteenth Century clothing.

Maureen enjoyed her time on *The Brady Bunch*. Acting and singing were a way for her to escape real life problems and by the fifth season she approached the show with aplomb. After it was cancelled, she wanted to continue acting, especially in the movies and in dramatic roles. "I had a reservoir of deep and dark emotions in me, and I was ready to show the world there was more to me than Marcia. I wanted to be known for serious work and winning awards."[6] For reasons that are complicated and involve Hollywood prejudice and eventually Maureen's own personal problems, she was never really able to land another breakthrough role. She received parts in many, many films but they were B-movies and she became disillusioned with her Hollywood dreams.

In the mid-1980s Maureen married Michael Cummings. They had a daughter Natalie and though there were ups and downs, everything has worked out well for Maureen's small family. In terms of acting, she lifted her head high and was finally able to land some more respectable roles such as *Get to the Heart: The Barbara Mandrell Story*. Like Chris Knight, she, too, has enjoyed a few reality show stints in CMT's *Gone Country* and *Outsiders Inn*. Her résumé is super long and she's proud to still be in the business after 40 years.

In 2008, Maureen wrote a tell-all memoir called Here's the Story: Surviving Marcia Brady and Finding My True Voice. In it, she tells readers of her personal life, *The Brady Bunch*, and her struggles and triumphs. It's a heartfelt book and took courage to write. As for Marcia Brady, Maureen says, "Now I can embrace Marcia, and when people of all ages, walks of life, and ethnicities say they wanted to be me or date me when they were little…I feel blessed to be that person."[7]

Filmography

Pre-Brady:

1. *Bewitched* – "And Something Makes Three" – Little Endora – December 3, 1964
2. *The Farmer's Daughter* – "Why Don't They Ever Pick Me?" – Christine – March 12, 1965
3. *Camp Runamuck* – "Runamuck" aka "Who Stole My Bathtub?" – Maureen Sullivan – September 17, 1965
4. *This Is the Hospital* – "Pilot" – unknown character – unknown date
5. *Bewitched* – "Trick Or Treat" – Little Endora – October 28, 1965
6. *Honey West* – "In the Bag" – Margaret Mary Driscoll – November 5, 1965
7. *Camp Runamuck* – "Tomboy" – Maureen Sullivan – January 7, 1966
8. *I Dream of Jeannie* – "My Master, the Doctor" – Susan – February 5, 1966
9. *My Three Sons* – "Ernie, the Bluebeard" – Sylvia Waters – November 11, 1967

Concurrent Brady:

1. *The Arrangement* – feature film – girl in Zephyr commercial – November 11, 1969
2. *Cold Turkey* – feature film – doll (voice) – February 19, 1971
3. *Marcus Welby, M.D.* – "The Day After Forever" – Sharon Boyd – February 27, 1973
4. *Young Marriage* – short film – Beth – September 9, 1973

Post-Brady:

1. *Happy Days* – "Cruisin' " – Hildie – February 11, 1975
2. *Harry O* – "Street Games" – Nancy Wayne – March 2, 1975
3. *The Turning Point of Jim Malloy* – TV movie – unknown character – April 12, 1975
4. *Jim Forrester* – "Bus Station" – Irene Kellogg – September 23, 1975
5. *The Streets of San Francisco* – "No Minor Vices" – Cindy Lawson – November 4, 1976
6. *Pony Express Rider* – feature film – Rose of Sharon – November 1976
7. *Gibbsville* – "All the Young Girls" – Alice Chapman – December 16, 1976
8. *The Hardy Boys/Nancy Drew Mysteries* – "Nancy Drew's Love Match" – Karen Phillips – January 20, 1977
9. *Delvecchio* – "One Little Indian" – Lynette Youndfellow – January 30, 1977
10. *Moonshine County Express* – feature film – Sissy Hammer – June 1, 1977
11. *The Love Boat* – "The Joker is Mild/Take My Granddaughter, Please/First Time Out" – Barbara Holmes – October 29, 1977
12. *The Love Boat* – "The Congressman Was Indiscreet/Isaac's History Lesson/Winner Takes Love" – Suzy Corbett – January 28, 1978
13. *Fantasy Island* – "Treasure Hunt/Beauty Contest" – Sally Quinn – March 11, 1978
14. *Wedge* – independent film – Wedge's girlfriend – 1978
15. *Fantasy Island* – "Best Seller/The Tomb" – Angela Brennan – October 14, 1978

BIOGRAPHIES

16. *Vega$* – "The Pageant" – Jenny Logan – November 15, 1978

17. *Take Down* – feature film – Brooke Cooper – January 1979

18. *Insight* – "When Jenny? When?" – Jenny – February 1, 1979

19. *Lou Grant* – "Sweep" – Tiffany – February 5, 1979

20. *Fantasy Island* – "The Stripper/The Boxer" – Jennie Collins - February 10, 1979

21. *A Vacation in Hell* – TV movie – Margret – May 21, 1979

22. *The Runaways* – "Throwaway Child" – Janet – June 5, 1979

23. *Skatetown, U.S.A.* – feature film – Susan – October 1979

24. *Fantasy Island* – "Aphrodite/Dr. Jekyll and Miss Hyde" – Jennifer Griffin – February 2, 1980

25. *The Love Boat* – "Another Time, Another Place/Doctor Who/Gopher's Engagement" – Celia Elliott – March 1, 1980

26. *The Idolmaker* – feature film – Ellen Fields – November 14, 1980

27. *Fantasy Island* – "High Off the Hog/Reprisal" – Trudy Brown – January 10, 1981

28. *The Love Boat* – "April the Ninny/The Loan Arranger/First Voyage, Last Voyage" – Cindy – January 17, 1981

29. *Texas Lightning* – feature film – Fay – June 1981

30. *The Love Boat* – "A Christmas Presence" – Lori Markham – December 18, 1982

31. *Fantasy Island* – "Love Island/The Sisters" – Stephanie Wilson – May 14, 1983

32. *Shout for Joy* – feature film – Alma Irons – September 24, 1983

33. *New Love, American Style* – "Love and the F.M. Doctor" – unknown character – 1986

34. *Return to Horror High* – feature film – Officer Tyler – January 28, 1987

35. *Day by Day* – "A Very Brady Episode" – Marcia Brady – February 5, 1989

36. *That's Adequate* – feature film – Space Princess – January 1990

37. *Herman's Head* – "When Hermy Met Maureen McCormick" – Maureen McCormick – November 18, 1993

38. *The Single Guy* – "Kept Man" – Valerie – October 10, 1996

39. *Panic in the Skies!* – TV movie – Tukey, Walker's Assistant/Flight Attendant – October 13, 1996

40. *Touched by an Angel* – "Clipped Wings" – Jodi – February 16, 1997

41. *Dogtown* – feature film – Didi Schmidt – 1997

42. *Johnny Bravo* – "Beach Blanket Bravo/The Day the Earth Didn't Move Around Much/Aisle of Mixed-Up Toys" – Franny (voice) – August 25, 1997

43. *Get to the Heart: The Barbara Mandrell Story* – TV movie – Barbara Mandrell – September 28, 1997

44. *Teen Angel* – 11 of 17 episodes – Judy Beauchamp – September 26, 1997-February 13, 1998

45. *Baby Huey's Great Easter Adventure* – straight to video – Nick's Mom – March 2, 1999

46. *Moesha* – "Isn't She Lovely?" – Saleslady – November 8, 1999

47. *The Million Dollar Kid* aka *Fortune Hunters* – feature film – Betsy Hunter – 2000

48. *Son of the Beach* – "South of Her Border" – Mrs. Strawther – August 15, 2000

49. *Passions* – 11 episodes – Rebecca Hotchkiss – July 5-August 17, 2000

50. *The Amanda Show* – Episode 2.28 – unknown character – 2001

51. *The A-List* – short film – unknown character – 2001

52. *Title To Murder* – feature film – Leah Farrell – May 15, 2001

53. *Son of the Beach* – "The Sexorcist" – Mrs. Strawther – June 26, 2001

54. *The Man from Elysian Fields* – feature film – unknown character – September 13, 2001
55. *Shock Video 2002: America Undercover* – TV movie – Narrator – December 22, 2001
56. *The Ellen Show* – "Shallow Gal" – Rita Carter – January 2002
57. *Jane White Is Sick and Twisted* – feature film – Nancy – January 27, 2002
58. *Johnny Bravo* – "It's Valentine's Day, Johnny Bravo!" – Pizza Girl (voice) – February 14, 2002
59. *Son of the Beach* – "Godfather Knows Best" – Mrs. Strawther – August 13, 2002
60. *The Brothers Garcia* – "Moving On Up" – Mrs. Bauer – September 21, 2003
61. *Scrubs* – "My Journey" – Maureen McCormick – October 9, 2003
62. *The Guardian* – "Beautiful Blue Mystic" – receptionist – January 13, 2004
63. *Stone & Ed* – feature film – Dream Mother – January 8, 2008
64. *Prayer Hour* – TV movie – Stage Mom – 2011
65. *Christmas Spirit* – TV movie – Sarah – November 30, 2011
66. *Snow White: A Deadly Summer* – feature film – Eve – March 16, 2012
67. *Naughty & Nice* – TV movie – Kate – November 9, 2014
68. *Big Baby* – feature film – Molly – November 2015
69. *Christmas Land* – TV movie – Glinda Stanwick – December 20, 2015
70. *Nightmare Next Door* – "Orange Grove Cruelty" – Marian Justi – January 24, 2016
71. *Accidentally Engaged* – feature film – Jeannette – March 5, 2016
72. *Rock Paper Dead* – feature film – Nurse Ruland – expected 2017

Eve Plumb

<u>*Birth*</u>: *April 29, 1958; Burbank, California*
<u>*Birth Name*</u>: *Eve Aline Plumb*
<u>*Siblings*</u>: *She's the youngest of three*
<u>*Marital Status*</u>: *Divorced once and re-married*
<u>*Kids*</u>: *None*
<u>*Favorite Brady Episode*</u>: *unknown*

Eve Plumb in 1969

Eve Plumb's parents Neely and Flora are the proud parents of three children; their oldest child Benjamin Neely Plumb, Jr. was born in 1943 and Flora – the third generation of her family to be named such – in 1944. Youngest child Eve was born in 1958. There's quite a spread between kids! Both parents were involved in show business. Mom Flora was a dancer and stage actress. Neely was a musician who played with the likes of Artie Shaw. He also had a very, very successful record producing career throughout the fifties, sixties, and seventies (see "Music" chapter under Eve's entry).

Eve became involved in acting when she was six years old. Ann B. Davis's book describes Eve's entry into Hollywood: "A children's talent agent moved next door to her family and quickly convinced her mother to take her on a commercial audition. She got the job, first time out, which started an active career in commercials and television shows."[8] She never had much of a problem auditioning, most likely because of her natural charm, acting ability, and gorgeous long blonde hair. Sister Flora was getting started around this time as well. (See the next chapter for more on Flora.) Eve appeared on many television series before she was a Brady, and was a guest of Art Linkletter on April 2, 1969 where she was interviewed about her role in a *Mannix* episode.

It's very possible that the world could have had a different Jan Brady. If Eve's pilots for *The Barbara Rush Show* and/or *Dick Tracy* had been picked up, she might have already been booked by the time Sherwood Schwartz started the *Brady* auditions! Luckily for us – and Eve – we got her. After *The Brady Bunch* ended, Eve chose to stick to acting, but wanted to mix it up a little by doing drama and get away from type casting. She landed the role as Dawn Wetherby in *Dawn: Portrait of a Teenage Runaway* in 1976. Dawn was a runaway teen who had to turn to prostitution in order to survive on the streets. It was a very gritty and memorable role for Eve. Her next role was in a suspense film, which was followed quickly by the sequel to *Dawn*.

Around 1980, she and her then-husband Rick Mansfield formed their own production company called Fleur de Lis Productions. Eve's father Neely also served as the company's vice president. They bought the rights to the book The Sweetheart: The Story of Mary Pickford and planned a movie in which Eve was going to play Pickford. Next, they went to the Bahamas to film a short called *Sea People*. They also had plans for a movie called *The Exchange*, which would be based on Rick's experiences in the armed forces. Unfortunately, none of the projects ever aired and the couple divorced in 1981.

In 1995 Eve remarried. Over the last 20 years or so, Eve has continued to act. Moreover, she has always had a talent for art and she put that skill to use for her second career. Eve likes to paint still pictures of cafés and you can see many of them on her website at http://www.eveplumb.tv/. She says on her homepage that "painting is a creative outlet for me when I'm not acting. It gives me a feeling of control over my creative life. An actor often has to wait for projects to come along, but I can paint any time of the day. I sometimes describe my art as 'spontaneous still life'."[9]

Filmography

Pre-Brady:
1. *The Barbara Rush Show* (as shown on *Vacation Playhouse*) – "Pilot" – Melissa – July 9, 1965
2. *The Smothers Brothers Show* – " 'Twas the Week Before Christmas" – little girl – December 17, 1965 (this may also have appeared in the series *My Brother the Angel*)
3. *The Big Valley* – "Hide the Children" – Sara Jane – December 19, 1966
4. *The Big Valley* – "Brother Love" – Ellen – February 20, 1967
5. *Dick Tracy* – "Pilot" – Bonnie Braids – 1967
6. *The Big Valley* – "Explosion! Part 2" – Lauren – November 27, 1967
7. *The Virginian* – "A Small Taste of Justice" – Kathy Cooper – December 20, 1967
8. *Lassie* – "Miracle of the Dove" – Terry – December 24, 1967
9. *It Takes A Thief* – "The Radomir Miniature" – Maritsa Radomir – April 9, 1968

10. *Adam-12* – "Log 71: I Feel Like a Fool, Malloy" – Cissy Franklin – November 2, 1968
11. *Mannix* – "The Edge of the Knife" – Marian Harriman – November 9, 1968
12. *Family Affair* – "Christmas Came a Little Early" – Eve Bowers – November 11, 1968
13. *Lancer* – "The Heart of Pony Alice" – Pony Alice – December 17, 1968
14. *Gunsmoke* – "Gold Town" aka "Goldtown" – Sue – January 27, 1969
15. *Then Came Bronson* – "Pilot" – unknown character – March 24, 1969

Concurrent Brady:
1. *In Name Only* – TV movie – unknown character – November 25, 1969
2. *The House on Greenapple Road* aka *The Red Kitchen Murder* – TV movie – Margaret Ord – January 11, 1970
3. *Here's Lucy* – "Lucy and Donny Osmond" – Patricia Carter – November 20, 1972

Post-Brady:
1. *Sigmund and the Sea Monsters* – "Now You See 'Em, Now You Don't" – Harriet – September 21, 1974
2. *ABC Afterschool Specials* – "Summer of the Swans" aka "Sara's Summer of the Swans" – Gretchen – October 2, 1974
3. *Dawn: Portrait of a Teenage Runaway* – TV movie – Dawn Wetherby – December 27, 1976
4. *Tales of the Unexpected* – "Force of Evil" – Cindy Carrington – March 13, 1977
5. *Alexander: The Other Side of Dawn* – TV movie – Dawn Wetherby – May 16, 1977
6. *Wonder Woman* – "The Pied Piper" – Elena Atkinson – October 21, 1977
7. *Telethon* – TV movie – Kim – November 6, 1977
8. *Insight* – "Is Anybody Listening?" – Jeannie – March 1, 1978
9. *The Love Boat* – "Gopher, the Rebel/Cabin Fever/Pacific Princess Overtures" – Vanessa Summerhill – May 20, 1978
10. *Little Women* – TV movie – Beth March – October 2, 1978
11. *Secrets of Three Hungry Wives* – TV movie – Vicki Wood – October 9, 1978
12. *Greatest Heroes of the Bible* – "Noah and the Deluge Part I and Part II" – Lilla – November 19 & 20, 1978
13. *Fantasy Island* – "Séance/Treasure" – Clare Conti – January 13, 1979
14. *Little Women* – "Pilot" – Lissa – February 8, 1979
15. *Fantasy Island* – "Hitman/The Swimmer" – Terry Summers – September 7, 1979
16. *The Love Boat* – "Celebration/Captain Papa/Honeymoon Pressure" – Teri Carlson – March 29, 1980
17. *Fantasy Island* – "Elizabeth's Baby/The Artist and the Lady" – Elizabeth Blake – January 17, 1981
18. *The Love Boat* – "Command Performance/Hyde and Seek/Sketchy Love" – Beth Heller – October 30, 1982
19. *One Day at a Time* – "Lovers and Other Parents" – Melissa – November 7, 1982
20. *The Facts of Life* – "The Best Sister: Part I and II" – Meg Warner – February 16 & 23, 1983
21. *The Night the Bridge Fell Down* – TV movie – Terry Kelly – February 28, 1983
22. *Masquerade* – "Spying Down to Rio" – unknown character – April 27, 1984
23. *Murder, She Wrote* – "Jessica Behind Bars" – Tug – December 1, 1985
24. *I'm Gonna Git You Sucka* – feature film – Kalinga's wife – December 14, 1988
25. *On the Television* – "Beach Party" – unknown character(s) – 1989

26. *The Super Mario Bros. Super Show!* – "Pizza Crush" – Jodie – November 17, 1989

27. *On the Television* – "Holiday Specials" – unknown character(s) – 1990

28. *Yesterday Today* – TV movie – Ricky's Mom – July 3, 1992

29. *The Making of ...And God Spoke* aka *...And God Spoke* – feature film – Mrs. Noah – 1993

30. *Lois and Clark: The New Adventures of Superman* – "Illusions of Grandeur" – Rose Collins – January 23, 1994

31. *ABC Weekend Special: Fudge-A-Mania* – TV movie – Ann Hatcher – January 7, 1995

32. *Fudge* – all 25 episodes – Ann Hatcher – 1995-1996

33. *Nowhere* – feature film – Mrs. Sighvatssohn – May 9, 1997

34. *Breast Men* – feature film – Mother – December 13, 1997

35. *Kenan and Kel* – "The Chicago Witch Trials" – teacher – October 29, 1998

36. *That '70's Show* – "The Keg" – Mrs. Burkhart – October 25, 1998

37. *Kill the Man* – feature film – Revolutionary #3 – January 24, 1999

38. *Manfast* aka *Holding Out* – feature film – Professor Mason – April 30, 2003

39. *All My Children* – unknown episode – June Landau – 2003

40. *Days of Our Lives* – Episode 1.10901 – Dora – August 29, 2008

41. *The Pox Show* – TV movie – Nurse Dremel – 2012

42. *The Sisters Plotz* – web series, all episodes – Celestia Plotz – 2012-2013

43. *Law & Order: Special Victims Unit* – "Monster's Legacy" – Angela Brooks – February 6, 2013

44. *Army Wives* – "Damaged" – Reba Green – June 2, 2013

45. *Blue Ruin* – feature film – Kris Cleland – September 22, 2013

46. *The Boy Who Stayed* – short film – Sam's Mother – July 30, 2014

47. *Grease Live!* – TV movie – Mrs. Murdock – January 31, 2016

48. *The Sisters Plotz* – feature film – Celestia Plotz – expected 2017

49. *Monsoon* – feature film – Gale – expected 2017

Susan Olsen

Birth: August 14, 1961; Santa Monica, California
Birth Name: Susan Marie Olsen
Siblings: She's the youngest of four
Marital Status: Divorced twice
Kid: Michael
Favorite Brady Episode: "Peter and the Wolf"

Susan Olsen's family is a lot like Eve's because her siblings are so spread out in age. Her oldest brother Lawrence Joseph, Jr. was born in 1938 in Iowa. The family moved to Miami, Florida where they lived until Larry Joe was 4. The next stop was California where their second child Christopher Robin was born in 1946. Then Linda Diane entered the world in 1956. Finally along came little Susan Marie in 1961. That's twenty-three years between the oldest and youngest! Larry, Jr. was the first of the Olsen kids to get in front of the camera, but all four eventually made it onto the small or large screen. (See the next chapter for more.)

As for Susan, she got her start on screen when she was just a baby in a fabric softener commercial. She made quite a few commercials between that age and three-years-old. At three, her mother DeLoice "Dee" decided to retire her. But when little Suzie was in kindergarten at Wilbur Elementary School in Santa Monica, she got the chance to audition to sing on *The Pat Boone Show*. She was picked out of everyone in her class and got to perform The Monkees' song "I'm a Believer" on the air. From that point, she was able to land a few guest-starring roles in some television series. Then in 1968 she auditioned for Sherwood Schwartz and we all know that she got the part.

This is one of Susan's first headshots when she was just a toddler. At that point, her agent was the famed Lola D. Moore. Courtesy of Susan Olsen.

After *The Brady Bunch*, Susan finished high school and went to college. In the 1980s and early '90s, she worked as a graphic designer. She had her own company called Man in Space. As part of that work, she created a series of shoes for Converse called Glow All Stars (marketed to adults) and Kids Glow (for kids). Then in 1995 Susan starred in a radio show on KLSX 97.1 out of LA called Ober and Olsen, named for herself and her co-host Ken Ober. The show lasted through early 2009 when KLSX was changed to "AMP Radio" as a top-40 station rather than a talk radio station. Then up until December 12, 2016 she had a show on LA Talk Radio called Two Chicks Talkin' Politics. Susan also keeps a Facebook page dedicated to Precious Paws, a program that rescues, spays, and neuters stray and unwanted dogs and cats and places them with good families.

In 2009, Susan co-authored a book called <u>Love to Love You Bradys</u> with Ted Nichelson and Lisa Sutton. The book chronicled the making of the Brady variety show. It's a very thorough, well-written reference guide to everything about the series, including costume designs, plot descriptions, and interviews with the Kroffttettes.

Susan has been married and divorced twice. Her second marriage brought her the joy of her life: a baby boy she named Michael after none other than Mike Lookinland.

FilmograPhy

Pre-Brady:
1. *The Pat Boone Show* – unknown episode, unknown date (probably 1966-7)
2. *Ironside* – "Barbara Who?" – Tracy Richards – February 29, 1968
3. *Gunsmoke* – "Abelia" – Marianne Johnson – November 18, 1968
4. *Julia* – "Paint Your Waggedorn" – Pamela Bennett – November 26, 1968
5. *The Trouble with Girls* aka *The Chautauqua* – feature film – auditioning singer – September 3, 1969

Concurrent Brady:

1. *Gunsmoke* – "A Man Called 'Smith' " – Marianne Johnson – October 27, 1969
2. *Disneyland* – "The Boy Who Stole the Elephant" – Lucy Owens – September 20 & 27, 1970

Post-Brady:

1. *Divorce Court* – unknown episode – litigant – 1986
2. *The Brady Bunch Movie* – feature film – reporter (scene deleted) – February 17, 1995
3. *Pacific Blue* – "Stargazer" – Cindy Russell – January 24, 1999
4. *Zombo* – short film – frumpy woman – 2009
5. *The Young and the Restless* – Episode #1.9494 – Liza Morton – September 1, 2010
6. *The Young and the Restless* – Episode #1.9515 – Liza Morton – October 28, 2010
7. *The Halloween Puppy* – TV movie – Rachel – October 2, 2012
8. *Child of the '70s* – 10 episodes – Nickel Laundry – 2013-2016
9. *Holiday Road Trip* – TV movie – Edna – December 1, 2013
10. *Mama Claus, Deck the Halls with Guts* – feature film – Mama Claus – November 1, 2015

Sherwood Schwartz and Family: A Veritable Brady Dynasty

Birth: November 14, 1916; Passaic, New Jersey
Birth Name: Sherwood Charles Schwartz
Death: July 12, 2011; Los Angeles, California
Siblings: He's the third of four
Marital Status: Married
Kids: Donald, Lloyd, Ross, & Hope
Favorite Brady Episode: unknown

Sherwood Schwartz was born to Russian immigrants and grew up between New York and New Jersey. He had desires early in life to become a doctor and when it came time for college Sherwood studied pre-med at New York University and biology in grad school at the University of Southern California. He says, "I actually started off in pre-med. In the 1930s the AMA decided there were too many Jewish doctors, so medical school admissions became tougher for applicants with Jewish-sounding last names. I decided to get a master's degree in biology from USC to make myself more competitive."[10] While at USC, Sherwood roomed with his older brother Al who was a comedy writer for Bob Hope at the time. At some point, Sherwood decided to try his hand at writing jokes, too, and Al brought them to Hope for comment. Bob Hope liked the jokes enough that Sherwood decided to leave doctoring behind and become a full-time comedy writer alongside his brother. The duo wrote for Hope's radio show throughout the 1940s and early 1950s. Then in 1954, Sherwood and Al both got jobs as writers for television's *The Red Skelton Show*. Sherwood became script supervisor and head writer for the show early on and received much acclaim for his ability to make Red funny. He was particularly well-known and lauded for a sequence he wrote for Skelton's character Freddie the Freeloader where there was no dialogue: just pantomime. Sherwood was nominated for two Emmys in comedy writing and won one in 1961.

When *The Red Skelton Show* ended in 1963, Sherwood was ready to move onto a new venue and had plans for a situation comedy of his own making. The sitcom would turn out to be *Gilligan's Island*, which lasted three years on CBS from 1964-1967. "The show deals with six people marooned on an island. It is the world in a microcosm. There are rich and poor, winners and losers, strong and weak," he says.[11] Add slapstick comedy and Bob Denver, Alan Hale, Jr., and four others and it makes for a hit.

The Fall 1967 season started with no *Gilligan's Island*, and instead Sherwood had a new series to his credit called *It's About Time*. This series starred Imogene Coca (who also had a guest role later in *The Brady Bunch*) and was about two astronauts who traveled back in time to "caveman" days. They lived there for a while getting to know a caveman family. Halfway through the season, the astronauts repaired their ship and came back to 1960s Earth. They brought along the cave-dwelling family and the rest of the season focused on the cavepeople adjusting to modern life in New York City. This CBS series lasted just one season, but Sherwood already had plans in the works for his next hit.

By the time *Gilligan's Island* was in its second season, Sherwood was making plans for *The Brady Bunch*. It would be three years before he was able to sell the new sitcom to ABC, though. (For more on this, read the Introduction chapter.) But once he did, the pilot was filmed, tested, and the show approved for one year. Sherwood not only created the series, but also wrote the theme song along with Frank DeVol. His brothers Al and Elroy would occasionally serve as writers on the show and his son Lloyd would also produce over the next few years. Sherwood served as executive producer throughout the series' five years. *The Brady Bunch* received mixed reviews during its run, but Sherwood always knew that at its core it had a good message, one about family support and love.

In 1973 – the year before *Brady* was cancelled – Sherwood and his brother Elroy created yet another new series starring their old friend Bob Denver from *Gilligan's Island*. This series was called *Dusty's Trail* and aired in syndication from 1973-1974. It was a Western with the same strain of comedy that *Gilligan's Island* had.

So the Fall of 1974 found Sherwood out two shows after both *The Brady Bunch* and *Dusty's Trail* were cancelled. In 1976 *The Brady Bunch Variety Hour* hit television sets, but Sherwood was completely left out of production. In effect, Sid and Marty Krofft (the creators of the variety show) got their signals crossed and never got permission from Sherwood to use his characters. But by the time the network realized, production was already underway and the show went on despite the lack of permission. You can read all about this in Ted Nichelson et al.'s book <u>Love to Love You Bradys</u>. But never fear, Sherwood would soon be back with the Bradys – now much more like themselves – when in 1981 the television movie *The Brady Girls Get Married* was produced. That was followed swiftly by *The Brady Brides* sitcom. (This time period also saw three different *Gilligan's Island* spin-offs such as *The Harlem Globetrotters on Gilligan's Island*.)

In 1982, Sherwood and his son Lloyd created the series called *Scamps* which starred Bob Denver and also had a very young Joey Lawrence in the cast. The series was very short-lived. The following year the father and son team was back at it again with a pilot movie *The Invisible Woman* that they hoped to turn into a series. This, too, featured Bob Denver. Unfortunately, the series was not picked up. Six years later, Sherwood was back to

BIOGRAPHIES

what he did best: *The Brady Bunch*. *A Very Brady Christmas* was considered one of the top two most successful television movies of 1988 (the other was *The Karen Carpenter Story*). It featured a grown-up Brady family and tenderness in all the right places. Sherwood's final scripted *Brady* reunion was in 1990: *The Bradys*.

Sherwood served as producer for the first two of three *Brady* spoofs in 1995 and 1996. He has been honored with a star on the Hollywood Walk of Fame. He passed away at the age of 94 in July 2011. At the time, he and his son Lloyd were producing a television movie of *Gilligan's Island*, set to air in late 2011 or early 2012. He and Lloyd also wrote a book which came out in late 2010 called <u>Brady, Brady, Brady</u> that told readers all about *The Brady Bunch* production from their point of view.

As the title of this section suggests, there are many Schwartzes involved with *The Brady Bunch*. Here's what they've all contributed to the *Brady* legacy:

Al Schwartz — Sherwood's Older Brother
Brady Connection: He co-wrote *"Kitty Karry-All is Missing," "The Possible Dream," "Will the Real Jan Brady Please Stand Up?" "Her Sister's Shadow," "Getting Davy Jones," "Cindy Brady, Lady," "Jan, the Only Child," "The Subject Was Noses," "The Great Earring Caper," "Never Too Young," "Try, Try Again," "The Cincinnati Kids," "Out of This World,"* and *"Welcome Aboard."* He co-produced *"The Cincinnati Kids"* and *"Miss Popularity."*

Elroy Schwartz — Sherwood's Younger Brother
Brady Connection: He wrote *"Vote for Brady," "Tiger! Tiger!" "The Hero," "The Winner," "Alice's September Song," "My Sister, Benedict Arnold," "The Big Bet," "Law and Disorder,"* and *"Greg Gets Grounded."*

Lloyd J. Schwartz — Sherwood's Son
Brady Connection: He directed *"Room at the Top."* He co-produced *"Adios, Johnny Bravo," "Mail Order Hero," "Snow White and the Seven Bradys," "Never Too Young," "Peter and the Wolf," "Getting Greg's Goat," "Marcia Gets Creamed," "My Brother's Keeper," "Quarterback Sneak," "Try, Try Again," "The Elopement," "Kelly's Kids," "The Driver's Seat," "Out of This World," "Welcome Aboard," "Two Petes in a Pod," "Top Secret," "The Snooperstar," "The Hustler," "The Hairbrained Scheme,"* The Brady Girls Get Married, *"Living Together,"* A Very Brady Christmas, *and the stage production "A Very Brady Musical."* He co-executive produced *"Gorilla of My Dreams," "The Newlywed Game," "Cool Hand Phil," "The Mom Who Came to Dinner," "The Siege," "A Pretty Boy is Like a Melody," "The Brady 500," "A Moving Experience," "Hat in the Ring," "Bottoms Up,"* and *"The Party Girls."* He co-wrote The Brady Girls Get Married, *"Living Together," "Gorilla of My Dreams,"* A Very Brady Christmas, *"The Brady 500," "A Moving Experience,"* and *"Hat in the Ring."* He played The Bear in *"The Cincinnati Kids."*

Barbara Mallory — Sherwood's Daughter-in-Law (married to Lloyd)
Brady Connection: She played Mrs. Powell in A Very Brady Christmas *and "The Brady 500."* She played Carol Brady in *"A Very Brady Musical."* She played Mrs. Whitfield in Growing Up Brady. *She was associate producer for "A Very Brady Musical."*

274

Hope (Schwartz) Juber — Sherwood's Daughter

Brady Connection: She played Jenny Wilton in "The Slumber Caper," Rachel in "The Big Bet" and "Greg Gets Grounded," Gretchen in "The Hairbrained Scheme," and Erica Hopkins in "The Brady 500." She co-wrote "The Siege." She co-wrote the spoof The Brady Bunch in the White House. She produced Still Brady After All These Years. She wrote music and lyrics for "A Very Brady Musical."

Laurence Juber — Sherwood's Son-in-law (married to Hope)

Brady Connection: He composed music for A Very Brady Christmas, The Bradys, the spoof The Brady Bunch in the White House, and "A Very Brady Musical."

Elliot Kevin Schwartz — Sherwood's Grandson (Lloyd & Barbara's son)

Brady Connection: He played Greg Brady in "A Very Brady Musical" stage production. The character of Kevin Brady (Greg's son) is named for him.

Robbie Rist

Robbie's headshot when he was with agent Toni Kelman. Courtesy of Robbie Rist.

Birth: April 4, 1964; La Mirada, California
Birth Name: Robert Anthony Rist
Siblings: None
Marital Status: Single
Kids: None
Favorite Brady Episode: unknown

Young "Cousin Oliver" graced *The Brady Bunch* with his presence in six episodes at the end of season five. Robbie and his colleague Allan Melvin played the only (non-core) recurring characters in the show. Oliver was one of Robbie's first roles, but certainly not his last. When you check out his filmography on imdb.com, you'll see that it goes on for pages and pages. Appearances include a television series called *Big John, Little John* (where he played Little John), *Lucas Tanner*, *The Mary Tyler Moore Show*, and *Kidd Video*. Robbie is well known for his voiceover work these days. Some of the animated characters he brought to life include Michelangelo of *The Teenage Mutant Ninja Turtles*, Choji Akimichi of *Naruto*, and most recently Stuffy the dragon from *Doc McStuffins*.

The aforementioned *Kidd Video* segment was the first time that Robbie got to showcase some of his musical skills on television. Music just happens to be another forte for this talented individual. Robbie is an excellent guitarist and his music has graced many, many albums. He has been in so many bands it's hard to keep track! He started playing guitar at age four. He's also proficient on drums and piano. Check out his Facebook page for more info.

Allan Melvin

Birth: *February 18, 1923; Kansas City, Missouri*
Birth Name: *Allan John Melvin*
Death: *January 17, 2008; Brentwood, Los Angeles, California*
Siblings: *None*
Marital Status: *Married*
Kids: *Mya and Jennifer*
Favorite Brady Episode: *unknown*

Although a Missourian by birth, Allan was raised in Manhattan and the Bronx, New York. Allan got his start as an entertainer doing standup and celebrity impressions. In 1946, he won the Arthur Godfrey's Talent Scouts radio show for his impressions and sound effects. He was quickly signed to NBC radio. He also joined the original Broadway cast of "Stalag 17." It wasn't long before Allan

Allan as Sgt. Henshaw in The Phil Silvers Show.

was on television. His first major role came on *The Phil Silvers Show* where he played Sgt. Henshaw. Allan became known as a great character actor, and the roles that came his way usually were for military men (*Gomer Pyle*, *The Dick Van Dyke Show*, and others). However, he also excelled at being someone's best bud; he had a long-standing role on *All in the Family*, which later morphed into *Archie Bunker's Place*. Like Robbie Rist, Allan Melvin also had a talent for voiceovers. He was the voice behind Hanna-Barbera's Magilla Gorilla. He also voiced Popeye's arch nemesis Bluto. Allan's filmography is very, very long and he kept participating in show business until the mid-1990s. In 2008, he died from cancer.

[1]Walters, Larry. Chicago Tribune. "Emmy? It's Not Useful to Schultzy." July 21, 1958. p. B7 Part 3.

[2]Kramer, Carol. Chicago Tribune. "Ann B. Davis Brushes Up Furniture Dusting." December 12, 1971. p. S_A1.

[3]Raddatz, Leslie. TV Guide. "Don't Tell His Pasadena Neighbors... but Robert Reed Is An Actor." April 4, 1970: Triangle Publications, Radnor, PA. p. 21.

[4]Lowry, Cynthia. Daytona Beach Sunday News-Journal. "Florence Henderson Has Grudge Vs. Hollywood." January 8, 1967. p. 6B.

[5]Momlogic. "Brady Kids on THEIR Kids Acting: 'No Way!'" November 6, 2008. Online video interview. http://www.momlogic.com/2008/11/brady_kids_on_their_kids_actin.php

[6]McCormick, Maureen. Here's the Story: Surviving Marcia Brady and Finding My True Voice. HarperCollins: New York, 2008. p. 77.

[7]McCormick, Maureen. Here's the Story: Surviving Marcia Brady and Finding My True Voice. HarperCollins: New York, 2008. p. 271.

[8]Davis, Ann B. et al. Alice's Brady Bunch Cookbook. Rutledge Hill Press: Nashville, TN, 1994. p. 144.

[9]Plumb, Eve. "Eve Plumb." Retrieved July 31, 2011. Online. http://www.eveplumb.tv/.

[10]Street, Nick. JewishJournal.com. "Sherwood Schwartz – creator of hit TV shows 'Gilligan's Island' and 'The Brady Bunch' – trades site." November 9, 2006. Website. http://www.jewishjournal.com/arts/article/sherwood_schwartz_creator_of_hit_tv_shows_gilligans_island_and_the_brady_bu/

[11]Scott, Vernon. Reprinted in the Beaver Country Times. "Reaching Them with TV: Schwartz a Big Man with Kids." March 15, 1972. p. D-7.

BIOGRAPHIES

CHAPTER 4: BONUS BIOGRAPHIES

Family is very important to the Bradys, so <u>Bradypedia</u> will take that to heart in a new way. Listed below are the filmographies and short biographies of *The Brady Bunch* actors' family members. You are among the first to ever see these real-life families presented together in one place. So sit back and enjoy reading about the siblings, parents, and kids you never knew!

Larry Olsen

Birth: May 16, 1938; Marshalltown, Iowa – "Lawrence Joseph Olsen, Jr."

Larry in Sergeant Mike, *1944*

As you just read in Susan Olsen's biography, she has older siblings who were actors as well. Both of her brothers were quite prolific film actors as children. The oldest is Larry, who is 23 years older than our beloved Susan. Larry got his acting start by luck. He says, "It sounds phony, but I was discovered on the street by Lola Moore, who was the famous agent for children. I was in a bank with my mother. Miss Moore was impressed with my looks and asked mother if she would be interested in my being in pictures."[1] Larry was cute, obedient, and willing: a winning combination. He started with small roles in Red Cross films and performing on stage, but quickly moved to major studio films. His first films were recorded when he was just five years old. Larry's major break came when he was cast as Curley in Hal Roach's comedies *Curley* and *Who Killed Doc Robbin*. (Hal Roach is the man who brought us *Little Rascals*, aka *Our Gang*.) *Curley* was a 1940s version of this earlier kid-centric show. *Curley* was a short film about a boy – played by Larry – who plays tricks on his new teacher. The later film *Who Killed Doc Robbin* is a mystery and features Curley and his pals exploring a mansion haunted by a man in a gorilla suit. The comedies were light fare but unfortunately did not do as well as their predecessors. Larry has very fond memories of being in show business. "It was a lot of fun and educational. It really was."[1]

1. Red Cross short(s) – unknown dates and title(s)
2. Pathé short – war propaganda film – unknown date and title
3. *The Chance of a Lifetime* aka *The Gamble of Boston Blackie* – feature film – Johnny Watson – October 26, 1943
4. *Happy Land* – feature film – Rusty age 5 – November 10, 1943
5. *None Shall Escape* aka *The Day Will Come* aka *After the Night* – feature film – Willie age 5 – February 3, 1944
6. *Address Unknown* – feature film – youngest Schulz boy – June 1, 1944
7. *The Seventh Cross* – feature film – Ludi Roeder – July 24, 1944
8. *Casanova Brown* – feature film – Junior – September 14, 1944
9. *My Pal Wolf* – feature film – Fred Eisdaar – September 25, 1944
10. *Sergeant Mike* – feature film – S.K. Arno – November 9, 1944
11. *Youth for the Kingdom* – feature film – boy – February 1945
12. *Lone Texas Ranger* – feature film – Whitey/Payne – May 20, 1945
13. *Divorce* – feature film – Michael Phillips – August 18, 1945
14. *Cloak and Dagger* – feature film – boy (scene deleted) – September 28, 1946
15. *Three Little Girls in Blue* – feature film – farm boy – October 1946
16. *Curley* – feature film – William "Curley" Benson – August 23, 1947
17. *Sitting Pretty* – feature film – Larry King – April 1948
18. *Who Killed Doc Robbin* – feature film – William "Curley" Benson – April 9, 1948
19. *Isn't It Romantic?* – feature film – Hannibal – October 6, 1948
20. *Kill the Umpire* – feature film – Johnny – April 27, 1950
21. *Winchester '73* – feature film – boy at rifle shoot – July 12, 1950
22. *Again...Pioneers* – feature film – Kenny Keeler – November 2, 1950
23. *Stop That Cab!* aka *On Four Wheels* – TV movie – blond boy – March 30, 1951
24. *Room for One More* – feature film – Ben Roberts – January 10, 1952
25. *The Story of Three Loves* – feature film – Terry – March 26, 1953
26. *Her Twelve Men* – feature film – Edgar – August 11, 1954
27. *Brigadoon* – feature film – boy – September 8, 1954
28. *Rawhide Riley* – TV series that never aired, five episodes and a pilot – 1952-1954

Christopher Olsen

Birth: September 19, 1946; Los Angeles County, California – "Christopher Robin Olsen"

Susan's second brother, Chris, had the benefit of an older brother experienced in show business, and thus his parents knew what to expect when they got young "Christie" started. He says, "My brother was doing a picture when I was a baby, and Mom didn't have a sitter for me and took me to the studio where my brother was filming. The director had been looking for a baby boy to be in another film, and there I was."[2] Chris was only 14 months old when he appeared in the feature film *The Iron Curtain*; his segment was filmed in Ottawa, Canada. From that point, he appeared in a series of war films and westerns. His films boast a stunning array of stars: Doris Day, Jimmy Stewart, Lucille Ball, Kirk Douglas, Walter Matthau, Danny Kaye, Glenn Ford, Rock Hudson, and more. Chris' most well-known role came in the Alfred Hitchcock film *The Man Who Knew Too Much*. Chris got to play the main characters' son who was kidnapped in Morocco. The film starred Doris Day (whom he shared a scene with five years earlier in *I'll See You In My Dreams*) and Jimmy Stewart. Chris was even lucky enough to sing a duet with Miss Day! A Paramount press release quotes Alfred Hitchcock: " 'This is one singer starting at the top,' " he said of Chris. In return, Chris had this to say of Alfred Hitchcock: "In the beginning, I think Hitchcock was somewhat indifferent towards me. He was an enigmatic, imposing figure. By the end of filming, he seemed a much friendlier fellow, and I left the film thinking he might have actually liked me."[2] The same year had Chris starring as another famous actor's son, this time in a movie called *Bigger Than Life*. James Mason played a man who became addicted to prescription pain killers and suffered serious psychological side-effects. The

Chris in The Man Who Knew Too Much, *1955. © Universal Studios. Courtesy of the Margaret Herrick Library.*

movie was controversial at the time because it brought addiction to the fore. It was recently released as a Criterion DVD, so you can now watch it at home. While filming the movie, James Mason taught Chris the fundamentals of playing the flute! After *Bigger Than Life*, Chris appeared in several more westerns and other films. He kept acting until he was 14.

1. *The Iron Curtain* aka *Behind the Iron Curtain* – feature film – Andrei Gouzenko – May 12, 1948
2. *A Life of Her Own* – feature film – Pete, Maggie's son – September 1, 1950
3. *I'll See You In My Dreams* – feature film – Donald age 4 – December 6, 1951
4. *The Marrying Kind* – feature film – Joey Keefer age 4 – February 1952
5. *My Pal Gus* – feature film – Tommy – December 1, 1952
6. *The Bad and the Beautiful* – feature film – Amiel's Boy – December 25, 1952
7. *Above and Beyond* aka *Eagle on His Cap* – feature film – Little Paul – January 2, 1953
8. *It Happens Every Thursday* – feature film (scene deleted) – Virgil – April 22, 1953
9. *Arena* – feature film – boy – June 24, 1953
10. *The Long, Long Trailer* – feature film – Tommy – February 18, 1954
11. *Four Star Playhouse* – "Detective's Holiday" – John Hepburn – March 4, 1954
12. *Knock on Wood* – feature film – Jerry at age 5 – April 6, 1954
13. *Big Town* – "Thirty Days to Live" – Billy Long – possibly April 22, 1954
14. *The Loretta Young Show* – "The Enchanted Schoolteacher" – unknown character – April 25, 1954
15. *Four Star Playhouse* – "Never Explain" – Steve Winters – October 7, 1954
16. *Leave It to Harry* – musical short – Whiz Kid – October 25, 1954
17. *Schlitz Playhouse of Stars* – "Spangal Island" – Jimmy – December 10, 1954

18. *December Bride* – "The Christmas Show" – Dannie – December 20, 1954
19. *The Ray Milland Show: Meet Mr. McNulty* – "Christmas Story" – boy – December 23, 1954
20. *Crashout* aka *Gunmen on the Loose* – feature film – Timmy Mosher – March 1955
21. *The Star and the Story* – "Desert Story" – unknown character – June 4, 1955
22. *Lux Video Theatre* – "Holiday Affair" – Timmy Ennis – December 22, 1955
23. *The Man Who Knew Too Much* – feature film – Hank McKenna – June 1, 1956
24. *The Naked Hills* – feature film – Billy as a boy – June 17, 1956
25. *The Fastest Gun Alive* aka *The Last Notch* – feature film – Bobby Tibbs – July 12, 1956
26. *Bigger Than Life* aka *One in a Million* – feature film – Richie Avery – August 2, 1956
27. *The Millionaire* – "The Harvey Borden Story" – Wilbur – November 28, 1956
28. *Cavalcade of America* – "Once A Hero" – Randy – December 11, 1956
29. *The Tall T* aka *Captives* – feature film – Jeff – April 2, 1957
30. *Cheyenne* – "Incident at Indian Springs" – Kenny Powell – September 24, 1957
31. *The Millionaire* – "The Carl Bronson Story" – David – October 9, 1957
32. *Sheriff of Cochise* – "Deep Fraud" – Timmy Weller – November 8, 1957
33. *The Tarnished Angels* aka *Pylons* – feature film – Jack Schumann – January 11, 1958
34. *Return to Warbow* – feature film – David Fallam – January 1958
35. *The Adventures of Ozzie and Harriet* – "David Loses His Poise" – Tommy – October 1, 1958
36. *Lassie* – "The Bundle from Britain" – Bud – November 30, 1958
37. *Lassie* – "Rock Hound" – Bud – April 5, 1959
38. *The Danny Thomas Show* – "Linda Wants to Be a Boy" – Chris – March 7, 1960

TIKI TALK

Chris worked with many talented, well-known actors and directors, including Alfred Hitchcock. But before Chris was "Hank" in *The Man Who Knew Too Much*, the newspaper Daily Variety[3] reported him as being signed for another Hitchcock film, *Strangers on a Train*. Unfortunately, it looks like Chris never ended up actually making the picture, but it would have been amazing for such a young boy to have appeared in two Hitchcock films by the age of nine!

Daily Variety[4] also had Chris cast in a 1952 film called *My Cousin Rachel*, but either his scene was cut from the final version or he simply ended up not being needed.

Þiane Olsen

Birth: May 14, 1956; Los Angeles County, California – "Linda Diane Olsen"

Finally, Susan's sibling Diane Olsen was an actress as well. She decided to "retire" when she was eight years old, but not before she had done some commercials. She was also cast in three television pilots which, unfortunately, were never picked up.[5] The names of those pilots are unknown.

ToÞÞ LookinlanÞ

Birth: March 1, 1965; Torrance, CA – "Eric Todd Lookinland"

Todd as Matt Kelly in The Brady Bunch.

Mike Lookinland's younger brother Todd is known to *The Brady Bunch* fans as Matt Kelly in the fifth-season episode "Kelly's Kids." But did you know he has a long résumé of television series and film appearances? In fact, Todd has appeared in a wide variety of shows. His filmography includes several dramatic television movies such as *The Suicide's Wife* and *A Sensitive, Passionate Man. Passionate* stars Todd as the son of an alcoholic. *Suicide* is about a family who tries to cope with their dad/husband's suicide. Todd is a great dramatic actor but is also gifted in comedies. *The Blue Bird* is perhaps the most well-known film Todd was in. The movie starred Elizabeth Taylor. It is based on a Russian fairy tale and in fact was filmed in Russia (then the Soviet Union). A 20th Century Fox press release says, "Todd Lookinland may be that mythical actor casting directors are always looking for: ten-years-old with eleven years' experience." Furthermore, Elizabeth Taylor said of him and his child co-star Patsy Kensit, "[they are] unspoiled, intelligent, and humorous. Two marvelous kids and great fun to work with."[6] Todd spent several months in the country, and he and his mother got to visit Moscow and a few other sites. Filming was done in Leningrad. Todd continued acting into his teens. As an adult, he served in the art and effects departments for film studios and even worked on *Star Wars Episode I* and *Men In Black* as a model maker. Today he lives in California and is married with two kids.

1. *Gunsmoke* – "P.S. Murry Christmas" – Jake – December 27, 1971
2. *Goodnight Jackie* aka *Games Guys Play* – unreleased feature film – Terry – 1973
3. *Guess Who's Been Sleeping In My Bed?* – TV movie – Adam Gregory – October 31, 1973
4. *Barnaby Jones* – "Secret of the Dunes" – Jimmy Mason – December 16, 1973
5. *Temperature's Rising* aka *The New Temperature's Rising Show* – 2 unknown episodes – unknown characters – unknown dates

6. *The Brady Bunch* – "Kelly's Kids" – Matt Kelly – January 4, 1974
7. *Gunsmoke* – "The Schoolmarm" – Lester Pruitt – February 25, 1974
8. *Apple's Way* – "The Accident" – Jeremy – May 5, 1974
9. *The New Land* – "The Word Is: Persistence" – Tuliff Larsen – September 14, 1974
10. *The New Land* – "The Word Is: Growth" – Tuliff Larsen – September 21, 1974
11. *The New Land* – "The Word Is: Acceptance" – Tuliff Larsen – September 28, 1974
12. *The New Land* – "The Word Is: Mortal" – Tuliff Larsen – October 5, 1974
13. *The New Land* – "The Word Is: Alternative" – Tuliff Larsen – October 12, 1974
14. *The New Land* – "The Word Is: Celebration" – Tuliff Larsen – October 19, 1974
15. *Gunsmoke* – "The Colonel" – Corporal Jimmy – December 16, 1974
16. *Petrocelli* – "The Kidnapping" – Jody – February 5, 1974
17. *The Blue Bird* – feature film – Tyltyl – April 5, 1976
18. *How the West Was Won* – TV miniseries – Joshua Hanks – January 19, 1976-February 13, 1977
19. *A Sensitive, Passionate Man* – TV movie – Dan Delaney – June 6, 1977
20. *Waiting for Godot* – TV movie – messenger – June 29, 1977
21. *Once Upon a Brothers Grimm* – TV movie – Hansel – November 23, 1977
22. *Mulligan's Stew* – "Winning the Big Ones" – Gary – December 13, 1977
23. *Wonder Woman* – "Séance of Terror" – Matthew R. Koslo – March 10, 1978
24. *Big Wednesday* – feature film – surfer #3 – May 1978
25. *The Suicide's Wife* – TV movie – Mark Harrington – November 7, 1979
26. *Beulah Land* – TV miniseries – young Leon Kendrick – October 7, 1980
27. *Every Stray Dog and Kid* – "Pilot" – Jeff Hatfield – October 21, 1981 (but filmed in 1979)
28. *Diff'rent Strokes* – "The Team" – Eddie Sanders – November 19, 1981
29. *Father Murphy* – "Buttons and Beaux" – T.J. McCandless – November 30, 1982
30. *The Karate Kid* – feature film – chicken boy – June 22, 1984
31. *A Perfect Place* – short film – the cheat – 2008

TIKI TALK

Here's another *Brady Bunch* connection for Todd. Lloyd Schwartz wrote a screenplay in 1973 called *Goodnight Jackie*. Lloyd also served as executive producer for the film. The director was Jerry London and the top-billed stars were to be Lana Wood and Wendell Burton. Another Schwartz fave – Jim Backus – would be in the film, too. *Goodnight Jackie* was the first project for the newly-formed endeavor called Calliope Productions, Inc. Filming began on June 4, 1973 and completed a few weeks later. Advertisements for *Jackie* boasted that the film was the first US-produced movie to be filmed in Fujicolor negative film. Unfortunately, the film was never released and we Brady fans cannot see it. But guess who else Brady-related was in the film aside from Todd? Barry Williams!

Terese Lookinland

Birth: June 4, 1959; Mount Pleasant, Utah – "Terese Lee Lookinland"

Mike's older sister, Terese, also tried her hand at acting. She was fresh-faced kid and grew into a beautiful young woman. She appeared in many commercials, including ones for Juicy Fruit and Skipper's Fish and Chips Chowder House.

Kelly, Scott, and Joe Lookinland

Mike's wife and sons have also dabbled in show business. His wife Kelly served as production and script assistants in several films. In fact, that is how the two of them met. She even had a cameo appearance in *Halloween 4* as a dead body. Their sons, Scott and Joe, have benefited from Mike's experiences as an actor. Most notably Scott played the "character" of Mike Lookinland in TV's *Growing Up Brady*. He bore a remarkable resemblance to a young version of his dad, right down to the mannerisms. Joe, too, appeared in a few pieces where his dad was working as a cameraman. Here are their filmographies as actors.

Kelly:

1. *Halloween 4: The Return of Michael Myers* – feature film – dead waitress – October 21, 1988

Scott:

1. *Growing Up Brady* – TV movie – Mike Lookinland – May 21, 2000

Joe:

1. *Walking Thunder* – feature film – McKay Baby – 1994
2. *Everwood* – "Giving Up the Girl" – Dougie Wilson – January 24, 2005
3. *Unaccompanied Minors* – feature film – bully – December 8, 2006

Edward Knight

Birth: July 12, 1927; New York City – "Edward Kozumplik"

Chris Knight's father, Edward, was born to Austro-Hungarian immigrant parents, Anton and Maria Kozumplik, as the youngest of six. Edward was a stage actor. He appeared on Broadway in the 1955 production of "The

BONUS BIOGRAPHIES

Lark," starring Julie Harris, Boris Karloff, and Christopher Plummer. He was also a member of the Shakespearewrights (a group Robert Reed would later join) and appeared in some of their productions, including "Hamlet" in 1956.

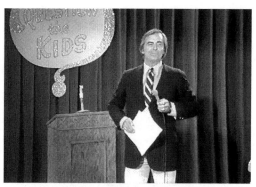

Edward as he appeared as Monty Marshall in The Brady Bunch

After his three eldest children were born, he moved the family to California. Here, Edward acted in television series, most of the time playing a strict (and often German) military officer of some sort on *Hogan's Heroes.* In March 1971, he and a woman named Patricia Kane opened a theatre in the San Fernando Valley called The Onion Company. The Onion was a non-Union theatre. At the time, the pair of actors were in a legal battle with the Union over an issue with contracts. They were in a two-person play and served as producers of the play as well. The Union accused them of acting without contracts, and Edward and Patricia appealed saying that they did so because they were also the producers; why would they enter into a contract with themselves? They were fined $26 by the Equity Union. Suffice it to say, The Onion Company was a bit rebellious. However, it was a place for serious actors to perform and even take classes on the craft. Edward appeared in many productions by the Company and produced many as well. Of note were "Who's Afraid of Virginia Woolf?" (he played George) and "Allison Wonderland" (he co-produced). Eve Plumb's sister, Flora, played the title character in the latter production.

Edward died in October 2009.

1. *Lock Up* – "The Sisters" – uniform cop – November 12, 1960
2. *The Detectives* – "The Airtight" – Stacey – May 1, 1961
3. *Cheyenne* – "The Young Fugitives" – Pat Kinsey – October 23, 1961
4. *77 Sunset Strip* – "The Deadly Solo" – Chris Kern – December 1, 1961
5. *Day in Court* – 2 unknown episodes – unknown characters – 1962-3?
6. *My Three Sons* – "The Girls Next Door" – Wes Marlowe – February 1, 1962
7. *Hawaiian Eye* – "Among the Living" – unknown character – May 30, 1962
8. *Combat!* – "The Medal" – Lt. Kohrs – January 8, 1963
9. *A Gathering of Eagles* – feature film – Pilot – June 21, 1963
10. *Combat!* – "A Distant Drum" – German Sergeant – November 19, 1963
11. *Wild Bill Hickok: The Legend and the Man* – "The Great Adventure" – Brady – January 3, 1964
12. *Hogan's Heroes* – "Top Hat, White Tie and Bomb Sights" – Major Klopfer – November 19, 1965
13. *Hogan's Heroes* – "I Look Better in Basic Black" – S.S. Captain Heinrich – April 1, 1966
14. *Hogan's Heroes* – "The Rise and Fall of Sergeant Schultz" – Gestapo Officer – October 21, 1966

15. *12 O'Clock High* – "Burden of Guilt" – Major Welch – December 2, 1966
16. *Hogan's Heroes* – "The Most Escape-Proof Camp I've Ever Escaped from" – Colonel Stieffer – March 10, 1967
17. *Hogan's Heroes* – "How to Win Friends and Influence Nazis" – Herr Grosser – October 21, 1967
18. *The Wild West* – "The Night of the Falcon" – General Lassiter – November 10, 1967
19. *Mission: Impossible* – "The Spy" – Nikos – January 7, 1968
20. *Hogan's Heroes* – "How to Escape from Prison Camp without Really Trying" – Colonel Nikolas – March 2, 1968
21. *Hogan's Heroes* – "Bad Day in Berlin" – Gestapo Major Metzger – December 7, 1968
22. *The Flying Nun* – "The Not So Great Imposter" – salesman – October 29, 1969
23. *Hogan's Heroes* – "Six Lessons from Madame LaGrange" – double agent – February 27, 1970
24. *Hogan's Heroes* – "The Experts" – Major Stern – September 27, 1970
25. *Hogan's Heroes* – "Look at the Pretty Snowflakes" – Corporal Dietrich – March 21, 1971
26. *Bonanza* – "A Place to Hide" – Sgt. Brown – March 19, 1972
27. *Mission: Impossible* – "Crack-Up" – driver – December 9, 1972
28. *Carola* – TV movie – Captain Clavaroche – February 6, 1973
29. *The Brady Bunch* – "You Can't Win 'Em All" – Monty Marshall – March 16, 1973
30. *The Magician* – "Pilot" – Todd – March 17, 1973
31. *The All-American Boy* – feature film – Dixie gang member – October 24, 1973
32. *The Streets of San Francisco* – "Shield of Honor" – unknown character – November 15, 1973
33. *Marcus Welby, M.D.* – "Death Is Only a Side Effect" – Dr. Mondrian – December 18, 1973
34. *Foxy Brown* – feature film – Adams – April 5, 1974
35. *Police Woman* – "Once a Snitch" – unknown character – January 4, 1977
36. *The Rockford Files* – "Dirty Money, Black Night" – Agent Fredericson – April 1, 1977
37. *A Killing Affair* – TV movie – Kagel – September 21, 1977
38. *Richie Brockelman, Private Eye* "Escape from Caine Abel" – Agent – April 14, 1978
39. *The Night Rider* – TV movie – Paul Hairston – May 11, 1979

David, Lisa, and Mark Knight

Chris' three siblings — Mark, Lisa, and David — also did their share of acting. Mark is the eldest, then Chris, then Lisa, and finally David. All three Knight siblings did some commercials and some modeling. Their only known television appearance, though, was made by David. He once appeared on *Emergency!* as a boy with his hand stuck in a vase. He had no lines.

1. *Emergency!* – "Cook's Tour" – David – February 12, 1972

Flora Plumb

Birth: October 14, 1944; Los Angeles, CA – "Flora June Plumb"

Flora is Eve Plumb's older sister. She began acting a little bit later than Eve did and appeared in several television episodes and films. But Flora's heaviest involvement in show business was on stage. One of her first main roles came in a UCLA production of "Carousel," which was put on in Japan in 1964. Next, Flora appeared back in the States as Heidi in a 1966 musical stage version of the famed children's book. Other stage plays she participated in in the late 1960s-1970s were "The Tempest" (playing Miranda), "Mimi, You Funny Little Honey of a…," "A Man's a Man," and "Idiot's Delight." In early March 1973, Flora was outside the Onion Company Theatre (remember Edward Knight's theatre?) for her play "That Was Laura but She's Only a Dream" when she was hit by a car. She suffered a broken leg and collar bone. It's likely she heard way too many jokes at the time about taking the phrase "break a leg" literally!

Flora, too, was influenced by the Plumb patriarch (their father, Neely) and recorded a single called "The Touch of Your Life upon Mine" (ABC 11313). "Touch" was the theme to the television movie *The Touch* and was produced by Neely Plumb and Lee Young. Flora was – and still is – actively involved with theatre. She attended the University of California-Los Angeles and received a degree in theatre.

1. *The Wild Wild West* – "The Night of the Plague" – Saloon Girl #1 – April 4, 1969
2. *Then Came Bronson* – "Your Love Is Like a Demolition Derby in My Heart" – Leona – November 19, 1969
3. *Bracken's World* – "Whatever Happened to Happy Endings?" – Teresa – February 13, 1970
4. *Marcus Welby, M.D.* – "Enid" – Enid Cooper – March 24, 1970
5. *On a Clear Day You Can See Forever* – feature film – unknown character – June 17, 1970
6. *Cover Me Babe* aka *Run, Shadow, Run* – feature film – unknown character – October 1, 1970
7. *The F.B.I.* – "The Witness" – Yvonne Demarest – December 13, 1970
8. *The Young Lawyers* – "Remember Chris Gately?" – Chris Gately – December 14, 1970
9. *Cade's County* – "Company Town" – Luanne Kingman – September 26, 1971
10. *The Mod Squad* – "Home Is the Streets" – Angie – September 28, 1971
11. *Dusty's Trail* – "Witch's Trail" – Priscilla – February 12, 1974
12. *Mannix* – "Rage to Kill" – Elaine – February 24, 1974
13. *Police Story* – "Love, Mabel" – Gail – November 26, 1974
14. *This Is the Life* – unknown episode – unknown character – unknown date
15. *Lovers and Friends/For Richer or Poorer* – unknown episodes – Eleanor Saxton Kimball – January 3, 1977 through 1978
16. *Malibu Beach* – feature film – Ms. Plickett – May 1978
17. *Lou Grant* – "Censored" – Mrs. Alden – February 4, 1980
18. *The Misadventures of Sheriff Lobo* – "The Haunting of Orly Manor" – Professor Nina Evans – March 18, 1980

19. *Quincy M.E.* – "Slow Boat to Madness: Parts I and II" – Lyla Crowley – November 11 & 18, 1981
20. *Silk Stalkings* – "Guilt by Association" – Patricia Parker – September 21, 1997
21. *The District* – "Untouchable" – Mrs. Emily Cartwright – January 25, 2003
22. *Mad Men* – "Red in the Face" – gaudy hat lady – August 30, 2007
23. *Death Panel* – short film – caring wife – March 3, 2010
24. *Guild Wars 2* – video game – Oska (voice) – August 28, 2012
25. *Song for Lindy* – short film – unknown character – July 2, 2015

The Bernstein Kids

Florence Henderson has four children with her first husband, Ira Bernstein: Joseph, Barbara, Robert, and Elizabeth "Lizzie." Each of the kids has been involved in show business in one capacity or another. In particular, Joseph and Barbara were both in *Brady Bunch* episodes. Robert and Lizzie did Tang commercials and ads with their mother in the late-1970s.

Joseph:

1. *The Brady Bunch* – "Eenie, Meenie, Mommy, Daddy" – tree – October 10, 1969

Barbara:

1. *The Brady Bunch* – "The Slumber Caper" – Ruthie – October 9, 1970
2. *The Brady Bunch* – "Everyone Can't be George Washington" – Peggy – December 22, 1972
3. *The Brady Bunch* – "The Hairbrained Scheme" – Suzanne – March 8, 1974
4. *Police Woman* – "Cold Wind" – student – October 17, 1975
5. *...And Your Name Is Jonah* – TV movie – Janice – January 28, 1979
6. *Nine to Five* – feature film – Buffy – December 19, 1980
7. *Ryan's Hope* – episode 1.1624 – Katherine Hayes – October 1, 1981
8. *Money to Burn* – feature film – photo girl – 1983
9. *Stitches* – feature film – Dee – November 1985
10. *Elvira's Halloween Special* – TV movie – unknown character – October 31, 1986
11. *Cheers* – "The Book of Samuel" – woman – December 11, 1986
12. *On the Television* – "Tobacco" – Connie Granger – unknown airdate
13. *On the Television* – "The Award Show" – unknown character – unknown airdate
14. *On the Television* – "Murder She Spelled Out Real Plain" – Greta Winworth – unknown airdate
15. *On the Television* – "The Search for Saints" – unknown character – unknown airdate
16. *On the Television* – "Golly, Ollie" – unknown character – unknown airdate
17. *On the Television* – "4-1-1 Info Line" – unknown character – unknown airdate

Robert:

He appeared in Tang ads with his sister Lizzie and mom. In adulthood, he was a television editor and worked on *The Bold and the Beautiful*, *Coming Up Roses*, *The Young and the Restless*, *Mama's Family*, and more.

Lizzie:

1. *Somebody's Daughter* – TV movie – young woman – September 20, 1992

[1]Goldrup, Tom and Jim. Growing Up on the Set: Interviews with 39 Former Child Actors of Classic Film and Television. McFarland and Company, Inc.: Jefferson, NC, 2002. pp. 218 & 225.

[2]SAMR. The Short Knight Hitchcock Blog: News, Interviews, and Ramblings on the Brilliantly Innovative, Enigmatic Sir Alfred. "Child Star Christopher Olsen, the Boy Who Knew Too Much." March 29, 2011. Website. http://shortknighthitchblog.blogspot. com/2011/03/child-star-christopher-olsen-boy-who.html.

[3]Daily Variety Vol. 70 No. 12 p. 11, December 21, 1950

[4]Daily Variety Vol. 76 No. 64 p. 9, September 5, 1952

[5]Interview filmed by Rich Stevens, retrieved July 7, 2011. http://www.youtube.com/watch?v=ZTqZAgit0tc

[6]Pashko, Stanley. Boys' Life. "A Webelos Scout in Russia." May 1976. p. 41.

CHAPTER 5: MUSIC

BRADY BUNCH RECORDS

All of the actors from *The Brady Bunch* except for Robert Reed and Ann B. Davis released music recordings and all of those folks had solo 45s except for Susan Olsen. Below are the musical endeavors of *The Brady Bunch* actors.

The Brady Bunch Albums

During the run of the original series, the Brady kids released five full length record albums and several 45 singles. Their first musical recording was actually the theme song to *The Brady Bunch* for the season two premiere. Sherwood Schwartz heard them singing on the set and decided that they would make a good replacement to The Peppermint Trolley Company's original theme song recording. Indeed they did. Their next venture was a Christmas album. The year after that saw the album Meet The Brady Bunch, which was much better received than the Christmas songs. At this point the group started touring the country as the Brady Bunch Kids (aka The Brady Bunch Singing Group). They traveled extensively over the summer and fall of 1972 and 1973. They appeared on numerous television shows as well, including *The Mike Douglas Show* and *American Bandstand*. By the time the show was cancelled in 1974 the group recorded two more albums: The Kids from The Brady Bunch and The Brady Bunch Phonographic Album. Finally, Chris Knight and Maureen McCormick joined forces to record an album of their own, entitled Chris Knight and Maureen McCormick.

Album #1:

Merry Christmas from The Brady Bunch
Paramount, #PAS-5026, 1971. *Songs:* *"The First Noel," "Away in a Manger," "The Little Drummer Boy," "O Come All Ye Faithful," "O, Holy Night," "Silent Night," "Jingle Bells," "Frosty the Snowman,"* "Silver Bells," "Rudolph the Red-Nosed Reindeer," "Santa Claus is Coming to Town," and "We Wish You a Merry Christmas."* Available as a 33 1/3 rpm record. Remastered in 1996 by MCA as a CD.
*This song also appears on the 1971 LP Home for the Holidays by various artists.

Front   Back

The 45 picture sleeves

This record was produced by Paramount in about a week. The kids had to learn the songs and record them very quickly, so they did not have much time to rehearse and it shows. "Frosty the Snowman" by Susan is really cute, though, and that song along with "Silver Bells" was chosen for a 45 single. "Frosty the Snowman" also appears on the Brady Bunch Sunshine Day CD that was released in 1995.

The kids promoted the album in a few ways, including a grand release event at the LA record store White Front. There were also magazine articles and ads for the LP.

Associated 45:

Frosty the Snowman. Paramount, #PAA-0062, 1970. *Songs: "Frosty the Snowman" and "Silver Bells."* Available as a 45rpm.

Front   Back

Front   Back

Front   Back

Front   Inside Cover 1

Inside Cover 2   Back

The LP picture sleeves

Album #2:

Meet The Brady Bunch

Paramount, #PAS-6032, 1972. *Songs: "We'll Always be Friends," "Day After Day," "Baby, I'm-A Want You," "I Believe in You," "American Pie," "Time to Change," "Me and You and a Dog Named Boo," "I Just Want to be Your Friend," "Love My Life Away," "Come Run With Me," "Ain't it Crazy," and "We Can Make the World a Whole Lot Brighter."* Available as a 33 1/3 rpm record. Remastered in 1996 by MCA as a CD.

After the moderate success of their first album, the Brady kids got a new manager in the person of Jackie Mills. Mills was a very successful producer and did not like the fact that he had to work with six actors who were decidedly not professional singers. Barry Williams says in his book, "Almost from day one, Mr. Mills openly bemoaned the fact that he was producing *our* new record instead of Rod Stewart's or the Rolling Stones'. He was publicly ambivalent about working with us, and throughout the project he expended very little energy."[1] Nevertheless, the album did reasonably well in sales, especially considering none of the top 40 radio stations played their music. Billboard Magazine reviewed the album: "ask any nine-year-old; this LP is going to be a big hit."[2]

Associated 45s:

We Can Make the World A Whole Lot Brighter. Paramount, #PAA-0141, 1972. *Songs: "We Can Make the World a Whole Lot Brighter" and "Time to Change."* Available as a 45rpm.

We'll Always Be Friends. Paramount, #PAA-0167, 1972. *Songs: "We'll Always Be Friends" and "Time to Change."* Available as a 45rpm.

MUSIC

Bonus Record:

Meet the Brady Bunch
#P-13307, 1972. American Forces Radio and Television Service (AFRTS) also had its own version of the record! Remember that *The Brady Bunch* was on the air during the last few years of the Vietnam Conflict. AFRTS existed to support members of the armed forces by broadcasting music to soldiers serving overseas. Thus, seven of the songs from the Brady album were recorded with seven- to sixteen-second military ads tagged onto the end of the tracks. This is a super rare version of the Brady classics. One side had six songs from The English Congregation and the other side were the Brady songs. Songs included were: *"We Can Make the World a Whole Lot Brighter," "Me and You and a Dog Named Boo," "We'll Always Be Friends," "Baby, I'm-A Want You," "American Pie," "Time to Change,"* and *"Ain't it Crazy."*

Album #3:

The Kids from The Brady Bunch
Paramount, #PAS-6037, 1972. *Songs: "Love Me Do," "It's a Sunshine Day," "Keep On," "Ben," "Playin' the Field," "Candy (Sugar Shoppe)," "In No Hurry," "Saturday in the Park," "Merry Go-Round," "You Need That Rock 'n Roll,"* and *"Drummer Man."* Available as a 33 1/3 rpm record. Remastered in 1996 by MCA as a CD.

Not long after Meet the Brady Bunch hit the shelves came the follow-up album The Kids from the Brady Bunch. The songs from these two albums were featured in the cartoon show *The Brady Kids*, hence the cartoon and picture puzzle cover for The Kids.

Associated 45s:

Candy (Sugar Shoppe). Paramount, #PAA-0180, 1972. *Songs: "Candy (Sugar Shoppe)"* and *"Drummer Man."* Available as a 45rpm.

Drummer Man. Dynamite Soul, #DS 7004. *Songs: "Drummer Man"* and *"I Want You Back" by artist Finger 5.* Available as a 45rpm.

Album #4:

The Brady Bunch Phonographic Album
Paramount, #PAS-6058, 1973. *Songs: "Zuckerman's Famous Pig," "I'd Love You to Want Me," "Colorado Snow," "Parallel Lines," "A Simple Man," "Everything I Do," "Yo-Yo Man," "Summer Breeze," "Charlotte's Web," "Gonna Find a Rainbow,"* and *"River Song."* Available as a 33 1/3 rpm record. Remastered in 1996 by MCA as a CD.

The final album the kids recorded as a group was, in most people's opinions, their best. The kids' voices had improved. They got a wonderful photographer to do the cover and liner pictures. Promotions were done all over the West Coast. This album featured two songs for the movie *Charlotte's Web*. The kids sang "Zuckerman's Favorite Pig" and "Charlotte's Web" at the movie premiere at the Avco Embassy in Westwood on April 7, 1973. *Charlotte's Web* was a Paramount cartoon, and who better to promote the film than Paramount's own Brady kids? This was the first major feature-length cartoon to hit theatres that was not developed by Disney. The film did swimmingly in the box office and sales of the Brady album and singles were high.

Nevertheless, no radio station would play their songs. So in response, fans and TV and radio stations gathered together to celebrate the Bradys. Record promotion executive Vikki Cooper said, "'So what we did was a big promotion on KHJ-AM in Los Angeles.' The station gave the first 1,000 people tickets to see the movie 'Charlotte's Web' and meet the Brady Bunch. At KLIV-AM in San Jose, Calif., the first 600 people to show up at a local theater were to get free tickets to the movie and the chance to meet the kids – 20,000 showed up. On April 21 at KTAC-AM in Tacoma, Wash., the movie and the appearance of the group drew so many phone calls that the phone company estimated 250,000 users experienced some trouble. …KOL-AM in Seattle did a picnic promotion with an Easter egg hunt to meet the Brady Bunch Kids."[3]

Associated 45s:

I'd Love You to Want Me. Paramount, #PAA-0229, 1973. *Songs: "I'd Love You to Want Me" and "Everything I Do."* Available as a 45rpm.

Zuckerman's Famous Pig. Paramount, #PAA-0205, 1973. *Songs: "Zuckerman's Famous Pig" and "Charlotte's Web."* Available as a 45rmp.

MUSIC

The Compilation CD

It's a Sunshine Day: The Best of the Brady Bunch. MCA Records, 1993. *Songs: "The Brady Bunch Theme," "Promo Intro," "It's a Sunshine Day," "We Can Make the World a Whole Lot Brighter," "American Pie," "Born to Say Goodbye," "Keep On," "Time to Change," "Sweetheart," "I Just Want to be Your Friend," "Merry Go-round," "Charlotte's Web," "Candy (Sugar Shoppe)," "Cheyenne," "Road to Love," "Gonna Find a Rainbow," "Truckin' Back to You," "Frosty the Snowman," "We'll Always Be Friends," and "Promo Outro."* Available as a CD.

Chris Knight and Maureen McCormick

Chris Knight and Maureen McCormick. Paramount, #PAS-6062, 1973. *Songs: "Spread a Little Love Around," "Little Bird (Sing Your Song)," "Hang on Baby," "Ben," "Over and Over," "Just a-Singin' Alone," "Road to*

Love," "Tell Me Who You Love," "There is Nothing More to Say," and "Good for Each Other." Available as a 33 1/3 rpm record.

FRONT   BACK

Because Chris was so popular with teenage fans, he was paired with Maureen to record their very own album. Barry might have made a better choice in terms of musical ability, but Chris trumped him in terms of potential sales. About half the songs on the album had already been recorded by Chris and Maureen for their single 45s, so only half the songs were new. There were two duets and the rest were solos.

This is the rarest of the full LPs the kids recorded because not long after it was released, the album was pulled off the shelves. Chris Knight didn't like the cover and was done with singing promotions. So, it didn't last long and received very little publicity.

Barry Williams

From the moment Barry recorded the Brady Christmas album, he felt that he needed to become a better singer. He took voice lessons and improved greatly. His first public attempt at singing since the Christmas album was "Till I Met You," which he co-wrote with Lloyd Schwartz and Sherwood Schwartz and which he performed on an episode of *The Brady Bunch*. He played guitar for the song as well, an instrument he started learning at age 12. It was well-received and Barry became a more confident musician. He signed with Paramount in 1971 to release an entire record, but the deal fell through and he only recorded six songs. Then, only two of those six were ever publicly released; this was his single "Sweet Sweetheart/Sunny." However, this wasn't what was originally planned with his unfinished solos. Originally, they wanted to release a song called "Cheyenne." But, again for reasons unknown, that song was replaced with the "Sweet Sweetheart/Sunny" mix, which is pictured below. (There were even ads placed in teen magazines for "Cheyenne," but at the last minute Paramount changed its mind and substituted the other tune.) The other three songs Barry recorded between 1971-2 were "Early Days," "It Ought to be Raining," and "All She Wants to Be," which are unfortunately lost to history. Luckily for Brady fans, though, "Cheyenne" was released for the first time ever to the public on the 1993 CD It's A Sunshine Day: The Best of The Brady Bunch.

Barry's next musical endeavors centered on the Brady Kids group. Then after the show was cancelled in 1974, he wanted to continue his passion for music. He signed on as the lead in a Broadway tour of "Pippin." Shortly thereafter came *The Brady Bunch Variety Hour*. At the same time the short-lived Brady series was being filmed, he recorded three songs for the soundtrack to the motion picture *The Further Adventures of the Wilderness Family* (aka *The Adventure Family*). In 1978 Barry again got a record deal. His single "We've Gotta Get It on Again" was supposed to be released on August 23, 1978, but it wasn't. He spent the next three years trying to get the entire album released but the company he signed with – Private Stock Records – dissolved before the album could be completed.

For many years Barry continued musical theatre. His return to recorded song came in 1999 when he released the CD The Return of Johnny Bravo. The following year saw The Real Greg Brady, a four-song mini-album. He also put out a compilation CD called Barry Williams Presents One-Hit Wonders of the '70s that featured some of his favorite songs of his 70's Sirius Radio satellite music show.

Sweet Sweetheart. Paramount, #PAA-0122, 1972. *Songs: "Sweet Sweetheart" and "Sunny."* Available as a 45rpm.

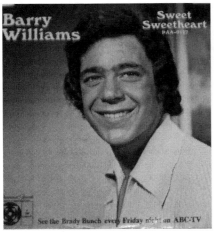

Sweet Sweetheart   *Wilderness Family*

The Further Adventures of the Wilderness Family. New Music Prod. 1978. *Songs: "Wisp of the Wind,"* "Preparing for Winter," "Welcome Back, Boomer," "Thanksgiving Dinner," "Snowflakes,"* "Hibernating Time," "Wisp of the Wing," "Wilderness Family,"* "Attacked by Wolves," "Yuletide Celebrations," "Mom's Really Sick," "Spring Comes to the Rockies," and "Wisp of the Wind (Reprise)"*.*
*Sung by Barry. Actually, his tracks are the only songs on the album; the rest are snatches of dialog from the film.

The Return of Johnny Bravo. Good Guy Entertainment, 1999. *Songs: "Johnny's Back," "Sunshine Medley: I Can See Clearly Now/Good Day Sunshine/It's A Sunshine Day," "Celebrate," "At This Moment," "Drift Away," "Rhythm of the Night/All Night Long," "Here Again," "To Love Somebody," "Happy Together," "Hip to Be Square," "These Are the Days of Our Lives," and "We Are the Champions."* Available as a CD.

The Real Greg Brady. Good Guy Entertainment, 2000. *Songs: "Backstreet Mix," "Kid of Rock Mix," "Chronic Mix," and "We Are the Champions."* Available as a CD single.

Davy Jones

Remember Davy Jones' appearance on *The Brady Bunch*? He sang a song called "Girl." Well, he actually recorded that song, and he sang it in concerts as well! The 45rpm recording of "Girl" is fairly rare; one sold on eBay in November 2011 for $170! BELL 45159X. The reverse side is "Take My Love."

Maureen McCormick

Maureen loves to sing and was one of the more eager participants in the Brady kids' group. She recorded and released more singles than any other Brady kid: three, for six songs total. She might have even released a fourth 7" single, but it never came to fruition. One of these unreleased songs was "Cinderella, Snow White, Little Bo Peep."[5] Maureen quite possibly could have recorded enough songs for her own solo LP, but that wasn't in the stars, either, with the exception of her joint effort with Chris.

Like Barry, Maureen did continue singing after *The Brady Bunch* ended, but not quite as immediately as he did. In 1981 she appeared in the film *Texas Lightning* and played a county singer. She wrote and sang the song "Typical Day" herself for the film. She was also a backup singer for Eddie Money in the early '80s. She provided back-up dialog on a song with Allan Holdsworth on a now-rare Occidental album called SOMA in 1986.

Then in 1996 Maureen released a county album called When You Get a Little Lonely. The album was mostly well-received and she toured the country promoting it. There has as of yet been no follow-up album. But in the 2000s, Maureen appeared on the first season of Country Music Television's reality show *Gone Country* where she sang for the chance at an album of her own. She lost to Julio Iglesias, Jr.

298

(No picture sleeves for any of her 45s.)

<u>Little Bird</u>. Paramount, #PAA-0246, 1973. *Songs: "Little Bird" and "Just a-Singin' Alone."* Available as a 45rpm.

<u>Truckin' Back to You</u>. Paramount, #PAA-0217, 1973. *Songs: "Truckin' Back to You" and "Teeny Weeny Bit (Too Long)."* Available as a 45rpm.

<u>Love's in the Roses</u>. Paramount, #PAA-0292, 1974. *Songs: "Love's in the Roses" and "Harmonize."* Available as a 45rpm.

<u>SOMA</u>. Occidental, #unknown, 1986. Available as a 33 1/3rpm.

<u>When You Get a Little Lonely</u>. Phantom Hill Records, 1995. *Songs: "When You Get a Little Lonely," "I'd Have to Call it Love," "Tell Mama," "Some Somebody," "We Must Have Done Something Right," "Cloud of Dust," "Go West," "Oh, Boy!," "Might As Well be Me," "I Do but I Don't," and "I Can't Say."* Available as a Cassette or CD.

Chris Knight

There are multiple picture sleeves available.

MUSIC

Poor Chris had a tough time singing. He was not exactly blessed with perfect pitch. Nevertheless, he was a really good sport about recording with the other kids. He even released his own solo 45 in 1973 called <u>Over and Over</u>. The single featured the title song as well as "Good for Each Other." Both of these songs also appear on the joint LP by him and Maureen, but they had to be re-recorded for the LP because his voice had changed slightly over the last year. Therefore, you can find *two* versions of these rare Chris Knight songs!

His parents put on the pressure even though they knew he was not a great singer: " 'My folks used to tease me about my voice and say that on the record it was "five kids and an IT"!' "[4] So by the time the Brady Kids tour ended in the summer of 1973, Chris had had it with music. That, in part, is why there was no other group record after <u>The Brady Bunch Phonographic Album</u>.

But believe it or not, Chris showed up for the variety hour show and even had a solo on screen with the song "Sing."

<u>Over and Over</u>. Paramount, #PAA-0177, 1973. *Songs: "Over and Over" and "Good for Each Other."* Available as a 45rpm.

<u>Eve Plumb</u>

Eve comes from a musical family so it was no great stretch for her to record her own 45 in 1972. Eve's father, Neely Plumb, was a record producer and also played several instruments. At one point he also had his own orchestra and recorded discs like <u>The Glowworm</u> with Lee Gordon and <u>Oh!</u>. Later he had a swingin' group called Neely Plumb and the Funky Fiddles. His production credits are quite extensive and include the *Batman Theme Song* LP, *The Sound of Music*, *The Good, the Bad and the Ugly*, *True Grit*, and Franco Zefferelli's *Romeo and Juliet*. He also arranged the famous and fun song "Purple People Eater." Mr. Plumb appeared in front of the camera once in the 1940 film *Second Chorus* playing the saxophone. No doubt the Plumb patriarch encouraged Eve's own musical endeavors.

But before she ever recorded <u>How Will It Be?</u>, Eve was a member of the Jimmy Joyce Children's Chorus. As part of the Chorus she recorded songs with Soupy Sales (a children's icon of the time), Anthony Newley, and on the 1967 *Dr. Dolittle* soundtrack. The soundtrack won an Oscar for best original song for "Talk to the Animals." It was also nominated by the Oscars for best original music score and for a Grammy for best original music score, both of which it lost. Once, Eve appeared on television singing with none other than Nancy Sinatra! Finally, according to a Tiger Beat book published in 1972, Eve has the honor of being the youngest-ever voting member of The National Academy of Recording Arts & Sciences.[5] (NARAS was unable to verify this, but they could not deny it either because their records do not include members' ages.)

So, Eve and Barry were the first two Brady kids to release singles, which happened in 1972. Eve's two songs were "How Will It Be" and "The Fortune Cookie Song." Her father arranged and conducted them both. "How

Will It Be" is half-spoken/half-sung and "The Fortune Cookie Song" is a goofy little tune with nonsense words as part of the chorus.

In 1974, Eve again joined forces with her father Neely. The Pat Williams Orchestra recorded a song called "California Love Story." Eve provided the voice narration for the song and Neely Plumb served as co-producer.

The Brady Three © Capitol Records

After *The Brady Bunch* was cancelled, the three youngest Bradys decided to continue singing. The trio was called "The Brady Three" (or sometimes "The Brady Bunch Three"). When Eve Plumb was asked about this venture and how it started, she said, "That came about because we [all six Brady kids] did have a song and dance act…that we took on the road. There comes a time when certain members of the group want to go one way and there are those that want to go the other way. So we came to an impasse and I guess we sort of split down the middle with the three of us – Mike, Susan, and myself – being in one camp and we decided to try to do that show ourselves. And I don't remember ever doing shows…I remember us getting outfits and taking pictures and rehearsing some songs and that was about it."[6] So the three youngest Brady kids had planned to tour the country with their own show and make records. Unfortunately, the group never got off the ground because the Paramount recording label went bust in 1975 just as the group was getting formed. However, the kids moved to Capitol Records. They managed to record a few songs in the studio for Capitol Records, but those are sadly now lost. They even had a concert schedule set up but of course had to disappoint the fans by canceling them because they had no songs to sing. The venues who would have heard them were the Hollywood Palladium in Oakland, the Sands Hotel in Las Vegas, a venue in Honolulu, and Knotts Berry Farm. It's really too bad they never performed because their mix of voices would have been interesting and fun to hear. Finally, also in 1975, Eve recorded with the Pat Williams Orchestra on his 7" single California Love Story, Capitol Records #CAP-3991.

How Will It Be?. RCA, #RCA-0409, 1972. *Songs: "How Will It Be?" and "The Fortune Cookie Song."* Available as a 45rpm. There is no picture sleeve for this 45, but there was sheet music, which did include a picture of Eve on the cover.

California Love Story. Capitol, #CAP-3991 (S45-91476A), 1974. *Songs: "California Love Story" and "A Lady Beside Me."* Available as a 45rpm. Eve's voice only appears on the "California" track. There is no picture sleeve with this record, either.

TIKI TALK

It seems that musicians either love or hate *The Brady Bunch.* Here's just the tip of the musical iceberg.

- •Eve Plumb has a whole band named after her called Eve's Plumb.
- •There is a CD by Peter Gabriel called Barry Williams Show, but the name is just a coincidence; Gabriel did not know about the real Barry Williams at the time.
- •Wonderful Broken Thing put out an album in 2007/8 called Looking for Mike Lookinland.
- •The Bruce Lee Band (aka the B. Lee Band) has two Brady-related songs: "Loved by Ann B. Davis" and "Mr. Hanalei."
- •Juicemaster has a 1993 song called "Jan's Theme."
- •The Italian thrash metal band Deathrage released a song called "Murdering the Brady Bunch."
- •Ed Farrow's got a song called "The Brady Bunch Medley."
- •There's a Norwegian emo post-rock band called Youth Pictures of Florence Henderson.
- •A band named The Brady Bunch Lawnmower Massacre formed in the 1980s.
- •The Dismembers recorded "I Hate The Brady Bunch" in 1988, the same year *A Very Brady Christmas* aired.

Mike Lookinland

Mike Lookinland is perhaps the most "unsung" of the Brady singers. He really does have a good singing voice but not much credit fell his way. Take, for instance, his minor-key lines in "Sunshine Day" that were done quite well. He also was the lead singer for the Brady version of "You Need That Rock 'n Roll," which can be heard on <u>The Kids from The Brady Bunch</u> album. It's too bad he didn't have any solo songs, a fact that is probably due to the other kids' statuses as teen idols. Mike was too young to be a teen heartthrob, but Barry, Chris, and Maureen fit that bill perfectly. So even though, for example, Chris could not sing as well as Mike, Chris is the one who was – er, forced – to put out a 45 and later an LP because he got more fan mail and turned more girls' heads.

After *The Brady Bunch* was cancelled in 1974, Mike, Susan, and Eve tried forming their own group. (See Eve's entry for more details.) When that fell through (or perhaps as part of the venture – it's unclear) Mike recorded his own solo 45 with the help of Eve's father Neely Plumb who served as producer.

When it came time for the variety show, Mike sang as part of the Brady group but was never given a solo. He played the piano in one episode but that's as far as the producers went to feature him.

FRONT   BACK

Mike's picture sleeve. © Capitol Records

<u>Love Doesn't Care Who's in It</u>. Capitol Records, #CAP-3914, 1974. *Songs: "Love Doesn't Care Who's in It" and "Gum Drop."* Available as a 45rpm.

<u>Susan Olsen</u>

Susan is the only Brady kid who did not branch out on his/her own into 45 singles or albums. But, as a young child of six she could be seen in the Elvis movie *The Trouble with Girls* singing a song. Five-year-old Susan also appeared with Pat Boone on his variety show singing "I'm A Believer." However, no original Susan songs were ever committed to vinyl. In the early 1990s she played bass guitar in a band in LA called Light Sweet Crude. In 1995, Susan said of the band: " 'It was alternative music - or an alternative to music,' Olsen said with a wry smile. 'But my husband at the time joined the band, which was a drag, because when we broke up, the band broke up.' "[7] Light Sweet Crude did not record any songs for posterity.

Florence Henderson

Aaaaaah, Florence. "Mrs. Brady" has the longest and most illustrious music career of all the actors. This is because she started her theatrical career at the age of 19 by appearing in the Broadway chorus for the musical *Wish You Were Here*. Leading roles followed quickly and over the next few years Florence was featured on the Broadway stage, appeared on magazine covers, and had guest spots on television shows. Her musical credits include *Fanny, Carousel, The Girl Who Came To Supper, Oklahoma!, South Pacific,* and *The Sound of Music*. Her first major role came in *Fanny* in 1954 when she was only 20 years old; she played the title character opposite Ezio Penza. She was a favorite leading lady of none other than Rodgers and Hammerstein.

During her early career Florence's voice can also be heard on vinyl for Oldsmobile ads in the 1950s and 1960s and on an Air Force recruiting disc called Find Yourself a Star in the early '70s. She was the spokesperson for Oldsmobile and appeared in several commercials, magazine ads, and radio ads all because of her fame on Broadway. The venture also got her on the television special called *Oldsmobile Music Theatre*. She became a regular guest

Florence Henderson the cover of the December 1963 Theatre Arts, the penultimate edition of the magazine

of such television stars & hosts like Jack Paar and Dean Martin. She also appeared and occasionally sang on *The Bing Crosby Show, Toast of the Town,* and *The Bell Telephone Hour.* Her list of credits can go on and on.

In 1959 Florence released her own solo album with songs covering a range of Broadway shows. The album was titled Selections from Gypsy and Flower Drum Song and did very well in sales. Today the album is somewhat hard to come by but it is worth it if you can find a copy.

By the time the late 1960s rolled around, Florence was ready for a steady job. In 1968-9 we all know that she got the part of Carol Brady. But also that year she spent several months filming a television movie/musical called *Song of Norway.* The show aired in 1970 and Florence had the lead female role. She also released two

45 singles in 1970, so she certainly did not shy away from music now that she was on scripted television. In fact, one *Brady Bunch* episode ended with her singing a solo at Christmas services. A few years later we saw her in a duet with Maureen McCormick in the episode "The Show Must Go On??"

TIKI TALK

Here's a little-known tidbit of information: during the first season of *The Brady Bunch* Florence had it in mind to form a singing group that would be made up of her, Barry Williams, Chris Knight, and Mike Lookinland. Nothing ever came of the idea, but wouldn't it have been interesting?

The post-*Brady* years were not quite as musically fulfilling as the pre-, but Florence did release some new songs. In both 1976 and 1979 she released more 45s. She would continue to make the occasional television guest appearance as well as some theatrical ones. In 1998 she released a compilation CD of the recordings from her Broadway youth called Mrs. Brady on Broadway. In her late 70s, Florence still appeared on the Broadway stage. In February 2010 she was the main attraction in New York's "Broadway Backwards." It was a little bit of improv, a little bit scripted, and a lot funny. Also appearing with her were Marion Ross of *Happy Days* and our very own Eve Plumb. (Florence and Eve had a scene together as jail birds and Eve even got to sing a song in this segment.) Let's hear it for Flo and her stunning career!

Wish You Were Here. RCA Victor #LOC 1000, 1952. *Songs: "Overture," "Camp Kare-Free Song,"* "Goodbye Love," "Ballad of a Social Director,"* "Shopping Around," "Mix & Mingle,"* "Could Be,"* "Tripping the Light Fantastic,"* "Where Did the Night Go,"* "Certain Individuals,"* "They Won't Know Me," "Summer Afternoon,"* "Don Jose of Far Rockaway,"* "Everybody Loves Everybody,"* "Wish You Were Here,"* "Relax!," "Flattery," "Finale."** Available as a 33 1/3 rpm. Remastered as a CD in 2008 and includes 7 bonus tracks.
*Includes Florence Henderson as part of the Ensemble.

Fanny. RCA Victor #LOC 1015, 1954. Remastered as a CD in 1996. *Songs: "Overture," "Octopus Song," "Restless Heart," "Never Too Late for Love," "Cold Cream Jar Song," "Why Be Afraid to Dance?," "Shika," "Welcome Home," "I Like You," "I Have to Tell You,"* "Fanny," "Panisse and Son," "Wedding Dance," "Finale Act I," "Birthday Song,"* "Love Is a Very Light Thing," "Other Hands, Other Hearts,"* "Montage," "Be Kind to Your Parents."** Available as a 33 1/3 rpm. Remastered as a CD in 1996.
*Includes Florence Henderson.

MUSIC

Carousel. RCA Victor #LPM 1048, 1955. *Songs: "Prologue: The Carousel Waltz," "You're a Queer One, Julie Jordan,"* "Mr. Snow,"* "If I Loved You," "June Is Bustin' Out All Over,"* "When the Children Are Asleep,"* "Blow High, Blow Low," "Soliloquy," "This Was a Real Nice Clambake,"* "Geraniums in the Winder,"* "What's the Use of Wond'rin,'" "You'll Never Walk Alone," "The Highest Judge of All," "Finale: Act II Graduation Scene."* Available as a 33 1/3 rpm. Remastered as a CD in 2008 with 6 bonus tracks.
*Includes Florence Henderson.

Selections from Gypsy and Flower Drum Song. RCA Camden Records #CAL 560, 1959. *Songs: "Grant Avenue," "I Enjoy Being a Girl," "Love, Look Away," "Sunday," "Like a God," "Some People," "Together Wherever We Go," "Small World," "Everything's Coming Up Roses," and "You'll Never Get Away from Me."* Available as a 33 1/3 rpm. "Small World" also appears on the double LP by RCA Victor called In Love Again, Volumes 3 & 4.

The Girl Who Came to Supper. Columbia #KOS 2420, 1963. *Songs: "Introduction," "Carpathian National Anthem," "My Family Tree," "I've Been Invited to a Party"* "When Foreign Princes Come to Visit Us," "Sir or Ma'am,"* "Soliloquies,"* "Lonely," "London Is a Little Bit of All Right/What Ho, Mrs. Brisket/Don't Take Our Charlie for the Army/Saturday Night at the Rose and Crown," "Here and Now,"* "Coronation Chorale,"* "How Do You Do, Middle Age?," "Curt, Clear and Concise," "The Coconut Girl (Welcome to Pootzie van Doyle)/The Coconut Girl/Paddy MacNeil and His Automobile/Swing Song/Six Lilies of the Valley/The Walla Walla Boola,"* "This Time It's True Love,"* "I'll Remember Her."* Available as a 33 1/3 rpm. Remastered as a CD in 1992.
*Includes Florence Henderson.

Oklahoma!. Columbia #OL 8010, 1964. *Songs: "Overture," "Oh, What a Beautiful Mornin'," "The Surrey with the Fringe on Top,"* "Kansas City," "I Cain't Say No," "Many a New Day,"* "People Will Say We're in Love,"* "Pore Jud Is Daid," "Out of My Dreams,"* "The Farmer and the Cowman," "All Er Nothin'," "Finale: Oklahoma."* Available as a 33 1/3 rpm. Remastered as a CD in 2002.
*Includes Florence Henderson.
**This song is also available on the 1992 CD called The Sullivan Years: Best of Broadway Vol. 1. It also appeared on the 2003 Hallmark CD Romance On Broadway: Classic Love Duets from the Broadway Stage.

The Sound of Music. 1964. The song "Climb Ev'ry Mountain" appears on the compilation LP The Sound of Richard Rogers' Music: Great Hits from the Great Write Way. It also appears on the double LP This Is Broadway from 1971.

South Pacific. Columbia #OS 3100, 1967. *Songs: "Act I: Overture," "Dites-mois,"* "A Cockeyed Optimist,"* "Twin Soliloquies,"* "Some Enchanted Evening,"* "Bloody Mary,"* "There Is Nothin' Like a Dame,"* "Bali Ha'i"* "I'm Gonna Wash That Man Right Outa My Hair,"* "A Wonderful Guy,"* "Younger Than Springtime,"* "Bali Ha'i (Reprise),"* "Act II: Happy Talk,"* "Honey Bun,"* "Carefully Taught,"* "This Nearly Was Mine,"* "Finale."**
*Includes Florence Henderson.

Song of Norway. ABC Records #ABCS-OC-14, 1970. *Songs: "Concerto Introduction," "Life of a Wife of a Sailor," "Freddy and His Fiddle," "Strange Music," "The Song of Norway," "A Rhyme and a Reason," "When We Wed," "The Little House," "Hill of Dreams," "I Love You," "Hymn of Betrothal," "Be a Boy Again," "Midsummer's Eve: Hand In Hand," "Three There Were," "The Solitary Wanderer At Christmastime," "A Welcome Toast," "Ribbons and Wrappings," "Wrong to Dream," "Solvejg's Song and National Anthem Concerto," "Finale."*

A Love Like Yours (Don't Come Knocking Every Day). Decca, #32666, 1970. *Songs: "A Love Like Yours (Don't Come Knocking Every Day)" and "What Do You Do When Love Dies."* Available as a 45rpm.

Conversations. Decca, #732619, 1970. *Songs: "Conversations" and "I'll Never Fall In Love Again."* Available as a 45rpm.

Great Stars of Christmas. RCA Victor #DPL 1-0132, 1975. Various artists singing Christmas songs. Florence's song is "My Favorite Things." Her song and several others from this LP were re-released the following year with a few new tracks. This second LP is called I Love Christmas: RCA Victor #DPL 1-0177. Then in the 1990s most of the songs were transferred to CD by BMG Music. Florence's song appears on Christmas Classics Vol. 2.

Born to Say Goodbye. ABC Records, #12274, 1976. *Songs: "Born to Say Goodbye" and "Can I Rely on You?."* Available as a 45rpm.

With One More Look at You, Manhattan Records #MR LA 953H, 1979. Available as a 45rpm.

Mrs. Brady on Broadway: A Collection of Songs from Her Performances in Musical Theatre. 1998. *Songs: "Cockeyed Optimist* from South Pacific," *"Many A New Day* from Oklahoma," *"Out Of My Dreams* from Oklahoma," *"I Have To Tell You* from Fanny," *"Be Kind To Your Parents* from Fanny," *"Night & Day* from Cole Porter Show," *"But Not For Me* from Gershwin Show," *"Wonderful Guy* from South Pacific," *"Wash That Man* from South Pacific," *"I've Been Invited To A Party* from Girl Who Came To Supper," *"Here & Now* from Girl Who Came To Supper," *"Wrong To Dream* from Song of Norway," *and "I Love You* from Song of Norway." Available as a CD.

Television Appearances and Concert Tours

The Brady Bunch Kids made quite a few appearances on television shows singing and dancing. They also traveled the country extensively during the summer of 1973 and performed at state fairs and other venues. Here is a listing of their appearances.

TELEVISION:

<u>*The Ed Sullivan Show Live from Las Vegas*</u>: On January 21, 1972, the kids appeared on the Entertainer of the Year Awards show hosted by Ed Sullivan. Barry Williams describes the experience in his book: "We were invited to sing the closest thing we ever had to a hit, 'Time to Change.' ...We took our place onstage alongside an incredible array of stars. Sonny and Cher performed, then Lily Tomlin, Danny Thomas, and of course the multitalented Edwina the Elephant."[8] (Actually, her name was Tanya and she won animal act of the year. You can see her in the James Bond movie *Diamonds Are Forever* pulling the handle of a slot machine in Vegas.)

American Bandstand: The Brady Kids appeared three different times on *American Bandstand*. The first episode was with José Feliciano, airing December 12, 1970. It was their Christmas show and the kids sang "Frosty the Snowman" and "Silent Night." Next came February 26, 1972; they sang "We Can Make the World a Whole Lot Brighter," "It's Time to Change," and Barry sang his single "Sweet Sweetheart." Donnie Elbert was the other guest that week. Finally, the kids appeared with Sailcat on August 26, 1972. This time they crooned to one song together and Maureen sang her single "Little Bird."

The kids and Tanya on The Ed Sullivan Show.

<u>*The Mike Douglas Show*</u>: The Brady Kids get to do the limbo with Mike Douglas and Liberace. They also sing on the show. Airdate June 17, 1973.

The Hollywood Bowl: On November 24, 1973, the Brady kids made an appearance at *The World of Sid and Marty Krofft at the Hollywood Bowl*. (The actual performance was filmed in July.) This was a live – but edited – televised performance and the kids sang "Proud Mary," and a medley that included Mike Lookinland wailin' to "A Whole Lot of Shaking Going On" and the rest of the Bunch singing songs like "Johnny Be Good" and "Rock Around the Clock." No original Brady songs were sung at this performance. Other performers were Johnny Whitaker, Jack Wild, and H.R. Pufnstuf. (If you look carefully, you can see Robert Reed in the audience!)

Unfortunately, filming the special was not exactly perfect. There were problems with the sound system, which forced the kids to sing without having a good ear turned to their back-up band. A reviewer for The Los Angeles Times said, "You can take the television performer out of television, but you'll be sorry if you do. ...It took the Brady Bunch 40 minutes to slog through 10 songs and matching cutesy dialog. ...Altogether not a giant evening at the Bowl. But by the time they get through with it, it will look better for TV."[9] Indeed it did look significantly better after edited for the special.

<u>Variety</u> found the performers favorable. "The six kept their cool and managed to sing and dance their way through a host of middle-road favorites, including 'Raindrops,' 'Saturday' and 'I Envy You.' Best of the lot was twelve-year old Susan Olsen whose precocious charm and natural stage presence proved remarkably alluring."[10]

<u>The Mike Douglas Show</u>: The Brady kids (and dad) were back on *Mike Douglas* a little older and a little more seasoned as performers. They were there to promote *The Brady Bunch Variety Hour*. Barry and Maureen sang a duet version of Paul Williams' song "I Won't Last a Day without You." The episode aired in early 1977.

CONCERT TOURS:

The Brady Kids in concert.

The Brady Kids played at state fairs and other venues across the nation to thousands of eager fans. Sometimes they were mobbed after their performances. Barry Williams recounts one such occasion in his book: "Our fans, six deep on all sides, yelled our names at the motor home, hoping that one of us might be inside [they weren't]. Next, they rapped on the doors, then pounded on the windows, and finally just plain shook the s**t out of that Winnebago until they'd actually tipped it over."[11] The Bradys certainly had their fair share of excited fans, but they never quite reached the level of their friendly rivals The Osmonds or *The Partridge Family* heartthrob David Cassidy.

The 1973 tour:
May 10: Savannah, GA
May 12: Raleigh, NC
May 13: Birmingham, AL
May 15: Augusta, GA
May 18: Knoxville, TN
May 19: Atlanta, GA
May 20: Greensboro, NC
June 7: Rose Festival – Portland, OR
June 8: Seattle, WA
June 9: Spokane, WA
June 10: San Francisco, CA
June 17-22: Knott's Berry Farm, CA
August 27: Minnesota State Fair
with appearances at the Steel Pier in Atlantic City and other shows in New Jersey squeezed in.

What did a performance by the Brady Kids look like? Well, for their summer 1973 tour they sang 14 songs per concert. The songs included "Candy (Sugar Shoppe)," "Drummer Man," "Saturday in the Park," "Save the Country," "Down by the Lazy River" (an Osmond Brothers classic), "I'm Going to Make You Love Me," and "Ain't No Mountain High Enough." Chris also soloed with "Good for Each Other" and Barry sang "You've Made Me So Very Happy." Barry & Maureen sang a duet of "You've Got a Friend."

Between songs the kids performed skits and told jokes. One skit involved Mike and Susan doing impersonations of Sonny and Cher. Most of us recognize the fringe-happy outfits and the blue and white striped ones, but the kids completed quite a few other costume changes during a stage performance. One skit had them in gowns and dinner jackets, for example. Finally, the kids talked about *The Brady Bunch* and answered some pre-determined questions about themselves, the show, and the tour.

The Savannah Morning News explains how the music worked: "The need for the quick rehearsal...is the fact that [the kids] don't carry their own band with them. Except for their musical director and drummer, they use an all-local group of musicians, and of course they have to take a little time getting used to each other."[12] Usually, the kids would arrive in the town the day before or early the day of the performance, rehearse their hearts out, and then perform. Then it would be off to the next city. It was a pretty grueling schedule for six new singers and dancers, but they managed okay.

Thousands of people would show up for their concerts. In San Francisco, they drew a crowd of 3,000 people: 800 more than "mascara rock star" David Bowie did in his two performances to the kids' one![13]

[1]Williams, Barry. Growing Up Brady: I Was a Teenage Greg. Good Guy Entertainment: Los Angeles, 1999. P. 129.

[2]Billboard. April 29, 1972. P. 56.

[3]Billboard. May 19, 1973. P.22.

[4]Teen Pin-ups. June 1973. P. 38.

[5]Reed, Rochelle. The Secret Lives of the Girl Stars. The Laufer Company: New York, 1972. p. 69.

[6]On Screen and Beyond. Episode 98 "Eve Plumb." February 14, 2010. http://onscreenandbeyond.com/ podcast/osb098EPlumb.mp3

[7]Westbrook, Bruce. Houston Chronicle. "Growing Up with Cindy: Olsen Makes the Most of 'Brady Bunch' Fame." March 17, 1995.

[8]Williams, Barry. Growing Up Brady: I Was a Teenage Greg. Good Guy Entertainment: Los Angeles, 1999. P. 130.

[9]Beigel, Jerry. Los Angeles Times. "At Hollywood Bowl." August 1, 1973. Part IV, p. 10.

[10]Daily Variety Vol. 160 No. 39.   July 31, 1973, p. 6.

[11]Williams, Barry. Growing Up Brady: I Was a Teenage Greg. Good Guy Entertainment: Los Angeles, 1999. P. 136.

[12]Savannah Morning News. 5/11/1973. Section D p. 1.

[13]Weekly Variety Vol. 271 No. 10. July 18, 1973. P. 45.

MUSIC

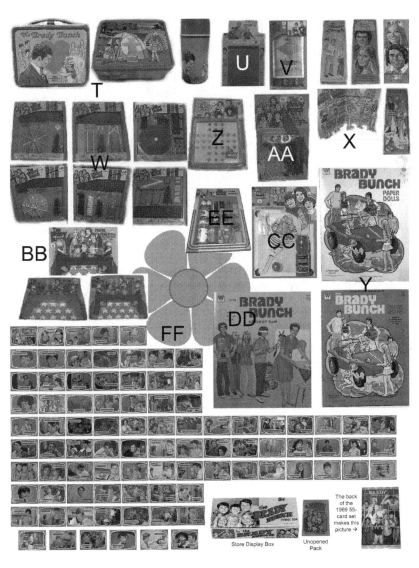

T

U

V

W

Z

AA

X

EE

CC

BRADY BUNCH PAPER DOLLS

BB

Y

DD

BRADY BUNCH

BRADY BUNCH

FF

MEMORABILIA

Store Display Box

Unopened Pack

The back of the 1969 55-card set makes this picture →

CHAPTER 6: MEMORABILIA

BRADY BUNCH MEMORABILIA

Two major toy companies took on *The Brady Bunch* toy market in the 1970s: Whitman Publishing and Larami. Both companies put out a load of toys and paper products that sold quite well. Today they are worth anywhere from $1 to $775.

Activity Books
(Image A)
There were two activity books printed in two consecutive years.
1) Whitman Publishing #1252, 1973, Paramount Pictures Corporation
Value = $12-15
2) Whitman Publishing, 1974, Paramount Pictures Corporation
Value = $15-20

Banjo & Guitar
(Image B)
Larami, 1973, Paramount Pictures Corporation
Value = $20 each

Barry Williams Fan Club
In 1970-1971 teen magazines ran ads for the Barry Williams Fan Club. Members of the Club received a 12x9 booklet about Barry that featured photographs and a short note from Barry on page 1. The booklet is 32 pages and includes a color cover (pictured) – the front is the same as the back – and 52 black and white photos inside. This item is super rare and its value is unknown...probably whatever someone will pay for it! Originally, it sold for $1.50. In addition to the Fan Club booklet, there are two known postcards in existence that advertised the Fan Club. The postcards are pictured below. Their value, too, is unknown but is probably somewhere between $5-$10 each.

Courtesy of Barry Williams

Board Game
(Image C)
Whitman Publishing, 1973
Value = $25 VG, $50 MIP
Players could be one of the six Brady kids in this camping-related game. The object of the game was to be the first to go around the board and successfully erect your tent.

Books, Vintage Fiction
(Image D)

There were eight Brady books written for kids during the time the original series was on the air. The first five books were written by William Johnston. The books feature Mike and Carol and there are quite a few errors in them that do not mesh with the television show. For example, the kids refer to their step-parents as "Mike" and "Carol" and the floor plan to the house is different. This is because the books were written by the author after he only saw the pilot episode and no more! The other three books by Jack Matcha are better informed. They are Scooby Doo-like adventures that center on the kids stopping criminals in their tracks.
Value = $1.00-$5.00 each, depending on condition
1) Johnston, William. The Brady Bunch. New York: Lancer Books, 1969.
2) Johnston, William. The Brady Bunch #2: Showdown at the P.T.A. Corral. New York: Lancer Books, 1969.
3) Johnston, William. The Brady Bunch #3: Count Up to Blast Down! New York: Lancer Books, 1970.
4) Johnston, William. The Brady Bunch #4: The Bumbler Strikes Again. New York: Lancer Books, 1970.
5) Johnston, William. The Brady Bunch #5: The Quarterback Who Came to Dinner. New York: Lancer Books, 1970.

6) Matcha, Jack. The Brady Bunch in the New York Mystery. Hollywood: The Laufer Company, 1972.

7) Matcha, Jack. The Brady Bunch in the Treasure of Mystery Island. Hollywood: The Laufer Company, 1972.

8) Matcha, Jack. The Brady Bunch in Adventure on the High Seas. Hollywood: Paramount Pictures Corporation, 1973.

Matcha, Jack. Teenage Mysteries Vol. 1. Hollywood: The Laufer Company, 1973. Eve Plumb appears on the cover of this book. The book contains six short mysteries, but none of them has Eve in them... she's just the model on the front. Volume 2 of this series is relatively easy to find, but good luck tracking down a copy of Volume 1.
Value = $50.00 because of its rarity

Courtesy of Tiger Beat

Resnick, Sylvia. Debbie Preston: Teenage Reporter – The Hollywood Mystery. Hollywood: The Laufer Company, 1972. From the back of the book: "Teenage reporter Debbie Preston is assigned to write a story about a TV musical that is being filmed in Hollywood. Appearing in the show are some of the greatest talents ever assembled – the Osmond Brothers, David Cassidy, Michael Gray, **Chris Knight**, The J-5 and a whole group of other superstars." Actually, Chris doesn't appear until page 105 in this 124-page mystery and is only mentioned twice thereafter. Mostly it centers on Debbie Preston and Michael Gray. The book has black & white photos of all the famous stars.
Value = $5.00 to $8.00, depending on condition

Books, Vintage Non-Fiction

There are several non-fiction books that contain tidbits, chapters, or even entire volumes on the actors who played the Brady kids. Some are easy to find; others are next to impossible to locate. Here is the list.

Courtesy of Tiger Beat

16's All Star Private Address Phone Numbers Autograph Book Top Secret Confidential!. New York: 16 Magazine, Inc., 1970. Contact information on Bobby Sherman, The Osmonds, The Jackson 5, The Cowsills, Ben Murphy & Pete Duel, Jack Wild, The Partridge Family, The Mod Squad, **Barry Williams**, and more.
Value = $10.00-$25.00 depending on condition

16's Most Wanted Bachelor Book. New York: 16 Magazine, Inc., 1971. This book contained info on Bobby Sherman, Mike Cole, David Cassidy, **Barry Williams**, Jack Wild, and many more. From a contemporary magazine ad: "It's the latest – and the greatest new book ever!!! Would you like to meet the most wanted bachelors in all teendom?? Would you like to learn all about their dating secrets and what kind of girls they

© *16 Magazine*

© *Young Readers Press*

like?? Would you like to learn their secret hangouts and how you could go about meeting them in the flesh?? If you would (and who wouldn't) you can join the posse – and go on your own bachelor hunt by getting a copy of '16's Most Wanted Bachelor Book!' "

Value = $50.00 because of its rarity

Arenson, D.J. Kids on TV. New York: Young Readers Press, Inc., 1972. This booklet contains a chapter on the kids from *The Brady Bunch*, and includes pictures from the pilot episode and more.

Hallinan, Tim. The Boys Tell the Girls. Hollywood: The Laufer Company, 1972. This book contains dating advice ostensibly given by six teen stars of the time: Donny Osmond, David Cassidy, **Chris Knight**, Michael Gray, Michael Jackson, and Jay Osmond. Readers are informed on topics such as looks, going steady, breaking up, and finding the boys of their dreams. It includes four black and white pictures of Chris.

Value = $50.00 because of its rarity

Hudson, Peggy. The Television Scene. New York: Scholastic Book Services, 1972. Unlike all the other books in this chapter, this one does not include an article on the Brady kids. Instead, it has a chapter called "Former Frustrated Cowboy: The Brady Bunch: Robert Reed." The article talks about Reed growing up on a ranch in Oklahoma and how he found his ambition for acting.

The Incredible Bachelor Book. New York: Reese Publishing Co., 1972. Similar to 16 Magazine's bachelor book printed the year before, Incredible contains information on music and television's most eligible bachelors. Featured single guys are The Osmond Brothers, The Jackson 5, Bobby Sherman, David Cassidy, and our own **Barry Williams**. The book came with an 11x16 pin-up of Donny Osmond.

Value = $50.00 because of its rarity

Chris Knight is credited as the author of two books Tiger Beat – The Laufer Company – issued about him in 1972. Tiger Beat was big on selling booklets like these and had much success with similar ones about David Cassidy and Donny Osmond. If you have a copy of either of Chris' books, count yourself luckier than a rabbit's foot, four-leaved-clover, and a horseshoe found all at once!

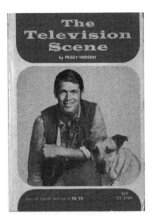

| *Courtesy of Tiger Beat* | © *Scholastic Books* | *Courtesy of Tiger Beat* |

Value = whatever you want to charge because these über rare books are almost impossible to find!

Knight, Chris. <u>Chris Knight's Photo Album</u>. Tiger Beat, 1972. From an advertisement in a TB magazine: "Designed just for Chris Knight fans, here's an absolutely fabulous keepsake photo history of Chris. It includes pix from babyhood 'til now, captioned by Chris himself so that you'll know every last detail about your fave Brady Boy! Plus these family photos, Chris has selected more than 30 brand new photos of him taken by Kenny Lieu, Tiger Beat's Official Photographer. None of these pictures have appeared in any other publication and you'll be the first to see them."

Knight, Chris. <u>The Secret of Chris Knight</u>. Tiger Beat, 1972. From an advertisement in a TB magazine: "For the first time you can learn all of Chris' secrets; what he wants out of life; what kind of girls appeal to him. Find out how Chris gets along with his real-life brother and sister as well as his TV family. Spend an entire fun-filled week with Chris, working and playing right along side of him."

McCormick, Maureen. <u>Every Girl Can Be Popular!</u> Tiger Beat, 1972. Chris wasn't the only one who attracted Tiger Beat's attention. Maureen was drafted to write a book about becoming popular. A fan site called Brady World has transcribed this book, and you can read the full text at http://www.bradyworld.com/mo/popular/book. htm.
Value = $25-$40, depending on condition

Reed, Rochelle. <u>The Secret Lives of the Girl Stars</u>. Hollywood: Laufer, 1972. This is a Tiger Beat book that has stories and facts on Marie Osmond, Susan Dey, Karen Valentine, **Eve Plumb, Maureen McCormick**, and Peggy Lipton. Most of the text is pretty superficial, which was par for the course in those days: how the girls do their hair, makeup, how they dress, diet, etc.
Value = $5.00-$8.00, depending on condition

© *Pyramid Books*   © *Pyramid Books*   *Courtesy of Tiger Beat*

Robinson, Richard. The Osmond Brothers and the New Pop Scene. New York: Pyramid Books, 1972. This book contains brief bios of all six Brady kids and their pictures, but focuses mainly on The Osmond Brothers. Value = $5.00-$8.00, depending on condition

Robinson, Richard. TV Superstars. New York: Pyramid Books, 1973. This book contains a chapter titled, "You Can Be a Brady" with short bios of the six kid actors. Photos of all six are also included. Value = $5.00-$8.00, depending on condition

Super-Stars!. Hollywood: Laufer, 1972. Ed. by the editors of Tiger Beat Magazine. Main features are on The Osmond Brothers, David Cassidy, and the Jackson Five. However, the book also includes bios on Bobby Sherman, Chad Everett, Elvis Presley, Michael Gray, Jack Wild, **Christopher Knight**, Mick Jagger, James Brolin, Ben Murphy, and Michael Cole. Value = $5.00-$8.00, depending on condition

More Stuff:

Bracelet
Pitts, 1973
Value = unknown

Brain Twister
(Image E)
"5 Tricky Puzzles"

Larami, 1973
Value = $10-15

Chess Set
(Image F)
Larami, 1973
Value = $10-15

Chess & Checkers
(Image G)
Larami, 1973
Value = $15-20

Chris Knight International Fan Club Kit
In 1973, Chris issued his own Fan Club Kit. Like Barry and Eve's kits, this is very rare. The Kit could be obtained by writing to his Fan Club, which was run by Cathy Carr out of Beverly Hills. The Kit consisted of:
1. A book cover for school text books
2. An 8x10 autographed photo
3. Three 8x10 photo sheets with four pictures printed on each
4. Three 5x7 photos
5. A three-page biography
6. A short letter thanking you for joining the Club
7. A membership certificate
8. A two-page fact sheet called "Popping Questions At Chris"

Value = $50-$75

Coloring Books
(Image H)
There were three coloring books printed in three consecutive years.
1) Whitman Publishing 1972, Paramount Pictures Corporation
Value = $12-50
2) Whitman Publishing #1657, 1973, Paramount Pictures Corporation
Value = $12-15
3) Whitman Publishing, 1974, Paramount Pictures Corporation
Value = $12-15

Comic Books
(Image I)
Here Comes The Brady Bunch: Family Fun For Everyone! Dell Publishing Company, Inc. 1970. Value = $25-$40. This is the first of two comic books published by Dell with a cover price of just fifteen cents. You can read the first story in the first issue online at: http://www.bradyworld.com/comic/front.htm. Poorly cut issues

of this comic will be missing Mike Lookinland's name on the cover. If you have a good copy, you can see his name at the bottom.

The Brady Bunch: Why Parents Get Gray or 3 +3 = Too Much! Dell Publishing Company, Inc. 1970. Value = $25-$40. This is comic book #2 and once again Mike Lookinland gets slighted on the cover. This time they mix up his name with Chris Knight's. They also misspell Maureen's name; they leave the "k" off "McCormick."

Dominoes
(Image J)
Larami, 1973 item no. 7885-7
Value = $10-15

Double Table Tennis Set
(Image K)
Larami, 1973
Value = $10-15

Eve Plumb Fan Club
In 1971, Eve formed a fan club in order to promote the release of her single "How Will It Be?" Members of the Fan Club received a letter from her, a postcard listing the release date of the single, and a photograph of Eve clutching a stuffed animal. This is another super, super rare item that is very difficult to find. It's worth whatever you'll pay for it!

Fan Club Kit
Tiger Beat, 1972
Value = $100-$150. The Kit included 1) a record with personal messages from each kid, 2) a booklet, 3) autographed portraits, 4) color stickers, 5) wallet-sized pictures, 6) membership card, and 7) birthday guide and fact sheet. Membership was a mere $2. And now for the very first time, YOU get to read what the Brady kids say on their record!!

Man: "Hello and welcome to The Brady Bunch Fan Club. Even through 'The Brady Bunch' has been one of your favorite TV shows for the past three years, this is the very first fan club ever formed for the group. The next few months should be exciting ones for all the Bradys because they'll be making records, doing personal appearances, and you can watch them every Friday night on ABC-TV. In between shows be sure to keep up on all their activities in the Tiger Beat family of magazines. Now meet The Brady Bunch in person."
Barry: "Hi, this is Barry Williams. Welcome to our Club. I know we'll be having lots of fun in the months ahead and I'm glad you'll be sharing it with us. I've got to admit that 1972 got off to a fantastic start. Within a few short months so many things happened that my head's been in a spin. Everything's been going so fast for us lately that sometimes I think it's all a dream. But fortunately it's not and what's best of all is that you're part of everything with us. I'm sure I'm speaking for everyone on the show when I say that our work week is just fantastic. Everybody's so close and we're all good friends that it's easy to forget we're acting. When we get together to

portray a family on TV, we really feel like brothers and sisters. But the best part about it is that it's not a put-on and we're as close as a family can be. I hope you can sense it when you watch our show because it really means a lot to us. And I also hope you remember that we have a date every Friday night on ABC.

Maureen: "Hi, this is Maureen McCormick and I'm very happy to have you in the Club. Over the last few months I've been receiving nice letters from people all over the world, and though I wish there was a chance for all of us to meet I'm sure this Fan Club

Courtesy of Tiger Beat

is the next best thing. It brings us all together in a special way: sort of like a bridge between our homes. And now that you're with us you'll be hearing the latest about all of our activities. Like Barry has said, it's hard to believe that so much is happening so fast and if the second half of this year is anything like the first it's sure to be exciting. I'd like to thank you for making it all possible because without your support this would never be happening. But most of all I'm happy to have you in the Club because it brings us close together. Thanks so much for joining.

Chris: "Hi, everybody, this is Chris and I'm so glad you joined our Club! There's going to be lots of things in store for you and I'd like to tell you about them now. First of all this September marks the fourth year our show has been in production and it's hard to believe that when it began I was only ten years old. So much has happened in the past three years and The Brady Bunch has really changed. We've begun recording and have released an album and now we've even got our own road show. We're going to be traveling a lot this year, especially in the summer and fall. More than anything I hope we'll meet when we come to your hometown. I mentioned our new album a while ago and it's called, 'Meet The Brady Bunch.' Already we've gotten some very nice letters from those of you who've heard it; I really hope you like the album because I know I had a lot of fun recording it. So until we meet keep a smile on your face and I hope to be seeing you soon."

Eve: "Hello, this is Eve Plumb, also known to my friends as Jan Brady. I can't begin to tell you how glad I am that you joined our Club because I know we're going to have a great time together. I can hardly wait for the next few months when we get our new show on the road. We'll be singing and dancing and maybe even doing some skits. I'm sure it's going to be fun. As a matter of fact, we're rehearsing right now and we're really enjoying it. I hope you stay tuned to our TV show, too, because there's going to be a lot going on. Remember last season when Davy Jones guest-starred with us? We'll, there's even more great people lined up for this year and the best part is they're also great to work with. So take care and until we come to your hometown be happy."

Mike: "Hi, I'm Mike Lookinland and I'd like to thank you for joining the Club. So many things have happened to us during the past year and now we've got our very own Fan Club. We've always liked fan clubs for many reasons, but the main one is because we can learn so much about each other. For the first time ever the

MEMORABILIA

thousands of miles between us don't seem that far apart and now with this record I feel like a guest right in your very own home. I hope someday we'll have a chance to meet so we can talk to each other in person. But until that time, please drop us a line so we can always be in touch.

Susan: "Hello, I'm Susan and I'm really glad to have this chance to talk to you right now. I just got through looking over a stack of letters on my desk and it makes me feel really happy inside to know that I've made so many friends through our TV show. My only wish is that we become better friends: that we get to know each other through this Club. If you have any questions about our show or even if you just want to say 'hi,' please write us a letter in care of the Fan Club because we'd love to hear from you."

Fishin' Fun
(Image L)
Larami, 1973, item no. 5359-5
Value = $10-15

Frame Tray Puzzle
(Image M)
Year unknown
Value = $10-$30

Goes Shopping
(Image N)
Larami, 1973
Value = $12-$18

Grand Canyon Adventure View-Master
(Image O)
Model #B568 3 reel Showtime, GAF Corporation, 1971, Paramount Pictures Corp.
Non-talking and talking models available
Value = $20-$30
Talking Model Value = $25-$40

The captions for the slides read:
Reel 1
1. The children ran downstairs to hear about the big surprise.
2. Their dad showed them a map of Grand Canyon Nat. Park.
3. It appeared they might spend all day loading the station wagon.
4. The Brady Bunch had their first canyon view at Mather Point.
5. Mike, like all park tourists, wanted to take pictures.
6. Alice read from guide book: "The canyon is a mile deep!"
7. Having rented a mule train, the Bradys headed "thataway"…

Reel 2

1. ...down Kaibab Trail, toward the bottom of the canyon.
2. Bobby and Cindy wandered away from camp and got lost.
3. Mike, Peter, and Marcia searched west of the campground.
4. As night closed in around them, Bobby tried to comfort Cindy.
5. Jimmy Pakaya, a runaway Indian boy, helped get them back.
6. "After this, no on leaves camp alone," Mike said sternly.
7. Later that night, the family gathered 'round a campfire.

Reel 3

1. Bobby filled a flashlight with beans for his Indian friend.
2. Jimmy agreed it was a pretty smart trick for a "pale face."
3. Hearing Jimmy's story, Mike was sure he should return home.
4. Jimmy came back early the next day with his grandfather.
5. The Chief shook hands and asked Bradys to join his tribe.
6. "It's an Indian custom," Eagle Cloud insisted. "You dance!"
7. Brady's Braves stopped atop the Canyon rim to say "goodbye."

Halloween Costume
(Image P)
Collegeville, 1972
Value = $40-60 because of its rarity
This is a plastic costume that just says "Greg" or "Marcia" on the package. The costume is a smock with picture of the *Meet the Brady Bunch* album on the chest and a mask that covers the eyes. The smock reads, "One of the Brady Bunch." (The date on the box says 1969, but that's just because that's the year the copyrights for the show began.)

Hand Tambourine
(Image Q)
Larami, 1973, item no. 4838-9
The tambourines came in yellow and red.
Value = $10-15

Hex-A-Game
(Image R)
Larami, 1973, item no. 5110-A
Value = $10-15

Jump Rope
Larami, 1973
Value = unknown

Kite Fun Book
(Image S)
Pacific Gas & Electric, 1976 Paramount Pictures Corporation
Printed by Western Publishing, Inc., Racine, WI
Value = $10-$20
The book is 15 pages and includes a short comic about the kids
going camping and running into a guy who has big feet (aka Big
Foot), some puzzles, and also of course directions on how to build
and fly a kite.

Kitty Karry-all Doll
Remco, 1969
Value = $45-$200 depending on condition
The original Kitty was issued in 1969 and you can see this date
and "Remco Ind., Inc. 19©69" stamped into the back of her neck.
If your doll does not have this stamp, it is a re-issued version and
worth far less! Her six pockets held a comb, a daisy, a notepad, a

Susan Olsen and Kitty Karry-all.

handkerchief, a mirror, and a pencil. "She's got a whole lotta pockets for a whole lotta fun!" The re-make was
done by Ashton Drake and her pockets are slightly larger and her hair is longer.

Lunch Box & Thermos
(Image T)
King Seeley Thermos, 1970
Value = $25 in fair condition without thermos; with thermos up to $375 in near mint or mint condition; $15-
35 for thermos alone

Magic Slate Paper Saver
(Image U)
Whitman Publishing, 1973
Value = $10-$15

Mosaic
(Image V)
Larami, 1973
Value = one sold in auction in 2001 for $133 (auction also included the Magic Slate)
This is a Lite-Brite-like peg board, except the pegs do not light up.

Outdoor Fun
(Image W)
Larami, 1973

Value = $10-$15 each
There were at least six different Outdoor Fun sets for kids to choose from.

Paper Dolls
(Image X)
Whitman Publishing #4784/7418, 1972
Whitman Publishing #4320/7209, 1973
Whitman Publishing #4340/7420, 1974
Whitman Publishing Paper Dolls Folder, #1976 and #1997, 1973
Value = $10-$30 depending on condition
The original artwork for the orange paper doll sold on eBay in December 2009 for $213.16! The original artwork for the blue paper doll sold at the same time for an astonishing $512.42!

Paper Dolls Cut-Out Book
(Image Y)
Whitman Publishing, 1973
Available with an orange background or white
Value = $15-$20

Peg Puzzle
(Image Z)
Larami, 1972
Value = $10-$15

Pick 'N' Play
(Image AA)
Larami, 1973
Value = $10-15

Pistol Ping Pong
(Image BB)
Larami, 1973 item no. 8301-A
Value = $10-15
These were available in a variety of colors, including green, red, and blue.

Purse
Larami, 1973
Value = unknown

MEMORABILIA

Spring with a Zing!
(Image CC)
Larami, 1973
Value = one sold in EX condition in 2001 for $121!
This toy package includes a plastic man connected to a parachute, a paddle with a ball and string attached to it adorned with a picture of the six kids, and a bottle of bubbles labeled "Monkey Bubbles."

Sticker Fun
(Image DD)
Whitman Publishing, 1973
Value = $15-$20

Super Market
(Image EE)
Larami, 1973
Value = unknown

Toy Tea Set
Larami, 1973
Value = unknown

Trading Cards
(Image FF)
There were two sets of trading cards issued, first in 1970 and then again in 1971. The 1970 set numbered 55 cards and were copyrighted 1970. The 1971 set numbered 88 cards and were copyrighted 1969. You can tell which set the card belongs to by looking at its copyright date. The backs of the cards were printed with one portion of a photo, which you had to put together like a puzzle.

Value of 1970 set = $500-$775
Value of 1971 set = $675-$800 a nearly-complete set (missing only 4 cards) was sold on eBay on June 9, 2010 for $721.
Individual cards will sell from between $2-$10 depending on condition.

The cards are all captioned.

1. The Brady Bunch
2. The Brady Girls
3. The Brady Boys
4. Ann B. Davis as Alice
5. Eve Plumb as Jan
6. Mike Lookinland as Bobby

7. Christopher Knight as Peter
8. Carol and Mike
9. The Family Pet!
10. Sweet Treat!
11. Peter, Greg And Bobby
12. Stuck In A Stockade!
13. Reporting For Duty!
14. "Here Comes My Fastball!"
15. Big Prize For Little Bobby
16. "Break It Up! It's Bedtime."
17. "What's Cooking, Alice?"
18. Big Noise!
19. Inferior Decorators!
20. Guess Who?
21. Make-up For Marcia!
22. Big Brother's Advice
23. Long Distance Phone Call!
24. The Music Man!
25. Christmas Celebration!
26. Musical Depreciation!
27. Ain't Love Wonderful!
28. "Sometimes I Hate Ice Cream!"
29. Homework Huddle!
30. A Couple Of Hungry Kids!
31. Backyard Playground!
32. Lollipop Lovers!
33. "I'm Ready For Action, Coach!"
34. Running A Fever!
35. King For A Day!
36. "Uh-oh, Here Come The Indians!"
37. Tired Ballplayers!
38. "Who Used My Toothbrush?"
39. "I'm The Umpire!"
40. Kitchen Conference!
41. "Something Smells Good!"
42. Trying To Get A Date!
43. Sorry For The Turkey!
44. Daydreaming!
45. "Say Something!"
46. Man To Man Talk!"*
47. Sandlot Stars!

48. "Flipped Your Wig?"
49. Soothing Greg!
50. A Boy's Room Is His Castle!
51. "Alice, You Grew A Beard!"
52. "Where's My Greasy Kid Stuff?"
53. Housekeeper!
54. "Someday Let's Eat Alone!"
55. [no caption]
56. "You Did It Again!"
57. Sloppy But Fun!
58. "Come And Get It!"
59. Big Sister!
60. "Talking It Over!"
61. A Small Disagreement!
62. A New Rock Star?
63. "What's The Noise?"
64. "Can I Keep The Bird?"
65. Meet Marcia Brady!
66. Meet Bobby Brady!
67. Meet Jan Brady!
68. Meet Cindy Brady!
69. Meet Peter Brady!
70. Trimming The Tree!
71. Meet Greg Brady!
72. Marcia's Pajama Party!
73. Having A Ball!
74. Christmas!
75. A Guitar Lesson!
76. Alice's Coffee Break!
77. Man To Man Talk*
78. Trouble At Home?
79. Greg's Big Date!
80. Practice Makes Perfect!
81. "What Was That?"
82. Bedtime Snack!
83. "What A Racket!"
84. Checking Homework
85. Greg Listens In!
86. A Tired Young Man!
87. "Feeling Better Yet?"
88. "Say Cheese!"

*There are two cards captioned, "Man To Man Talk," nos. 46 & 77. The images are slightly different. Both show Mike Brady talking to Greg. No. 46 is slightly more zoomed in than no. 77 where one can see a bit more of the boys' room in the background.

Now you, too, can write the caption for a Brady trading card. It's easy: just think of something silly to say and don't forget the exclamation point at the end!

_____

(Your Caption)

MEMORABILIA

CONCLUSION

The Brady Bunch is a pervasive part of American popular culture. You've now read about the original series and all of the spin-offs – those filmed and those not – that cover roughly four decades of material. The music was a wide-spread phenomenon that had an impact on many teens of the 1970s and persists through today, the refrains of "It's a Sunshine Day" and the show's theme song being the most obvious hangers-on. The collectible trading cards and toys are still relatively easy to find on sites such as eBay. The actors and producers have written six books collectively about their experiences filming the series, and many of the actors are still recognizable on today's reality television shows. There was even a convention in 2014 in New Jersey devoted solely to *The Brady Bunch* and its fans. It's no wonder that the Bradys are one of television's most identifiable fictional families.

It is a combination of likeable characters, simple story lines, happy endings, and inundation that makes the show so long-lasting. The first generation of Bradys is now gone: Sherwood Schwartz, Ann B. Davis, Robert Reed, and Florence Henderson. Their absence leaves a mark on American culture that won't go away for a long, long time. Their stories, as well as the Bradys' stories, are ingrained in our television past and present. The future of television is yet to come, and I for one would not be surprised if there's still a little something left of the Bradys yet to be told.

BIBLIOGRAPHY

Almost every issue of teen magazines from 1970-1975 and 1977 contains something about the Brady kids. Magazines include Tiger Beat, 16 Magazine, 16 Magazine SPEC, Tiger Beat Star, Tiger Beat Spectacular, FaVE!, Flip Teen Magazine, Teen Pin-ups, Teen Beat, Teens Now, Teen's Star, and a few others.

"3 Tots Join 'Brood.' " Daily Variety Vol. 141 No. 20, 3 October 1968: 11.

Albert, Stephen W. and Diane L. "A Pre-Marcia-Brady Maureen McCormick Joins the Kids on *Camp Runamuck*." The TV Collector Vol. 2 No. 79, July-August 1995: 14-29.

Aradillas, Elaine. "Maureen McCormick: How I Lost 36 Pounds." People 5 April 2010: 126.

"Barry Williams One of the Bunch." Summer Weekly Reader Vol. 10 No. 8, July 6, 1971.

Beigel, Jerry. "At Hollywood Bowl." Los Angeles Times 1 August 1973: Part IV p. 10.

Bergman, Anne. "She's Getting Past the Bradys, Sort Of." Los Angeles Times 7 October 1994: F12.

"Birdina Proudly Eyes Results of Teaching Young Film Stars." Tucson Daily Citizen 8 March 1952: 1.

"Brady Bunch Set." Los Angeles Times 4 June 1973: Part IV I13.

"Brady Bunch Star Gets Her Health Back." The Hartford Courant 2 September 1970: 20.

Brady, James. "In Step with Florence Henderson." Parade Magazine 6 May 1990: 26.

"Brady Kids Start Tour." Savannah Morning News May 11, 1973: D1.

"The Brainy Bunch." Cracked Annual, 1973: 1-5.

Brenoff, Ann. "Hot Property: Here's the Story of a Lovely Lady." Los Angeles Times 27 July 27.

Broadcasting: The Businessweekly of Television and Radio Vol. 38, October 6, 1969: 46.

Brown, Les. "A.B.C. Cuts 10 Night Shows and Favors Fare for Families." New York Times 25 April 1974: 78.

Browning, Norma Lee. "Mother Brady Loves the Kids On and Off TV." Chicago Tribune 21 March 1971: S1.

"Cassius M. Davis." Daily Variety Vol. 124 No. 33, 22 July 1964: 11.

"Christopher Olsen." Daily Variety Vol. 91 No. 55, 21 May 1956: 15.

Daily Variety Vol. 81 No. 61, 2 December 1953: 10.

Daily Variety Vol. 112 No. 42, 3 August 1961: 10.

Daily Variety Vol. 113 No. 47, 8 November 1961: 8.

Daily Variety Vol. 115 No. 41, 1 May 1962: 9.

Daily Variety Vol. 124 No. 33, 22 July 1964: 11.

Daily Variety Vol. 133 No. 34, 21 October 1966: 10.

Daily Variety Vol. 142 No. 3, 10 December 1968: 14.

Daily Variety Vol. 159 No. 4, 9 March 1973: 8.

Daily Variety Vol. 160 No. 4, 11 June 1973: 5.

Daily Variety Vol. 160 No. 8, 15 June 1973: 5.

Daily Variety Vol. 168 No. 9, 18 June 1975: 2.

Dam, Julie K.L. and Samantha Miller. "The Brady Bunch Where Are They Now? True Confessions and Behind-the-Scenes Memories from TV's Favorite '70s Family." People 13 December 1999: 72-79.

Davis, Ann B, Ron Newcomer, and Diane Smolen. Alice's Brady Bunch Cookbook. Nashville, TN: Rutledge Hill Press, 1994.

DeBlasio, Ed. "How Much Longer Can Robert Reed Get Away with It?" TV Radio Mirror August 1963: 32-33 & 78-79.

Edelstein, Andrew and Frank Lovelace. The Brady Bunch Book. New York: Grand Central Publishing, 1990.

"Edward Knight Starring in 'A View from the Bridge.'" Daily Variety Vol. 144 No. 1, 6 June 1969: 8.

Edwards, Bill. "Onion to Sprout in Valley." Daily Variety Vol. 151 No. 5, 12 March 1971: 6.

Edwards, Bill. "Spotlight on Legit: Equity Spurs Theatre Expansion Here." Daily Variety Vol. 156 No. 43, 2 August 1972: 11.

Edwards, Bill. "Spotlight on Legit: Lure of Road Greater than B'way?" Daily Variety Vol. 156 No. 6, 11 August 1972: 6.

"Eve Plumb." Daily Variety Vol. 128 No. 24, 9 July 1965: 6.

"Eve Plumb." Daily Variety Vol. 143 No. 20, 2 April 1969: 26.

"Every Stray Dog and Kid." Daily Variety Vol. 193 No. 12, 23 September 1981: 10.

Fields, Randy. "What Do Brady Kids Do? Well, for Starters They Sing, Dance, Tell Jokes and Put On a Family-Type Show." Savannah Morning News May 6, 1973: F1.

"Flora Plumb." Daily Variety Vol. 145 No. 54, 19 November 1969: 8.

Gansberg, Alan L. "Plumb, Mansfield Acquire Properties for Features, TV." Hollywood Reporter 24 July 1980: 6.

Gill, Alan. "How Much Influence Does He Have with the Jury? Robert Reed's Contributions to 'The Defenders' Are Beginning to be Recognized." TV Guide 18-24 May 1963: 22-23.

Gliatto, Tom, Maria Eftimiades et al. "Here's the Story…of How The Brady Bunch, the Syrupy '70s Sitcom, Became a '90s Sensation – and How Its Kid Cast Copes with Adulthood and a Dad's Death." People 1 June 1992: 80-88.

Goldrup, Tom and Jim Goldrup. Growing Up on the Set: Interviews with 39 Former Child Actors of Classic Film and Television. Jefferson, NC: McFarland & Company, 2002.

"Gross-Krasne Resumes 'Big Town' Shooting." Daily Variety Vol. 81 No. 62, 3 December 1953: 6.

"Growing Boy." Daily Variety Vol. 51 No. 32, 18 April 1946: 15.

Hallinan, Tim. The Boys Tell the Girls. Hollywood: Laufer, 1972.

Harford, Margaret. "'Burlesque' Billed at the Hartford." Los Angeles Times November 20, 1966: M21.

Harford, Margaret. "'Heidi' Gets Santa's Call for Musical." Los Angeles Times December 14, 1966: E22 Part V.

Henderson, Florence and Joel Brokaw. Life is Not a Stage: From Broadway Baby to a Lovely Lady and Beyond. New York: Center Street, 2011.

Higgins, Mary Jane. "The Secret Robert Reed Tried Not to Tell!" TV Picture Life March 1971: 33 & 57-59.

Hobbs Daily News-Sun [Hobbs, NM] December 26, 1976: 45.

"Hollywood Bowl." Daily Variety Vol. 160 No. 39, 31 July 1973: 6.

Hudson, Peggy. "Former Frustrated Cowboy The Brady Bunch: Robert Reed." The Television Scene January 1972: 45-50.

Irwin, Kim. "Using Your Head: SM Workshop Offers Migraine Sufferers Tips on How to Cope." The Outlook 22 January 1998: B2.

Jaques, Damien. "Brady Bunch's Greg Is Now an Emperor's Son." The Milwaukee Journal 11 August 1978: TV Section 1.

Johnson, Lauren. The Brady Bunch Files: 1,500 Brady Trivia Questions Guaranteed to Drive You Bananas!. New York: Renaissance Books, 2000.

Kay, Terry. "Meet Chris Olsen: Fifth-Grader's Many 'Parents' Are All Famous Movie Actors." Freeport Journal-Standard 17 August 1960: 18.

Knight, Chris. Chris Knight's Photo Album. Hollywood: Laufer, 1972.

Knight, Chris. The Secret of Chris Knight. Hollywood: Laufer, 1972.

Kramer, Carol. "Ann B. Davis Brushed Up Furniture Dusting." Chicago Tribune 12 December 1971: S_A1.

Kramer, Carol. "Brady Bunch Star Serves Up 'Pudding' on Show Business." Chicago Tribune 13 April 1970: 1A_11.

Lane, Lydia. "Alumna Snubs the Snack Cart." Los Angeles Times 16 April 1981: Part V 19.

Lane, Lydia. "Dance Classes for the Posture." Los Angeles Times 16 September 1976: Part IV 4.

Laurent, Lawrence. "'The Brady Bunch.'" The Ledger. [Lakeland, FL] Reprinted from The Washington Post 5 December 1971: 32.

Laurent, Lawrence. "The Brady Bunch's Formula Has Been Around Before." Milwaukee Journal. Reprinted from The Washington Post 7 November 1971: 15.

"Legit Review: Allison Wonderland." Daily Variety Vol. 158 No. 15, 27 December 1972: 3.

"Legit Reviews." Daily Variety Vol. 147 No. 9, 18 March 1970: 14.

"Legit Reviews: Who's Afraid of Virginia Woolf?" Daily Variety Vol. 166 No. 11, 20 June 1972: 5.

Lincoln, Rachel. "Maureen McCormick: Time to Change." Children July 1998: 32-34.

Lombard, Brian. Bradypalooza: The Unauthorized Guide to TV's Favorite Family. Baltimore: PublishAmerica, 2004.

"Lomita to Hold Annual Parade, Race Sunday." Los Angeles Times September 22, 1974: C55.

Lord, Marcia. "The Brady Bunch Takes a Bow: A Closer Look at TV's Biggest Family." TV Family August 1972: 39 & 58-60.

Lowry, Cynthia. "It's Alias Ann B. Davis: Schultzy, Alice – All the Same." Daytona Beach Morning Journal December 24, 1971: TV Section 16-17.

Lowry, Cynthia. "Series a Cliff Hanger for One of Its Stars." Chicago Tribune 9 July 1970: B27.

MacMinn, Aleene. "A Nice Change: Brady Bunch Show from King's Island." Los Angeles Times 22 November 1973: Part IV F38.

"Many Nations Flavor Disk." Billboard Newspaper 15 August 1970: 8.

Marin, Rick. "'Bradys' is Schlock full of Causes." The Washington Times February 9, 1990: E1.

Margaret, Mary. "Marcia Brady's Dark Past." People 2 April 2007: 67-68.

Martin, John. "The Dance Bennington Festival." New York Times August 3, 1941: X8.

"Maureen McCormick." Biography Magazine April 2000: 32.

McCormick, Maureen. Every Girl Can Be Popular! Hollywood: Laufer, 1972.

McCormick, Maureen. Here's the Story: Surviving Marcia Brady and Finding My True Voice. New York: HarperEntertainment, 2008.

McCormick, Maureen. "A Very Brady Confession." Newsweek 10 November 2008: 64.

McCormick, Maureen. "My True Story." People 27 October 2008: 72-79.

McFarland, Sabrina. "Where Are They Now?" Us Magazine 28 November 1988: 64.

McLellan, Dennis. "TV Personality Allan Melvin Dies After Battle with Cancer." The Post and Courier [Charleston, SC] January 20, 2008: 5B.

McMurphy, Jean. "As Schultzy on TV Ann Davis Not Content to Get Her Man." Los Angeles Times 6 April 1958: Part VII G2.

"Miami Boy Signed for Film Series." Miami Daily News 6 September 1946: 2nd Sect., Eve., 1.

"Mike Lookinland." Daily Variety Vol. 145 No. 65, 5 December 1969: 27.

"Mike Lookinland." Daily Variety Vol. 150 N. 43, 5 February 1971.

Momlogic. "The Brady Kids on THEIR Kids Acting: 'No Way!'" November 6, 2008. Online video interview. http://www.momlogic.com/2008/11/brady_kids_on_their_kids_actin.php.

Moran, Elizabeth. Bradymania: Everything You Always Wanted to Know – and a Few Things You Probably Didn't. Holbrook, MA: Adams Media Corporation, 1995.

"Motion Picture Mothers Observe Thirty-First Birthday." Van Nuys News June 23, 1970: 19.

"Movie Moppet Has Highest Paid Coach." The Amarillo Globe-Times 2 November 1956: 21.

Nichelson, Ted et al. Love to Love You Bradys: The Bizarre Story of The Brady Bunch Variety Hour. Toronto: ECW Press, 2009.

"Odyssey to Open House with 'Man's a Man.'" Daily Variety Vol. 144 No. 11, 20 June 1969: 19.

"Parliament Bldg. to be Filmed by Hollywood Co." The Evening Citizen [Ottawa, Canada] November 27, 1947: 30.

Pashko, Stanley. "A Webelos Scout in Russia." Boys' Life May 1976: 41.

"Planted." Daily Variety Vol. 76 No. 64, 5 September 1952: 9.

Raddatz, Leslie. "Don't Tell His Pasadena Neighbors…But Robert Reed Is an Actor." TV Guide 4 April 1970: 21-23.

Reed, Rochelle. The Secret Lives of the Girl Stars. Hollywood: Laufer, 1972.

"Reunion before Renown." Life 20 September 1954: 169-174.

Rizzo, Monica. "Maureen McCormick: 'I Have to Start Over.'" People 22 June 2009: 152.

"Robert Reed: A Little Mannix Cures the Blahs." Los Angeles Times June 21, 1970: 39C.

Rossiter, Patrick. "'Bunch' Capture Audience." Savannah News Press Classified May 12, 1973: B6.

Rubino, Anthony. Life Lessons from the Bradys. New York: Plume, 1995.

Ruditis, Paul. The Brady Bunch Guide to Life. Philadelphia: Running Press, 2004.

SAMR. "Child Star Christopher Olsen, the Boy Who Knew Too Much." The Short Knight Hitchcock Blog: News, Interviews, and Ramblings on the Brilliantly Innovative, Enigmatic Sir Alfred. March 29, 2011. Online. http://shortknighthitchblog.blogspot.com/2011/03/child-star-christopher-olsen-boy-who.html.

Saunders, Rubie. "Barry Williams: TV's Triple-Talented Teen-Ager." Young Miss Vol. XIX No. 180, April 1972: 18-21.

Schenectady Gazette. August 29, 1970: TV Sect. 3.

"'Schultzy' Davis Returns to TV." Oakland Tribune 30 June 1963: Sect. TV/Radio 1.

Schwartz, Sherwood and Lloyd J. Schwartz. Brady, Brady, Brady: The Complete Story of The Brady Bunch as Told by the Father/Son Team Who Really Know. Philadelphia: Running Press, 2010.

Scott, Vernon (UPI). "Reaching Them with TV: Schwartz a Big Man with Kids." Beaver Country Times March 15, 1972: D-7.

Scura, John. "Eve Plumb Says Growing Up on TV Seemed Normal. 'But I Never Knew Anything Else.'" Us Magazine 26 May 1981.

"See Flora Plumb." Daily Variety Vol. 135 No. 58, 24 May 1967: 9.

"Short Shorts." Daily Variety Vol. 70 No. 12, 21 December 1950: 11.

Stoddard, Sylvia. TV Treasures: A Companion Guide to The Brady Bunch. New York: St. Martin's Press, 1996.

Street, Nick. "Sherwood Schwartz – Creator of Hit TV Shows 'Gilligan's Island' and 'The Brady Bunch' Trades Sitc." JewishJournal.com. November 9, 2006. Online. http://www.jewishjournal.com/arts/article/sherwood_schwartz_creator_of_hit_tv_shows_gilligans_island_and_the_brady_bu.

"Sue Olsen Grows Up in 'Brady.'" Schenectady Gazette 8 June 1974: TV Sect. 15.

Sullivan, David. "Jack Lemmon, Miss Harris in CTG's 'Delight.'" Los Angeles Times March 18, 1970: F1-F2 Part IV.

"Talent Countdown." Billboard Newspaper 19 May 1973: 22.

"Telepix Review 'Then Came Bronson.'" Daily Variety Vol. 143 No. 15, 26 March 1969: 28.

Thomas, Kevin. "UCLA Acting Prize – A Theatre Surprise." Los Angeles Times January 28, 1967: 18 Part I.

"Today 3PM Eve Plumb as Special Guest of Art Linkletter." Daily Variety Vol. 143 No. 20, April 2, 1969: 26.

"Tomorrow Night Maureen McCormick 'Bewitched.'" Daily Variety Vol. 129. No. 38, 27 October 1965: 11.

"Tonight Eve Plumb as Little Girl on The Smothers Brothers Show." Daily Variety Vol. 129, 17 December 1965: 19.

Von Blon, Katherine. "Comedienne Shines at Cabaret Concert." Los Angeles Times 23 November 1957: B2.

Weekly Variety Vol. 253 No. 13, 12 February 1969: 40.

"What Barry Williams Wants Most Out of Life." Binky Vol. 78, May 1971.

"What's Doing in Orange County." Los Angeles Times May 10, 1974: OC-C16.

"Where Are They Now?" Chicago Tribune August 27, 1961: SW11.

"White Drops 'Flicka' Reins." <u>Daily Variety</u> Vol. 93 No. 16, 27 September 1956: 1.

Williams, Barry with Chris Kreski. <u>Growing Up Brady…I Was a Teenage Greg</u>. Los Angeles: Good Guy Entertainment, 1999 2nd edition.

Witbeck, Charles. " 'Brady Bunch' Hangs On for New Season." <u>Toledo Blade</u> 11 August 1970: 18.

Wolters, Larry. "Emmy? It's Not Useful to Schultzy." <u>Chicago Tribune</u> 21 July 1958: Part 3 B7.

Wolters, Larry. "Radio TV Gag Bag." <u>Chicago Tribune</u> 10 May 1959: Part 8 G40.

Zylstra, Freida. "Cooking's a Family Affair." <u>Chicago Tribune</u> 17 September 1971: Sect. 2 B3.

INDEX

A

B

E

F

G

H

I

J

K

S

INDEX

X

Y

Z

ABOUT THE AUTHOR

Erika Woehlk lives in Missouri and works professionally as an archivist. In her spare time, she enjoys writing and wildlife photography. She grew up watching *The Brady Bunch* in reruns after school. This is her second book.

Made in the USA
Middletown, DE
14 December 2020